2nd Edition

S/NVQ
Level
3

The Teaching Assistant's Handbook

Secondary Schools

Supporting teaching
and learning in schools

D0495242

Louise Burnham
Luisa Diaz

Heinemann is an imprint of Pearson Education Limited, a company incorporated in England and Wales, having its registered office at Edinburgh Gate, Harlow, Essex, CM20 2JE. Registered company number: 872828

www.heinemann.co.uk

Heinemann is a registered trademark of Pearson Education Limited

Text © Louise Burnham & Luisa Diaz, 2008

First published 2008

12 11 10 09 08
10 9 8 7 6 5 4 3 2 1

British Library Cataloguing in Publication Data is available from the British Library on request.

ISBN 978 0435449 39 1

Edited by Catherine Baker & Karen Hemingway
Designed by Wooden Ark Studio
Typeset by Tek-Art, Croydon, Surrey
Original illustrations © Pearson Education Limited, 2008
Illustrated by Mark Beech and Tek-Art
Cover design by Siu Hang Wong
Cover photo/illustration © Getty
Printed in the UK by Scotprint

Websites

The websites used in this book were correct and up-to-date at the time of publication. It is essential for tutors to preview each website before using it in class so as to ensure that the URL is still accurate, relevant and appropriate. We suggest that tutors bookmark useful websites and consider enabling students to access them through the school/college intranet.

Contents

Introduction   **v**

Mandatory units

Unit 3   Help to keep children safe   **1**
Unit 18 Support pupil's learning activities   **29**
Unit 19 Manage pupil behaviour   **51**
Unit 20 Develop and promote positive relationships   **77**
Unit 21 Support the development and effectiveness of work teams   **103**
Unit 22 Reflect on and develop practice   **121**

Optional units

Group A Supporting pupil's learning

Unit 23 Plan, deliver and evaluate teaching and learning activities under the direction of a teacher   **141**
Unit 24 Contribute to the planning and evaluation of teaching and learning activities   **155**
Unit 28 Support teaching and learning in a curriculum area   **169**
Unit 30 Contribute to assessment for learning   **187**

Group B Meeting additional support needs

Unit 34 Support gifted and talented pupils   **199**
Unit 35 Support bilingual/multilingual pupils   **213**
Unit 36 Provide bilingual/multilingual support for teaching and learning   **231**
Unit 38 Support children with disabilities or special educational needs and their families   **241**
Unit 39 Support pupils with communication and interaction needs   **253**
Unit 40 Support pupils with cognition and learning needs   **265**
Unit 41 Support pupils with behavioural, emotional and social development needs   **277**
Unit 42 Support pupils with sensory and/or physical needs   **289**

Group C Providing pastoral support

Unit 47 Enable young people to be active citizens   **301**
Unit 50 Facilitate children and young people's learning and development through mentoring   **317**

Group D Supporting the wider work of the school

Unit 55 Contribute to maintaining pupil records   **331**
Unit 57 Organise cover for absent colleagues   **345**

Group E Working with colleagues

Unit 62 Develop and maintain working relationships with other
         practitioners   **361**

Index   **374**

The following units can also be found on the Heinemann website
(www.heinemann.co.uk/)

Unit 8   Use information and communication technology to support
         pupils' learning
Unit 31 Prepare and maintain the learning environment

About this book

Welcome to this handbook for the National Vocational Qualification (NVQ) or Scottish Vocational Qualification (SVQ) for Teaching Assistants at secondary education level. If you are using this handbook, you will be setting out or have already begun to train for work as a Teaching Assistant. This handbook has been written for assistants in secondary schools although if you are working in a primary school you may find that many ideas and principles will apply to you as well.

You may find yourself referred to under the general title of 'Teaching Assistant' within your school, but you may also be called a 'Classroom Assistant', 'School Assistant', 'Individual Support Assistant', 'Special Needs Assistant' or 'Learning Support Assistant'. These different titles have come about due to the different types of work which assistants are required to do within the classroom. At the time of writing, assistants are being increasingly required to take on a more leading role alongside teachers and are being given more responsibility. You may be one of a large team of assistants within a big urban primary school, or you may be part of a much smaller team of adults in a village school.

Some background information about the NVQ

The structure of the NVQ requires you to achieve **ten** units of competence from the national occupational standards. There are **six** mandatory units that each candidate must achieve. These mandatory units are longer than the optional units as they contain more information. In addition, each candidate must achieve **four** of the optional units. The optional units are split into five groups A, B, C, D and E. You may choose any combination of units from these groups, but with **no more than two** units taken from group E.

Apart from this restriction, optional units may be selected from within the same group or from across different groups. Selections of optional units will be a matter of choice for the candidate in consultation with the school. Always bear in mind career aspirations and employment requirements.

This book covers a selection of these optional units with the focus on applying the knowledge to situations that can be found in primary schools. For each unit we have identified what you will need to know and understand from the knowledge points (or K points, i.e. K1, K2, K3 etc) at the start of the chapters. The chapter then gives information and activities related to these items of learning. At the end of each unit there is a portfolio activity, showing you how to collect relevant information from your experiences. There are places in which information overlaps between units. Full cross-references have been inserted throughout the book for these instances. Throughout each chapter there are a number of features to help with your studies.

Louise Burnham and Luisa Diaz would like to thank the following people for their help and advice during the writing of this book:

Val Hughes and Sandhurst Junior School in Catford for a copy of their teaching assistant feedback form in Unit 24.

Lewisham LEA for a copy of a teaching assistant's job description.

Elayne Gough from Stillness Junior School, Forest Hill for her SHEEP mnemonic in Unit 38.

Tony Donohue from Downderry School in Downham for looking through Unit 50 on mentoring.

Andy Cobb from Lewisham College for his inspirational teaching ideas!

Yasmin Ahmad from Haberdasher Aske's Knights's Academy in Bromley for allowing us to reproduce her literacy lesson plan, and Arzu Han for her help.

Graham Jameson, headteacher at Edmund Waller school in New Cross for his example of a school staffing structure in Unit 18.

Catherine Baker for her wonderful motivational comments and Karen Hemingway for her attention to detail.

Beth Howard and Alistair Nunn at Heinemann for their guidance and support throughout the project.

Anne Rae for her excellent work in checking the book's suitability for readers in Scotland.

Photo acknowledgements

The author and publishers would like to thank the following for permission to reproduce photographs:

page 247 – Alamy Images/Brian Mitchell

All other photos © Pearson Education Ltd/Ian Wedgewood

3 Help to Keep Children Safe

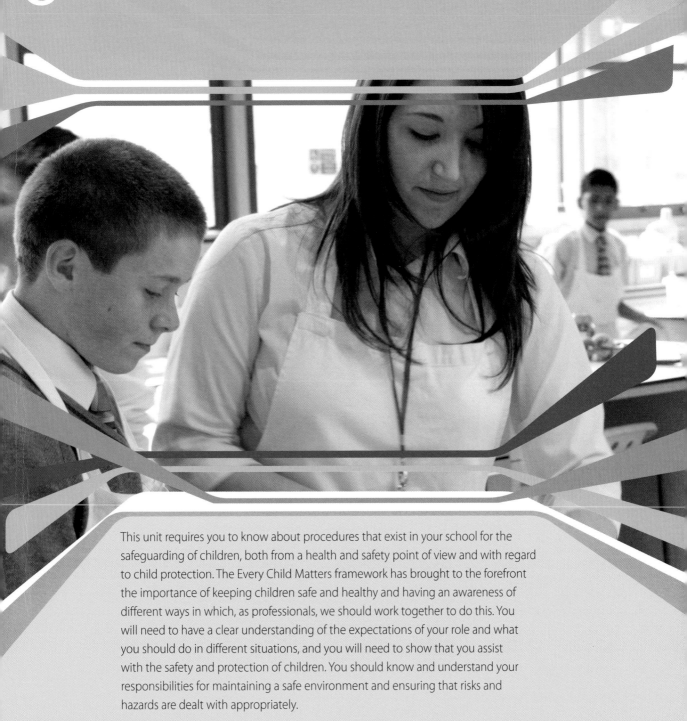

This unit requires you to know about procedures that exist in your school for the safeguarding of children, both from a health and safety point of view and with regard to child protection. The Every Child Matters framework has brought to the forefront the importance of keeping children safe and healthy and having an awareness of different ways in which, as professionals, we should work together to do this. You will need to have a clear understanding of the expectations of your role and what you should do in different situations, and you will need to show that you assist with the safety and protection of children. You should know and understand your responsibilities for maintaining a safe environment and ensuring that risks and hazards are dealt with appropriately.

What you need to know and understand

For this unit, you will need to know and understand:

- Setting's safety, safeguarding and protection and emergency procedures, what these are and why they must be followed, including controls on substances harmful to health and other key aspects of health and safety

- The laws governing safety in your home country, including the general responsibility for health and safety that applies to all colleagues and to employers

- The duty of all within the sector to safeguard children, including the difficulties in situations where your concerns may not be seen to be taken seriously or followed through when following normal procedures

- Regulations covering manual handling and the risks associated with lifting and carrying children

- Safety factors and recognised standards of equipment and materials for children. Importance of using equipment that is appropriate for the age, needs and abilities of the child. The importance of following manufacturers' guidelines

- Routine safety checking and maintenance of equipment. Safe storage of hazardous materials and disposal of waste

- Safe layout and organisation of rooms, equipment, materials and outdoor spaces

- How to adapt the environment to ensure safety for children and young people, according to their age, needs and abilities and taking into account disabilities or special educational needs, e.g. keeping the floor tidy to limit hazards for children/young people with visual difficulties

- When and how to use safety equipment such as safety gates, socket covers, window and drawer catches, cooker guards, safety harnesses. Safety in respect of animals, plants, sand pits and outdoor spaces

- Good hygiene practice: avoiding of cross-infection, disposal of waste, food handling, handling body fluids. Issues concerning spread of HIV and AIDS virus and hepatitis

- Familiarity with adult/child ratio requirements, according to regulatory and setting requirements

- How to supervise children/young people safely, modifying your approach according to their age, needs and abilities. The balances between safety and risk, and challenge and protection for children and young people

- Policies and procedures of setting for responding to and recording accidents and emergencies. Basic first aid required in an emergency and how to apply it, recognition of and response to choking, unconsciousness, breathing difficulties, bleeding, anaphylactic shock, burns. Awareness of location and contents of first aid box. How to treat common minor injuries that may be dealt with on site, such as minor skin abrasions, cuts, bumps

- The importance of following instructions about children's diets carefully to avoid known allergic reactions. How you would recognise allergic reactions

- Policies and procedures of setting to deal with children/young people's illness. How to recognise when children/young people are ill, including when they cannot communicate, e.g. fever, rashes, headache, crying and breathlessness

- The emergency procedures within settings and the types of possible emergency. This must include:
    - a   procedures for fires
    - b   security incidents
    - c   missing children or persons.

- Types and possible signs and indicators of child abuse: physical, emotional, sexual abuse, bullying and harassment, neglect and failure to thrive not based on illness. This must include:
    - a   behavioural changes such as regression, withdrawal, excessive attention seeking, aggression and negative behaviour
    - b   physical indicators such as unlikely bruising, burns, marks, genital irritation or damage, hunger, being dirty, lack of health care

- Recognition that social factors, e.g. substance abuse, may increase a child's vulnerability to abuse

- Safe working practices that protect children/young people and adults who work with them

- Ways to encourage children/young people to be aware of their own bodies and understand their right not to be abused, according to their age, needs and abilities. These may include:
    - a   use of appropriate descriptive language
    - b   activities involving discussion about their own bodies

- The importance of consistently and fairly applied boundaries and rules for children/young people's behaviour, according to their age, needs and abilities, and the avoidance of stereotyping (See also Unit 19, K5, page 56)

- How to respond to children/young people's challenging behaviour, according to their age, needs and abilities and in line with the policies and procedures of the setting (See also Unit 19, K9, page 62)

- *The importance of encouraging and rewarding positive behaviour* (See Unit 19, K8, page 60)

- Safety issues and concerns when taking children/young people out of the setting

- The legislation, guidelines and policies which form the basis for action to safeguard children and young people

The setting's safety, protection and emergency procedures

All schools need to ensure that they take measures to protect all adults and pupils while they are on school premises. This means that there will be procedures in place for a number of situations that may arise, including the following.

Accidents and first aid

There should be enough first aiders in the school at any time to deal with accidents. First aid boxes should be regularly checked and replenished. (See also K13, page 18.)

School security and strangers

This includes making sure that all those who are in school have been signed in and identified. Schools may have different methods for doing this, for example visitors may be issued with badges. If staff notice any unidentified people in the school, they should challenge them immediately. If you are on playground duty and notice anything suspicious, you should also send for help. Schools may also have secure entry and exit points, which may make it more difficult for individuals to enter the premises. (See also K16, page 20.)

Fire procedures

There should be clear procedures in place so that everyone on the premises knows what to do in case of fire. (See also K16, page 20.)

Emergencies

These do sometimes occur and schools should have procedures in place to deal with them. (See also K13, page 15.)

Personal hygiene

Pupils should develop routines and good practice for general personal hygiene and understand its importance.

General health and safety

Health and safety should be a regular topic at staff meetings and during assemblies, so that everyone's attention is drawn to the fact that it is a shared responsibility.

Controls on substances harmful to health (COSHH)

Anything that may be harmful should be stored out of pupils' reach or locked in a cupboard, for example, cleaning materials or medicines. COSHH legislation gives a step-by-step list of precautions that need to be taken to prevent any risk or injury.

▲ Figure 3.1 Fire notices must be displayed in prominent places around the school

K1 Portfolio activity

Investigating safety, protection and emergency procedures

Using a copy of your school's health and safety policy, highlight the procedures your school has in place for the areas above. If a particular area is not documented in the policy, find out whether it is recorded elsewhere. If you are unable to find the information recorded anywhere, you will need to speak to your headteacher or health and safety representative in order to find out about it. Then write a reflective account under each heading.

Laws governing safety

The Health and Safety at Work Act 1974 was designed to protect everyone at work through procedures for preventing accidents. The procedures everyone in the workplace is expected to observe are described below.

Reporting any hazards

Everyone should be alert to any hazards in school that are likely to cause injury to themselves or others. The school is required to carry out an annual risk assessment to determine which areas and activities are most likely to be hazardous, the likelihood of specific hazards occurring and those who are at risk. Pupils and staff need to be vigilant and immediately report any hazards that they notice to the appropriate person. This may be the school's health and safety representative, the headteacher or another member of staff. You should be aware of the designated person to whom you should report health and safety matters.

Following the school's safety policy

The school has an obligation to have a safety policy, which should give information to all staff about procedures that the school has in place for ensuring that it is as safe as possible. All new staff joining the school should be given induction training in safety procedures and what to do in case of emergencies. Safety should be a regular topic at staff meetings.

Making sure that their actions do not harm themselves or others

Staff must also ensure that any actions they take are not likely to harm or cause a danger to others in the school. This includes tidying up and putting things away

▼ Figure 3.2 How can you encourage pupils to assess and manage risks?

after use. You must also consider the effects of not taking action, for example, if you discover a potential danger, it is your responsibility not to ignore it but to report it as appropriate.

Using any safety equipment provided

Staff need to ensure that safety equipment that is provided for use when carrying out activities is always used. This includes the safe use of tools used for subjects such as Design Technology or the use of gloves when handling materials in Science activities. There should be guidelines in the school's policy for the safe use and storage of equipment.

All staff working in a school have a responsibility to ensure that pupils are cared for and safe. The Children Act 1989 (Children (Scotland) Act 1995) also requires that staff protect children as far as possible when they are in their care. This includes preventing any risks that may occur.

K2 Portfolio activity

Investigating legal requirements for safety

Find out about and briefly describe the requirements of the following:

- Health and Safety at Work Act 1974
- Children Act 1989
- Every Child Matters

The duty of all within the sector to safeguard children

Under the Health and Safety at Work Act, it is the responsibility of everyone in the school to ensure that safety is maintained and in particular that vulnerable groups such as children are safeguarded. Standards for safety are also set by the Department for Education for each country and are monitored by the body responsible for school inspections, for example, Ofsted in England and HMIE in Scotland. As well as having an awareness of health and safety, all routines should be planned carefully with safety in mind so that incidents are less likely to occur. Pupils should also be encouraged to think about safety when they are in the learning environment, so that they develop their own awareness.

If you notice and report something, which you consider needs to be addressed through the correct channels but which is not subsequently followed through, you should take the matter further. You should approach the headteacher or governing body (local authority, in Scotland), who should have a committee that manages general facilities and should be able to advise you on what the next steps should be.

Pursuing safety issues

Carrie has been concerned about a safety issue in her Year 7 (S1) Art class. As building work is taking place in school, the class has been placed in a temporary classroom with only 28 desks for 30 pupils. There is barely enough space in the room for the pupils and two adults to move around. She has spoken to various senior managers about it as two pupils are more often than not left struggling to sit and draw comfortably. It is November and behaviour in the class has deteriorated noticeably since the start of the academic year.

Carrie has been told that there is no funding for new furniture and the room is too small to accommodate it, so nothing can be done.

- Should Carrie continue to be concerned or has she passed the responsibility on?
- Is there anything else she could do?

Regulations covering manual handling and the risks associated with lifting and carrying children

If you are asked to lift and carry pupils or equipment as part of your job, you should receive appropriate training. By the time a child is of secondary age, it will be impossible for you to lift them on your own and it is unlikely that you will be asked to. However, if you are working with pupils who have special educational (Additional Support for Learning (ASL)) needs, lifting them with hoists or other equipment may be part of your daily routine. You should be aware of the risk of spine and back muscle injury and should make sure that you follow the correct procedures. A quarter of all accidents involving staff in schools are caused by moving heavy objects.

▲ Figure 3.3 When lifting a pupil, two adults should grasp each other's wrists to make a four-handed seat and the pupil should put an arm around each of the adult's shoulders, before the adults stand up together

As part of the Manual Handling Operations Regulations 1992, your employer should make sure that you always follow correct guidelines when lifting pupils or equipment. You should also be aware of the dangers of bending over small desks or tables as this can also lead to problems – it is always better to crouch down and keep a straight back. Under the Health and Safety at Work Act, all adults have a duty to look after themselves.

Keys to good practice

Lifting and carrying

✓ Only lift if absolutely necessary.
✓ Check the weight of the object or pupil before you start to lift.
✓ If necessary, share the load with another person.
✓ Make sure you are holding the pupil or object securely.
✓ Bend your knees and keep your back straight as you lift.
✓ If the pupil or object is too heavy, put it down again slowly and do not attempt to continue.

Safety factors and recognised standards of equipment and materials for children

All materials and equipment used in schools must fulfil recognised standards of safety. The most widely used, although not legally required, safety symbol is the Kitemark, which shows that an item has been tested by the British Safety Institute. In addition, before items can be offered for sale within the European Union, they must carry a CE symbol to show that they meet European regulations.

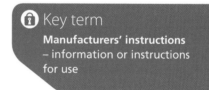

ⓘ Key term

Manufacturers' instructions – information or instructions for use

◀ **Figure 3.4** How many of these safety symbols do you recognise?

Always make sure that any equipment to be used by pupils is age and ability appropriate. The **manufacturers' instructions** and guidelines are intended to be a realistic means of checking that equipment is not misused. A pupil who is too young or too old may be unable to use the equipment safely and may hurt themselves and others as a result.

Considering the suitability of materials and equipment

Find and list as many items in your classrooms that display the Kitemark as you can. How have the age and needs of the pupils you work with been taken into consideration when choosing materials and equipment? Show one way in which manufacturers' guidelines are followed.

Routine safety checking and maintenance of equipment

The person responsible for health and safety in your school should routinely carry out safety checks or make sure that these take place on a regular basis. There should be regular walkabouts or other means of making sure that hazards are not being left unreported. Where hazards are discovered, for example, items stored on top of cupboards, which could fall down when the cupboard is opened, these should be recorded immediately. Safety checks should also be made on all equipment that could be hazardous if neglected. All electrical items used in school should have annual checks, carried out by a qualified electrician. Equipment such as fire extinguishers should also be checked annually and checks recorded on the outside of the extinguisher.

Hazardous materials should always be locked away (see K1, page 4). (For disposal of waste, see K10, page 13.)

Safe layout and organisation of rooms, equipment, materials and outdoor spaces

Safe layout and organisation of rooms

Rooms should be organised safely and there should be adequate space to move around comfortably for the number of people using them. Everyone should be able to access

Figure 3.5 Pupils need to be sitting properly in order to be able to write correctly

materials and equipment as required. The furniture should be an appropriate size for the age of pupils, so that they are able to sit comfortably when working.

Preparing learning materials and equipment

All secondary schools use a variety of materials that need to be prepared daily. Some, such as putting out glue and scissors in an Art class, will be easily achieved, but others, for example where pupils are using different materials to design and make a game in Design Technology, may take longer to organise. As there is more than one class in a year group, there may be several classes needing to use similar materials in the same week and it is important to check that there are enough to go around.

You will often have to make sure that there are sufficient general classroom resources in all classes. This includes getting out items such as Maths equipment, text books or even new exercise books. If you or other adults are working in other areas in the school, it should be made clear to you exactly what resources to use and where to find them. It should also be made clear to you where particular items are stored and whether you have access to storage areas and store cupboards. Teachers should ensure that items that are needed will be available at the time and that other classes will not be using the same resource area. Some schools may have rotas and procedures in place for ensuring that all classes have equal access to resources and facilities.

Outdoor spaces

Outdoor areas used by pupils should be safe and boundaries should be inspected regularly to ensure that they are secure. Outdoor areas should be checked before pupils go into them to ensure that they are tidy and that any litter, broken glass or animal mess has been cleared up. If you are responsible for putting out equipment, make sure that pupils are aware how it should be used and reinforce rules wherever possible to remind them how to behave.

▼ Figure 3.6 There are many hazards that can be caused by a badly controlled environment

How to adapt the environment to ensure safety for children and young people

All children should be given equal opportunities and this should be remembered in the learning environment. All pupils, including those with special educational (ASL) needs, should be considered when planning and setting out materials and resources. The environment may often need to be adapted for the needs of particular pupils within the class.

Factors to be considered include the following:

- **Light** – This may need to be adjusted or teaching areas changed if a visually impaired pupil's eyes are light sensitive.
- **Accessibility** – A pupil in a wheelchair needs to have as much access to classroom facilities as others. Furniture and resources may need to be moved to allow for this.
- **Sound** – Some pupils may be sensitive to sounds, for example a child on the autistic spectrum who is disturbed by loud or unusual noises. It is not always possible for such noises to be avoided, but teaching assistants need to be aware of the effect that they can have on pupils.

Portfolio activity K7 K8

Demonstrating outdoor and indoor safety

Show your assessor how the learning environment in which you work fulfils safety requirements. You will need to look at a variety of indoor and outdoor spaces and equipment, and include a description of how you make safety checks before use.

Next, look at and evaluate a classroom in your school and assess whether its layout takes the following into account:

- accessibility for all pupils, particularly those with special educational (ASL) needs
- maximum use of space
- good use of storage areas
- safety issues
- accessibility of materials.

When and how to use safety equipment; safety in respect of animals and outdoor spaces

The kind of safety equipment shown in Figure 3.7 is more likely to be used where there are very young children, for example in nurseries and other early years settings. However, if you are working in a special needs school or in a setting where pupils need additional supervision, you may be required to use this type of safety equipment with older pupils. Safety codes are sometimes used in schools to deter pupils from entering a particular area such as a kitchen or ICT suite. You should always use manufacturers' guidelines when setting up equipment and it should be checked regularly. Any broken or incomplete equipment should be removed and disposed of.

Keeping animals

You may keep animals in school, although this may vary from one school or local authority to another, or there may be opportunities for staff or pupils to bring them into school as part of a topic or activity. Pupils can learn a great deal from contact with and caring for animals. However, animals should always be handled carefully and pupils should be taught to treat them with respect and be mindful of health and safety issues. Tadpoles, for example, can die if they are kept in very warm classrooms. You must make sure that whenever animals are kept in school, health and safety requirements are carefully considered and that there is adult supervision at all times.

▲ Figure 3.7 When would you use this type of equipment?

Keys to good practice

When animals are in school

✓ Make sure pupils wash their hands after handling animals.
✓ Always supervise pupils' contact with animals.
✓ Keep animal cages, tanks and other areas clean.
✓ Ensure that there are rotas and routines for feeding animals.

Safety in outdoor environments and spaces

Pupils should be encouraged to use the outside environment as much as possible. However, there can be dangers if outside areas are not monitored carefully. Ponds and sandpits used for long jump should be covered when not in use, as both can be hazardous and uncovered sandpits can attract foxes and dogs. Equipment should always be appropriate to the space available and should be put away safely. Plants can also be dangerous – thorns or nettles should be kept back and any poisonous plants noted and/or removed.

K9 Portfolio activity

Procedures for checking and maintaining safety of equipment and outdoor spaces

Can you think of any other safety equipment which is used in your school? What are the procedures for checking and maintaining it? How are outdoor spaces monitored and maintained?

Good hygiene practice

You should be a good role model for pupils and always follow good practice yourself with regards to hygiene. This includes washing your hands before any activity involving foodstuffs, such as lunchtime or cooking activities. If you are giving first aid, you must make sure you follow the appropriate procedures.

Principles of cross-infection

When working with pupils, you are vulnerable to picking up and also to carrying infection, so you should keep up to date with your own immunisations for diseases such as mumps, flu and meningitis. However, most childhood illnesses are most infectious before the symptoms occur and many pupils come to school with coughs and colds. Your school may have its own policy for these circumstances. For example, some pupils seem to have a permanent cold during winter and it would not be practical for them to be out of school for long periods. You should be aware of the signs of the common illnesses (see page 19).

Appropriate systems for disposing of waste and for handling body fluids

Your school will have a policy that follows local and national guidelines for handling body fluids and disposing of **waste**. When dealing with body fluids, you should always wear latex gloves, disposing of them after use. There should be special bins for first-aid waste, which should be disposed of appropriately.

> **🔒 Key term**
> **Waste** – unwanted materials, soiled clothing, body fluids, dressings, cleaning cloths

Issues concerning the spread of HIV/AIDS virus and hepatitis

The virus that causes AIDS is called the HIV virus. It is only spread through body fluids (i.e. blood, semen, breast milk and vaginal fluids). The most common ways of HIV being passed from one person to another are through unprotected sex, sharing of needles or from mother to child during pregnancy, birth or breastfeeding. HIV cannot be spread through casual contact, or tears or sweat as these body fluids are not infectious.

Although there are different forms of hepatitis, it is caused by a virus that attacks the liver. It is also transmitted through blood-to-blood contact, sharing needles and general poor hygiene.

Adult/child ratio requirements

Adult to child ratios will vary according to the setting and the age group of the children. In school, it may vary according to local authority requirements within and outside school hours. Look at your school policy or local education authority requirements for the adult to pupil ratio in your school. As a rough guideline, however, there should be one teacher for every 30 pupils in maintained schools and one adult for every five pupils on school trips and out-of-hours activities.

How to supervise children safely

When supervising pupils, you should be aware of the kinds of risks to which they are exposed and how likely these are to happen bearing in mind the age and/or needs of the pupil. Younger, less mature pupils are more likely to have accidents due to a lower awareness of risk and danger. If you are working with pupils who have learning disabilities (ASN in Scotland), they may also be less likely to have a fully developed awareness of danger: you need to modify your supervision according to the needs of the pupils and their level of awareness.

You may be involved in risk assessment activities, in particular if you are taking pupils off school premises. Always encourage pupils to talk and think about any risks when they are working with you, so that they develop their own awareness of danger.

Most activities carry some element of risk. Many educationalists now believe that the current tendency for many parents to keep their children indoors and take them everywhere by car is detrimental and over-protective, as it does not allow them to explore and discover the world for themselves. Therefore, it is important for all children to have the opportunity to take some risks.

(See also K24, page 27.)

K12 Portfolio activity

Balancing learning experiences against the risks involved

Think about the areas of risk for the following groups. How does the risk involved balance with the learning experience?

- Taking a group of pupils with learning difficulties to the park
- Working with a Year 7 (S1) Drama group in the playground
- Going on a Citizenship walk to local shops with Year 9 pupils
- Working with Year 8 (S2) on a Design Technology activity, using hot glue guns and hacksaws
- Doing a traffic survey with a Year 11(S5) group
- Taking a Year 7 (S1) group to the nearby athletics track each week

Policies and procedures for responding to and recording accidents and emergencies

In any environment where pupils are being supervised it is likely that there will be incidents or injuries at some time. You may find that you are first on the scene in the case of an accident or emergency and need to take action. If you are the only adult in the vicinity, you must make sure you follow the correct procedures until help arrives. It is vital to send for help as soon as possible. This should be the school's qualified first aider and, if necessary, an ambulance.

You will also need to support and reassure not only the casualty but also other pupils who may be present. Children quickly become distressed and, depending on what they have witnessed, may be in shock themselves. Make sure that you and any others on the scene are not put at unnecessary risk.

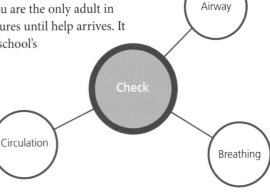

▼ Figure 3.8 The three key elements to check when giving first aid

Airway

Check

Circulation

Breathing

Warning! If not trained in first aid, and if at all unsure about what to do, you should only take action to avert any further danger to the casualty and others.

Resuscitation

If you are the first on the scene and find a casualty is not breathing, you may need to attempt resuscitation. This is known as Cardio Pulmonary Resuscitation (CPR). In all cases you should call for an ambulance immediately. Before carrying out CPR, check that there is no further risk to the casualty or to others.

For children from 1 year to puberty:

- Gently tip the head back by lifting the chin. Check the nose and mouth for any obstructions.
- Pinch the child's nose, place your mouth over the child's mouth and give five rescue breaths.
- Give chest compressions using the heel of your hand in the centre of the child's chest. After 30 compressions, give two further breaths.
- Continue until emergency help arrives.

For adults:

- Place the heel of your hands (hands linked one over the other) on the casualty's chest and press down 30 times.
- Your compressions should depress the chest to a third of its depth (4–5cm).
- Compressions should be completed at a rate of 100 times a minute.
- After 30 chest compressions, gently tilt the casualty's head back and lift the chin.
- Give two rescue breaths.
- Continue the sequence until the casualty responds or emergency help arrives.

(For procedures for administering CPR to other age groups, see www.bbc.co.uk/health/first_aid/procedures_index/index.shtml).

▲ Figure 3.9 When carrying out CPR you must place the victim in the correct position to avoid further injury

Different emergencies and what you should do

Burns and scalds

Cool the affected area immediately using cold water. Do not remove any clothes that are stuck to the burn.

Electrocution

Cut off the source of electricity by removing the plug. If there is no way to do this, stand on dry insulating material, such as newspaper or a wooden box, and push the victim away from the source using something wooden, such as a chair. Do not touch the victim until the electricity has been switched off. Then, place the victim in the recovery position (see pages 16–17).

Choking or difficulty with breathing

Encourage the victim to cough to dislodge the blockage. Bend the casualty over with the head lower than the chest and slap between the shoulder blades five times using the heel of the hand.

Poisoning

If possible, find out what the pupil has taken or swallowed. Stay with the pupil and if they become unconscious, call an ambulance and put the pupil in the recovery position. Do not try to give the pupil anything to drink. Take the suspected poison to hospital with you.

Falls: fractures

Treat all cases as actual fractures. Do not attempt to move the casualty. You will need a qualified first aider to come to the scene. Support a fractured leg by tying it to the other leg, using a wide piece of fabric such as a scarf or tie. If the knee is broken, do not try to force it straight. If you suspect a fractured arm, support it in a sling and secure it to the chest. If the arm will not bend, secure it by strapping it to the body.

Faints or loss of consciousness

Treat those who feel faint by sitting them down and putting their head between their knees. If they do faint, lie them on their back and raise their legs to increase blood flow to the brain. Loosen clothing at the neck and keep the patient quiet after regaining consciousness.

Anaphylactic shock

This is a severe allergic reaction and can be due to ingestion of a particular food, such as nuts, or caused by insect stings. It may cause constriction of air passages and can be fatal. Sit the casualty up and find out if they have any medication. Seek emergency help. If they lose consciousness, open the airway and start resuscitation.

Bleeding

Reassure the pupil and keep them calm if distressed. Elevate the wound if necessary and put a dressing on it. If there is a foreign body in the wound, do not attempt to remove it. Press on or around the wound to stop the bleeding.

Breathing difficulties or asthma attack

Ensure that the pupil has nothing in their mouth. Make sure they have their inhaler and encourage them to breath slowly. Keep them away from others in a quiet area. Call for help if there is no improvement.

Putting a casualty into the recovery position

If you are dealing with an unconscious person, you will need to place them in the recovery position. This will prevent any blood, vomit or saliva from blocking the windpipe. You should always do this unless you suspect that the victim has a fracture of the spine or neck.

1. Kneel beside the victim and turn their head towards you, lifting it back to open the airway.
2. Place the victim's nearest arm straight down their side and the other arm across their chest. Place the far ankle over the near ankle.
3. While holding the head with one hand, hold the victim at the hip by their clothing and turn them onto their front by pulling towards you, supporting them with your knees.

4. Lift the chin forward to keep the airway open.
5. Bend the arm and leg nearest to you, and pull out the other arm from under the body, palm up.

If you are treating a casualty, you should be aware of the dangers of contamination from blood and other body fluids. If possible, always wear protective gloves when treating an open wound or when in contact with other body fluids. Many infections such as HIV and hepatitis can be passed on through contact with these fluids.

You should always stay with the casualty and give support by your physical presence, and also as much care as you are able. If you feel that you are not able to deal with the situation, you should always do what you can and reassure the patient as much as possible while sending for help. Where a pupil has been injured badly, their parents or carers should be notified immediately. They will need to know exactly what is happening and if the child is being taken to hospital they will need to know where.

How to treat common minor injuries such as minor skin abrasions, cuts, bumps

Minor injuries such as cuts and grazes will usually be dealt with as they occur by a first aider. It is unlikely that creams and lotions will be applied; most school first aiders will clean minor injuries with cold water. A note should be sent home stating what has happened so that the parent is informed. It is particularly important that parents are aware if their child has had a bump on the head.

▼ Figure 3.10 A sample accident report form

Sunnymead Secondary School
Accident report form

Name of casualty ……………………………………………………………………..

Exact location of incident …………………………………………………………….

Date of incident ………………………………………………………………………

What was the injured person doing? ………………………………………………..

How did the accident happen? ………………………………………………………

What injuries occurred? ………………………………………………………………

Treatment given ………………………………………………………………………

Medical aid sought ……………………………………………………………………

Name of person dealing with incident ………………………………………………

Name of witness ………………………………………………………………………

If the casualty was a child, what time were parents informed? …………………….

Was hospital attended? ………………………………………………………………

Was the accident investigated? …………………… By whom? …………………….

Signed ………………………………………………… Position …………………….

Remember that following all injuries or emergencies, even minor accidents, a record should be made of what has happened and the steps taken by the staff present.

Awareness of location and contents of first aid box

The appropriate contents of a first aid kit

You should know the location of safety equipment in school and the identity of trained first aiders. It is strongly recommended (in Scotland, it is a legal requirement) that there are first aiders in all educational establishments. They need to have completed a training course approved by the Health and Safety Executive (HSE), which is valid for three years. You should also be aware of the location of first aid boxes in the school. The school's trained first aider should be responsible for ensuring adequate supply and regular restocking of the first aid box. Supplies should be date stamped when they are received as they have a five-year shelf life. If you find that there is not sufficient equipment, you must report that to the health and safety officer.

There is no mandatory requirement for the contents of first aid boxes but they should include certain items, as shown in Figure 3.11.

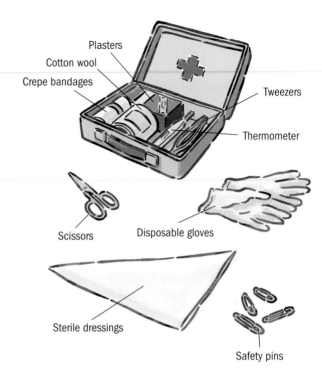

▲ **Figure 3.11** Items to include in a first aid box

How to recognise and avoid allergic reactions

There are an increasing number of children who have allergic reactions to foods such as nuts or intolerances to foods such as wheat. All school staff should be aware of the identities of pupils who have these reactions and clear instructions on how to deal with each case must be readily available. In particular, lunchtime supervisors need to be kept informed. There may be a book containing photographs of relevant pupils, information about their condition and contact telephone numbers. In some schools, photographs and information may be displayed on staffroom walls. Care must always be taken to keep such information as confidential as possible.

K14 Case study

Maintaining awareness of pupils' allergies

Jemma is supervising at lunchtime. A new pupil starts to have difficulty breathing and his friend calls Jemma over. She finds out that the pupil has a nut allergy and is sitting close to a pupil who has peanut butter in her sandwiches.

- What should Jemma do first?
- What should have happened to prevent this situation from occurring?

Policies and procedures for dealing with children's illness

Signs and symptoms of some common illnesses

All staff should be aware of the types of illnesses that may occur in children and also be alert to physical signs that show children may be incubating illness. Incubation periods can vary between illnesses, from one day to three weeks in some cases. Remember that some children, such as those with special educational (ASL) needs, may not be able to communicate exactly what is wrong. General signs that children are 'off colour' may include:

- pale skin
- flushed cheeks
- rashes
- different (quiet, clingy, irritable) behaviour
- rings around the eyes.

Common illnesses and their characteristics

Illness and symptoms	Recommended time to keep off school and treatment	Comments
Chickenpox – patches of itchy red spots with white centres	For five days from onset of rash. Treat with calamine lotion to relieve itching.	It is not necessary to keep at home until all the spots have disappeared.
German measles (rubella) – pink rash on head, trunk and limbs; slight fever, sore throat	For five days from onset of rash. Treat by resting.	The child is most infectious before diagnosis. Keep away from pregnant women.
Impetigo – small red pimples on the skin, which break down and weep	Until lesions are crusted and healed. Treat with antibiotic cream or medicine.	Antibiotic treatment may speed up healing. Wash hands well after touching the child's skin.
Ringworm – contagious fungal infection of the skin; shows as circular flaky patches	None. Treat with anti-fungal ointment; it may require antibiotics.	It needs treatment by the GP.
Diarrhoea and vomiting	Until diarrhoea and vomiting has settled and for 24 hours after. No specific diagnosis or treatment, although keep giving clear fluids and no milk.	
Conjunctivitis – inflammation or irritation of the membranes lining the eyelids	None (although schools may have different policies on this). Wash with warm water on cotton wool swab. GP may prescribe cream.	
Measles – fever, runny eyes, sore throat, cough; red rash, which often starts from the head, spreading downwards	Give rest, plenty of fluids and paracetamol for fever.	This is now more likely with some parents refusing MMR inoculation.
Meningitis – fever, headache, stiff neck and blotch skin; dislike of light; symptoms may develop very quickly	Get urgent medical attention. It is treated with antibiotics.	It can have severe complications and be fatal.
Tonsillitis – inflammation of the tonsils by infection. Very sore throat, fever, earache, enlarged red tonsils, which may have white spots.	Treat with antibiotics and rest.	It can also cause ear infection.

The Department of Health has issued a useful poster, 'Guidance on infection control in schools and nurseries', to schools, which could be displayed in the first aid area as a quick reference. It clearly sets out some common illnesses and their characteristics. Some of these are listed in the table on page 19, although the list is not exhaustive. Staff must be alert to the signs and symptoms of these common illnesses and notice changes in behaviour that indicate that children may be unwell.

Younger pupils often develop symptoms more quickly than adults, as they may have less resistance to infection. Most schools will call parents and carers straight away if their child is showing signs or symptoms of illnesses. If pupils are on antibiotics, most schools will recommend that they stay off school until they have completed the course.

K15 Portfolio activity

Dealing with ill pupils appropriately

Either write a reflective account detailing how you have dealt with an incident when a pupil was ill or ask your assessor to speak to a first aider or other staff member who can confirm that you acted appropriately and in compliance with school policy.

Emergency procedures

Procedures for fires

Schools may need to be evacuated for different reasons, for example, in the case of fire, bomb scare or other emergency. Your school is required to have a health and safety policy, which gives guidelines for emergency procedures and you should make sure that you are aware of these. Fire notices should be displayed at various points around the school, showing what to do in case of a fire and where to assemble in case of building evacuation. All adults should know what their role requires them to do and where to assemble pupils.

The school should have regular fire drills – around once a term – at different times of the day (not just before playtime for convenience!) so that all adults and pupils are aware of what to do wherever they are on the premises. Fire drills should also be practised at lunchtime or during after-school or breakfast club, when there are different staff on site and when pupils are in different environments. Records should be kept of all fire drills, any issues that occur and the action taken.

Security incidents

It is important that all staff are vigilant and make sure that unidentified people are challenged immediately. Do this by simply asking whether you can help the person or by asking to see their visitor's badge. (In Scotland, unauthorised visitors are extremely unlikely due to the security entry system, which causes all secondary entrances to lock automatically after all pupils are in school, and allows visitor entry through the main entrance only after identification and authorised release of the door. Vigilance is, however, always advisable.)

Missing children

Fortunately it is extremely rare for pupils to go missing, particularly if the school follows health and safety guidelines and procedures. On school trips you should periodically check the group for whom you are responsible, as well as keeping an eye on pupils supervised by helpers. If for some reason a pupil does go missing, raise the alarm straightaway and make sure that you follow school policy.

Keys to good practice

Health, safety and security arrangements

✓ Always be vigilant.
✓ Use and store equipment safely.
✓ Check both indoor and outdoor environment and equipment regularly and report anything that is unsafe, following the correct procedures.
✓ Challenge unidentified persons.
✓ Check adult/child ratios in all situations.
✓ Ensure you are aware of procedures at the beginning and end of the day.
✓ Make sure you are thoroughly prepared when carrying out unusual activities or when going on trips.
✓ Use correct procedures for clearing up blood, vomit, urine or faeces.

Types and possible signs and indicators of child abuse

As an adult working with children, you need to have an understanding of the different signs that may indicate that a child is being abused. Although you will do your best to ensure a child's safety while they are in your care, you also need to look out for any signs that they are being mistreated when they are out of school. The signs may include both physical and behavioural changes. There are four main types of abuse.

Physical abuse

This involves being physically hurt or injured. Physical abuse may take a variety of forms and be either spasmodic or persistent. Injuries may come from children being hit, kicked, shaken, punched or beaten.

The signs of physical abuse are often quite straightforward to spot and can include bruises, cuts, burns and other injuries. However, you should be aware that such injuries can also be caused by genuine accidents. If you notice frequent signs of injury or if there appear to be other signs of abuse, it is important to take action. Less obvious signs of physical abuse may include fear of physical contact with others, reluctance to get changed for PE, wanting to stay covered up, even in hot weather, and aggression.

Emotional abuse

This involves the child being continually 'put down' and criticised, or not given love or approval at a time when they need it the most. It includes bullying, discrimination and racism, which may also take place outside school. This could take the form of name calling, humiliation or teasing. Increasingly, it can also take place through mobile phones and the Internet.

The signs of emotional abuse are that the child is withdrawn and lacks confidence, shows regression or is 'clingy' towards adults, and has low self-esteem. Children who suffer from emotional abuse are likely to be anxious about new situations and may show extremes of behaviour or appear distracted and unable to concentrate.

Sexual abuse

Sexual abuse involves an adult or young person using a child sexually, for example, by touching their bodies inappropriately or by forcing them to look at sexual images or have sex.

The signs of sexual abuse may include sexual behaviour inappropriate to the child's age, genital irritation, clinginess or changes in behaviour, regression and lack of trust of adults. Sexual abuse can be almost impossible to identify and its signs can be caused by other kinds of abuse. It is therefore important that any signs are seen as possible, rather than probable, indicators.

Neglect

This means that the child is not being properly cared for and not having its basic needs met by parents or carers.

Basic needs include shelter, food, love, general hygiene and medical care. The signs of neglect may include being dirty, tired, hungry, seeking attention and generally failing to thrive.

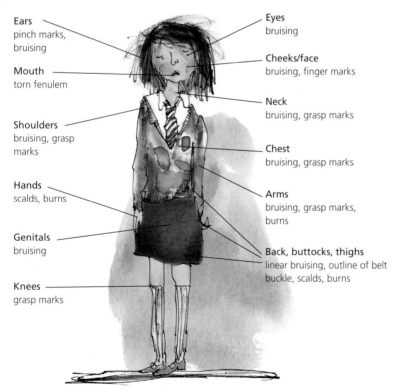

Ears
pinch marks,
bruising

Mouth
torn fenulem

Shoulders
bruising, grasp
marks

Hands
scalds, burns

Genitals
bruising

Knees
grasp marks

Eyes
bruising

Cheeks/face
bruising, finger marks

Neck
bruising, grasp marks

Chest
bruising, grasp marks

Arms
bruising, grasp marks,
burns

Back, buttocks, thighs
linear bruising, outline of belt
buckle, scalds, burns

Figure 3.12 There are many signs that may indicate some form of abuse

As a teaching assistant you are in a good position to notice changes in pupils' behaviour and other signs of possible abuse. You should always look out for the indicators above and, if you are at all concerned, speak to either your class teacher or the school's Child Protection Officer (usually the headteacher). They will follow the school's child protection policy and, if necessary, follow local authority guidelines for informing social services. Always keep a note of what happened, what you reported and who you told.

Case study K17 K18

Identifying and acting on signs of possible abuse

Marie has been working in Francesca's class for six months. Recently she has noticed that Francesca, who is usually happy and settled, has become very withdrawn and less involved with her friends. She appears very reluctant to join in during class activities and at playtimes, and her clothing does not appear to have been washed. She has not had her PE kit in school for two weeks. Marie knows that Francesca's mother has been treated for alcoholism in the past, but as far as she knows this is not currently an issue. She speaks to the class teacher and tells her about her concerns.

- What signs is Francesca showing that may be indicators of abuse?
- How should Marie and the class teacher proceed?

Recognition that social factors may increase a child's vulnerability to abuse

If you know that a pupil comes from a home background where there are likely to be pressures on the family, for example if there is a parent or older sibling who misuses drugs or alcohol, it is possible that the pupil is more vulnerable to abuse. However, it

▼ Figure 3.13 You may need to report to others possible cases of abuse.

is very important that you do not jump to any conclusions or assume that abuse has definitely taken place.

Safe working practices that protect children and adults who work with them

It is important to follow safe working practices to ensure that pupils are protected from abuse. Child protection is the responsibility of all who work with children and you need to be aware of your school's policy for recording and reporting suspected abuse. Records will need to be kept of what pupils have said and when they said it, as well as notes, dates and times of any meetings that have taken place between the school and social services. If a pupil reports anything that is a cause for concern, the school needs to make sure it is followed up.

Adults who work with children also need to protect themselves by making sure that they are never on their own with individual pupils for any length of time or, if they have to be, that they are in an area that is open to others.

K19 Portfolio activity

Investigating protection and behaviour policies

List the different ways in which your school protects both pupils and adults through the use of safe working practices. You may need to look at your school's child protection and behaviour policies.

How to encourage children to be aware of their own bodies and understand their right not to be abused

All children have a right to be safe and feel protected. The UN Convention on the Rights of the Child, which was signed by the UK in 1989, sets out the rights of all children to be treated equally and fairly. These include:

- the right of all children to grow up in an atmosphere of happiness, love and understanding
- the right to be as healthy as possible
- the right to grow and develop to the best of their ability
- the right to live in a safe environment.

Children must be protected from things that threaten to infringe these rights. This means that forms of abuse or abduction, taking them out of school without cause or making them work on activities harmful to their health must be prevented.

Children need to be taught how to keep safe in a number of different ways. As well as encouraging their awareness of health and safety issues, you should support their development by helping them to have a positive self-image. Children need to have plenty of opportunities and encouragement as they grow up in order to develop their independence and learn about their likes and dislikes. They should also be aware that they have a right to be safe and know what to do if they do not feel safe. If you are talking to pupils about their bodies, using activities you have planned with the teacher, be aware that people use different terms to describe body parts and functions, such as going to the toilet, when speaking to pupils. If pupils confide in you and tell you what has happened to them, they may need time or additional help to use the right language or to draw what has happened. The curriculum should include giving pupils information about organisations that exist to protect them, such as the NSPCC (in Scotland, Children 1st, formerly SSPCC), Childline and Kidscape.

Keys to good practice

Keeping pupils safe

✓ Ensure that pupils are taught to keep themselves safe.
✓ Encourage pupils to talk about their worries and speak to others.
✓ Use age-appropriate language when speaking to pupils.
✓ Never promise not to tell others if a pupil discloses that they have been abused.
✓ Set an example by encouraging co-operation and positive behaviour.

Portfolio activity K20

Supporting positive self-image and awareness of rights

How does your school encourage positive self-images in pupils? What kinds of activities or discussions might staff encourage in order to develop pupils' awareness of their rights? Investigate the different forms of support that might be available through outside organisations to help with this.

The importance of consistently and fairly applied boundaries and rules for children's behaviour

As discussed in Unit 19, it is important that all staff are consistent when managing pupils' behaviour. Children need to have boundaries that they can understand and are regularly reinforced by adults. If it is not clear to them how they are expected to behave or if adults give them conflicting messages, children become confused and upset, and find it hard to know how to behave next time. Although all children will test boundaries for behaviour, if they are met with the same response each time they will be less likely to repeat it. Rules should be appropriate for the age or ability of the pupil and the language used should make the expectations of adults clear.

When managing pupils' behaviour, be careful of stereotyping or making assumptions about how they will behave. If pupils are expected to behave well or badly, they will usually live up to the expectation.

Case study

Applying boundaries and rules

Barbara is working in a Year 8 (S2) Science class as a teaching assistant. There is also a work experience student and a student teacher, as well as the class teacher. This afternoon, Barbara notices that the student teacher, who is supervising pupils completing an online activity, is allowing four pupils to sit around one computer when the rule is two. When Barbara asks her about it, she replies that the pupils were upset when she had told them only two at a time and wanted to be together. She also tells Barbara that she has not allowed James and Hanif to use the computer together because 'they always terrorise each other'.

- Should Barbara say anything to the student about what she has told the pupils?
- Why is it important that the adults in the class give pupils the same messages?
- What might have been a more appropriate way of managing James and Hanif?

How to respond to children's challenging behaviour

Pupils who display challenging behaviour need to know what will happen if they regularly and persistently do this. As well as consistent boundaries, managed by all staff and agreed through school policies, there should also be age-appropriate sanctions. Be aware that what may deter younger pupils may not always work for older ones.

Portfolio activity

Managing inappropriate behaviour in different age groups

Consider the sanctions used in your school for managing inappropriate behaviour. Do they vary in line with different age groups? If not, are some more effective than others at deterring pupils of different ages? Give reasons for your answer.

Importance of encouraging and rewarding positive behaviour

(See Unit 19, K8, page 60)

Safety issues and concerns when taking children out of the setting

You need to be aware of safety issues when taking pupils out of school. If you are taking a large number of pupils on an outing or residential trip, a member of staff should undertake a risk assessment beforehand. This means that they will check what kinds of risks there might be and the likelihood of the risk occurring. The level of risk may be dependent on a number of factors:

- the adult/child ratio
- where you are going
- how you will get there
- your planned activities on arrival.

The facilities will need to be checked to make sure they are adequate for the needs of the pupils, for example, if you are taking a pupil with a disability (ASN in Scotland). As well as a risk assessment, preparations need to include other considerations. A trip must always be planned thoroughly so that the adults are prepared for whatever happens. Preparations include the need to:

- seek and gain parental consent
- arrange for suitable safe transport
- take first aid kit and a first aider with you
- take appropriate clothing for the activity or weather
- make lists of adults and the pupils for whom they will be responsible
- give information sheets to all helpers, including timings and any safety information
- make sure that pupils you have concerns about are in your group rather than with a parent.

Portfolio activity K24

Identifying safety issues for trips

Outline the different safety issues you need to be prepared for when undertaking each of the following:

- a Year 9 (S3) trip to a theme park
- a Year 7 (S1) trip by train to a local museum
- a Year 8 (S2) visit to a Tudor castle and gardens
- a Year 10 (S4) five-day trip to the Ardèche.

Legislation, guidelines and policies which form the basis for action to safeguard children

The Every Child Matters guidelines, which led to the Children Act 2004, came about as a direct result of the Laming Report following the death of Victoria Climbié. The report was highly critical of the way in which the Climbié case was handled and made 108 recommendations to overhaul child protection in the UK. The main points that emerged were that:

- there should be a much closer working relationship between agencies such as health professionals, schools and welfare services
- there should be a central database containing records of all children and whether they are known to different services
- there should be an independent children's commissioner for England to protect children and young people's rights (a Children's Commissioner for Scotland has been in post for several years)
- there should be a children and families board, which is chaired by a senior government minister
- Ofsted will set a framework that will monitor children's services.

The Children's Act 2004 required that these recommendations became a legal requirement and as a result the Every Child Matters framework was introduced to implement the Act and the wider reform programme.

(For a full outline of the Laming Report, see www.victoria-climbié-inquiry.org.uk. For more on Every Child Matters, see Unit 38, page 245.)

For your portfolio...

K6
K7
K8
K9
part of
K13
K14
K15

A good way of producing evidence for this unit is to go for a health and safety walkabout with your assessor. You can point out any hazards and carry out your own safety check of facilities and equipment in all areas of your school. This could include fire extinguishers and exits, first aid kits, access to first aid, how the school routinely checks equipment and stores hazardous materials, and any accidents you have recorded. You could record the walkabout, include it as evidence in your portfolio and ask your assessor to use it as part of the assessment process. They might ask witnesses in school whether you always follow health, safety and security procedures yourself and encourage pupils to do the same. For the school's policies for dealing with health emergencies, including allergic reactions, you could carry out a simulated activity showing how you would respond to different symptoms.

K17
K18

For the child abuse section of the unit, you may need to have a professional discussion with your assessor to show that you know and understand the different indicators of abuse and how you should respond to any concerns you may have.

Websites

www.barnardos.org.uk

www.bbc.co.uk/health/first_aid

www.hse.gov.uk – Health and Safety Executive

www.kidscape.org.uk – a charity to prevent bullying and child abuse

www.nch.org.uk – The Children's Charity

www.redcross.org – The Red Cross

www.scotland.gov.uk/childrenscharter

www.sja.org.uk – St John Ambulance

www.teachernet.gov.uk – gives a list of charities that work together with schools

www.unicef.org.uk – The United Nations Children's Fund

Other sources of information

Protection of Children (Scotland) Act 2003

Contact details

helpline@nspcc.org.uk

nspcc helpline: 0808 800 5000

18 Support Pupils' Learning Activities

This unit will examine how you can most effectively support pupils and teachers when undertaking teaching and learning activities in school. This is one of the most important aspects of your role as a teaching assistant. All learning will take place under the direction of a teacher, but you may be asked to support individuals, groups or even whole classes. The unit will identify what you need to do in order to support planned learning activities and applies not only to classroom activities but also to any setting where teaching and learning takes place such as extended hours provision or educational visits.

The unit will define the type of support you may be asked to give in the presence or absence of the teacher. It will give you some idea of the kinds of problems you may encounter and how to deal with them. You will also need to look at the different ways in which you promote independent learning and the importance of doing this. This will include developing relationships with pupils to enable you to provide an appropriate level of assistance while encouraging them to make their own decisions about their learning. Many of the knowledge base standards for this unit overlap with those in Units 23 and 24; Unit 18 can be used whether or not you are directly involved with planning and evaluation.

What you need to know and understand

For this unit you will need to know and understand:

- The nature, extent and boundaries of your role in supporting teaching and learning activities, and its relationship to the role of the teacher and others in the school

- The importance of having high expectations of all pupils with whom you work

- The relevant school curriculum and age-related expectations of pupils in the subject/ curriculum area and age range of the pupils with whom you are working

- The teaching and learning objectives of the learning activity and the place of these in the teacher's overall teaching programme

- The key factors that can affect the way pupils learn including age, gender and physical, intellectual, linguistic, social, cultural and emotional development

- How social organisation and relationships, such as pupil grouping and the way adults interact and respond to pupils , may affect learning

- School policies for inclusion and equality of opportunity and the implication of these for how you support teaching and learning activities

- How to use and adapt learning support strategies to accommodate different learning needs and learning styles

- School policy and practice in relation to the use of praise, assistance and rewards and how to use these to maintain pupils' interest in learning activities

- How to monitor the pupils' responses to teaching and learning activities

- When and how to modify teaching and learning activities

- How to monitor and promote pupil participation and progress

- The sorts of problems that might occur when supporting learning activities and how to deal with these

- The importance of working within your own sphere of competence and when you should refer to others

- The importance of independent learning and how to encourage and support this in pupils

- Strategies for challenging and motivating pupils to learn

- The importance of active listening and how to do this

- How to help pupils to review their learning strategies and achievements and plan future learning

The nature of your role in supporting teaching and learning activities

In order to support pupils effectively you should have a very clear idea about exactly where you fit into the school structure and your role within it. You should also have an up-to-date **job description** that is a realistic reflection of your duties (for more on this see Unit 22). Your job description may divide your responsibilities under different headings such as:

- teaching and learning
- administrative duties
- standards and quality assurance
- other duties.

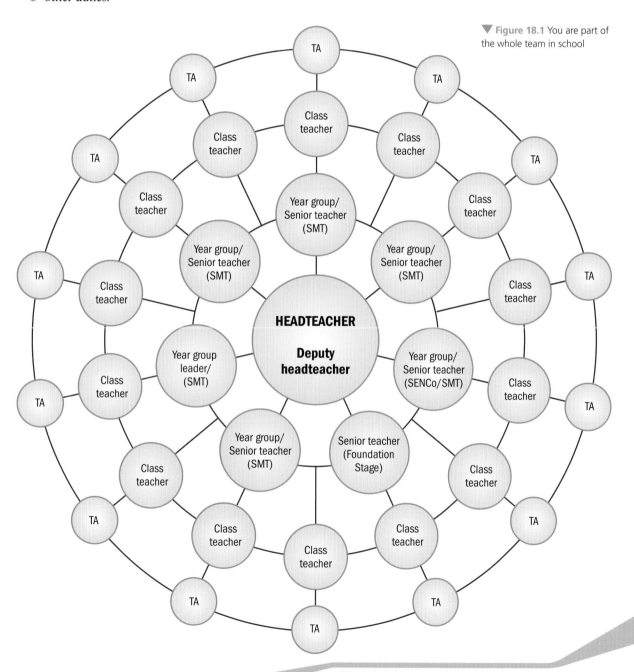

▼ **Figure 18.1** You are part of the whole team in school

Teaching assistants are likely to have a number of responsibilities, both in and outside the classroom. These responsibilities may vary widely between schools and roles, although there will be many areas that overlap. However if you are being asked to support teaching and learning as one of the main aspects of your role, you should be working closely with teachers and have access to detailed plans (see also Unit 23). You should also be able to ask for additional support yourself if you feel you are not trained to carry out some of the duties asked of you.

Depending on your role within the classroom, the amount of support you are required to give individual pupils may vary. A teaching assistant who is employed specifically to work with a pupil who has special educational (Additional Support for Learning (ASL)) needs, for example, may have much more detailed information on the individual than a teaching assistant who is supporting learning within the whole class (see Unit 38). However, if you are new to a group, ask the class teacher whether there is anything specific you should know about the pupils. There is more information on this in the units on special educational (ASL) needs (see Units 38–42).

When supporting learning you may be working with individuals, groups or the whole class. You may need to provide support using a variety of different strategies.

You are supporting the class teacher and the pupils in your class, but you are also part of the whole school team. Teaching and learning activities need to be planned and you may or may not be involved at the planning stage. However, you should have some advance notice of what you will be doing so that you can prepare yourself. This may involve discussing plans with the teacher before the class or having access to planned activities, for example plans may be in a departmental or class-planning folder stored in a shared location. You also need to know about ability groupings within the department, for example the pupils may be in set groups for different subjects depending on their acquired levels and skills.

Importance of having high expectations of all pupils with whom you work

Research has shown that where individuals are encouraged and told that they will be able to achieve, they are more likely to do so. This is often known as the Pygmalion effect – if a person thinks that we are clever, they treat us this way and we will learn to think that we are. High expectations of learning and behaviour should be part of a whole school approach and give pupils a sense of pride in their achievements. It is vital for pupils to feel part of a whole school and whole class, and to understand the importance of the contribution of each individual. In this way, pupils will develop a positive attitude to learning. In a similar way, negative self-expectations will often lead to negative work or behaviour.

▲ Figure 18.2 High expectations build success

The relevant school curriculum of the pupils with whom you are working

During the first three years (Years 7–9)(S1–3) at secondary school, when pupils are aged 11–14, teachers in schools work to the National Curriculum for Key Stage 3 and the Secondary National Strategy for School Improvement. From the age of 14 to 16 (Years 10 and 11)(S4 and 5), they work to the National Curriculum for Key Stage 4, as well as the Secondary National Strategy for School Improvement. For the purpose of this unit, you need to understand that schools and classroom teachers are working to curriculum plans such as the National Curriculum Programmes of Study and departmental Schemes of Work to ensure that attainment targets are met and appropriate National Curriculum levels achieved. Your role when supporting teaching and learning is to interpret these curriculum plans and help the classroom teacher to deliver them. (In Scotland, all pupils work within the 5–14 curriculum guidelines (currently being redeveloped to become A Curriculum for Excellence to incorporate a continuum of ages 3–18) at the level appropriate to their level of attainment/ability before progressing to Access levels 1–3 and/or Intermediate 1 or 2.)

Key Stages 3 and 4

Pupils will be learning through curriculum plans based on the National Curriculum document and taught by subject specialists. (For Scotland, see the comment about A Curriculum for Excellence above.) In the secondary setting, there is a more formal and subject-based approach to the way the curriculum is organised, compared with the primary school. However, with the changes to the curriculum, many schools are opting for a more cross-curricular approach to learning, which may slightly obscure the traditional subject boundaries. For example, ICT and Numeracy may be taught together in a project rather than as separate lessons.

Each of the subjects should have a member of staff responsible for making sure that the subject areas are monitored throughout the school, to attend curriculum courses to remain up to date, and to offer curriculum support to other members of staff. These subject leaders will usually be called subject co-ordinators, subject managers or Heads of Department, for example 'English Head of Department'. They will also need to devise school curriculum policies for each subject, which should outline the school's approach to planning and delivering the subject, and will tie in with national guidelines.

(See below for a Portfolio activity relating to this section.)

The curriculum is slightly different in the four areas of the United Kingdom and is undergoing a process of change.

Portfolio activity K3

Investigating the National Curriculum

Investigate the National Curriculum for the country and the age range in which you are working. What recent changes have taken place? (You will find some useful websites at the end of this unit.)

Teaching and learning objectives of the learning activity and the place of these in the teaching programme

The learning objectives of a lesson define what we are hoping pupils will learn during that session and therefore what pupils will be assessed against. For example, the learning objectives of a French lesson on the perfect tense might be 'to be able to recognise at least six irregular verbs in the perfect tense' (although some in the class may be expected to conjugate a minimum of six irregular verbs in the perfect tense independently). Teaching assistants need to be clear on the learning objectives of the activities they are supporting. Plans should be available and show a clear progression in the work pupils are being asked to do so that learning objectives build on each other. You should also have had at least some discussion with the teacher about the pupils and how you will be approaching the task, and you need to be clear on how what you are doing fits in with the overall plans. Usually teachers put the learning objective on the smartboard or whiteboard at the beginning of the session so that all pupils are aware of what they will be learning. This is sometimes displayed as the WALT (We Are Learning To…) or WILF (What I'm Looking For…). (See also Unit 23, page 141 for more details on planning with the teacher.)

Key factors that can affect the way pupils learn including age, gender and different types of development

A key influence on children's learning is their age and stage of development. However, children are all individuals and there will be other factors that also affect them. These are based on their own experiences and personalities, which will be different for each child. You need to consider these factors when supporting pupils in order to understand the needs of each one.

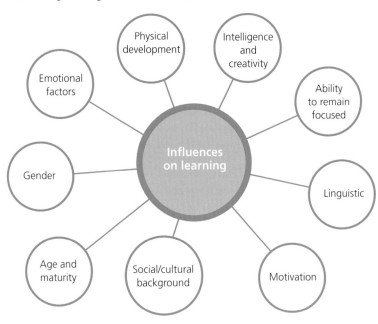

▲ Figure 18.3 Children's learning has many different influences

Intelligence and creativity

Each pupil has his/her own talents and aptitudes, and so will be more or less able at different tasks within the classroom. They may also perceive themselves to be better or worse than other pupils, and this may affect their motivation. For example, if they notice that another pupil is particularly good at a creative task such as Art, they may think that their own work is not as good and feel inadequate. As pupils will always have strengths and weaknesses in different areas, the role of the adult will be to encourage them and instil an awareness that all of us are different and that this is a positive thing.

Social and cultural background

A pupil's background will have an influence on their learning as they may come to school with a variety of experiences. Some pupils may have had a wide range of social interactions with others, while others may have had very little. Different cultures will mean that pupils will see things from different perspectives. Where pupils' experiences are socially limited, they may lack confidence with others, find the setting difficult to adjust to or take longer to relate to other adults.

Age and maturity

As we have already seen, children will develop at an individual pace and so in any group of pupils there will be some who are more mature than others. Also, due to the way in which some schools have their intakes, there may be pupils in the same class or group who are almost a year apart in age. At an earlier age, this may make a big difference to the range of abilities that exist in the class. Adults should therefore be aware of this factor when monitoring pupils' learning.

Linguistic ability

This is a key area in children's learning. Language is the route by which we build on our understanding and gradually learn to rationalise and have abstract thought. Pupils have different experiences of social interaction and a range of vocabularies, and we need to build on these through discussion, role play and wider experiences. Where pupils speak more than one language they may need more support to develop their understanding (see also Unit 36).

Physical factors

There is a wide range of physical factors that may affect learning. Pupils may have special educational (ASL) needs, for example a hearing impairment, which may mean that they need extra support to access the curriculum fully. Some pupils may not have developed full muscle control and find fine or gross motor skills a challenge (for more on this see Unit 42).

Motivation

This will directly affect the pupil's learning as motivation is the pupil's desire to learn and the interest that they have in a task. Where a pupil is not interested, does not see the purpose or is unable to do a task, he or she may quickly become demotivated. The adult should therefore be aware of this and make sure that the task is at the right level, is enjoyable and makes sense to the pupil.

Emotional factors

Naturally, children will be affected by whether their home life is happy and settled. They may have been living with parents who are going though a divorce or they may have been bereaved. Sometimes they may be deeply affected by something seemingly insignificant to an adult, such as not being allowed to wear their fashionable trainers or having an argument with a sibling. Any of these things may have an impact on the pupil's ability to learn. You may need to take them away from the situation and talk to them to find out what is upsetting them and give them reassurance before attempting to continue. If the pupil is too upset or unsettled to work, it is not a good idea to try to make them do so.

Gender

The sex of a pupil may affect their learning, particularly if they have been given greater or fewer opportunities owing to their gender. It is important that we do not favour boys or girls in school when directing questioning and do not have expectations of one sex over another. For example, research shows that girls are generally quicker to read, but this could be due to the expectations of adults.

Ability to concentrate

Pupils of different ages vary in their ability to concentrate on tasks and to sit and listen when required, although pupils of the same age may have a similar concentration span. Teachers should be aware of the length of time the pupils in their class are able to focus on a task, so that the work given or the amount of time they are required to sit still is not too demanding for them. Where one pupil's ability to concentrate is markedly different from that of his or her classmates, this may affect the learning of both the individual and of the rest of the class.

Very young children are unable to concentrate for long on one activity and will copy adults and other children, seeking reassurance about what they are doing. As they become older, the length of time children are able to focus on activities increases, although they may be easily distracted and find writing difficult. By the time pupils reach secondary school, most can concentrate on a task for a given time without distractions, even though some of them may enjoy distracting others!

How to recognise when a pupil is losing concentration

A pupil who is not focused on the teacher or the task may:

- start to disturb other pupils
- be distracted and fidgety
- misbehave and try to gain attention
- start daydreaming.

Where pupils are not concentrating on a given task, the teacher or teaching assistant must ensure that they try to engage them again as soon as possible. This can be done through re-involving them in the task. You can do this by:

- removing any distractions. This will refocus the pupil's attention on what they are doing
- giving praise where possible for good work which pupils have completed to give them encouragement
- noticing the good behaviour or work of others so that you are giving positive attention to those pupils who are focusing on their work
- making yourself available and approachable so that pupils are able to ask you for help if they are finding an activity challenging. You need to develop a good relationship with pupils so that they will respect and respond to you
- being able to manage spontaneous opportunities that may arise when pupils are working and remembering to make learning fun
- varying the pace of learning if pupils are finding a task too easy or too difficult. You may need to backtrack to ensure pupils understand the task or find ways of extending the task if they complete it quickly.

How social organisation and relationships may affect learning

Another way in which pupil learning may be affected is by the group they are working with. Depending on the age of the pupils and their stage of development, they may be easily distracted or influenced by the opinions of others. Some pupils may be concerned about what their peers think of them and be reluctant to put their ideas forward in case they are wrong. Others may want to show off to their classmates in order to gain attention. If there has been a disagreement or particular problem during playtime, pupils may be unable to concentrate on their learning if they are upset or agitated. As the adult, you need to be aware of and manage these kinds of issues and their effects on pupil's learning. (See also page 42 on monitoring pupils' responses to learning activities.)

Case study K11

Managing circumstances that affect pupils' learning

You are supporting a boy with a low concentration span in a cross-curricular Year 7 (S1) Maths and Cooking lesson. Over the lesson the pupils have been asked to complete four different activities in groups. The task is a carousel activity where pupils are required to spend 15 minutes completing the activity at each table. The pupil you are working with has done some of the first activity (calculating measurements), but is now eager to move on to another table where he sees pupils are using scales to measure the weight of the ingredients to make a cake.

- What could you do to try to re-involve the pupil in the task with you?
- Are there any other strategies that you could use to make sure that the pupil completes the activity?

As the adult in the group, you may need to ensure that pupils remain focused on what they are required to do. You may also need to modify or adapt what you are doing with pupils so that they are able to achieve the learning objectives.

School policies for inclusion and equality of opportunity and their implication for supporting teaching and learning activities

All pupils should be able to fully access all areas of the curriculum. The advent of the Every Child Matters Framework and the focus on personalised (individualised) learning in all sectors of education has also made this high on the educational agenda. The reasons for this are:

Human rights
- All children have a right to learn and play together.
- Children should not be discriminated against for any reason.
- Inclusion is concerned with improving schools for staff as well as for pupils.

Equal opportunities in education
- Children do better in inclusive settings, both academically and socially.
- Children should not need to be separated to achieve adequate educational provision.
- Inclusive education is a more efficient use of educational resources.

▲ **Figure 18.4** An activity which involves pupils working together gives them social opportunities

Social opportunities

- Inclusion in education is one aspect of inclusion in society.
- Children need to be involved with all of their peers.

All schools should have codes of practice concerning equal opportunities and inclusion. These will sometimes form part of the policy for special educational (ASL) needs but are usually separate. You should be familiar with your school's policies on inclusion and equal opportunities. (See further information on inclusion in the learning environment in Unit 31.)

Always be aware of the needs of different pupils, whatever these may be. Remember that these may become more apparent as you get to know particular pupils. Those who may be vulnerable could include pupils:

- who have special educational (ASL) needs
- who speak English as an additional language
- who are new to the setting
- who are gifted and talented
- whose culture is different from the predominant culture of the setting
- who are in foster care
- whose parents' views are not consistent with those of the school.

Investigating the school's inclusion or equal opportunities policies

Find a copy of your school's inclusion or equal opportunities policies. For your portfolio, you need to show what its implications are for how you support teaching and learning of pupils. You can do this by:

- highlighting the relevant parts of the text and putting this into your portfolio
- summarising the main points of the policy.

When supporting pupils for different activities, assistants may find themselves in a variety of situations. An individual teaching assistant, for example, will be assisting and supporting a particular pupil and will usually work alongside or close to that pupil. As that pupil may have a Statement of Special Educational Needs (Co-ordinated Support Plan), they need that adult support to ensure that they have full access to the curriculum.

Usually, teaching assistants are asked to work with a group of pupils. In this situation, it is vital that all pupils are given the same opportunities to give their thoughts and opinions.

How to use and adapt learning support strategies to accommodate different learning needs and styles

Pupils have different approaches to learning, owing to the fact that we are all individuals and absorb information differently. By understanding the way in which different individuals learn best, we are able to support pupils more effectively. For learning to take place, information needs to be presented in a way that is relevant to the learner. As you get to know pupils, you will be able to identify how they learn best. The way in which you support their learning should depend on the learning styles and needs that they have.

Learning styles

Gardner (1993) describes a model of seven intelligences. This varies from traditional views of how we learn. Gardner's theory has implications for how we teach pupils, as it states that all seven intelligences are needed to function productively in society. Traditionally, our education systems have placed a strong emphasis on verbal and mathematical intelligences. In the light of Gardner's thought, we need to teach pupils a broader range of talents and skills. The seven intelligences are listed below.

Logical mathematical intelligence

This consists of the ability to think logically and sequentially, and reason deductively. It is most often associated with scientific and mathematical thinking. Those who learn best in this way tend to be very organised in their thinking.

Linguistic intelligence

These people will have the ability to manipulate language, both in order to express themselves and as a means of remembering information.

Spatial intelligence

Those who have spatial intelligence will find it easy to manipulate images or pictures in order to solve problems, for example when following instructions such as furniture assembly.

Musical intelligence

This means that these individuals will respond to musical pitches, tones and rhythms. They may find it easier to retain information if they learn it while listening to music or through rhythms.

Bodily/kinaesthetic intelligence

Those who learn in this way are more likely to need to learn things in a physical way, for example through practical tasks.

Personal intelligences

These include *interpersonal* feelings, or how people relate to others, and *intrapersonal* intelligence – the ability to understand one's own feelings and motivations. These two intelligences are separate from each other.

Naturalist intelligence

This includes those who can distinguish among, classify and use features of objects in the environment, for example a pupil who is able to talk about the features of different makes of car.

Although everyone is born possessing the seven intelligences, pupils come into the classroom with their own unique set of intelligences, which have been developed to a greater or lesser extent. This determines how easy or difficult it is for them to learn information when it is presented in a particular way. Pupils need to be given different methods of learning within the framework of lessons to accommodate these different learning styles; for example, practical tasks are best suited to kinaesthetic learners. You need to be aware of these ideas in order to support learning activities.

For more on learning styles, you can go to www.support4learning.org.uk/education/learning_styles and take a learning styles test.

Learning needs

Pupils' learning will also depend on their needs and abilities. We have looked at background factors that may influence how children learn on page 34, but they may also have additional learning needs, sometimes defined as special educational (ASL) needs. (See also Unit 38, which explains additional strategies.) Special educational (ASL) needs are listed below.

Physical and sensory

If a pupil has a physical or sensory impairment, they may need to have the learning environment adapted to enable them to participate fully. For example, a pupil in a wheelchair should have access to the same resources and facilities as all other pupils.

Communication and interaction

Pupils with communication and interaction needs may need support to help them with their understanding of language. You need to develop strategies that help you to check on this.

Social and emotional

Pupils who have social and emotional needs will be affected in terms of their behaviour. They may seem distracted or distract others and need extra support to stay focused.

Cognition and learning

These pupils may find some learning activities more challenging than others in their peer group. They may need you to make activities more accessible to them by modifying them (see page 265).

Gifted and talented pupils

These pupils may have additional work set for them or be encouraged to work with others. They should not always be sent out of the class to work with a 'gifted and talented group'.

Case study K8

Adapting strategies for pupils' differing needs

You have been asked to work with a group of Year 7 (S1) pupils on an activity to look through a poem and identify the way in which the poet has described different experiences using his senses. You have read the poem to the pupils and they now have to think of some descriptive phrases of their own.

Pupil A has dyslexia and is full of original ideas.
Pupil B has some difficulty in remaining focused for too long.
Pupils C and D are of average ability.
Pupil E is average and very musical.
Pupil F is above average in Maths but finds language activities challenging.

- Looking at the 'Keys to good practice' on page 49 and bearing in mind the needs of the pupils, how could you adapt the strategies you used for the different pupils in the group?
- If planned carefully, how might this take some of the pressure off you as the adult?

School policy and practice in relation to the use of praise, assistance and rewards

Be aware of your school policy for the use of praise, assistance and rewards as they are all valuable tools when supporting pupils' learning and you need to use them. They may be written down as part of your school's behaviour or inclusion policies, or it might be assumed that staff just 'know' them. Make sure you are aware of which you can and cannot use when supporting learning.

Praise and encouragement

As you will be working with pupils who are learning all the time, it is vital that you use praise and encouragement to keep them on task and motivate them in their learning. This kind of reward is very effective, although it must be clear to pupils why they are being praised. It is important as you get to know pupils to praise their efforts as well as their achievements. They will need to have recognition for what they do, and this could take several forms:

- **verbal praise** – this could be simple praise while pupils are working, for example by saying 'well done, that's a very good description' or by asking the pupil to go and show the teacher at a convenient moment and so gain another adult's attention
- **material praise such as house points and merits** – there could be a school policy on how these are used and you should be aware of this. Some schools will leave it to the class tutor to use reward systems that they find the most beneficial, whereas others may prefer a consistent whole school approach.
- **school recognition of a good effort**, such as the pupil gaining a school certificate, will offer motivation at all stages of learning.

Assistance

Teaching assistants need to be aware that their role is that of an enabler, rather than to do the task for pupils if they are having difficulties. It is important to remember to find different ways of encouraging pupils to arrive at the answer or complete the task themselves, for example through questioning and encouragement. If you need to give pupils too much support, they clearly do not understand the task and you will need to inform the class tutor.

K9 Case study

Using rewards

Femi has recently started a new job. In her last school, she always kept a packet of sweets in her pocket to give pupils if they had done well. She has continued to do this in her new school. Jack in her group has today completed an activity for the first time this week and has tried very hard, so she gives him a sweet. She is surprised when the class teacher tells her that she is not allowed to do this because it is not school policy.

- Do you think that anyone is in the wrong?
- What might be Femi's next steps?
- How else might Femi encourage Jack if he has done well?

When and how to monitor the pupils' responses to teaching and learning activities and promote pupil participation and progress

Monitoring responses

Your role is such that you will be constantly monitoring pupils' responses to learning activities and finding new ways to engage them where necessary (see How to recognise when a pupil is losing concentration on page 36). We have already looked at adapting work to accommodate different learning styles and the importance of using praise and rewards as two examples of this.

Pupils will find some subjects more stimulating than others or need help to achieve learning objectives. It is important that you monitor their responses and check what they know because you will need to feed back to the teacher whether they have achieved the learning objective.

Modifying activities

As part of the support you are required to give, you need to be able to modify activities where necessary. This is because some pupils may find tasks more challenging than others (see also Managing problems below). An example of this might be if, when working on a new concept in Maths, some pupils need more help and practice than others in understanding what they need to do. You may need to describe things in a different way or find a new angle if a pupil cannot grasp what is being taught.

Monitoring and promoting pupil progress

You might monitor and promote pupil participation in different ways.

Instructing pupils

- Talk through with pupils what they have to do.
- Give pupils a starting point so that they are able to focus.

Questioning pupils

- Use open-ended questions – what/when/why/how? – rather than questions that invite 'yes' or 'no' answers.
- Find out what the pupils already know or remember from last time.
- Involve all the pupils in a group.
- Probe, using questions, if pupils are unable to understand the task.

Explaining to pupils

- Explain any words or phrases that pupils are not clear about.
- Remind pupils of key teaching points.
- Model the correct use of vocabulary.
- Ensure all pupils understand the teacher's instructions.

Problems that might occur when supporting learning activities and how to deal with these

It may be that assistants who are supporting individuals, groups or the whole class encounter **problems** when supporting learning activities. These could take different forms, but could relate to any of the following factors.

> **Key term**
>
> **Problems** – the barriers and hindrances to supporting planned learning activities

Learning resources

The task will usually require certain resources such as pencils, paper, worksheets or textbooks, Maths apparatus, paint pots, Science equipment and so on. If you have been asked to set up for the task, make sure that you have enough equipment and that it is accessible to all the pupils. Where you have equipment that needs to be in working order, check that you know how to use it, that it is functioning and that pupils will be able to use it. If the teacher or another adult has set up for your task, it is still worth doing a check to ensure that you have everything you need. In this way you avoid potential problems before they arise.

The learning environment

This relates to the suitability of the area in which pupils are working. Problems may arise in the following circumstances.

- **Insufficient space to work** – If pupils are working on weighing, for example, and there is no room for them all to have access to the scales, they may quickly lose their focus on the task. There may not be space around the table or work area for the number of pupils that you have been asked to work with. You should always ensure that you have sufficient space for people and equipment before you start.
- **Too much noise** – The pupils may be working with you in a corner of the classroom, but any other kind of noise will be a distraction, whether it is from other pupils in the room or from some kind of outside disturbance such as grass cutting or a nearby road. It may be possible in this situation for you to investigate another area within the school, which is free from this kind of noise, or to inform the teacher that the noise level within the classroom is preventing the pupils from benefiting from the activity.
- **Disturbances from other children** – This can often be a problem if you are working in the classroom because tasks with close adult supervision can often seem exciting to other pupils. They may be naturally curious to find out what the group or individual is doing, and if there is a continual problem, the teacher should be informed. A good diversion is often to say that they will all be having a turn as long as they allow others to have theirs.

K13 ## Case study

Managing disturbances outside your group

You have been asked to work in the classroom on a practical task of science investigation with a group of Year 7 (S1) pupils. Although you have sufficient space to carry out the activity, you quickly find that due to the interest generated, pupils from other groups are repeatedly disturbing your activities because they are interested in finding out what is happening.

- How could you ensure that other pupils do not continue to disturb you?
- What could you say to the pupils with whom you are working?

Pupils' ability to learn

Here, again, there may be a variety of reasons why pupils are not able to achieve.

- **Pupils' behaviour** – If any pupils are not focused on the task due to poor behaviour, you need to intervene straight away. If they are able to continue interrupting, they will do so and you will be unable to continue with the task. Always praise the good behaviour of any pupils who are doing what is required of them, as this sometimes makes the others try to gain your attention by behaving well. If there is a particular pupil who is misbehaving and disturbing others, a last resort is to remove them from the group and work with them later.

- **Pupils' self-esteem** – Sometimes a pupil with low self-esteem may not think that they are able to complete the task that has been set. Some pupils are quite difficult to motivate and you need to offer reassurance and praise wherever you can to improve their self-esteem. However, it is very important to remember that your role is one of a facilitator and that you are not there to complete the task for the pupil. Some pupils may just need a little gentle reassurance and coaxing to 'have a go', while others may be more difficult to work with and require you to use your questioning skills.
- **Pupils' lack of concentration** – There may be a few reasons for pupils finding it hard to concentrate on the task that has been set. These could include an inability to complete the work (the teacher has made the task too difficult) or the pupil may complete the task quickly and need more stimulation. Some pupils with special educational (ASL) needs have a very short concentration span and the task may be taking too long to complete. If this is the case, you will need to stop the pupil and continue with the task later.
- **Pupils' range of ability** – You may find that you are working with a class or group of pupils whose wide range of ability means that some of them are finished before others. If you are faced with a situation where one pupil has finished while others are still working, you may need to have something else ready for them to move on to. For example, if a group of Year 9 (S3) special educational (ASL) needs pupils are working on an activity to find words in a text that include the sounds 'ch' and 'sh', you could ask those who finish early to make their own list of words including the two sounds.

Unclear or incomplete information

Sometimes the teacher may set activities that are not suitable for the pupils involved or you may not have clear or complete information to support the activity. You may need to change the activity to make it more achievable for the pupils by going back and checking with the teacher.

Importance of working within your own sphere of competence and when you should refer to others

As a teaching assistant you are working under the direction of a teacher, even if you are working with a large group of pupils on your own. If you are working at S/NVQ Level 3 or above, you will have a certain amount of experience and will often be able to resolve issues as they arise when supporting pupils' learning (for example, see the potential problems on pages 43, 44 and above). However, even though you may be very competent and experienced you are still working in the role of a teaching assistant. This means that you should know the boundaries of your responsibilities and be aware of when to refer to the class teacher or senior managers in the school.

Broadly speaking, you will need to refer to others in situations that you cannot resolve or which:

- disrupt the learning of pupils working with you
- are indicators that a pupil does not understand the teaching points despite being approached in different ways
- show that a pupil has a very good understanding and is working at a higher level than others in his or her group
- are issues of which others need to be aware (e.g. child protection concerns or incidents that have happened at home)
- put others in danger.

Case study

Managing disruptions within your group

Carole is working with a group of Year 8 (S2) pupils on a Science activity. She is a very experienced assistant and regularly works with groups and individuals on activities set by the teacher. Today the group are quite lively and one pupil in particular is calling out and distracting the others. Carole uses all the strategies she knows to re-focus the pupil but he continues to disrupt the group.

● What would you do in this situation?
● Why is it important to refer incidents like this?

Portfolio activity

Referring incidents to other staff

Write a reflective account of an incident that you have needed to refer to another member of staff.

Importance of independent learning and how to encourage and support this in pupils

Pupils need to be given opportunities to learn and discover things for themselves where possible. In this way, they have ownership of their learning. A teacher or assistant who stands at the front of the class for too long and talks to pupils without engaging them soon loses their attention. You need to learn skills and strategies for developing pupils' independent learning. You will find that there are a variety of ways in which pupils are given tasks to do within the learning framework.

Instruction

Pupils may be given a task that involves following a series of steps. This will lead them to arriving at a set outcome, for example when learning to make a cake or a kite.

Collaboration and problem solving

This method of learning involves groups of pupils working together to discuss or discover ideas. An example might be pupils finding the best material to make a bag to carry potatoes. Through doing this, they will also learn how to work as part of a team and listen to others' views.

Facilitation

This method involves giving pupils the tools to carry out a task and then allowing them the freedom to devise their own outcome. An example of this might be showing them how to mix colours and then allowing them to experiment to find different shades.

There is much work going into personalised learning and how we can effectively support all pupils in the assessment of their own learning. Learning objectives need

▲ Figure 18.5 Pupils should be encouraged to work as independently as possible

to be clear and pupils should know why they are carrying out each activity as they do it. They should also be encouraged to peer and self-assess to check what learning has taken place. It is important for pupils to have as many opportunities as possible to be responsible for their own decision-making: this encourages their independence and creativity, as well as giving them more confidence in their abilities.

Strategies for challenging and motivating pupils to learn

As well as encouraging them to carry out the task as independently as possible, pupils may need you to further challenge and motivate them to learn. Depending on the way that the task has been set, offer as much encouragement as is needed while allowing pupils to develop their own self-help skills. If they tell you that they have finished, it is always worth keeping an additional challenge or related task, which is related to the activity that they have completed, up your sleeve.

Importance of active listening and how to do this

As a teaching assistant, you may have more opportunities than teachers for getting to know individual pupils, particularly if you are working as an individual teaching assistant, because you will have more time to talk to them and develop relationships with them. This means that you can gain an insight into what motivates individuals, their interests and abilities, and how to keep them focused on learning activities. As you get to know each pupil, you will recognise when they are achieving or not achieving to their own ability.

You need to be careful when giving pupils attention for bad behaviour, as this can cause it to be repeated – although it is not always possible to ignore. An effective strategy for behaviour management is to 'catch them being good'. This is particularly helpful when building relationships with pupils as they will respond well to positive attention, however small. It can include the use of positive eye contact, smiles and quiet praise.

When listening to pupils, staff should also be aware that they need to show they are interested in what the pupils are saying or *actively listening*. It is very frustrating when we are talking to another person and find that they are not listening and we need to repeat what we have said. We can also show that we are listening through the use of body language and the amount of interest we display, including how we respond. If we only appear half-interested, this also gives the pupil the message that we do not value what they are saying. It is important for pupils to gain the approval of adults and most will respond better to a member of staff who is taking the time to listen to them. This also means that pupils will be more likely to talk to staff and confide in them if there is anything wrong, as these kinds of factors will influence their learning.

K15 K16 Case study

Encouraging focus on learning activities

You have been asked to work with a group of pupils who are individually designing and making a puzzle.

- How could you encourage those with different learning styles and promote their independence without giving them too much help?
- What would you do if you had a pupil who was reluctant to carry out the task and did not want to continue?

How to help pupils to review their learning strategies and achievements and plan future learning

Pupils are often asked to think about their own learning and how they best approach what they are doing. At secondary level, they will be thinking about how they have worked in different subjects and will discuss their strengths and areas for development. For example, pupils are encouraged to attend annual review days with their parents to discuss progress with their teachers. Sometimes teaching assistants will attend the annual review days too.

When the pupils have completed a task, staff may review it with a group, with individual pupils or as a whole class. This means that pupils should discuss what they were asked to do and how they went about it. They may then discuss whether they think that the task went well and what they felt was successful or unsuccessful, and why. This encourages them to think about the strategies and ideas they used, and also to compare their method with that of others. It is important for pupils to look at different ways of doing tasks so that they are aware that there may not be a right or wrong way; some pupils are lacking in confidence and worried about 'getting it wrong'.

You can use either the portfolio activity or the case study below for your portfolio, but do not need to complete both.

Portfolio activity K18

Using strategies for pupils to review their achievements

Write a reflective account to show an example of a strategy that you have used in class to help pupils to review their learning achievements. How did this help them to plan for future learning activities?

Case study K18

Facilitating pupils' review of achievements

You have just completed a Design Technology activity with a group of Year 9 (S3) pupils who have had to make a toy for a young child. They have been given a variety of materials to look at and have discussed the different qualities of each.

- What types of questions could you ask the pupils to encourage them to think about their work?
- How could you reassure a pupil who felt unable to review what they had done?

Keys to good practice

Supporting pupils during learning activities

✓ Ensure both you and the pupils understand what you are required to do.
✓ Use a range of questioning strategies.
✓ Remind the pupils of the main teaching points.
✓ Model the correct vocabulary.
✓ Make sure you actively listen to all the pupils.
✓ Encourage the pupils to work together in pairs.
✓ Help pupils to use the relevant resources and ensure there are enough.
✓ Reassure pupils who are less confident about their ideas.
✓ Listen carefully to pupils.
✓ Give positive praise wherever possible.
✓ Have high expectations of pupils.
✓ Adapt work where necessary.
✓ Inform the teacher of any problems that have taken place, which you have been unable to resolve.
✓ Provide a level of assistance that allows pupils to achieve without helping them too much.

K3
K4
K8
K11
K13

For your portfolio...

Write a reflective account of a learning activity you have undertaken with a group of pupils.

Drawing closely on the knowledge base for this unit, include the following:

- information you had before the activity such as learning objectives, the needs of the pupils and any specific criteria you needed to follow
- the year group and stage of the curriculum at which the pupils are working and where the lesson fits into the daily, weekly or yearly plans
- how you included all the pupils and whether you have had to adapt or modify the activity to accommodate different learning needs or styles
- any problems that have occurred and how you dealt with them.

Make sure you evaluate how the activity went and think about all the pupils in the group.

Further resources

Gardner, H (1993) *Multiple Intelligences: The Theory in Practice* (New York; BasicBooks)

Websites

England: www.nc.uk.net – National Curriculum for England

Northern Ireland: www.ccea.org.uk/ – Council for the Curriculum, Examinations and Assessment

Scotland: www.ltscotland.org.uk/ – Learning and Teaching Scotland

Wales: http:old.accac.org.uk – Curriculum and Assessment Arrangements for Wales

www.support4learning.org.uk (learning styles) – signpost to relevant advice for learning

www.everychildmatters.gov.uk – Government website to promote the framework for the provision of services to children

19 Manage Pupil Behaviour

For this unit you will need to show that you are able to manage pupil behaviour. This will be in a variety of contexts, including around the school, on school trips and in different learning environments. You will need to be able to show that you understand and implement agreed classroom management strategies and are part of a whole school approach to encourage positive behaviour.

You will also need to be able to encourage pupils to take responsibility for their own behaviour within the framework of a code of conduct. If they are given clear boundaries and high expectations within which to work, they will be more likely to adhere to them. It is important for all adults to take a proactive approach to managing behaviour so that pupils are aware of the consequences before they act, rather than afterwards. Pupils should also have opportunities to be involved in the evaluation and review of behaviour strategies.

What you need to know and understand

For this unit you will need to know and understand:

- The school's policies for pupil care, welfare and discipline, including the promotion of positive behaviour and classroom management

- The school's agreed code of conduct

- The roles and responsibilities of yourself and others within the school setting for managing pupil behaviour

- The importance of shared responsibility between all staff for the conduct and behaviour of pupils in corridors, playgrounds and public areas within the school and your role and responsibilities in relation to this

- The benefits of the consistent application of good classroom management and behaviour strategies

- The stages of social, emotional and physical development of children and young people and the implications of these for managing behaviour of the pupils with whom you work

- The importance of modelling the behaviour you want to see and how to do this

- The importance of recognising and rewarding positive behaviour and how to do this

- The agreed strategies for managing pupils' negative or inappropriate behaviour

- The school's policy and procedures for rewards and sanctions

- How to assess and manage risks to your own and others' safety when dealing with challenging behaviour

- The importance of working within the remit of your role and responsibilities and your own sphere of competence and when you should refer to others

- The specialist advice on behaviour management which is available within the school and how to access this if needed

- How to evaluate classroom management and behaviour strategies and your own contribution to implementing these

- School arrangements for reviewing behaviour and the effective use of rewards and sanctions including pupil councils, group reviews, class reviews and whole school policy review

- The range and implications of factors that impact on behaviour of all pupils, e.g. age, gender, culture, care history, self-esteem

- Stereotypical assumptions about pupils' behaviour relative to gender, cultural background and disability, and how these can limit pupils' development

- The home and family circumstances and care history of pupils with whom you work and how to use this information appropriately to anticipate and deal effectively with difficult situations

- Agreed strategies for managing and meeting the additional needs of any pupils with learning and behavioural difficulties

- The performance indicators included within any behaviour support plans for pupils with whom you work and the implications of these for how you work with the pupil(s) concerned

- How to support pupils in using peer and self-assessment to promote their learning and behaviour

- The triggers for inappropriate behavioural responses from pupils with whom you work and actions you can take to pre-empt, divert or diffuse potential flash points

- How to support pupils with behavioural difficulties to identify and agree behaviour targets

- How to encourage and support pupils to review their own behaviour and the impact of this on themselves, their learning and achievement, on others and on their environment

- School procedures for collecting data on pupils' learning and behaviour, including the use of rewards and sanctions, and tracking pupil progress, and your role and responsibilities in relation to this

School's policies for pupil care, welfare and discipline

When managing pupils' behaviour, all staff will need to be aware of **school policies.** This means that you should know where they are and have read them, so that pupils understand when you apply sanctions and behaviour management strategies. The school's behaviour policy is important as it gives guidelines to all staff on how they should manage pupil behaviour. This needs to be consistently applied by all staff in the school. The introduction of the Every Child Matters Framework has had an impact on the way schools address issues of care, welfare and discipline, and takes its root from the case of Victoria Climbié. Under this framework and the Children Act 2004, agencies such as Social Services and Education work together closely to take responsibility for children's welfare. (In Scotland, the main legislation affecting the way schools deal with issues of care, welfare and discipline is the Protection of Children (Scotland) Act, the text of which is available at www.opsi.gov.uk/legislation/scotland/acts2003/20030005.htm.) Other school policies will also have an impact on managing behaviour, for example the health and safety, child protection, and anti-bullying policies. (See also page 64.)

All staff need to be know procedures for promoting positive behaviour and it should be a regular item at meetings.

> **ⓘ Key term**
>
> **School policies** – the agreed principles and procedures for promoting positive pupil behaviour including, as relevant to the school, policies for: behaviour management, bullying, the care and welfare of pupils, use of language, treatment of other pupils and adults within the school, equality of opportunity, movement within and around the school, access to and use of school facilities and equipment.

School's agreed code of conduct

It is imperative in any school for pupils to be aware of a **code of conduct** so that they have a clear understanding of how to behave. Pupils need to be aware of the boundaries within which to manage their behaviour so that they understand what is expected of them.

> **ⓘ Key term**
>
> **Code of conduct** – an agreed set of rules by which all pupils are expected to behave

These rules should be written in such a way that the pupils are given positive targets, for example 'I will walk quietly around the school' rather than the negative 'Do not run in school'. Where the language may be difficult for some pupils (e.g. where English is an additional language or for pupils with Autistic Spectrum Disorder (ASD)) to understand, for example 'treating others with respect', staff should make sure that they understand its meaning. The rules should be discussed frequently with pupils, during tutor periods and during assembly times, so that they remember them.

Where possible, pupils should be involved in devising school or classroom rules so that they have more ownership of them. You should say to them, for example, 'As a class we agreed that taking other people's property is not acceptable' rather than 'Leave Sajida's things alone'. This also encourages them to take responsibility for their actions.

As well as this list of school rules, pupils should be encouraged to behave in a positive way through watching the behaviour of adults. Pupils soon notice if an adult is not acting in a way that they would expect, or if there are inconsistent expectations between adults. When a pupil is behaving particularly well, remember to praise this behaviour so that it is recognised. Pupils need to be praised for work and behaviour, effort and achievement genuinely and frequently. This reinforces good behaviour and builds self-esteem.

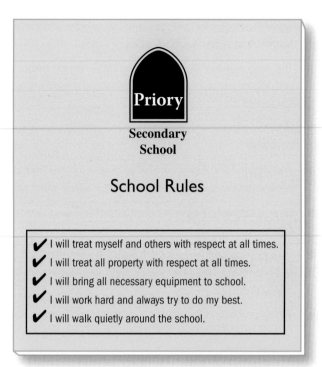

Priory

Secondary School

School Rules

✔ I will treat myself and others with respect at all times.
✔ I will treat all property with respect at all times.
✔ I will bring all necessary equipment to school.
✔ I will work hard and always try to do my best.
✔ I will walk quietly around the school.

▲ **Figure 19.1** A simply and attractively laid out code of conduct will appeal to pupils

Portfolio activity

K1 K2 K3

Investigating your school's behaviour policy

Using a copy of your school's behaviour policy, highlight and annotate it before putting it in your portfolio to show:

- what your responsibilities are under the policy
- any school rules or codes of conduct
- how positive behaviour is promoted within the school.

If you are unable to keep and use a copy of your policy, you can still note these points down and put them in your portfolio as evidence.

Responsibility for managing pupil behaviour

Your role and responsibilities and those of others

As a teaching assistant, you need to be aware of your role in managing pupils' behaviour. If you have any worries or concerns about how to deal with pupils' behaviour you must always refer to the class teacher. Your school's behaviour policy (see above) will give guidelines for

  Thinking point

How do pupils in your school address teaching assistants and other support staff? Do they use first names or surnames (e.g. Mrs Jones)? Do you think this makes any difference to the way in which pupils in the school perceive the responsibilities of support staff?

all staff, but teachers have the ultimate responsibility for managing the behaviour of pupils within the class and the headteacher has responsibility for all the pupils.

Keys to good practice

Managing behaviour

✓ Have high but realistic expectations of work and behaviour. Pupils will be aware of how they should behave and will be praised when they behave well. Adults need to give praise such as 'I know how well you can work when we come into the library', rather than 'This class never works quietly in the library'.

✓ Create a working environment where pupils can achieve and where their work and efforts are seen to be valued, thus developing their self-esteem. This can be done not only verbally but through displays of pupils' work and sharing with other pupils and adults in the school.

✓ Make expectations of behaviour and work clear and consistent, ensuring instructions have been understood. If pupils are unsure of what they need to do, it is very difficult for them to automatically behave in a way which adults expect.

✓ Work consistently as a staff so that the same expectations apply throughout the school. This is vital so that pupils understand that all staff are working together throughout the school.

✓ Be aware of your own values and opinions. Ensure that you do not make assumptions about people on the grounds of gender, race or disability.

▶ **Figure 19.2** Can you manage behaviour in different areas of the school?

The importance of shared responsibility

Managing behaviour does not only apply to the classroom. You may also have to manage behaviour in specialist areas such as ICT suites when pupils may be more excitable. At transitional periods of the day such as lunchtimes or between lessons, pupils will be moving around the school and you need to ensure that they are acting appropriately.

Benefits of the consistent application of good classroom management and behaviour strategies

If *all* members of the **school community** are using the same principles and strategies when managing behaviour, it is far more likely that the pupils will respond positively. Workforce remodelling has had an impact on the number of different professionals who are now working in schools. Support staff and midday supervisors, as well as those running extended school provision should know the importance and impact of consistent strategies. Individual class teachers sometimes have their own methods that work well, but all staff involved with those particular pupils should know about those methods.

Key term

School community – all personnel contributing to the work of the school including pupils, teachers, support staff, volunteer helpers, parents and carers, and other professional agencies

Stages of development and their implications for managing pupils' behaviour

It is important for all adults who have contact with pupils in secondary school settings to be aware of the different stages of children's development. You need to understand the way in which children learn and develop socially, emotionally and physically. In this way you will be able to support and enhance the learning process through a wider understanding of pupils' needs.

Physical development

As a teaching assistant, you will be working with pupils who should have already developed a whole range of skills through a wide range of physical activities. These may be gross motor skills, such as walking and running, or fine motor skills like holding a pencil or scissors. However, you may support pupils with special educational (Additional Support for Learning (ASL)) needs, who have difficulties with their gross and/or fine motor skills. These pupils may feel a little apprehensive and reluctant to join in with others and may need reassurance from you.

Pupils undergo health checks at various stages to make sure that they are developing normally and to draw attention to any potential problems. If a pupil is not reaching the expected milestones, investigations and any necessary action can then be taken straightaway.

Both boys and girls at secondary school will also go through major physical changes during puberty. The age at which adolescents reach puberty varies and some girls may begin the changes as early as Year 7 (S1), whereas for others it may be as late as Year 10 (S4). During puberty, the hormonal changes can lead to mood swings and therefore unusual or uncharacteristic behaviour.

Gross motor skills

These are skills that involve large movements through the use of children's arms and legs and may include running, hopping, skipping, playing football or dancing.

Fine motor skills

These are manipulative skills which involve finer hand control. They are vital for activities such as writing, drawing recognisable pictures, cutting with scissors and completing jigsaws. These finer skills are vital for being able to write effectively.

Basic stages of physical development

Age	Stage of development
0–3 months	Infant starts to have control of its head.
3–6 months	Baby starts to roll from side to side and, when on its front, pushes itself up with its arms.
6–9 months	Baby starts to grasp objects and sit unsupported. Baby may start to move by trying to crawl or shuffle.
9–12 months	Baby has started to crawl or even walk, and starts to reach for objects.
1–2 years	Baby starts to build using blocks, make marks with crayons, turns pages in picture books. Baby is gaining in confidence and enjoys repetitive play, and games and songs with a known outcome, such as 'Pat-a-cake' and 'Round and round the garden'.
2–3 years	Child uses a spoon, puts on shoes, begins to use a preferred hand and walks up and down stairs with confidence.
3–4 years	Child turns pages of books, puts on coat and shoes, throws and kicks a ball, washes and dries hands with help.
4–5 years	Child draws a person, cuts out simple shapes, completes simple puzzles, is starting to hop.
5–6 years	Child forms letters, writes name, dresses and undresses, runs quickly, uses large apparatus.
6–7 years	Child writes with even spacing, ties laces, can complete more complex puzzles, chases and plays with others.
7–11 years	Child is refining physical skills such as running, jumping and skipping.
12–14 years	In early adolescence there is rapid physical development, although there is also great variety among peers. Some pupils will have reached puberty before starting secondary school. Others will not reach puberty until 14 years old. As a result there may be a great variance in height and other aspects of development.
15–18 years	Physical changes are slower, although boys will still be growing at a fast pace. A good time to perfect skills and talents, competition or performances.

When pupils arrive in secondary school, the majority will already have developed a large number of physical skills through practising and refining different physical activities from an early age. Pupils may also start to learn a new range of skills at secondary school through increased opportunity to use a wider variety of tools, apparatus and equipment, such as tools in Design Technology. As they develop and change physically, pupils need to develop greater control of both gross and fine movements. They need to have opportunities to develop these skills within the learning environment, through a variety of indoor and outdoor activities.

If pupils' growth patterns are very different from their peers, this may sometimes have an effect on their behaviour. For example, some pupils may start to become much taller than their peers and develop some of the first signs of puberty earlier than others. Girls, in particular, can become much taller than boys and this can put pressure on them to behave differently. There may also be pupils who are very small for their age and this can sometimes affect how they are treated by their peers. Growth patterns can also affect social and emotional development.

Social and emotional development

The social and emotional development of pupils is directly linked to the way in which they relate to others. Pupils need to interact with others so that they have opportunities to gain confidence. If there are physical difficulties, for example a hearing problem, these may affect the way in which pupils relate to others and cause a delay in their overall development. For example, they may withdraw socially, find communicating difficult or suffer a language delay. All of these could have a negative effect on their developing self-esteem.

Stages of social and emotional development

Age	Stage of development
Years 4–7 (P5–S1)	Pupils will already be aware of how they fit into groups, the co-operation necessary and what the acceptable levels of behaviour are. They will be aware of their own achievements and capable of self-criticism. Friendships will already be important to them. Throughout they will be growing in maturity and be able to take on greater responsibilities. They will respond well to small group activities. They will have a strong need to feel accepted and worthwhile. Leaders should provide reassurances and support.
Years 8–10 (S2–4)	This age group will be keen to plan activities together and enjoy teamwork. They may enjoy taking part in activities that are away from home. This is a time of emotional swings and the biggest period of challenges to a pupil's self-concept. Staff need to take time to talk about values with this age group.
Years 11 and 12 (S5–6)	Give teenagers opportunities to interact in mixed groups. They are learning to co-operate with others at an adult level. They need increasingly greater responsibilities to allow for independent thinking and decision-making. Consistent treatment by staff is important. Be willing to listen to and accept each one as an individual.

Pupils who are entering secondary school are just beginning to gain the confidence to take on greater responsibility and become independent. As they are developing their maturity, they will still be fine-tuning their ability to show desirable behaviour, and that behaviour will be largely affected by their peers. Adults need to give pupils as many opportunities as possible to develop independent skills and to praise them as much as they can for good behaviour. In this way, pupils start to develop a positive self-esteem.

Self-esteem can be high or low, positive or negative. It is how we feel about ourselves and leads to our self-image, that is how we think about or perceive ourselves. Pupils develop a positive self-esteem when they feel good about themselves and when

High self-esteem

I like myself

I am good at my work

I like school

I have lots of friends

I have fun trying out new things even if I am not always good at them

This is me

I don't like trying new things because I won't be able to do them

I'm not good in school because I don't like it

I am not good at my work

I don't like myself

Low self-esteem

▲ Figure 19.3 Think about how pupils might think about themselves

they feel valued. The way in which we treat pupils has a direct effect on this so it is important that we encourage and praise them, value each pupil as an individual and celebrate differences and similarities.

The rate at which a child develops socially and emotionally depends on the opportunities that have been given for them to interact with others. Where a pupil has come from a large family, for example, there may have been many opportunities to interact with others and form relationships. If a child has had very little contact or social interaction with other children, it may be more difficult for them to understand how relationships with others are formed. There may also be less understanding of social codes of behaviour, such as taking turns or waiting for others to finish speaking.

Social and Emotional Aspects of Learning (SEAL) is a whole school framework, which has been introduced in many primary schools. It is organised into seven themes, which are then revisited and built on during primary school. Pupils are encouraged through the seven themes to explore their own feelings, relationships with others, self-awareness and responsibilities. (For more information, see www.teachernet.gov.uk/SEAL.) (In Scotland, the curriculum is currently Personal & Social Education (PSE) in primary school and Personal, Social & Health Education (PSHE) in secondary schools.)

It is hoped, therefore, that when entering Year 7 (S1) most pupils will be at the expected stage of social and emotional development. Secondary schools capitalise on the work undertaken by SEAL and continue to provide support for the social and emotional development of the pupils. This may be through assemblies, learning mentors, peer mentoring, emotional health sessions, personal, social and health education (PSHE) sessions or across curriculum subjects. PSHE is backed by the National Healthy Schools Programme (NHSP), which outlines what schools need to do to achieve national healthy school status.

Case study

Encouraging pupils' social development

Melissa has come into your Year 7 (S1) group highly intellectually advanced for her age. She quickly settles into school and has no difficulties interacting with teachers. She has good organisational skills and responds well to school routines. However, you have noticed that Melissa does not have good relationships with other pupils. You have heard her saying to them that she is very good at reading and doesn't need to work as hard as they do. You have noticed that she is often on her own at playtimes and the other pupils in the class are reluctant to interact with her.

- What can you say about Melissa's behaviour and her stages of physical, social and emotional development?
- Do you think that there is any cause for concern?
- How could you manage Melissa's behaviour and encourage her to form good relationships with others in the class?

Modelling, recognising and rewarding positive behaviour and how to do this

It is important for all pupils, but especially for those who tend to be 'told off' more than others, that we recognise and reward positive behaviour. Even as adults we like to be noticed for something good that we do. Research has shown that we need to be given six positives for every negative in order to balance this out. It is always much easier for us to focus on negative aspects of a child's behaviour and react to them. When recognising and rewarding positive behaviour, however, you must not forget to notice those pupils who *always* behave appropriately.

These ideas are linked to Behaviourist Theory, which was developed by Burrhus Frank Skinner in the 1940s. He suggested that children respond to praise and so repeat behaviour that gives them recognition or praise for what they do. This may take the simple form of verbal praise, which is very powerful, or house points, letters home or merit marks. Pupils who receive praise or attention for positive behaviour, such as kindness towards others, are more likely to repeat this behaviour.

Pupils also attempt to gain attention through undesirable behaviour, so be aware of this and try to ignore it where possible, instead giving attention to those pupils who are behaving well.

Modelling the correct behaviour

You will need to demonstrate that you are a good role model in all areas of behaviour within the school. Pupils will take their lead from adults and need to see that they too are behaving appropriately and responsibly. This is also true for good manners! Be careful when speaking to others that you are showing the same respect that we are asking pupils to show.

Notice when pupils are behaving well or trying hard

This is important because it will help to build positive relationships and shows that you care about the pupil.

Use positive recognition such as merit marks

Most schools use these kinds of systems and have assemblies and evenings to celebrate work and behaviour.

Follow up on important issues

Always make sure you follow up, particularly if you have said that you will. There is little point in saying to a pupil that you will be telling their teacher how pleased you are with their behaviour if you then forget to do so. The pupil will then think that you do not really think it is important.

Build trust with all pupils to maintain positive relationships

Do all you can to show pupils that you are interested in and value them. As you get to know them, you will remember particular things about them. Giving your trust to pupils encourages them to take more responsibility, for example, allowing them to work at pupil reception.

Ensure pupils know why they are being rewarded

You must be clear on exactly what you are praising or rewarding, for example 'I am giving you this merit mark because you have been so helpful to others this morning'.

Making sure directions are unambiguous

Make sure that you communicate clearly to pupils so that they understand what you are asking. Some pupils with special educational (ASL) needs, such as dyspraxia (Developmental Co-ordination Disorder (DCD)), may find directions confusing, especially if there are too many instructions at once or if they are occupied doing something else. If you communicate through questioning, for example, pupils may think that there is some choice involved. If we want pupils to do as we ask, we need to say things as though we mean them!

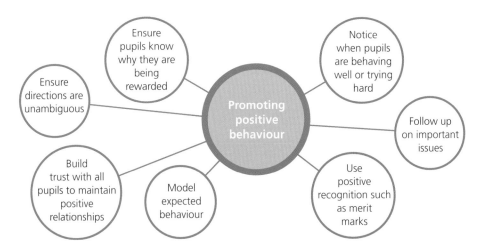

▲ **Figure 19.4** Staff behaviour can positively reinforce pupils' behaviour

Case study

Monitoring behaviour management strategies

Jack is in Year 11 (S5) and has ADHD. He has difficulty in controlling his behaviour sometimes, although he is aware that he can get excited and tries hard. Recently there has been a succession of teachers in the English class as the regular teacher has been in hospital. You are a teaching assistant and are there for Year 11 (S5) English. You have noticed recently that the classroom behaviour management strategies have not been consistent, as the teachers all come in with different ideas. This has had an impact on the class as a whole and also on Jack, who is finding it increasingly difficult to settle to his work.

- Outline the steps you might take, including who you would speak to about the situation.
- Why is it important that you bring this to the attention of other staff?

Agreed strategies for managing pupils' negative or inappropriate behaviour

Your school should have a scale of sanctions for instances when behaviour is undesirable despite modelling and encouraging good behaviour. All staff should be able to apply these and pupils should be aware of this. There should be a structured approach, which is clear and defines what is expected and the consequences of **inappropriate behaviour**. Consequences could be:

- time out or name on the board
- miss one minute or longer of break
- miss 5 minutes of break
- be sent to a referral class
- be sent to the headteacher or teacher speaks to the parents.

It is important that pupils see a clear structure to what happens if they choose not to pay attention to the school rules that are in place. They are much more likely to adhere to the rules if they know exactly what will happen if they do not. In this situation, adults are prepared for the types of behaviour which may occur and are teaching pupils that they are responsible for their actions.

> **Key term**
>
> **Inappropriate behaviour** – behaviour that conflicts with the accepted values and beliefs of the school and community

Portfolio activity

Managing inappropriate behaviour

Write an account of a situation in which you have had to manage pupils' negative or inappropriate behaviour. Make sure you include your school's strategies and how you have implemented these in stages.

Keys to good practice

Managing unwanted behaviour

✓ Intervene early so that the problem does not escalate. If a situation arises where you are the first to be aware of unacceptable behaviour, intervene straightaway.

✓ Repeat directions calmly rather than reacting to what the pupil is saying or doing, for example 'I have asked you to line up by the door'.

✓ Make sure you send for additional help if needed, especially if there are health and safety issues.

✓ Give eye contact to the pupil who is misbehaving. Sometimes all that is needed is a stern look at a pupil so that they see an adult is aware of what they are doing.

✓ Relate any negative comments to the behaviour, rather than the pupil, for example 'Simon, that was not a sensible choice', is more acceptable than 'Simon you are not a sensible boy'.

✓ Remove items that are being used inappropriately. If a pupil is using an item such as a pair of scissors or piece of outdoor equipment to hurt or threaten another pupil, this should be gently taken away. The pupil should then be told why the item has been removed and when they can have it back.

✓ Use proximity; move closer to a pupil who is misbehaving so that they are aware of an adult presence. This will usually prevent the behaviour from continuing. You can use this practice in whole class teaching time, when the teacher is at the front, to calm or prevent inappropriate behaviour by having an awareness of who to sit beside.

✓ Time out is sometimes used when older pupils are consistently misbehaving and need to be given some time to calm down before returning to a situation. It can be applied within the classroom or on the playground.

✓ Use an agreed scale of sanctions of which all in the school community are aware.

School's policy and procedures for rewards and sanctions

Your school's behaviour policy should give a clear indication of the procedures you can use when implementing rewards and sanctions. Make sure that both you and the pupils are aware of what will happen if their behaviour is not acceptable.

All adults in the school should be able to give rewards and sanctions, although some will be specific to certain members of staff. An example of this might be certificates, which may only be handed out by the headteacher in Friday assembly. (See also page 74.) If, as a teaching assistant, you are not sure about what you can pass on to pupils, you need to find this out so that you are ready at the appropriate moment!

Case study

Using rewards within school policy

Nicola has just started working as a teaching assistant. She gets on well with the teacher and pupils, although some of the pupils demonstrate quite challenging behaviour. She decides to take some sweets into school and give them out to pupils when they have behaved well during sessions with her.

- Does it matter if Nicola starts using the sweets?
- What should she do if they don't work?
- Why is it important for her to make sure she is aware of school policy?

How to assess and manage risks to your own and others' safety when dealing with challenging behaviour

You need to know how to manage risks to yourself and others. If you are in any doubt about your ability to do this, you must always refer to another member of staff. Your school's behaviour and health and safety policies should give guidelines for dealing with challenging behaviour and also the use of restraint, which may be based on local guidelines.

Pupils will not always be aware of risk and dangerous situations, so when speaking to them, always point out the consequences of what they are doing.

When you are assessing risks to safety, they may be caused by:

- a pupil who is violent or aggressive
- a situation, such as an argument, which has got out of control.

> **? Thinking point**
>
> Find out about your school's policy regarding the use of restraint. Are there guidelines from your local authority? Have you ever needed to refer to them?

▲ **Figure 19.5** Talking with pupils can help define dangerous situations

Importance of working within your role, responsibilities and sphere of competence and when to refer to others

Make sure that you know what your own responsibilities are with regards to behaviour management. This includes the use of rewards and sanctions. In most schools teaching assistants have the same responsibilities as teachers, although there will be some incidents in which you need to call for another member of staff.

You should refer to others if:

- you or others are in any danger
- you are dealing with a difficult situation on your own
- you are not comfortable with dealing with a pupil, for example, if they are behaving unpredictably
- pupils are not carrying out your instructions and you are not in control of the situation.

If you need to, you can ask another pupil to go and get adult help.

Portfolio activity K12

Managing behaviour within your responsibilities

In pairs, look at the scenarios below. Decide which of these you would be comfortable dealing with yourself and which you would need to refer to others.

- A Year 8 (S2) pupil is having a temper tantrum because he is not allowed to sit by the window.
- An special educational (ASL) needs pupil is refusing to join in with your group's activity because he doesn't want to.
- A playtime argument between two Year 7 (S1) boys over a football has become aggressive.
- You have discovered a case of bullying during your speech and language group activity.
- An incident you have come across in the corridor has left a Year 10 (S4) pupil very upset.
- A pupil has reacted uncharacteristically when being told that she has to stay and finish her work.

How would you deal with the situations you could manage yourself?

Specialist advice on behaviour management available within the school and how to access it

In some situations, where a teacher or supervisor has used all the ideas and strategies already available, it may be necessary to ask for extra help and support. If you are in a mainstream school, you should have a Special Educational Needs Co-ordinator

(SENCo)(Additional Support for Learning (ASL) teacher) or learning mentor on the staff. (In Scotland, each school will have a Principal Teacher (Support for Learning) who manages all pupils with additional support needs.) There may be different situations which require the help of outside agencies; as a teaching assistant you will not be asked to contact them, but you should have an awareness of the support that is available.

Support available within the school

- **SENCo or supervisor (ASL or principal teacher)** – They should be the first point of contact for behaviour support and devising additional strategies for use within the classroom. They will also contact other professionals outside the school.
- **Other class teachers** may also be able to offer support, particularly if they have had to deal with similar behaviour patterns.
- **Headteacher or deputy** – You should be able to speak to those in the senior management team of your school if you have particular concerns about a pupil or situation.

Support available outside the school

- **Behaviour Unit** – This unit is usually run by the local authority and offers support and suggestions for dealing with pupils who have behaviour problems. They may also come into schools to observe or work with specific pupils.
- **Educational psychologists** – These professionals visit all schools regularly to support pupils and the adults who work with them. They offer help and advice on a variety of special educational (ASL) needs problems, and may assess pupils and devise individual programmes. They are also involved with assessing those pupils who may need a Statement of Special Educational Needs (Co-ordinated Support Plan).

How to evaluate classroom management and behaviour strategies and your own contribution to implementing these

Evaluation of behaviour strategies should be an ongoing process. What works one week with a pupil or group of pupils may not always work in another! Work with the class teacher and other staff to evaluate the kinds of systems that are used within the class. **Classroom** and **behaviour management strategies** should be reviewed through careful monitoring of outcomes.

ℹ Key terms

Classroom management strategies – agreed procedures for managing learning and behaviour in the classroom, for example: being in the classroom before pupils arrive, greeting pupils at the door, lining up and entry/exit procedures, using seating plans

Behaviour management strategies – a set of broad principles and procedures for promoting positive pupil behaviour that have been agreed by the governing body/parent council and school community of consistent implementation over time by everyone within the school, for example the use of rewards and sanctions, buddies, one-to-one support, time out, counselling, behaviour and anger management techniques

Supporting class management strategies

Raj, an experienced ICT teacher, has a lively Year 9 (S3) class. They work well together but can be disruptive and need to be closely managed. Although he works within the school behaviour policy, he has found it necessary to implement an additional set of procedures to maintain positive behaviour. Raj has decided to use the following strategies and has asked Sue, a teaching assistant who is in his class, to support him in this.

- All pupils have a set place to sit in the class.
- When pupils enter the class at the start of the lesson, there is calm music playing in the background. They go straight to their tables and start a warm-up activity.
- There is a lot of emphasis on the togetherness of the Year 9 (S3) class and how they work together. This means that they take pride in their class and are responsible for their behaviour.

Raj has also asked Sue to meet him to discuss the strategies they are using and how they might set alternatives if these become less effective.

- How do you think that these additional strategies might help the Year 9 (S3) class to work together?
- Why is it important that Raj and Sue work together and make sure they evaluate the effectiveness of the strategies?
- Does it matter that Raj has implemented these strategies in addition to the school rules?

School arrangements for reviewing behaviour and the effective use of rewards and sanctions

Many schools have arrangements in place for reviewing whole school issues such as the effective management of behaviour. It is often the case that pupils will discuss what their own class rules should be. Where pupils are more involved with decisions around managing behaviour they are more likely to be effective.

School councils are being increasingly used in both primary and secondary schools and are linked to the Citizenship curriculum. In Wales they have become a compulsory part of school life, following legislation by the Welsh Assembly. They discuss a range of issues, but a report by Ofsted in November 2006 cited them as having one of the most positive impacts on whole school behaviour, as pupils have a voice in managing issues that affect them. Councils are comprised of an elected representative group of pupils who play an active role in dealing with issues such as bullying. An organisation called School Councils UK has the support of the DCSF and the HMIE in Scotland, and gives advice and guidance for setting up and running councils.

 Key term

Review of behaviour – opportunities to discuss and make recommendations about behaviour, including bullying, and the effectiveness of rewards and sanctions, including class, year and school councils, class or group behaviour reviews, and whole school policy reviews

Factors that impact on the behaviour of pupils

Pupils enter schools with a variety of backgrounds and experiences, all of which have affected the way in which their individual personalities react to others. Some pupils come from secure and loving family backgrounds, while others may have had very unsettled experiences or a series of different homes and carers. Some may have experienced many social situations, while others' experience may be limited to family members or friends. These experiences affect the child's ability and confidence when socialising with others. There may also be other short-term factors that affect how they behave on any one day, such as the death of a pet or an argument with a friend. You will need to be sensitive to the causes of any uncharacteristic behaviour, and in your role it may be more possible for you to spend time with pupils and find these out.

Age, gender, culture, care history, self-esteem

Age

The pupil may develop physically or socially particularly quickly or slowly for their age. This can affect the way that others see them, which in turn will impact on their behaviour. For example, a pupil who is particularly small for his or her age may have been 'babied' at home and find it difficult when faced with the need for increasing independence.

Gender

It may be that a pupil enters school with limited experiences due to gender, for example, a boy who has not been allowed to experience sewing or cooking. As a result of this, the pupil may not expect that both sexes may be able to participate in all tasks at school.

Medical

A pupil who was premature at birth may have delayed physical development and this can also be the cause of immature behaviour. Some pupils who have medical intervention for specific problems such as poor hearing may be less confident about becoming involved with tasks within the classroom. Other pupils may have to take medication such as Ritalin for ADHD and this can affect their behaviour. If the dosage of Ritalin is too high, a pupil may become withdrawn and lethargic. If the dosage is too low, a pupil's behaviour may become very hyperactive and impulsive.

Disability

It is now a statutory requirement to encourage the inclusion of children with disabilities into mainstream schools. According to the Disability Discrimination Act 1995, a person has a disability if 'he or she has a physical or mental impairment that has a substantial and long-term adverse effect on his or her ability to carry out normal day-to-day activities'. The inclusion of pupils with a disability is to encourage more positive integration of disabled people into society, and to give pupils a greater understanding of the needs of others. The impact of inclusion will mean that there are more pupils in mainstream schools who may have disabilities.

Culture

Pupils will enter school from a variety of cultures. Some of these may encourage particular behaviours from men and women that differ from those in school. For example, some cultures may not encourage women to go out to work, which contrasts with the fact that in secondary school settings, although there are more male teachers than in primary schools, teaching assistants are predominantly female.

Self-esteem

All pupils' self-esteem, or how they view themselves, is directly affected by whether they feel valued by others. A pupil whose self-esteem is low may display behaviours that are disruptive or may withdraw and be timid in class. There may be several reasons why a pupil has low self-esteem. These could include poor relationships at home or a family that spends little time with the pupil.

Stereotypical assumptions about pupils' behaviour and how these can limit pupils' development

Stereotyping pupils can limit their development just as they are building up their own ideas about how similar or different we all are. If they hear adults making remarks which are prejudicial, they will grow up thinking that there is no harm in that type of behaviour. The pupils who are the subject of such remarks will also be damaged further by the reinforcement of low self-esteem and low expectations. You will therefore need to be aware of your own assumptions and opinions about pupils' behaviour. For example, beware of stereotyping pupils when giving them tasks. 'I need some sensible girls to take this message for me' may sound to the boys that only girls can be sensible. Care should also be taken in other situations. For example, it should not be assumed that a pupil with a disability should necessarily be excluded from activities; he or she should be included wherever possible.

How to use information about pupils appropriately

If you are working closely with one or more pupils you should be able to get to know background information about them that will help you to manage their behaviour. This may be through observing and talking to them, but it may also be information that has been passed on to the school by parents or carers, or through discussion with the teacher. You should have access to any information on the pupil or pupils that the school has on record, although you will need to be aware of the school policy on confidentiality. Do not pass on or discuss any information with those who do not have a valid reason to know it.

I am the only child and my parents have just separated

I have never been away from my mother before

I live with my mother and her partner, who also has two children

I am from a large extended family with several brothers and sisters

I am living with foster parents, and have been in several nurseries

I have a childminder and both my parents work

◄ **Figure 19.6** Get to know pupils' backgrounds but know when to keep information confidential

Case study

Supporting pupils with behaviour targets

Harry is in Year 10 (S4) and has been in your school for about a year. He has an Individual Education Plan (IEP) with behaviour targets and is known in the school as being a 'difficult' pupil to work with. You work in the special educational (ASL) needs department for one morning a week with Harry. You ask to speak to the class teacher and SENCo (ASL teacher) about him so that you can get a better idea about strategies that might work with him. You have a very fruitful discussion with them and find out that Harry has lived in a series of care homes and that this is his fourth secondary school. You are also told that next week he is going to be living with a new carer.

- How might this information help you to gain a greater understanding of Harry's behaviour?
- What legislation should you be mindful of in this situation?
- Could the school have handled this better?

Agreed strategies for managing and meeting the additional needs of pupils with learning and behavioural difficulties

Your school needs to have agreed strategies and policies for managing pupils who have additional needs. Pupils who have learning and behavioural difficulties can be the most challenging, as their behaviour may be disruptive to other pupils' learning.

School policies that relate to pupils' learning and emotional development may include the following.

- **Special educational needs policy** – This will give guidelines to staff about managing the behaviour of pupils with specific needs.
- **Behaviour policy** – This will give staff strategies and guidelines on managing behaviour in school.
- **PSHE policy** – This will give details of the way in which staff carry out the National Curriculum with regard to personal, social and health education.
- **Inclusion and equal opportunities policies** – These policies will promote the school's ethos and procedures in these two areas.
- **Anti-bullying policy** – Since September 1999, schools have been legally required to implement anti-bullying policies.
- **Child protection policy** – This has an effect on the way staff are alert at all times for signs of abuse or neglect in pupils. It will give you an indication of the key points that you need to observe and the person you need to go to in order to report any concerns.
- **Anti-racism policy** – Schools are also now required to have a clear anti-racism policy.

These policies give you guidelines for managing pupils with learning and behavioural needs in school. However, you may also need to refer to the school SENCo (ASL teacher) or seek outside help if these pupils cause challenges that you and the class teacher find difficult to mange in the classroom. If you are at all concerned, it is always best to seek help and advice.

Case study K19

Supporting pupils with special educational needs

Robert is in Year 7 (S1) and is on the Special Educational Needs Register. He finds it hard to concentrate in class and is waiting to be seen by the Educational Psychologist. You and his class teacher have tried various strategies to help him to focus, but it is taking a long time for his appointment with the Educational Psychologist to come through and, in the meantime, his behaviour in class is quite disruptive to other pupils.

- What could you do in this situation?
- Why is it important that you seek help as soon as possible rather than wait for the Educational Psychologist?

Performance indicators within behaviour support plans and their implications for how you work with the pupils concerned

If you have pupils in your school who have specific behavioural difficulties, they should be invited to review their behaviour and any targets they have on a regular basis. This will give them the opportunity to think about and discuss the impact of what they do. If you are involved in reviews with pupils, you should know them well and they should be comfortable working with you.

Swingate Secondary School — Behaviour Support Plan

Summer Term 2008 — School Action/Action Plus

Support Began: Jan 2008 — Review date: July 2008

Name: Michael Davies — Class: Year 9

Supported by……………………

Targets

1. To come into class without disturbing others
2. To work in a group with adult support and remain on task for 5 minutes

Signed……(teacher) M. Davies……(pupil)……(parent)

Figure 19.7 Behaviour support plan

You may need to work alongside your class teacher or SENCo (ASL teacher), as well as the pupil concerned, to devise targets for Behaviour Support or Individual Education Plans. Usually these plans are specific and outline the steps to be taken by staff to support the pupil when working towards the target and the resources to be used. There may also have been suggestions for targets from outside agencies that you can work on. When working with and setting targets, make sure that they are SMART (see Unit 50 page 324) and that the pupil is aware of why they need to work on them. It is also important to have realistic expectations of both the pupil and staff. When working towards the targets, you can then discuss with the pupil why the targets have been agreed and ask them about any issues that arise.

How to support pupils in using peer and self-assessment to promote their learning and behaviour

Pupils need support in the development of peer and self-assessment, but the rewards for the wider school community will be a positive one. The rationale behind peer and self-assessment is that pupils will be able to identify the purpose and understand the meaning of their experiences, and take a more active role in their learning. They will be more closely involved in the learning and behaviour-setting process, which will give them more responsibility and motivation.

Self-assessment is the process by which pupils make decisions about their own learning and what they need to do in order to progress. They will look at the criteria against which their learning is measured and think about what they need to do in order to achieve the benchmarks. (See also Unit 18.)

In **peer assessment,** pupils work in pairs or groups to reflect on learning goals and to question one another in ways which they may not do if there was a teacher present. They may be asked to comment on how their peers have performed against learning criteria.

Your role in each of these processes is to check that pupils are clear about the learning intention, are questioning what they know and what they need to know, and how they are going to get there. You may need to ask them questions to help them to progress (e.g. 'How are you getting on? What can you do next?') or to ask them to find ways of extending what they are doing.

Triggers for inappropriate behavioural responses from pupils and actions you can take to deal with potential flash points

As you get to know pupils, you may find that you are able to identify triggers to their inappropriate behaviour. Knowledge of the pupil will also help you when dealing with such behaviour, as you will be able to predict what works and what doesn't. For example, it may be enough to remove them from the situation. An awareness of the pupil's needs is very important if they have specific behavioural difficulties.

Supporting pupils with autism

James, in Year 9 (S3) , is autistic. Ellen is the teaching assistant who works with him. Today the class are going into the hall during History because there is a visitor who will be talking to them about the Second World War. Ellen knows that this may be a trigger for James to become distressed and to behave inappropriately, as he finds changes in routine difficult.

- Should James still go to the hall with the other pupils?
- If you were working with James, what might you do and say to him?
- How will an awareness of James' needs help in this situation?

How to encourage and support pupils to review their own behaviour and set new behaviour targets

It can be helpful with pupils to draw up a contract for behaviour so that they can recognise and proactively take responsibility for their actions. It will then be clearer to them exactly what they are required to do. Your role, when reviewing behaviour, will be to encourage pupils to think about what they have done and the consequences of their actions for themselves and for others.

Helping pupils review their behaviour

Michael, in Year 7 (S1), has an IEP, which has targets for behaviour. He has difficulty in socialising with others and will often call out and show attention-seeking behaviour in whole class situations. Through discussion with the class teacher and with Michael, the SENCo (ASL teacher) has helped to develop specific targets. These are to:

- develop his social skills through regular one-to-one sessions with a teaching assistant and a small group
- interact fairly with others at playtimes
- take 'thinking time' when he wants to call out.

During classroom teaching, Michael has shown improvement and is trying hard to remember what he has agreed. However at playtimes and lunchtimes, he has been unable to do this.

- Why do you think that Michael is less likely to behave appropriately on the playground and during lunchtimes?
- Should Michael be involved in reviewing these targets?
- Make some suggestions for how a whole school approach could be implemented and the kinds of strategies that would help Michael.

This will be in relation to the impact their behaviour has had on themselves and others, and on their learning and achievement. When reviewing targets and asking pupils about their progress, you need to be sensitive in the way you approach them and the kind of questioning you use. It is likely that other members of staff would also be involved.

School procedures for collecting data on pupils' learning and behaviour

Your school should have a system for collecting data on pupils' learning and behaviour so that all staff can work together to support both. Make sure that you are aware of any difference between the kinds of rewards you give pupils for behaviour and those you give for good work, as these can often become confused, which does not give a clear message to pupils about exactly why they are being rewarded.

Depending on the procedure in your school, there may be an ongoing record system, such as giving house points, for managing behaviour or pupil progress.

Examples of some of the rewards that may be given to pupils include:

- house points
- certificates
- awards for achievement in games or PE
- merit marks
- being sent to headteacher/deputy/year group leader/teacher for verbal praise
- written encouragement on pupils' work
- special assemblies to recognise achievements
- additional, sought-after responsibilities.

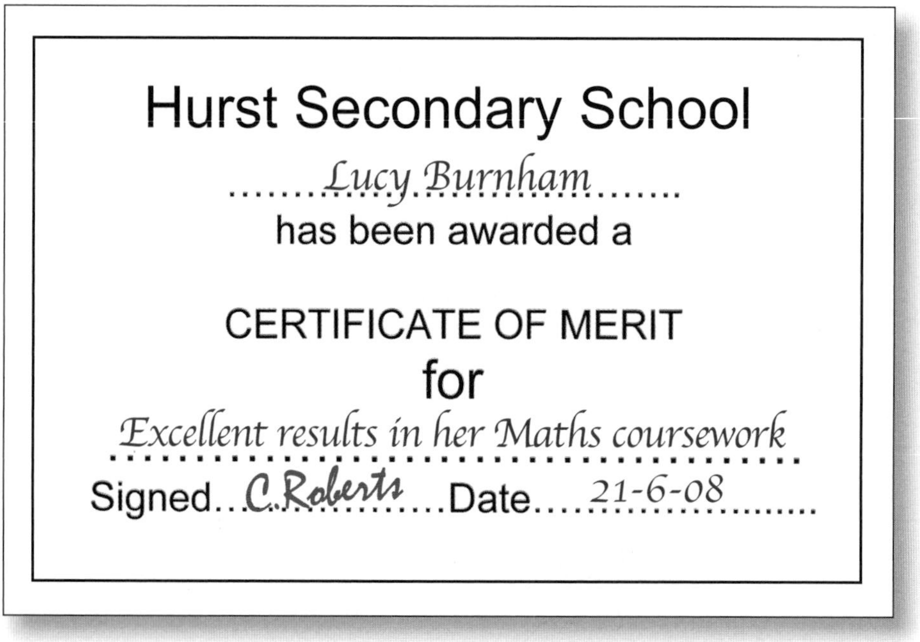

Hurst Secondary School

............Lucy Burnham.......
has been awarded a

CERTIFICATE OF MERIT
for

Excellent results in her Maths coursework
Signed...C.Roberts....Date.....21-6-08.........

▲ **Figure 19.8** Example of a certificate

Collecting data on pupils' learning and behaviour

At Darnfield Secondary, there are two systems – one for collecting data on pupil learning and another for behaviour. Where pupils have made a particular effort or achieved well, this is recorded by class teachers. They are then awarded a bronze certificate when they have collected 50 merits for good work. Behaviour is recorded in a separate system, which allows for 'Golden time' during tutor time on Fridays. If pupils' behaviour is not acceptable on three occasions during the week, they are not able to take part in Golden time.

● What system does your school have for collecting data on pupils' learning and behaviour?
● How successfully is this implemented?
● What is your role?

For your portfolio... **K9 K11 K12 K19 K22**

Write a reflective account of a situation in which you have had to manage risk to yourself or others due to pupil behaviour. Outline the background and events leading up to the incident. In order to cover the knowledge base above, make sure that you indicate how you followed school policy, assessed and acted on the risk involved and took into account the needs of any pupils who have learning and behavioural difficulties.

You will need to check with your assessor whether you have covered all of the knowledge base.

Further resources

Rogers, B (2004) *How to Manage Children's Challenging Behaviour* (London; Paul Chapman Publishing)

Rogers, B (2006) *Classroom Behaviour: A Practical Guide to Effective Teaching, Behaviour Management, and Colleague Support* (London; Paul Chapman Publishing)

Websites

www.everychildmatters.gov.uk

www.schoolcouncils.org

www.teachernet.gov.uk/SEAL

www.teachers.tv/video/122 (video resources on behaviour management)

20 Develop and Promote Positive Relationships

As you are working with pupils, a central part of your role is to help them to develop positive relationships with others. Pupils will not only develop their cognitive skills while at school: they need to learn how to work and play together co-operatively and respect individuals from other backgrounds and cultures. Although in schools we often spend a lot of time talking about emphasising the importance of forming and maintaining positive relationships, pupils will need good role models to help them to do this. They will witness how adults interact with one another and work together, which in turn will influence how they behave. Pupils will also need to feel that they are valued and respected by others around them and this will form a sound basis for their learning. You should demonstrate good relationships in your interactions with all pupils and adults in order to be an effective role model.

You will have contact with a range of teachers and possibly other professionals, as well as parents and pupils. You will need to demonstrate that you know and understand the boundaries of the information that can be passed on and the importance of observing school policies around confidentiality.

What you need to know and understand

For this unit you will need to know and understand:

- The importance of good working relationships in the setting

- Relevant legal requirements covering the way you relate to and interact with children and young people

- Relevant legal requirements and procedures covering confidentiality and the disclosure of information

- Relevant legal requirements covering the needs of disabled children and young people and those with special educational needs

- The types of information that should be treated confidentially: who you can and cannot share this information with

- The meaning of anti-discriminatory practice and how to integrate this into your relationships with children, young people and other adults

- How you adapt your behaviour and communication with children/young people to meet the needs of children/young people in your care of different ages, genders, ethnicities, needs and abilities

- Strategies you can adopt to help children/young people to feel welcome and valued in the setting

- What is meant by 'appropriate' and 'inappropriate' behaviour when interacting with children and young people, the policies and procedures to follow and why these are important

- The importance of encouraging children and young people to make choices for themselves and strategies to support this

- The importance of involving children and young people in decision-making and strategies you can use to do this

- How to negotiate with children/young people according to their age and stage of development

- Strategies you can use to show children and young people that you respect their individuality

- How to balance the needs of individual children/young people with those of the group as a whole

- The importance of clear communication with children and young people and specific issues that may arise in bilingual and multilingual settings

- Why it is important for children/young people to ask questions, offer ideas and suggestions and how you can help them do this

- Why it is important to listen to children and young people

- How to respond to children and young people in a way that shows you value what they have to say and the types of behaviour that could show that you do not value their ideas and feelings

- The importance of being sensitive to communication difficulties with children and young people and how to adapt the way you communicate to different situations

- How you can help children and young people to understand the value and importance of positive relationships with others

- The importance of children and young people valuing and respecting other people's individuality and how you can encourage and support this

- Why it is important for children and young people to understand and respect other people's feelings and how you can encourage and support this

- Why it is important to be consistent and fair in dealing with positive and negative behaviour

- Strategies you can use to encourage and reinforce positive behaviour

- Strategies you can use to challenge and deal with different types of behaviour which are consistent with your organisation's policies

- Why it is important for children and young people to be able to deal with conflict themselves and what support they may need from you, according to their age, needs and abilities

- Why it is important to encourage and support positive relationships between children/young people and other adults in the setting and strategies you can use to do this

- Why positive relationships with other adults are important

- Why it is important to show respect for other adults' individuality and how to do so

- The importance of clear communication with other adults and how this can be achieved

- The importance of being sensitive to communication difficulties with other adults and strategies you can use to overcome these

- How and when it may be necessary to adapt the way you communicate to meet the needs of other adults

- Typical situations that may cause conflict with other adults and how to deal with these effectively

Importance of good working relationships in the setting

In whatever profession you are employed, it is very important to have good working relationships with others. This is because it is through the development of these relationships that you will be able to carry out your role more effectively, which benefits everyone. If you are lucky enough to work in an environment where colleagues work positively together, you will find this enormously supportive.

Although your main point of contact in school may be the Special Educational Needs Co-ordinator (SENCo)(Additional Support for

> **ⓘ Key term**
>
> **Setting** or **service**
> – anywhere children and young people's care, learning and development takes place and where children or young people are normally present under adult supervision

Learning (ASL) teacher), there are other groups or individuals with whom you will form working relationships. Depending on how much you are working with a particular pupil, you may be involved with some of these other people on a regular basis. Alternatively, working as a teaching assistant and having limited hours in school, you may find that you come into contact with very few people other than teaching and other support staff.

You need to show that you have good working relationships with all those with whom you work. This in turn will create a happy and welcoming atmosphere, which will form a positive environment for pupils.

Adults in school with whom you may have regular contact

- **Other assistants or support staff** – You may meet formally and informally to discuss issues.
- **Administrative staff, midday supervisors, bursars, caretakers** – You will have contact with other support staff who will have different roles in the school.
- **Teaching staff** – You will work with them on a daily basis.
- **Parents** – They may come into school for annual review days. You may also have close contact with them if you support an individual pupil with learning needs.
- **Year group leaders** – You may need to discuss ideas as a year group.
- **SENCo (ASL teacher)** – You may have regular contact with the SENCo (ASL teacher) if you are working as an individual teaching assistant.
- **Assistants' manager** or **co-ordinator** – You should have regular meetings with a line manager to gather information and discuss school issues.
- **Headteacher/Deputy** – You should have some contact with senior management, which may take the form of meetings and exchanging information.

▼ **Figure 20.1** How good are your relationships with other adults in your work environment?

Professionals from outside agencies also visit the school in order to work with and advise on pupils who have special educational (Additional Support for Learning (ASL)) needs. If you are an individual teaching assistant, you may be asked to join in with meetings and discuss the pupil's progress. Extend your good practice and positive relationships to include your work with them. Professionals from outside school with whom you are likely to come into contact may include:

- speech and language therapists
- educational psychologists
- language support teachers for EAL pupils
- sensory support teachers
- learning support staff
- behaviour support staff
- specialist teachers, for example for pupils with autism
- occupational therapists or physiotherapists, who usually work with pupils outside school, but may also offer advice
- social services.

Legal requirements relevant to your work in school

Legal requirements covering the way you interact with pupils

Adults who work with children in any setting need to have some idea about current legislation as it will affect their practice. There is an increased awareness of how important it is to recognise the uniqueness of each child and to have respect for their human rights. The legislation is constantly under review and you need to keep up to date through reading relevant publications.

United Nations Convention on the Rights of Children (UNCRC)

In 1989 the first international convention took place around children's rights. This was because it was felt that children under 18 needed to have special care and protection. In it were devised a 'universally agreed set of standards and obligations' for children's human rights and a set of minimum standards to be observed by all governments. In all 54 different articles were agreed, surrounding areas such as non-discrimination, developing children to their fullest potential, the right to education, the right to be with their parents, the right to be heard. It set out that the best interests of the child should be acknowledged at all times. (All 54 articles can be seen on the UNCRC website at www.unicef.org.crc.) The UK has taken on board many aspects of the convention's thinking in legislation that has been devised since 1989.

Portfolio activity K2

Investigating relevant legislation

Find out what you can about the legislation below and give a short presentation to others in your group.

- Human Rights Act 1998
- Children Act 2004

Relevant legal requirements and procedures covering confidentiality and the disclosure of information

In schools we ask parents and carers for a range of information so that we are able to care for pupils as effectively as we can while they are with us. However, we may only ask for information that is directly relevant, such as health or medical information, records from previous schools, or records for pupils who have special educational (ASL) needs. All this is **confidential information** and must only be used for the purpose for which it was gathered. If the information needs to be passed on to others for any reason, parental consent needs to be given. This usually involves parents signing a consent form.

Key term

Confidential information – information that should only be shared with people who have a right to have it, e.g. teachers, line manager or an external agency

Under the Data Protection Act 1998, any organisation that holds information on individuals needs to be registered with the Data Protection Commission. This is designed to ensure that confidential information cannot be passed on to others without the consent of the individual concerned. There are eight principles of practice that govern the use of personal information. It must be:

- processed fairly and lawfully
- only used for the purpose for which it was gathered
- adequate, relevant and not excessive
- accurate and kept up to date where necessary
- kept for no longer than necessary
- processed in line with the individual's rights
- kept secure
- not transferred outside the European Union without adequate protection.

Relevant legal requirements covering the needs of disabled children and those with special educational needs

Special Educational Needs (SEN) Code of Practice 2001 and Disability Discrimination Act 1995

Under the Disability Discrimination Act 1995, it became a requirement for premises not to discriminate against disabled people. As part of the SEN Code of Practice 2001 this was also extended to schools, which meant that schools could not discriminate against disabled pupils. This means that an increased number of pupils with special educational (ASL) needs now attend mainstream schools.

Every Child Matters Framework and the Children Act 2004

This legislation stresses the importance of more integrated services and sharing of information between professionals. It came into being after the tragic case of Victoria Climbié, when there was no communication between health and social workers.

Types of information that should be treated confidentially: who you can and cannot share this information with

You will need to be aware of a range of information in your role as a teaching assistant, from issues around the school to the individual needs of the pupils with whom you work. You should know how and when to share any information you have access to. If you are at all concerned or unclear about who you can speak to, your first point of

▶Figure 20.2 Be careful not to divulge confidential information

You'll never guess what I found out this morning…

contact should be your line manager, or, in the case of pupils with special educational (ASL) needs, the SENCo (ASL teacher).

Some teaching assistants working in schools are also parents of pupils at the same school, and other parents may sometimes put pressure on them to disclose information. Do not pass on any information about the school or the pupils before being certain that this is the correct thing to do. By passing on information without following the correct channels you will be abusing your position of professional trust and this can be very damaging.

Also be very careful if taking photographs for displays or if filming pupils for any purpose; again parental permission needs to be given for this. You should not take pictures of pupils for your portfolio!

Case study K5

Keeping information confidential

You have a new pupil in Year 8 (S2) who is on the autistic spectrum and he is being monitored by all staff during his settling in. You have been asked to support him as much as you can and have been given information on his background and access to reports from other professionals. At present his behaviour can be unpredictable and a parent who comes into school to run a lunchtime drama club has witnessed this. She has then spoken about it to other parents. A few days later, at the Year 8 (S2) annual review day another parent asks you about the pupil. She wants to know where he has come from and why he is in a mainstream school. She says it is 'not the right place for him'.

● What would you say to her?
● What would you do if other parents continued to ask you about the pupil and voice their opinions?

You should not pass on information to:

- other pupils in the school
- other parents
- other professionals, unless parents have been consulted
- visitors.

Anti-discriminatory practice

How to integrate anti-discriminatory practice into your relationships

When you are working in school you may find that you meet pupils, families and also other staff with ideals and approaches that are very different from your own. This should be seen as a positive aspect of your work in school as we all learn from each other. Depending on the location and catchment area of the setting, you may experience a range of diversity issues.

Anti-discriminatory practice forms the basis of an environment in which there is no discrimination towards individuals on the basis of race, gender, culture or ethnicity. No adults or pupils should be the victims of discrimination in schools and fair treatment should be given to all individuals. The term '**inclusion**' is often used when referring to pupils who have special educational (ASL) needs, but it is also used in a wider sense to describe equal opportunities for all in the learning environment. It is through the development of trust and positive relationships that children and adults of all backgrounds will learn to respect one another.

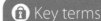
Key terms

Anti-discriminatory practice – taking positive action to counter discrimination, which involves identifying and challenging discrimination and being positive in your practice about differences and similarities between people

Inclusion – a process of identifying, understanding and breaking down barriers to participation and belonging

K6 Case study

Recognising and addressing discrimination

Kwakye is a male teacher in a secondary school. He enjoys his job and working with his female colleagues, and is a valued member of staff. However you notice that often in the staff room, he is teased and almost bullied by female colleagues. They often say that he is a man, so is unable to multitask, or that as a man he won't be able to deal with sensitive issues. You have noticed that he is spending less and less time in the staffroom with colleagues.

- Do you think that these kinds of comments matter?
- Would you say anything to Kwakye?
- Why is it important that these kinds of issues are addressed?

Self-awareness of your own values and beliefs is an important part of your work with others. Be aware that your own thoughts and opinions have been shaped by your experiences and background. This in turn may affect how you react and respond in different situations.

Investigating anti-discriminatory procedures and policies

Find out what procedures and policies your school has in place for dealing with anti-discriminatory practice. Write an account of the ways in which your school might bring these to the attention of staff and pupils.

Adapting your behaviour and communication with pupils to meet the needs of all pupils in your care

In order to build relationships with pupils, you need to adapt your behaviour and communication accordingly. Pupils of either gender and all ages, ethnicities, needs and abilities need to feel secure and valued, and your interactions with them should demonstrate this. Through positively communicating with and being involved with pupils, you will show them that they are part of the school community. However, this is not the same as giving all pupils attention whenever they demand it!

Age and maturity

By the time pupils reach secondary school they should be able to co-operate and concentrate for longer periods independently. They will not, however, be able to concentrate fully for a whole period (1 hour) unless the activities and the pace of tasks are varied. As they grow more independent, pupils are able to take on more responsibility.

Gender

Both boys and girls need to have positive role models. In many secondary schools, although there are several male teachers, there is still a lack of male teaching assistants. Boys and girls should also have equal access to activities – cooking, construction activities and creative tasks should be available to all pupils.

Ethnicity

Pupils from all **ethnicities** need to feel that they 'belong' in the school. There should be a wide range of representation through Citizenship and assemblies, celebrating different festivals, invited visitors and so on. In some cultures, the 'norms' of communication may be different from our own so be sensitive to this, for example, giving eye contact when speaking to pupils.

Needs and abilities

Depending on pupils' needs and abilities you will need to adapt the amount of time given. If you are employed to work specifically with one pupil, you need to make sure you support them without doing the work for them.

> **🛈 Key term**
>
> **Ethnicity** – refers to a person's identification with a group that shares some or all of the same culture, lifestyle, language, skin colour, religious beliefs and practices, nationality, geographical region and history; everyone has an ethnicity

Strategies you can adopt to help pupils to feel welcome and valued in the setting

All staff should help to make pupils in the school feel welcome and valued at all times. Pupils need to feel settled and confident in order to learn, but the kinds of strategies you adopt will depend on the circumstances and age of the pupil.

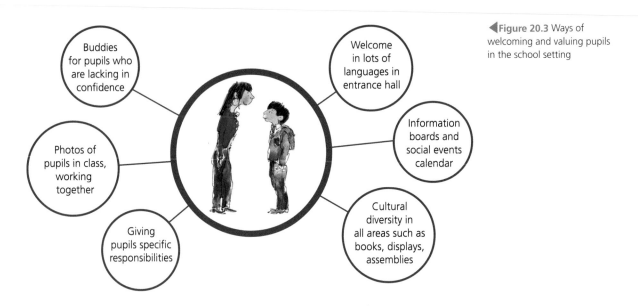

◄ **Figure 20.3** Ways of welcoming and valuing pupils in the school setting

Buddies for pupils who are lacking in confidence

Welcome in lots of languages in entrance hall

Information boards and social events calendar

Photos of pupils in class, working together

Cultural diversity in all areas such as books, displays, assemblies

Giving pupils specific responsibilities

Younger pupils may appreciate a colourful and lively learning environment, while older pupils may be more interested to hear about social events in the school and local community. Encourage the participation of pupils and their families in school events in order to make them feel welcome.

K8 Portfolio activity

Reflecting on policies for welcoming and valuing pupils

Write a reflective account of the kinds of strategies your school uses to welcome and value all pupils. You may want to give examples of particular initiatives you have been responsible for or to show how you have been part of whole school practice to help pupils feel welcome.

What is meant by 'appropriate' and 'inappropriate' behaviour when interacting with pupils

As a professional in any setting, you need to be fully aware of the way in which you can interact and behave with pupils in your care and the implications of this. Make sure that you are friendly but firm with

ⓘ Key term

Appropriate behaviour – behaviour that demonstrates the child is respected and valued; behaviour that is not abusive or derogatory to the child, either physically, emotionally or sexually

them, while knowing that both of these approaches have limits. If you are too friendly, pupils will not understand that there are boundaries that they need to adhere to, and may not respect your authority. If you are too firm with pupils, there may be issues around child protection. You may notice how other adults' interactions affect the responses of pupils. We have a responsibility to pupils to show them respect so that they in turn will respect others.

How we speak to pupils and what we say to them

Always show that you value pupils through the way in which you address them. It is important that you speak to them in a way that maintains the relationship of professional carer to child. Pupils will often question you, for example, they may ask you how old you are. It is sometimes best to answer these kinds of questions with humour, but at times you may have to explain that giving them personal information or talking about your home life is not appropriate.

Physical contact

Adults are often nervous about any kind of physical contact with pupils. Sometimes, in cases where pupils are behaving aggressively and in danger of hurting themselves or others, they may need to be restrained. Your school should have a policy for dealing with this, which may in turn come from local authority guidelines. You may also want to speak to other members of staff for advice and guidance. Always follow the school's guidelines and policies in case there is any later comeback. It may also be a good idea to belong to a union (see union websites on page 102).

Case study K9

Maintaining appropriate contact

Kelly, in Year 9 (S3), seems to have very low self-esteem. She is very quiet and reserved in class and does not speak to adults very much. However, you are the male teaching assistant and she has started to follow you around. She interacts with you during lessons/tutor time and wants to walk around with you when you are on playground duty. You have tried to initiate some Drama activities during the tutor period to involve other pupils, but she does not want to interact with them.

- Should you have any cause for concern?
- Would you mention this to anyone or adjust your behaviour?
- What would be the most appropriate/inappropriate thing to do in this situation?

Encouraging young people to make choices and supporting their decision-making

An important part of learning is for pupils to learn to make choices for themselves. As part of the new Citizenship curriculum, pupils are encouraged to have the confidence and assertiveness to have their own voice, make decisions about issues within their community and use negotiating skills to present their ideas to community decision makers. A strict and authoritarian structure is likely to cause problems, as pupils will feel they have little say in what they are asked to do.

One strategy which is often used with pupils is discussing targets for work and behaviour with pupils and involving them in setting their own, so that targets are not imposed on them without their involvement. Another regularly used strategy is the use of school councils. These work very effectively in encouraging pupils to think about and discuss different sides of an issue and then come to a decision, which will be adopted by the school. (See also Unit 19, page 67).

(See also Unit 19, page 67).

K11 Case study

Setting class rules on behaviour

It is the beginning of a new school year. The Year 7 (S1) teacher needs to speak to your new class about the kind of behaviour you expect to see in the tutor period. You have decided that you will involve the pupils in discussing a set of class rules.

- Why might this be a worthwhile exercise?
- What support would you need to give the pupils?
- Have you been involved in similar activities in your own school?

How to negotiate with young people according to their age and stage of development

You need to use negotiation skills when working with pupils. It may be harder to negotiate with pupils in Key Stage 3 (Upper Primary stages) as they are only just beginning to develop maturity and need lots of reassurance and support. By Year 11 (S5), teenagers are learning to co-operate with others at an adult level, so it should be easier to negotiate with them.

Pupils also need to develop negotiation skills for themselves. Younger pupils may find it hard to make decisions due to peer pressure and the need to feel accepted. They may be easily influenced to accept decisions made on their behalf by their peers and therefore have little chance to practise their decision-making skills. You therefore need to provide opportunities for them to develop these skills, such as presenting business cases through the Citizenship curriculum.

K2 Case study

Supporting pupils' involvement with decision-making

In Perry Vale Secondary, there has been a great deal of discussion around the school uniform. Pupils have not been wearing items on the uniform list and the headteacher has spoken about the issue several times in assembly. Many of the pupils are saying that they don't see why they need to wear a uniform. The School Council has been asked to discuss the matter. After drawing up a list of advantages and disadvantages, they have decided to speak to the school about the advantages of wearing a uniform.

- What would be the benefits of using this approach?
- How could school staff support the School Council in following through their decision?

Strategies you can use to show young people that you respect their individuality

All children are individuals and should be treated as such. They will each have their own strengths and interests, and your responses to them should recognise this. You can show them that you respect their **individuality** through your interactions with them and the way in which you work with them. Pupils are very likely to approach you as you spend more time with them: as you get to know them and their personalities and backgrounds, this will become easier.

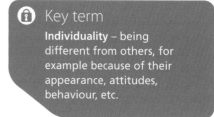

Key term

Individuality – being different from others, for example because of their appearance, attitudes, behaviour, etc.

How to balance the needs of individual young people with those of the group as a whole

When you are working with groups of pupils, you may find it difficult to balance the needs of individuals with those of the group. This will be because pupils often seem to require different levels of attention: some may be able to work and organise themselves independently, whereas others may need the reassurance of an adult. At times you will need to arrange the positions of different pupils in the group, as well as your own, so that you are able to give this reassurance just by your physical proximity. If pupils are encouraged to work and make decisions for themselves, they will not need as much adult support and will have more confidence.

Keys to good practice

Developing pupils' individuality while working in groups

✓ Encourage all pupils to put forward their own ideas.
✓ Know the names of all pupils.
✓ Acknowledge that some pupils will have strengths in a particular area and encourage this.
✓ Know the needs of all pupils, such as any special educational (ASL) needs.
✓ Enable pupils to express themselves in different ways, for example through creative activities.
✓ Sit close to pupils who need more reassurance.
✓ Be sympathetic if individuals find some things difficult.

Importance of clear communication with pupils

When communicating with pupils, we need to be very clear and unambiguous in what we say. They need us to communicate what is expected of them so that they learn to communicate well themselves. Sometimes we forget the importance of making sure that pupils understand what we mean, and might ask them 'What did I just ask you to do?' when they can't answer the question!

Issues arising in bilingual and multilingual settings

In bilingual or multilingual settings, where two or more languages are spoken, it is particularly important that instructions or expectations are clarified to pupils. All pupils may occasionally struggle to understand what they are being asked to do. For bilingual and multilingual pupils, who may speak one or more languages well, we may sometimes forget that their understanding of English can sometimes be less developed than that of other pupils.

In Wales, where pupils are taught in Welsh, there may be gaps in their understanding of either Welsh or English, which might cause misunderstanding. Some pupils may be more fluent than others or have limited experience of Welsh outside school.

K15 Case study

Supporting EAL pupils

Vijay is in Year 9 (S3) and has been in school for six months. He did not speak English when he started, but has picked up quite a lot and is managing well. The Science teacher has just given the class a complicated list of things to do at the beginning of the session and you notice that Vijay is unsure what to do and is looking worried.

- Why is it important that you go and speak to Vijay?
- What strategies could you use to help him and others in the class to check their understanding?

Why it is important for pupils to ask questions and offer ideas and suggestions, and how you can help them do this

For pupils to be able to communicate effectively, they should be encouraged to ask questions and put their own ideas forward. Pupils should feel relaxed and confident enough in school to be able to do this, as it is by questioning and finding out that they learn. They should also be able to offer their own suggestions and ideas so that there is a two-way dialogue between adults and pupils rather than a one-way flow of instructions. This also encourages the formation of positive relationships.

Why it is important to listen to pupils

During a busy school day, it is sometimes hard to find time to listen to pupils. However, listening to what they have to say is important as it reinforces self-esteem, values what they are saying and is a crucial part of building relationships. Making conversation and finding out the answer to questions also builds on the language skills that are vital to pupils' learning.

Children and adults of all ages need to feel that they are heard. You may need to reflect on how you do this and the opportunities you give pupils to talk. Your communication skills should enable you to both actively and reflectively listen to pupils, using a variety of strategies.

How to respond to pupils in a way that shows you value what they have to say

You need to show pupils that you value their contributions when they are speaking in a number of different ways. Children learn to communicate through the responses of others: if they do not feel that their contribution is valued, they will be less likely to initiate different forms of communication. To avoid giving pupils the message that you do not value their ideas and feelings, you should always make sure you adopt the following strategies.

Find opportunities to speak

Make sure that pupils are given sufficient opportunity to talk. Some pupils have very little chance to put their own ideas forward and express themselves with adults. They may lack confidence and need to be given a chance to 'warm up' first so that they feel able to do so.

Give eye contact

If you say that you are listening, but are looking away and are busy doing something else, this will give the pupil the message that you are not really interested in what they are saying. Make sure that if a pupil is talking, you are giving them your attention.

Use body language and facial expressions

Make sure that you show your interest by the way in which you act when speaking to pupils. Also make sure that you smile and react positively to what they are saying.

React and comment on what they are saying

You may need to repeat back to pupils to check on your understanding, particularly if they have used incorrect language: for example 'I bringed my book in today'; 'You have brought your book in today? Oh good, that means we can change it'.

Be interested, responding and questioning to maintain conversation

It is important to model and invite the 'norms' of conversation with pupils so that they build up an understanding about how it works. They will do this through experience, so show that you are interested and respond to their questions.

Importance of being sensitive to communication difficulties with pupils and adapting the way you communicate

Care and sensitivity should be taken with pupils who have communication difficulties, as they need to take their time and feel unpressured when they are speaking. Some pupils may not have many opportunities to speak, or may be anxious or nervous. You need to adapt the way in which you communicate according to their individual needs. If they have speech disorders, such as a stammer, or conditions that make it difficult for them, they should be allowed to take their time. Try not to fill in words for them or guess what they are going to say, as this will add to their distress.

You may need additional training, for example in sign language, to be able to communicate effectively or know the most effective strategies to use. In some cases where pupils have special educational (ASL) needs, you may need to have additional equipment in order to communicate with each other.

▲ **Figure 20.4** You may need to adapt your communication method

Helping young people to build positive relationships

As adults working with children, we need to help them to understand the value and importance of positive relationships. Over time pupils will learn to do this in school in different ways. They will be encouraged to work in pairs, groups and as a class to listen to one another and acknowledge ideas. They will learn to think of others and have respect for their feelings. They will also find out how positive relationships with others will enhance what they do. By observing our interactions with pupils and other adults, they should be able to see the effects that positive relationships with others have.

Importance of pupils valuing and respecting other people's individuality and how you can encourage and support this

It is important that schools encourage pupils to learn to value and embrace diversity and individuality. The learning environment should be one in which all cultures, ages and personalities are valued and respected. Often as pupils become older and form friendship groups, they can become nervous about being different and standing up for what they think. Adults will need to listen to what they have to say and encourage them to speak confidently.

Supporting pupils with religious needs

It is tutor time and you are in the Year 7 (S1) tutor room. You notice that some pupils are huddled around a Year 7 (S1) pupil who is not eating the sweets brought in for a pupil's birthday. When you go over to find out what is happening, he tells you that he is fasting because it is Ramadan. The other pupils ask you what this means and why he can't have any sweets.

- How would you deal with this in the short term?
- Why should you follow it up and how would you do this?
- What procedures does your school have in place for supporting pupils who celebrate different religious festivals?

Why it is important for pupils to understand and respect other people's feelings and how you can encourage and support this

It is important for pupils to learn to understand and respect the feelings of others. Depending on their past experiences, pupils may have a greater or lesser experience of doing this. We often speak to them in school about thinking about the consequences of their actions and how they might have affected others. Through personal, social and health education (PSHE) sessions, assemblies and role play, we might encourage them to think about considering others' feelings.

Pupils also need to be able to understand how their own feelings might affect their behaviour and you may need to talk to them about this. For example, saying to a pupil, 'I know you are upset because you could not do cooking today' will help them to make the link between emotion and behaviour. In this way they are more able to understand how to think about others.

One effective way of encouraging pupils to understand and respect others' feelings is through discussion and activities such as drama therapy, where pupils are asked to show how they perceive others' feelings through characters in a role play. A whole class forum is another good way of helping pupils listen to others and respect their feelings.

Reflecting on your school's support of positive relationships

Write a reflective account of the different ways in which your school supports the development of positive relationships between pupils.

- How have you been involved?
- What kinds of activities does the school encourage and have you seen the benefits of this way of working?

If you have had any specific training, you should also mention this.

Strategies such as the Restorative Justice programme are also popular in schools. These are taken from the criminal justice system and have worked well as a method of resolving behaviour issues and learning from what happens. The table below, taken from the Transforming Conflict website, an organisation which promotes restorative justice, shows how you can encourage and support pupils as they learn to understand how the impact of what they do affects others.

Restorative justice in schools, from www.transformingconflict.org

Retributive justice	Restorative justice
Negative behaviour is 'breaking the rules'	Negative behaviour is adversely affecting others
Focus on blame/guilt/who was the culprit	Focus on problem solving and expressing needs and feelings
Adversarial relationships	Dialogue and negotiation
Imposition of pain/unpleasantness to punish and deter	Restitution, leading to reconciliation
Attention to rules	Attention to relationships
Conflict represented as impersonal and abstract	Conflict identified as interpersonal with value for learning
One social injury replaced by another	Focus on repair of social injury
School community as spectators	School community involved in facilitation
People affected by behaviour are not necessarily involved	Encouragement of all concerned to be involved
Accountability defined in terms of punishment	Accountability defined as understanding the impact of the action

Communication and young people's behaviour

Why it is important to be consistent and fair in dealing with positive and negative behaviour

It is vital to have a whole school approach when dealing with behaviour, as this gives a clear message to pupils. The way in which you manage behaviour also has a strong impact on the relationships you have with pupils, as it is one area where effective communication is essential. The school should have a clear scale of sanctions and strategies for you to use for behaviour management, such as school rules and a reward system. (See also Unit 19).

You need to be consistent and fair in school because pupils will always notice and pick up on any differences in the way in which adults manage behaviour. It is also important for pupils to see that adults are able to remain calm and fair when dealing with issues of behaviour. This enables them to recognise the limits of what is acceptable and what is not. If adults are inconsistent, this will send out confusing messages to pupils about how they should behave.

Reinforcing positive behaviour

Positive praise is a very powerful tool when managing behaviour. As adults, we need to notice the positive as much as we can, because it can be human nature and easier for us to notice and comment on the negative. Commenting on the negative brings the pupil down and makes them feel that they are only getting attention when they do something they shouldn't. Children respond straightaway to positive comments and any acknowledgement that we have noticed them. Also make sure that you are clear about what you are praising, rather than assuming that the pupil knows.

Well done, Omar, you have done really good research today.

▲ Figure 20.4 Be clear about why you are praising a child

Dealing with negative behaviour

Negative behaviour should be dealt with quickly and the pupil should be very clear on the reasons for any sanctions. If you react strongly without speaking to them first, for example, 'Go straight to Mr Barnes!', the pupil may not be clear on your reason. Pupils need to know that it is the behaviour rather than themselves that is the focus of your reaction. For example, 'You forgot that in this school we always go up the stairs on the right-hand side, Maria' will always be more effective than 'What a silly girl you are, Maria, for pushing up the stairs on the left'. By labelling the behaviour rather than the pupil, we are giving them an opportunity to move away from it.

As soon as possible afterwards try to notice the same pupil doing something positive and praise them for that. (See Unit 19 for further strategies for dealing with negative behaviour.)

Keys to good practice

Reinforcing positive and dealing with negative behaviour

✓ Notice positive behaviour at all times – including politeness and good manners!
✓ Keep an eye out for additional ideas, for example if pupils have behaved well give them a choice over the activity they complete in the last lesson of the week.
✓ Use class as well as whole school systems and devise them together with the pupils.
✓ Be clear if you have told pupils off exactly why you are reprimanding them.
✓ Make sure you tell pupils that it is their behaviour that is bad, not them.
✓ 'Catch them being good' as soon as you can afterwards.

Why it is important for young people to be able to deal with conflict themselves and what support they may need

Conflicting points of view and ideas will be a natural outcome of encouraging pupils' individuality. We all have our own thoughts and feelings, and pupils need to learn how to deal with this. They will also have to learn what behaviour is acceptable in the school environment, and be able to listen to and respect the thoughts of others. Older pupils should be encouraged to have discussions and debates around different points of view, as this gives them perspectives other than their own. Learning to talk through and resolve issues themselves will give them a valuable skill.

When you should intervene

You need to recognise that adults should not always intervene when there are areas of conflict and that if we want pupils to learn to resolve issues, we need to give them opportunities to do so. The best strategy is for them to discuss or negotiate issues themselves. However, there are times when you need to intervene and speak to pupils, for example if at any time they become aggressive or unkind.

Very young or immature pupils

These pupils may find it hard to put themselves in the place of others. You may need to point out how important it is to be considerate of how others may be feeling. For example, if they want to take part in an activity that another pupil is doing, they will have to wait.

Pupils with specific needs or abilities

Such pupils, for example if they are autistic, may find empathising with others very difficult. You need to adapt how you respond in order to support them and you may need to ask for specialist advice. Where pupils have limited understanding due to their needs, it may be more difficult to explain to them and you may have to speak to them sensitively to resolve conflict.

K26 Case study

Intervening in pupils' decision-making

You are working close to a group of Year 7 (S1) pupils who are carrying out an investigative activity. They have to discuss and find out about reversible and irreversible changes in materials. The pupils have started well, but are now arguing about the best method they can use to test the materials and which materials to look at. You are observing them and decide to wait and see whether they are able to resolve the argument themselves. After some time, one of them suggests that they work in pairs to consider different materials, as this will be a better use of time.

- Do you think that this is the best outcome?
- Would the pupils have benefited from adult intervention? If so, how?

(See also page 94 on restorative justice.)

Why it is important to encourage and support positive relationships between young people and other adults and strategies you can use

It is very important for you to support positive relationships between pupils and other adults in the setting. You are in a position in which pupils notice and take their lead from your behaviour and the way in which you relate to others. If they see negative behaviour and comments being made by adults, they will learn to think that this is acceptable. Always make it clear that you have positive views about others when working with them.

Case study K27

Encouraging positive relationships between pupils and adults

You are working in a Year 9 (S3) History class alongside the class teacher who is completing a training course over 12 weeks. This means that one day per week the pupils have another teacher, Mr Knightley, who does part-time supply work at the school. Although the class likes Mr Knightley, you have noticed that some of them are making negative comments about him and this has started to affect their behaviour during the afternoon session.

- Is there anything you can do to support the teacher both in the session and outside it?
- Why is it important to try to keep the relationship positive?

Communicating with other adults

Why positive relationships with other adults are important

As **adults**, we need to show pupils how to get along with one another and we should model the kind of behaviour we expect from them. If we are able to show them that we value and respect others they are much more likely to learn to do the same.

Having **positive relationships** with other adults is also important because we will be more likely to communicate information to one another. Parents and other professionals who come into the school are more likely to offer support if communication is strong and effective. This will in turn benefit the pupils.

> **Key term**
>
> **Adults** – in this context, includes children's family members, colleagues and other professionals

> **Key term**
>
> **Positive relationships** – relationships that benefit the children and young people and their ability to participate in and benefit from the setting

Why it is important to show respect for other adults' individuality and how to do so

Having respect for others is a crucial part of being able to have a positive relationship with them. We cannot do this unless we value others, respect their views and show that we do this. We can do this in a number of ways.

- Listen to all adults, let them put their ideas forward and encourage discussion.
- Find out how individuals like to be addressed and then speak to them in the preferred way, for example Ms Malone, Miss Matharu.
- Encourage pupils to respect other children and adults by acting as good role models.
- Celebrate diversity through assemblies, activities and displays.

It is important for you to remember that we are all individuals and that you should not expect others to share the same ideas. We also need to ensure that we do not make any assumptions about adults, particularly if we know very little about them or their background.

K29 Case study

Respecting other adults' individuality

Mary, a new teaching assistant in your school, has come to speak to you because she has had a disagreement with a physiotherapist who has come to visit one of the pupils. She tells you that the physio has given her a long list of exercises to do with the pupil and that she doesn't have time to do them and has told the physio so. Moreover, she says that the physio became unhappy when Mary got her name wrong and addressed her incorrectly. Mary says that it is enough to try to remember the names of all the pupils and she shouldn't be expected to learn the long-winded surnames of everyone that comes into school.

- What issues need to be considered here?
- What might you say to Mary?
- Should you speak to anyone else about this?

Importance of clear communication with other adults and how this can be achieved

We communicate with each other in many different ways. Communication occurs not only through the spoken and written word but also through the way in which we respond to others, for example, how soon we reply to an email or phone message, how attentive we are when we talk to them, how we dress. In schools, everyone is very busy and it is important that we have structures in place that ensure that all staff, professionals, parents and governors have access to any information that is available. Clear communication should not be left to chance.

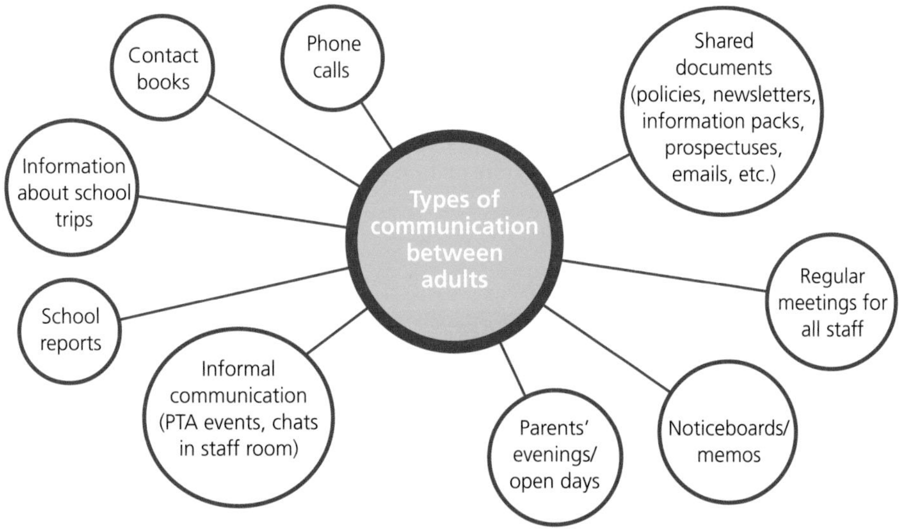

Figure 20.5 Effective communication comes in many forms

The diagram shows "Types of communication between adults" connected to:
- Contact books
- Phone calls
- Shared documents (policies, newsletters, information packs, prospectuses, emails, etc.)
- Information about school trips
- School reports
- Informal communication (PTA events, chats in staff room)
- Parents' evenings/ open days
- Noticeboards/ memos
- Regular meetings for all staff

Your school will have a range of types of planned communication with other adults. For those who work in the school, or when dealing with other professionals, there will be meetings and discussion, although there will also be informal communication. Where it is vital that information is passed on, it should always be done in a more formal situation.

You may need to suggest that a meeting is held or have an idea for discussion – do not be worried about putting your thoughts forward.

Portfolio activity K30

Investigating ways of passing on information to adults

Think about and record the different ways in which your school passes information to adults outside school. They may be parents, carers or outside agencies. You may want to list the methods of communication under 'Formal' and 'Informal' headings.

Importance of being sensitive to communication difficulties with other adults and adapting the way you communicate

It is important that we are sensitive to the needs of other adults, particularly if they have communication difficulties. It is possible that you will adapt the way you communicate with them without realising that you are doing it. We often change the way we react to others depending on the way in which they react to us. For example, if you are speaking to a parent or carer who is hearing-impaired, you might make sure that you are facing them and giving eye contact so that they can lip-read. However, if you have contact with adults who have other communication difficulties, you may need to reflect and make sure you adapt your means of communication.

Often, schools send out or gather information in a particular way, for example through letters. Depending on their individual needs, the recipients may not be able to access this method of communication easily, and this will not always be apparent. You may need to observe sensitivity, for example, if you need to ask a parent or carer why they have not responded to a note that was sent home.

If you need to communicate with other adults who speak English as an additional language, you may need to have a translator and meet together if information you are communicating to one another is difficult to convey.

K31 K32 Case study

Being sensitive to communication difficulties

Yasser's mother has come up to the school because she is unhappy about the way in which an incident on the playground was dealt with. English is not her first language. She has an appointment to see the tutor and says that she is very angry that you spoke to Yasser and sent him to the referral room (which is your school's policy for managing negative playtime behaviour). You are upset as Yasser's behaviour was out of turn and you acted according to school policy. The class tutor has invited you to come in and speak to her and you are reluctant to do so.

- Should you go and speak to Yasser's mother even if you do not want to?
- How might you reflect on the incident before going to meet with the parent?
- How might communication difficulties have influenced her reaction?
- What strategies can you think of to prevent this from happening again?

Situations that may cause conflict with other adults and how to deal with these effectively

As adults we can sometimes misread or perceive information wrongly. We may think that someone has communicated something to us when they have not. We sometimes blame others for saying things that could be ambiguous or for having a different point of view from ourselves.

Where there are areas of conflict with other adults, you will need to show sensitivity and try to resolve the situation as soon as possible. The longer a problem is allowed to go on, the more difficult it will be to put right.

Poor communication

Often areas of conflict occur when communication has not been effective. This may be because letters have not been passed on by parents or pupils, because of a lack of time or a misunderstanding. The best way to resolve areas of poor communication is to discuss them to establish a cause and then find a way forward together. The important thing is not to ignore the problem or talk to everyone else about it except the individual concerned.

Opposing expectations

Sometimes adults may not have the same ideas about the purpose of an activity or meeting, or come with a different idea in mind. Always clarify exactly the aims of what you are there to do and why.

Different values and ideas

Parents and schools may sometimes have different methods of dealing with situations. Whereas the school may request that pupils do things in a particular way, parental views may be very different.

External factors

You may be working with an individual who has considerable home pressures or other issues, which are affecting how they communicate. External professionals are likely to have time and other pressures of which you are not aware. As we get to know people we can identify if they are behaving in an uncharacteristic way and will be able to ask if there is anything wrong or if we can help.

Lack of confidence

Sometimes adults can act in an aggressive way if they are not sure about what they are doing or if they lack confidence. This may come across in a personal way to others, but is more to do with how they perceive themselves and their own abilities. You may need to be sensitive to this and offer them encouragement and support.

Keys to good practice

Communicating with adults

✓ Make sure you are friendly and approachable.
✓ Encourage parents to come into the school wherever possible.
✓ Ensure you use the correct form of address when speaking to others.
✓ Observe confidentiality.
✓ Do not make assumptions about others.
✓ Provide or obtain any vital information promptly.
✓ Be sympathetic to the needs of others.
✓ Prepare for and contribute to meetings.
✓ Acknowledge the help and support of others as much as you can.

For your portfolio... K28 K30 K33

Your school has an open door policy and parents and other adults are always welcome. Recently a parent has complained to you that the open door policy is not a reality. She said that teachers are always too busy to speak to her and it is so difficult to get into the school because of the security measures that she does not feel the term 'open door' is particularly accurate. She complained that she mentioned it to the headteacher some time ago, but nothing seems to have been done about it.

● What would be your first reaction in this situation?
● What else could you do or say in order to support the parent?
● Can you think of any other strategies the would help to deal with the complaint?
● Why is it important that you and the school act to resolve this matter?

In this unit you will need to show that you know what to do in sensitive situations, such as in the last case study, where there are communication issues or relationships between adults or pupils have broken down. You may or may not have had to deal with them.

If you have not had to deal with such situations, you can use the portfolio activities and case studies in this unit to show that you know what procedures you would follow. If you have been involved in a situation where communication has broken down, and do not want to write a reflective account about it, you can tell your assessor about it during a professional discussion. They can then record that you have told them and whether you have acted appropriately. The actual incident and individuals involved will not need to be named. This will avoid writing any sensitive information in your portfolio.

Websites

www.askatl.org.uk (Association of Teachers and Lecturers)

www.dfes.gov.uk (SEN Code of Practice 2001 England and Wales)

www.everychildmatters.gov.uk

www.pat.org.uk (Professional Association of Teachers)

www.restorativejustice.org.uk – Restorative Justice Consortium

www.transformingconflict.org

www.unicef.org/crc/

www.unison.org.uk (trade union for people delivering public services)

21 Support the Development and Effectiveness of Work Teams

While you are working in a school it is important to demonstrate that you are one of a team. Nobody can work in isolation and you will need to show how you work alongside others and demonstrate a knowledge and understanding of their roles as well as the importance of taking a proactive role yourself. Teams in secondary schools comprise the different groups of people who work together in order to achieve shared objectives for supporting individuals or groups of pupils, for example in year groups, as well as the whole school team. You will need to be able to contribute to the effectiveness of the team and work alongside others for the benefit of pupils. This means that you will need to show that you can recognise and respond to issues affecting team effectiveness. You should also be able to contribute in your own way to the development of the team through providing support and advice to others.

What you need to know and understand

For this unit, you will need to know and understand:

■ The principles underlying effective communication, interpersonal and collaborative skills and how to apply these within the teams in which you work

■ The relationship between your own work role and the role of other members of the work team

■ The value and expertise you bring to a team and that brought by your colleagues

■ The importance of respecting the skills and expertise of other practitioners

■ Your role within the team and how you contribute to the overall group process

■ The range of interactive styles which individuals have and how these may affect ongoing work

■ The differences between work and personal relationships and how work relationships can be maintained effectively

■ The sorts of situations where team members may require help and advice and how you should respond to these

■ Indicators of problems with team working and the actions you should take in response to these

■ Methods of handling and minimising interpersonal conflict

■ School policies and procedures for dealing with difficulties in working relationships and practices, including confidentiality requirements

■ The range of learning styles and preferences within the work team and the implications of these for the way in which you offer support to colleagues

■ The broader contexts in which everyone works and the particular situations of colleagues which might affect how they work and tackle problems at particular points in time

■ The sort of information and expertise you have which could benefit team members and how to share these with others

■ The value of sharing how you approach your role with other members of the team

Principles underlying effective communication, interpersonal and collaborative skills and how to apply these within the teams in which you work

Effective communication skills

Good communication is an essential part of working as a **team**. The principles of effective communication include the following aspects.

Listening to what others have to say

This is important: often people listen to one another, but do not really hear what others are saying. This may be because they are thinking about something else or are too eager to put their own point of view across.

ⓘ Key term

Team – people with whom you work on a long-, medium- or short-term basis, relating to the support provided for a specific pupil or a group of pupils

Making sure that you contribute to team discussions

You may not feel confident in volunteering your ideas: perhaps you are new to the team or find it difficult to put ideas forward. You should remember that all contributions are important, and your point of view is as valid as anyone else's.

Providing regular opportunities for talk

This is important in a school, where everyone is busy and may not have time for discussions when one member of the team needs to talk about a particular issue. For teams to communicate effectively within a school, there need to be systems in place that contribute to this. It helps to have a clear staff structure and clearly defined roles, which will make it easier for individuals to see where they fit into the school as a whole and how their role is defined. Communication should also take place through meetings between different groups within the school, for example the senior management team, the teaching staff, the year group, teaching assistants, individual support assistants and those working within a particular class. These meetings provide regular opportunities for discussion and exchange of information, which may be written or verbal.

Effective interpersonal skills

These are sometimes the most difficult skills to have because within any team there will be a number of personality types. Individuals need to have the skills to relate to one another well and be sympathetic, supportive and helpful. Members of the team should be sensitive to the needs and feelings of others, and encourage those who they know are finding work challenging or difficult, which may be due to other issues outside school.

There may be a combination of factors that makes it difficult for individuals to focus on and tackle problems in the work environment. In order to get around this, it is important to read each other's body language so that you can pick up on when it is not a good time to approach another member of the team with a problem. There may also be a member of the team who is much more of a speaker than a listener. This can be a problem if the person does not give others the chance to have their say.

Effective collaborative skills

Members of the team need to be able to work together. In his *Team Development Manual*, Mike Woodcock outlines nine 'building blocks' which lead to team effectiveness. These are:

- have clear objectives and agreed goals
- be open about facing issues and resolving them

- work in an atmosphere of mutual support and trust
- have appropriate leadership, which suits the task, team and individual members
- conduct regular reviews to reflect on performance as a team and as individuals
- have good relationships with other groups
- have sound procedures for working together and taking decisions, with all members being consulted and involved
- encourage and foster individual development of all team members
- work together cohesively but be free to disagree when necessary, i.e. allow both co-operation and conflict to get results.

Teams within a school should be able to apply these skills to their own environment and experience to ensure that they are supporting other members of their team. It is important to remember that although you are working as a team, individuals have their own strengths, which should be recognised and valued.

Relationship between your own work role and the role of other members of the work team

You may find that there are a variety of different teams in which you work within school on a short-, medium- or long-term basis. Although your role may be the same in each, these different teams will focus on different areas. These may be:

- **Supporting a particular pupil** – Teaching assistants who work with individual pupils may work alongside others such as the Special Educational Needs Co-ordinator (SENCo)(Additional Support for Learning (ASL) teacher) or other professionals who come into school to give special educational (ASL) needs support (see Unit 62, page 368 for the types of these professionals).
- **Within the class** – Teaching assistants will work with the class teacher, but there may also be other adults or teaching assistants within the class who work together.
- **Within a year group** – The school may be large and have three or four classes within a year group. Year groups may work very closely together and support one another in planning and moderating pupils' work.
- **Within the school** – All members of staff are part of a team and should support one another. For example, the Maths co-ordinator will be able to offer help and advice to any member of staff on any maths activities.

In each of these situations, members of the team need to understand their role and how it fits in with the roles of other team members. The most important part of any role within a team is communicating effectively with others. There should be clear and consistent methods of communication so that all team members feel that their opinions are valued.

K1 K2 K5 Portfolio activity

Using your skills for working in a team effectively

Using the headings in the bullet list above, indicate the different teams you belong to in school and where you fit in. Write a reflective account to show how you use effective communication, collaborative and interpersonal skills in your dealings with others.

Value and expertise you bring to a team and that brought by your colleagues

Depending on your own experiences, you bring a unique level of expertise to the school. You may have had specific training or experience, for example in an area of special educational (ASL) needs, and be able to offer advice to others. Remember that each individual in the school has their own experience and expertise, which at some point may be useful to another person. If you find that you are in a situation requiring advice or support, always consider going to others in your team in the first instance.

Case study K3

Seeking advice

Michaela, a teaching assistant working with Year 7 (S1), has been asked to support a new, visually impaired pupil. She does not have any experience of working with a pupil with these needs. There have been a few staff changes including the headteacher recently, but she is aware that there was a visually impaired pupil in the school two years before and knows that one of the teachers involved in supporting her is still at the school.

- Who should she go to first for advice?
- Would it be more appropriate for her to ask for external support?

Importance of respecting the skills and expertise of other practitioners

If you are working in a team you should always respect the opinions and knowledge that others bring. This is because in order to have a good working relationship with them, you need to show that you consider their opinions and experience. Bad feelings can quickly cause problems and unrest within teams.

Case study K4

Respecting the skills and expertise of others

You are part of a large secondary school, which holds weekly or fortnightly meetings for all teaching assistants, as required. This week, two of the teaching assistants who work in the Citizenship department are speaking to the group about some of the strategies they have been using to manage playground behaviour, following a course they attended. Some of the group are talking over what they are saying and are clearly not listening.

- Why is it important that schools give all staff opportunities to feed back to colleagues following development opportunities?
- Give two reasons why all staff should be attentive in this situation.

Your role within the team and how you contribute to the overall group process

As a member of any team, you should be invited to contribute to the group process, i.e. the task being undertaken by the group, such as supporting a particular pupil. You may belong to a number of different teams as part of your role and you need to be able to work with other team members so that you complement one another, regardless of the personalities involved (see also K2).

- **Working under own initiative** – You should be able to identify when something needs doing in the class or school that you are able to carry out without discussing it first with teachers. As you grow in experience you will recognise how you can support your team through your contributions, both large and small.
- **Planning with teachers** – You should plan alongside teachers or at least have access to plans so that you have a clear understanding of what you are expected to do within the class. Plans should show the role of other adults as well as learning intentions and whether activities are whole class, group or individual.
- **Attending meetings** – Meetings should give you a clear idea of how what you are doing fits into the school or team as a whole.
- **Taking part in extra-curricular activities** – It is likely that as well as doing your job, you will have other roles in school, such as working with the PTA, supporting a club or after-school activity, or contributing to another area of school life like helping with the school fair. Through these roles you are also contributing to school enrichment activities as well as supporting your colleagues.
- **Having a clearly defined job description** – It is important that your job description is up to date so that you can be sure that you are fulfilling your role and be clear of where you fit into your team.

▲ Figure 21.1 Key functions in the group process

Range of interactive styles which individuals have and how these may affect ongoing work

Individuals in any team have a range of interactive styles. This means that they have different personalities and may approach things in their own ways, which will usually be a strength, but may sometimes cause problems! There are a number of personality 'types', which are referred to in the work of Isabel Myers, based on the theories of Carl Jung. These form the basis of the Myers-Briggs identity test, which is often referred to and used in business training to encourage managers to think about how they relate to their teams. These 16 personality types all have their own strengths and focuses, and none of these is 'right' or 'wrong'. Although you are not working in a business context, it is interesting to consider how your own personality affects the way in which you relate to others and the success or challenges within your team.

> **? Thinking point...**
> Consider the different teams you belong to, whether at work or to do with leisure activities, family, college, etc. How do the different personalities in each context affect team dynamics?

Case study (K6)

Using the potential of different interactive styles

Demitri has been working as a teaching assistant in a small rural secondary school for some years. He has achieved his NVQ 3 and is considering applying for his HLTA (higher-level teaching assistant) status as he is often asked to manage the other teaching assistants and they go to him for advice. There are three other teaching assistants who have also been in the school for some time.

The school has been asked to support a community opera, which is taking place in the local town. Representatives from local colleges and choirs will be involved and it is open to anyone who wishes to take part. The school has also been asked for two large groups of pupils to be part of the production. Demitri has asked the other teaching assistants for their support for the project, which involves being present at rehearsals over a number of weeks, followed by three performances. The pupils will be involved in the performance and the teaching assistants will be required to support them, manage behaviour and help with costumes.

Identify how the different personality types below might react to this situation and how that may affect the project.

- Diane is quiet and has a good sense of humour.
- Maureen often gossips with others and is usually at the centre of most things in the staffroom.
- Denise has been in the school for a long time and makes it clear that she knows all there is to know.
- Jamie is enthusiastic in most situations and has good relationships with all.
- Hilary is not receptive to new ideas and will usually find fault with them.

Stages in team development

Research surrounding the effectiveness of teams shows that they pass through certain stages before they operate effectively. One of the most succinct definitions was reached by Tuckman (1965) and others, who believed that all groups need to go through a process of maturing before they are able to function efficiently, due to the different personalities within them. The process has been divided into four stages:

- **Forming** – Team members are just starting to get together and a leader emerges. Members need to have a clear sense of identity and purpose.
- **Storming** – Team members start to view themselves as more of a team and have reached an understanding of what is expected of them. There may be a challenge to the leader during this stage. Members need to have clear roles and opportunities for participation within the group.
- **Norming** – This term defines the stage at which the team organises itself into work groups and starts to develop different areas of activity. At this stage, the team needs to establish a culture around shared norms and values all members agree on.
- **Performing** – This is the ideal state to which all teams aspire. The group are comfortable with one another and work effectively together.

These four stages may not have clear boundaries and teams may sometimes become 'stuck' at a particular stage, or go backwards and not develop fully. In his book,

Effective Teambuilding, John Adair suggests that there may also be a fifth phase of development, the Dorming phase, when the team falls into a state of complacency about its achievements and does not continue to move forward. This is usually avoided through consistent communication and planning.

Differences between work and personal relationships and how work relationships can be maintained effectively

As the role of support staff has become 'professionalised' over time, it has become even more important to be mindful of issues around work and personal relationships. As a teaching assistant, you may work in a school attended by your friends' children and this can mean that you need to be particularly aware of confidentiality. You may be approached by other parents who want to know how their child is doing in class. It is important to refer queries through the appropriate channels and remain professional in this situation, so that work relationships can be maintained.

K7 # Case study

Personal relationships in a professional setting

Anthonia works in a large school in which her mother is the deputy headteacher. All of the staff are aware of this. Anthonia has recently been allocated a job in school that several other teaching assistants requested. One of the others is unhappy about this, due to Anthonia's connection with the senior management team, and issues a formal complaint.

● Could Anthonia have done anything different in this situation?
● What might be a satisfactory outcome?

Situations where team members may require help and advice and how you should respond to these

If you are experienced and/or approachable, others may come to you for help or advice. You should always think about your role and theirs within the team when doing this, while remaining supportive. When you do not feel that it is appropriate for you to deal with a particular issue, you may need to refer to someone else in the team. You must remain non-judgemental about others and not allow your own opinions to intrude or cloud any decisions you may have to make. You may also find that you have an area of expertise that is helpful to others and in this situation you should offer the help needed.

Recognising suitable situations for giving advice

As an experienced teaching assistant, you have been approached by a member of your team, who is having difficulties in her working relationship with her Science class teacher. She says that the teacher does not value her and she regularly has to ask for time to discuss the work she has done with her group because the teacher is always in such a hurry.

- What would be the most appropriate advice to give?
- How would you respond if your colleague asked you to speak to the teacher on her behalf?

Indicators of problems with team working and the actions you should take in response to these

Apart from clashes of personality, there are other areas that may cause problems within a team. One of the main areas is that of conflict. Members of an effective team need to confront any differences they have rather than ignore them. In his book, *Managing Disagreement Constructively*, Herbert Kindler identifies the following four main areas of conflict that occur within teams.

- **Having inaccurate or incomplete information** – In this situation, team members may have access to different information and feel that they have not been fully informed as to what is happening. This may also cause them to interpret information in different ways. This emphasises the importance of openness within teams.
- **Having inappropriate or incompatible goals** – Staff may not agree on strategies for managing one area of their work. However, if everyone in the team ensures that they have the same aims at the outset, these types of conflicts should be avoided.
- **Having ineffective or unacceptable methods** – It is important for the team to have shared values so that some members do not seem to say one thing and do another.
- **Having antagonistic or other negative feelings** – This is usually due to left over resentment that has built up over time. Conflict caused by old wounds is difficult to diagnose and often difficult to heal or resolve.

The school may have policies and procedures in place for dealing with difficulties and conflicts within working relationships. These will include areas such as confidentiality and all members of teams should be aware of issues surrounding the exchange of information. If you speak to another member of your team about an issue that concerns other people, be aware that this may be harmful to or get back to those concerned. Be aware of who you need to speak to on a professional level if you find that there are problems within your team or group, which are affecting your work.

Kindler also states that conflict exists at six levels:

- **Conflict within the individual** – This means that one person has to choose between actions or goals that are incompatible with one another; for example, a teaching assistant who has been offered ICT training after school each Thursday, but has other commitments at home.

- **Conflict between two people** – This occurs when individuals disagree about joint outcomes. It is most likely if team members do not have the same ideas about the team's work objectives.
- **Conflict within a group** – Group or team members disagree on important issues, such as which topic to plan for the term.
- **Conflict between groups** – Different groups or teams within the school disagree about the way in which something is done, for example, year groups who would prefer to do things in a different way from one another.
- **Conflict within an organisation** – A school finds that members of staff do not agree with a particular decision.
- **Conflict between organisations** – This is not so relevant to schools, but could occur, for example, when two schools that are geographically close have an area of disagreement.

If you find yourself experiencing conflict or difficulty, try to identify on what level it is occurring and be ready to articulate that to the appropriate person so that the problem doesn't fester and become worse.

K9 # Case study

Resolving problems with team working

In her second year as a teaching assistant, Karine has been placed with the same Maths teacher as in the previous year. She is unhappy about the decision because there is a personality clash and she had specifically requested to work with another teacher. She goes to see the headteacher, who tells her that it is important to work through difficulties and that she needs to learn to work with a range of personalities.

- What do you think about the headteacher's reaction?
- What should Karine do if she remains unhappy?

Methods of handling and minimising interpersonal conflict

Remember that as part of a team you will always get along with some personalities better than with others, but that this does not mean that you cannot relate in some way to all members of your team through your common purpose. You may also find that work or home pressures affect the way in which team members relate to one another. It is important to try to minimise conflict so that bad feeling and resentment does not build up over time. In order to do this, make sure that you try to resolve any issues as soon as possible through the appropriate channels. Communication is the most important factor, as many conflicts arise due to misunderstandings or the lack of time to discuss what is happening. If you find that another member of your team appears to be making your work more difficult due to their attitude or opinions, you need to try to resolve the situation or refer to a senior member of staff.

Keys to good practice

Working in teams

✓ Be considerate and respectful towards others in your team.
✓ Carry out your duties well and cheerfully.
✓ Do not gossip or talk about other people in your team.
✓ Make sure you discuss any problems as they arise.
✓ Speak to the appropriate team member if you need help.
✓ Prepare for and contribute to meetings.
✓ Acknowledge the support and ideas of other team members.

School policies and procedures for dealing with difficulties in working relationships and practices, including confidentiality requirements

You should be familiar with your school's policy for dealing with difficulties in working relationships and practices. It is usually known as the grievance policy and will give you information and details about how to approach any problems you may face when working with others. As an example, most policies advise a set way of dealing with issues as they arise. **Confidentiality** is particularly important in this situation and speaking to others or gossiping about issues that are being addressed through grievance procedures can be very harmful. There should be separate guidelines for individuals wishing to raise a grievance and for collective disputes.

> 🔒 **Key term**
>
> **Confidentiality** – only providing information to those who are authorised to have it

◀ **Figure 21.2** Example of a grievance policy

GRIEVANCE POLICY

Informal procedure (recommended course of action)

1) Speak directly and confidentially to the person or persons with whom you have a grievance. If agreement is not reached the issue should be taken directly to the headteacher. If the grievance is with the headteacher, take the issue to the chair of governors.

2) The headteacher or chair of governors will act as mediator and encourage both parties to resolve the issue as soon as possible and to avoid using the more formal procedure. Parties may be represented by a trade union representative or colleague if required. If the issue is not resolved within seven days of the grievance being raised, it should progress to the next level, i.e. the formal stage.

3) A record of the mediation meeting and any agreed actions by both or either party should be kept on file so that it can be referred to if required.

Formal procedure

1) If the informal procedure does not resolve the issue or it has not been resolved to the satisfaction of both parties, a letter should be sent to the Clerk to the Governors outlining progress so far. This should then be addressed by the grievance sub-committee of the governing body.

2) A meeting will be called between all parties by the grievance sub-committee and each person given the opportunity to put forward their side. There will be opportunities for questioning and responses by all.

3) If there is still no resolution, the matter may be passed to the Director of Education of the local authority and/or the unions.

Portfolio activity

Showing an awareness of your school's grievance policy

In order to present evidence here, you could copy and highlight your school's grievance policy to show the course of action you would need to take when addressing any difficulties in your team. Alternatively, you could discuss the issue with your assessor and ask them to record the discussion for you. (Also see the Portfolio activity at the end of this unit.)

Range of learning styles and preferences within the work team and the implications of these for the way in which you offer support to colleagues

All individuals work slightly differently and it may take some time for you to become used to the different styles and preferences held by others in your team. Be aware that their learning styles may be such that they find it easiest to absorb information in a particular way, for example if you tell them something verbally they may find it hard to remember. (See Learning styles in Unit 18 on page 39 for the different ways individuals absorb and process information.) As you get to know them, you may find that others have strengths or weaknesses in a particular area or work better if particular support is given to them. You may need to adapt how you offer support, where it is needed, to accommodate this.

Case study

Adapting support for different learning styles and preferences

Alia is the manager of a group of teaching assistants in a special behavioural unit attached to a mainstream school. She meets with the teaching assistants each week to discuss what is happening in school and which professionals are coming in to work with individual pupils, as well as issues which have arisen. Alia knows her team well and can identify which members need her to give them additional information or present it in a different way. For example, one of her team has dyslexia, so Alia has started to produce a visual weekly plan of professionals who are attending. Alia's dyslexic colleague finds the visual plan much easier to take in and has also asked for the information to be available to them online in advance of meetings.

- How might this approach benefit all of the team?
- What other strategies might Alia use for members of the team who are:
  a) poor at personal organisation and unlikely to remember things
  b) in need of lots of reassurance during the course of their job
  c) very capable but easily bored?

Broader contexts in which everyone works and the particular situations of colleagues which might affect how they work and tackle problems at particular points in time

Whatever their personality type or learning style, all your colleagues will have their own day-to-day issues and problems to deal with. It is unlikely that you will know what these are, but if, for example, you notice that a colleague is not their normal self, it would be appropriate to offer support to acknowledge this. Support staff may work in a range of school situations and you may not know what pressures they are under as part of their job. Many members of the team will have families and all will have a life outside school, which at different times may have an impact on their ability to provide the same level of support in school. You should be sensitive to any changes in behaviour or ability to juggle the demands of home and school, or to cope with what they have been asked to do at work.

Case study K13

Acknowledging situations that affect colleagues' work

Mandy is on playground duty, which is shared between all the teaching assistants on a rota system. As staff are not allowed take coffee onto the playground for health and safety reasons, they are on duty for 10 minutes and are then relieved by another member of staff for the second 10 minutes. Mandy has just worked the whole playtime and has not had a coffee because Romena has not come out to take over. After looking for Romena, she goes straight to see the deputy headteacher as she has had a long morning and this is the second time Romena has not been where she should be that week. The deputy headteacher tells Mandy that Romena's son has been in hospital and that she has been very worried about him and is preoccupied with an operation he is due to have that week.

- What might have been an alternative approach?
- How could the situation be resolved if Romena was unable to fulfil her duties for the time being?

Information and expertise you have which could benefit team members and how to share these with others

You may have information or expertise that would benefit others in your team and you should support others by passing on anything that may be useful. In some schools you may be required to feed back information on courses you have attended or, if you are experienced, you may be working with others who would benefit from some of your ideas.

Case study

Using your expertise and experience to support colleagues

Debbie has been working as a teaching assistant in her school for four years and prior to this was at another local secondary school. She has recently completed her NVQ 3 and is considering starting a higher level teaching assistant course next year after her own children have left school. She is very interested in exploring the different options and qualifications available to support staff.

Debbie has been approached by Ali, a teaching assistant who is being assessed for his NVQ 2, and asked for some advice about balancing work and study as he is finding this difficult. As Ali is a colleague, Debbie suggests some of the strategies she used when she was studying for her NVQ 3 so that Ali can use the ones he finds helpful.

- How might supporting Ali benefit Debbie?
- In what other ways might she support other teaching assistants in her school who are working on formal qualifications?

Value of sharing how you approach your role with other members of the team

When you are working in a team it is important to have opportunities to share and discuss various approaches and also to listen to the ideas of others. It is likely that you will have opportunities to do this with other members of your team both formally and informally and will do this on a regular basis. There will be benefits to team members who are less experienced, and also to those who may have more fixed ideas about how they approach things!

▼ Figure 21.3 Share best practice with your colleagues

Formal approach

This will usually be directly through meetings, INSET or other training when you will be invited to discuss strategies and ideas. This will help you ensure that you are following school policy in your own practice and give you the opportunity to raise any concerns. You may also be able to listen to those who have used similar approaches so that you can discuss what has worked or been less effective.

Informal approach

If you have good communication skills, it is also likely that you will be talking to other members of your team about how you approach your role on an informal basis. This is valuable in giving you the opportunity to share different aspects of your role and also another perspective on issues or concerns as soon as they arise. Others may also be able to suggest alternative sources of information or help.

You may also have opportunities to share ideas with others who are not directly involved in your own team but have similar experiences and are able to share these, for example other support staff in school cluster groups (Associated School Groups) or collaboratives.

Case study K15

Offering informal advice

Davy has just spent his break talking to Pat, another teaching assistant who works in the juniors (Middle Stages). She has just had a difficult session with a pupil she is supporting and talks about the kinds of problems that are coming up. Davy knows the pupil well from working with him the previous year and is able to talk to Pat about the kinds of strategies he used that she may find useful.

- In what ways will this informal chat be useful?
- How else might Davy help Pat in the long term?

For your portfolio...

K1
K2
K3
K4
K5
K9
K10
K11
K14

In order to gather evidence for this unit, you need to show how you support other members of your team and also how you deal with any issues that have arisen. Your assessor may be able to observe you in a team meeting, which will cover K1, K2, K3, K4, K5 and K14. You will also need to have a professional discussion or write a reflective account to show how you have dealt with any issues that have arisen (K9, K10 and K11) If you write an account, be careful how you do this if your portfolio is likely to be seen by others in your team.

References and further reading

Adair, J. (1987) *Effective Teambuilding* (location?; Pan)

Kindler, H.S. (1996) *Managing Disagreement Constructively* (Los Altos, CA; Crisp Publications)

Tuckman, B.W. 'Developmental sequences in small groups' *Psychol. Bull.* 63: 384–99, 1965

Woodcock, M. (1989) *Team Development Manual* (Aldershot; Gower Publishing)

Websites

Both of these sites enable you to take a test to discover your personality type:

www.humanmetrics.com/cgi-win/JTypes1

www.personalitypathways.com/type_inventory.html

22 Reflect on and develop practice

There will always be changes taking place in education that will have an impact on you and the work you carry out in schools. New areas of development may be based on legislation such as the Children Act 2004, on new frameworks like Every Child Matters or on updated initiatives such as the Secondary National Strategy for School Improvement (in Scotland, A Curriculum for Excellence). It is good practice to reflect regularly on what you do both within the classroom and in a wider context, so that you can build on your knowledge and experience and identify any areas of change.

This unit is also about your own continuing professional development. As part of your NVQ, you will need to have some form of professional appraisal, which includes thinking about your practice and setting targets for development: many schools are doing this already for teaching assistants. Appraisals will usually be carried out by your line manager, but some schools are asking their higher-level teaching assistants to appraise other assistants (the post of higher-level teaching assistant does not exist in Scotland). You should not be anxious about the appraisal process; it is not meant to be threatening and is designed to enable you to have some input into your career development.

What you need to know and understand

For this unit you will need to know and understand:

- Why reflection on practice and evaluation of personal effectiveness is important

- How learning through reflection can increase professional knowledge and skills

- How reflection can enhance and use personal experience to increase confidence and self-esteem

- Techniques of reflective analysis:
    a)   questioning what, why and how
    b)   seeking alternatives
    c)   keeping an open mind
    d)   viewing from different perspectives
    e)   thinking about consequences
    f)   testing ideas through comparing and contrasting
    g)   asking 'what if?'
    h)   synthesising ideas
    i)   seeking, identifying, and resolving problems

- Reflection as a tool for contrasting what we say we do and what we actually do

- How to use reflection to challenge existing practice

- The difficulties that may occur as a result of examining beliefs, values and feelings

- How to assess further areas for development in your skills and knowledge through reflection, feedback and using resources such as the Internet, libraries and journals

- How to develop a personal development plan with objectives that are specific, measurable, achievable, realistic and with timescales

- The availability and range of training and development opportunities in the local area and how to access these

- The importance of integrating new information and/or learning in order to meet current best practice, quality schemes or regulatory requirements

Why reflection on practice and evaluation of personal effectiveness is important

The role of the teaching assistant has in recent years become that of a professional. As part of any professional job role it is important to be able to carry out **reflective practice**. This will be especially important when working with pupils as your personal effectiveness has a considerable impact on them and their learning.

Reflective practice means thinking about and evaluating what you do and discussing any changes that could be made. It relates not only to your **professional development**, but also to how you carry out individual activities with pupils and other aspects of your role. You will need to reflect on a regular basis and should have opportunities to discuss your thoughts and ideas with your colleagues. By doing this you can identify areas of strength as well as exploring those that need further development. Teaching assistants have quite diverse roles within schools and inevitably you will find that you are more confident in some situations than others. By reflecting on your practice and how you work with others, you will come to be more effective in your role and gain in confidence.

ⓘ Key terms

Reflective practice – the process of thinking about and critically analysing your actions with the goal of changing and improving occupational practice

Professional development – ongoing training and professional updating

How learning through reflection can increase professional knowledge and skills

Your role when supporting pupils' learning

You should be able to think about activities you have carried out with individuals or groups of pupils and evaluate how the sessions went. Even if you always work in a particular way, which seems to go well, consider different ways of approaching the work you do with pupils. Here are some questions you could ask yourself at the end of a session.

- What went well?
- What went not as well as anticipated? Why?
- Did the pupils achieve the learning objectives for the session?
- What would I change if I did the activity again?

▲ Figure 22.1 Allow time for reflection

▼ Figure 22.2 How well do you think about and evaluate the work you do with pupils?

In this way your evaluation will encourage you to develop and change what you are doing if needed to ensure that you are working effectively with the pupils. It may be helpful, if you have not evaluated your work before, for your class teacher or line manager to observe you working with pupils. They may then go through the evaluation with you afterwards and be able to offer suggestions and help you work though ideas.

Your professional development

In most areas of work, professionals need to think about their role on a regular basis. This involves looking at your job description and thinking about areas for development. Think about how you can develop in your role so that you are always giving yourself opportunities to extend your knowledge and practice. (See also 'How to develop a personal development plan' on page 129 for the kinds of questions you can ask yourself.)

K2 # Case study

Engaging in further training

Sobiga has been working in the same department (English) for four years. She enjoys her work with the pupils and gets on well with the departmental teachers. She has been asked to go on a training course to develop her numeracy skills as she has never been confident with Maths.

Sobiga goes on the course reluctantly, but is very pleased with her progress and surprised that she is enjoys it and is able to do the work easily. She goes back to school and says that she is thinking about going on a course to retake her Maths GCSE as she does not have the qualification.

- How has the Maths course benefited Sobiga?
- How does this show that she is reflecting more on her practice?
- How will this help in other aspects of her role?

Working with colleagues and other adults

This important aspect of your work is about your relationships with your colleagues and others. Think about how you relate to others and the support you offer to them both individually and within different school teams, such as year groups, subject teams or key stages. If you support pupils who have special educational (Additional Support for Learning (ASL)) needs, you may also work with other professionals outside school such as speech and language therapists, or educational psychologists. (See also Units 20 and 62.) You may also work with parents, particularly if you work closely with one pupil. You may need to think about ways in which you can develop your relationship with a parent so that the child is supported more effectively.

You should think about:

- how you greet other adults
- whether you offer help or support to them if you can
- whether you recognise their contributions to the team
- how you respond to any issues that may arise
- whether you actively listen to their concerns
- whether you are positive and offer encouragement to others.

Planning, assessment and feedback

As a teaching assistant, you may or may not be involved with devising plans, but it is important that you have an awareness of the process and have opportunities to speak to the class teacher about pupils' progress following the activities. Part of your role is supporting teaching and learning, and so your feedback to the teacher will form part of the cycle of planning. You should know how the teacher plans for the class and also for the groups and individuals with whom you will be working. You will need to consider:

- whether you know and understand the learning objectives for each session
- whether any of the pupils have particular targets to work on and your role in this
- pupils' backgrounds or circumstances, which may affect their behaviour or learning
- how you feed back to the teacher (is this written or verbal, at a set time or spontaneous?)

Managing pupils' behaviour

This can be one of the most challenging aspects of your work. In order to manage behaviour effectively, you need to be firm and consistent with pupils and be part of a whole school approach. It is also important to be proactive and not reactive when managing behaviour, in other words setting firm boundaries and ensuring pupils are aware of the consequences, and pointing out both their responsibilities and those of others. Be aware of the contents of your school's behaviour policy. This includes knowing what strategies you can use to manage behaviour and what sanctions to apply if pupils are not behaving appropriately. Reflect on what aspects of behaviour management you are confident with and which areas may need development. (See also Unit 19.)

? Thinking point

Managing pupils' behaviour

Think about occasions on which you have had to confront pupils about their behaviour.
- Do you know what strategies you can use to manage behaviour?
- Does your school have a scale of sanctions which all adults can apply?
- How do you reward positive behaviour?
- What aspects of behaviour management do you find challenging?

Case study K1

Reviewing behaviour management policy

Mary always supports the same group for Year 11 (S5) English. There is a pair of pupils in the group who do not work well together and Mary feels that the teacher only puts them with her so that she does not have to deal with their 'difficult' behaviour. Mary perceives them as being hard to manage and concentrates her attention on the pupils who she feels want to learn. She usually just separates the two pupils when issues start to arise. However she has started to reflect on the way she manages their behaviour and has realised that her approach is also impacting on the behaviour of the pupils.

- Devise a plan of action for Mary to use with the group to manage behaviour.
- Why is it important for Mary's own practice that she adjust what she is doing?
- How might the pupils benefit from Mary's new approach?

Keys to good practice

Reflective analysis

✓ Be honest with yourself and others.
✓ Make sure you evaluate successes as well as failures.
✓ Include *all* areas of your work.
✓ Ask a colleague for help if required.

How reflection can enhance and use personal experience to increase confidence and self-esteem

Reflecting on your work will give you opportunities to improve your practice and therefore empower you as you are using skills that you have developed yourself. It is important to take time out to think about what you are doing in your work with pupils; you have a professional duty to consider the impact of what you do. By thinking about this and knowing why particular strategies or approaches have worked, you can then repeat them. In identifying aspects that have been less successful, you can ask for more support. Remember that it is not a question of whether you got it 'right' or 'wrong', but of making sure you can build on all the positive aspects of the work you do as a positive means of developing your career. Effective questioning of your experiences will help you to find a starting point for your reflective analysis. As a tool, it enhances your experiences because it enables you to take more control over what you do and helps you to develop your confidence.

K3 Case study

Applying reflective analysis techniques

Chris is a teaching assistant supporting pupils in Years 7, 8 and 9 (S1, 2 and 3). He has always worked with older pupils in the past and this is a change of role for him. He enjoys working with the younger pupils and has good relationships with them and staff.

However, he is not confident of how what he is doing fits in with the curriculum. He is given plans, but is not really clear on what they mean. The class teacher with whom he is working asks him if he would like to find out more about the Key Stage 3 curriculum (in Scotland, Levels D and E of the Curriculum Guidelines 5–14) and go on a course when it is available. He is not keen to go as he feels he will be the only man on the course and does not particularly enjoy training days, although he knows it will help his practice.

Chris finds the course extremely beneficial and is much more able to understand the plans and how the different activities benefit the pupils. He asks the class teacher whether it will be possible for him to attend another training day on Science, as this is a part of the curriculum that he feels less confident in delivering.

● How is Chris starting to reflect on his personal experience?
● How might the pupils benefit from his awareness?
● Think about how Chris is applying some of the techniques of reflective analysis as listed in the next section.

Techniques of reflective analysis

It is important to be able to use different techniques when reflecting on what you do. Start by being open to questioning yourself on different aspects of your role and thinking about them one by one (see also page 121). In areas where you feel you are strongest, think about why this is and what experience, knowledge and skills are helping you to achieve this. In areas where you may feel less confident or are weaker, think about what you need in order to help you to develop experience, knowledge and skills. As you reflect on what you do, you may find that you need the support of your class teacher or line manager. Apply the techniques of reflective analysis to different areas of your work so that you can use them to think about your role. As you do this, you can start to develop a plan of action to go on your personal development plan during your appraisal (see page 129).

The different ways in which you could look at your role are listed below.

- **Questioning what, why and how** Make sure you are able to ask questions around all areas of your practice (see pages 133–4).
- **Seeking alternatives** Constantly look out for different ways of doing things even if your approach seems to work well, for example through asking others how they might approach a similar idea, topic or theme.
- **Keeping an open mind** Be open to taking new ideas on board without being dismissive or critical, for example when there is a new initiative or scheme taken on by the school.
- **Viewing from different perspectives** Be receptive to the thoughts and views of others and look at things from their point of view, for example taking into account the views of colleagues, parents and pupils.
- **Thinking about consequences** Think about how any changes in your role might affect other areas of your work, for example changing the amount of support a pupil has will affect the pupil.
- **Testing ideas through comparing and contrasting** Look at different approaches, possibly those you have thought of yourself or others suggested to you or that you have read about.
- **Asking 'what if?'** Be one step ahead by questioning in different situations.
- **Synthesising ideas** Adapt ideas so that they fit with what you are doing in school.
- **Seeking, identifying and resolving problems** Identify and resolve problems as another opportunity to develop your skills, for example be aware that problems don't go away – they need to be managed proactively!

Reflection as a tool for contrasting what we say we do and what we actually do

In all aspects of your role, you need to be able to think about your practice. Your school can offer you support and provide you with the experience you need. Taking a step back and looking at things from a different point of view is often an enlightening exercise – the important thing to do is to ask the right questions so that you are learning from the experience. You may also have the opportunity to benefit from other tools such as observations of your practice, peer assessment and feedback from your assessor. These are all useful ways of helping you to think about how your practice comes across to others. You may find that some of your reflections come as a surprise and you were not expecting what you find out. If the school has an ethic of personal

Figure 22.3 Reflection can also take place informally

reflection anyway, it will be easier for you to engage in it, as you will be more used to the process. This is particularly true when it comes to uncovering the difference between words and actual practice – if the school has an open and accepting ethos where everyone is engaged in reflection and expects to learn through mistakes, the process will be less threatening.

K5 Portfolio activity

Reflecting on your practice

As part of your NVQ, your assessor needs to come into school and observe your work with pupils. They will then give you feedback on what they have seen around your work with pupils and relationships with adults, and give you areas for development.

When you have received your feedback, think about any areas in which development issues have been raised or where you have been given particular credit. Answer the following questions fully and use them in your portfolio.

- Are these areas different from what you had expected?
- Were there any issues that came up as part of your observation which surprised you?
- Why is it important for everyone working with children to reflect on their practice?

How to use reflection to challenge existing practice

It is important to remember that in your work with pupils, you are part of a whole school. If you are reflecting on your practice and find that you need to change or develop the work that you are doing, discuss this with those with whom you work as it also affects them. This could mean that if you are in a school that is less receptive to change or where staff do not reflect on their work as a matter of course, it may be difficult for you to approach others. You may need to be very tactful and sensitive in order to put your ideas across in a way that does not appear threatening.

A good starting point might be speaking to your line manager, as they may be able to advise you on your ideas. Staff or year group meetings may also be an opportunity for you to put forward proposals, and this gives others the chance to respond. You need to think about how you communicate your thoughts so that you do not appear to be criticising the way others operate. Always ensure that you build in a means of reviewing and evaluating any changes that are considered.

Case study K6

Gathering evidence of professional development

As part of her NVQ, Helen needs to have a professional review meeting with her line manager so that targets can be set for review. She has discussed this with her assessor and is keen to identify areas for development because she has started to reflect on her practice. She asks her line manager whether this is possible because, at present, teachers in the school have professional development meetings, but not teaching assistants. Her line manager is not enthusiastic about the idea; she says it will make more work for her, but that she will speak to the headteacher. There is no comeback, so Helen starts to talk to her assessor to find out whether there are other ways for her to gather evidence of professional development.

Three weeks later, the headteacher asks Helen about the evidence she needs to gather. She says that it would be good practice for all the teaching assistants in the school to have performance management meetings and tells Helen it will be an item for discussion at the next staff meeting.

- How did Helen show sensitivity in her request for professional development?
- Should she have gone straight to the headteacher in retrospect?
- How might the school benefit from Helen's request?

Keys to good practice

Challenging existing practice

✓ Discuss any proposals sensitively and explain your reasons.
✓ Listen to what others have to say.
✓ Allow time for changes to be considered.
✓ Evaluate any changes as part of the review cycle.

Difficulties that may occur as a result of examining beliefs, values, and feelings

As you examine your existing practice you may find that the process is challenging and sometimes hard. You will need to reflect not only on the practical side of your work with pupils, which can be a difficult process in itself, but also on your own attitudes and beliefs. Reflection can lead you to reconsider issues that you may not even have thought of as relevant. When you start to think about all aspects of your role, you may find this hard as beliefs can be very difficult to change.

By going through different aspects of your work in school, you will start to identify areas in which you are not as successful as others. Your reflections will enable you to draw conclusions about your work, which may not be an easy process. Remember that it is a process and that by working through it and addressing areas of your performance, you will improve your practice in the long run.

K7 Case study

Reflecting on professional practice

Saida works as an individual teaching assistant with a bilingual pupil and is in school for 10 hours a week. She tends to come into school, do her job and go home as she works as a childminder in the afternoons. She does not really speak to other staff apart from the class teacher, although she does meet with the local co-ordinator for bilingual pupils. Saida has been asked to reflect on her practice and is starting to think about her role within the school and her relationships with her colleagues. As she lacks confidence, Saida is finding this process challenging.

- Give at least two reasons why Saida might find this process difficult.
- What might you do first if you were in her position?
- How might the school support her in this process?

How to assess further areas for development in your skills and knowledge

As much as possible, keep up to date with issues in education and particularly for teaching assistants through reading publications and looking on the Internet. Your school staff room probably has a selection of relevant publications, but you will also

K8 Case study

Recognising opportunities for professional development

Sharlene is a teaching assistant in a school where there is only a small group of teaching assistants. They have all been there for a long time and do not seem to be keen to develop in their roles. Sharlene is looking on the local authority website and finds that there is to be a conference for teaching assistants in two months' time. There are to be workshops on different areas of interest for assistants and also a keynote speech on 'Managing your Practice'. She asks her headteacher whether she can attend and is told that she can.

- How is Sharlene being proactive in her own professional development?
- By attending the conference, what other opportunities will Sharlene have available to her?
- How might Sharlene encourage others in her school to join her?

need to keep up to date through research or listening to news items. This is because education is always undergoing change and developments and you may find further opportunities or ideas. Also keep a close eye on local developments, for example what the local authority are offering for teaching assistants in terms of additional training, updated information on qualifications or pay and benefits.

How to develop a personal development plan with SMART objectives

As part of your professional development you may be asked by your line manager to have an **appraisal.** During your appraisal you will be monitoring **processes, practices and outcomes** from your work. The appraisal system is designed to help members of staff to consider their own professional performance on a regular basis. This should ensure that they think about their performance and continuing professional development.

> **Key terms**
>
> **Appraisal** – a regular meeting to discuss your development progress
>
> **Processes, practices and outcomes** – how you do things, what you do and what you achieve

The main consideration is that the appraisal process is a positive and non-threatening one. Each member of staff, including headteachers, is appraised by the person who has responsibility for managing them. In the case of the headteacher, this is usually done by the governors. With teaching staff, the process is an ongoing cycle which takes place annually. As an assistant, you may be appraised by your line manager or the member of staff responsible for teaching assistants. In the case of individual teaching assistants, this may be done by the school's Special Educational Needs Co-ordinator (SENCo)(Additional Support for Learning (ASL) teacher).

Teaching assistants should find that the appraisal process is a good opportunity to discuss issues that may not otherwise be approached. It is also useful for discussing with your line manager anything you have done which you feel has been more or less successful than you had anticipated.

How the appraisal system works

The general appraisal form on page 130 gives you some idea of how the initial discussion with your line manager might be structured. However, this is a basic outline and further ideas such as whether you would like a more formal observation of your work may be recorded. If this is the case, the

Figure 22.4 Do you know what to prepare for your appraisal?

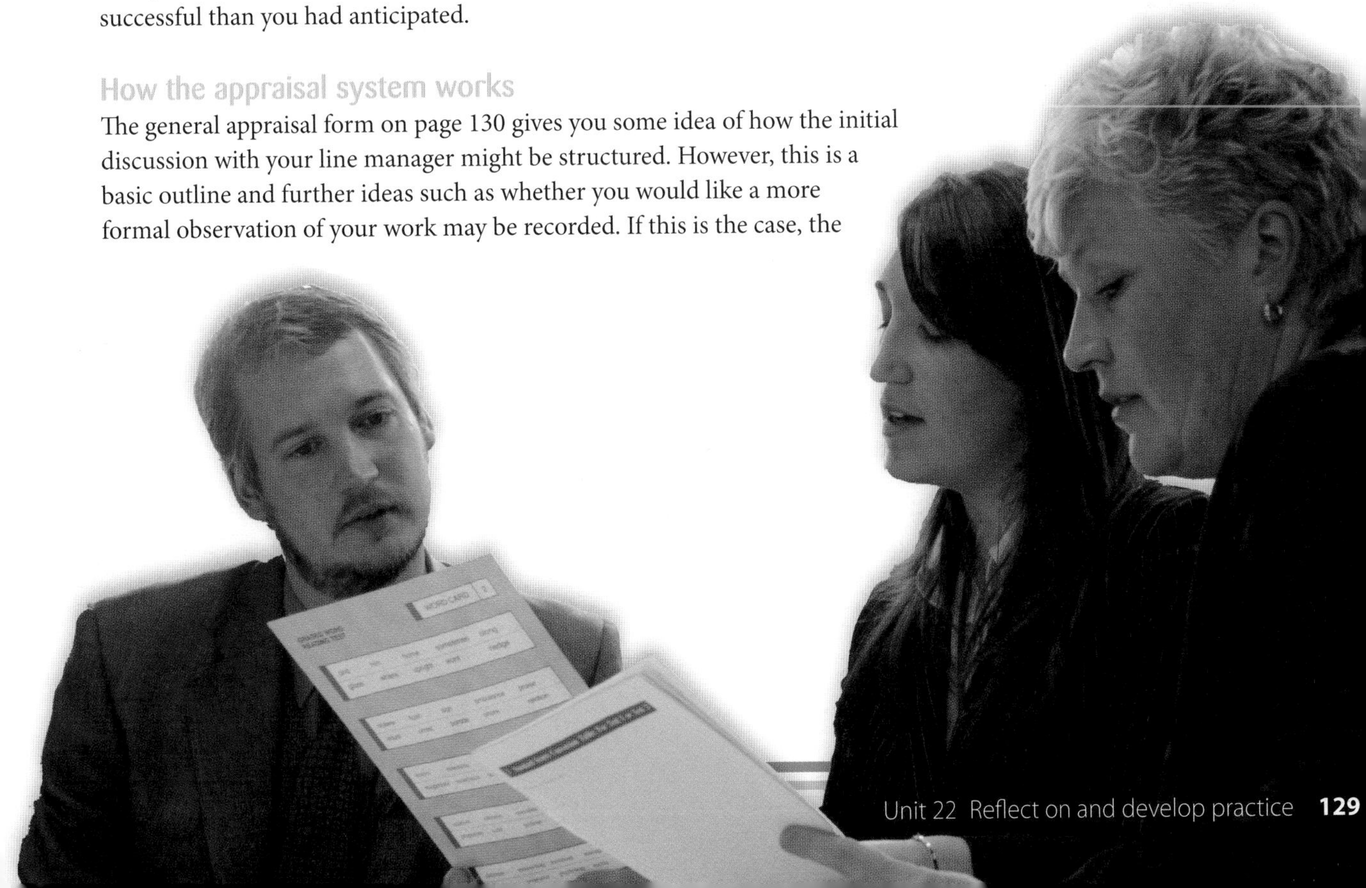

focus and timing of the observation should be decided at the initial meeting. An observation may take place if you or your manager feel that you would benefit from some feedback concerning your work: for example, if you are not sure that your methods for giving pupils praise are as effective as you would like. You will then agree on any action to be taken and on new targets for the coming year. Following the meeting, copies of the appraisal form will be given to you and to the headteacher for record-keeping, but will be confidential. Before the meeting:

- check through your job description
- be prepared by having some ideas of your strengths and successes
- think about areas you may wish to develop.

K5 Portfolio activity

Preparing for appraisal

Before you meet with your line manager, think about your current role and how it matches your job description. To help you to think about your appraisal, try completing the questions on the self-appraisal form below.

General self-appraisal

It woud be useful if you could bring this information with you to your initial meeting, to help you to identify your needs as part of the appraisal process.

1 Do you feel that your job description is still appropriate? Do you feel that there are any changes that need to be made?

2 What targets were set at the last appraisal/when you started your job? Have you achieved your targets?

3 What are the reasons for not having achieved your targets?

4 What aspect of your job satisfies you the most?

5 What aspect of your job has not been as successful as you had anticipated?

6 Are there any areas of your work that you would like to improve?

7 What training have you received? Has it been successful?

8 What are your current training needs?

▲ Figure 22.5 Typical self-appraisal form

To support pupils effectively, you should have a very clear idea about exactly where you fit into the school structure and your role within it. You should have an up-to-date job description, which is a realistic reflection of your duties. A starting point for your appraisal will then be to go through the job description and review any changes that have taken place over the past year.

Sample teaching assistant job descriptions are also available on www.teachernet.gov.uk/management/staffingandprofessionaldevelopment/jobdescriptions/.

As well as a job description, there may also be a Person Specification, which should set out the personal qualities that are relevant to the particular post. It may include some

▼ Figure 22.6 Example of a job description

Job Description

Title: Teaching Assistant

Post: Level 3

Main purpose of the job:

Under guidance of teaching staff: implement work programmes to individuals/groups, including those requiring detailed and specialist knowledge in particular areas; assist in whole planning cycle and management/preparation of resources; provide cover for whole classes for short periods under an agreed system of supervision.

Summary of responsibilities and duties:

Support for pupils

- Use specialist (curricular/learning) skills/training/experience to support pupils.
- Assist with the development and implementation of independent education plans.
- Establish productive working relationships with pupils, acting as a role model and setting high expectations.
- Promote the inclusion and acceptance of all pupils within the classroom.
- Support pupils consistently whilst recognising and responding to their individual needs.
- Encourage pupils to interact and work co-operatively with others and engage all pupils in activities.
- Promote independence and employ strategies to recognise and reward achievement of self-reliance.
- Provide feedback to pupils in relation to progress and achievement.

Support for teacher

- Work with the teacher to establish an appropriate learning environment.
- Work with the teacher in lesson planning, evaluating and adjusting lessons/work plans as appropriate.
- Monitor and evaluate pupils' responses to learning activities through observation and planned recording of achievement against pre-determined learning objectives.
- Provide objective and accurate feedback and reports as required to the teacher on pupil achievement, progress and other matters, ensuring the availability of appropriate evidence.

of the strengths listed below. You do not have to use these for your appraisal, but it may be worth going through them and bearing them in mind.

Be a good communicator and enjoy working with others

It is vital that an assistant is able to share thoughts and ideas with others, and is comfortable doing this.

Use initiative

Teaching assistants need to be able to decide for themselves how to use their time if the teacher is not always available to ask. There are always jobs that need doing in a classroom, even if this just means sharpening pencils or making sure that books are tidy and in the right place.

Respect confidentiality

It should be remembered that in a position of responsibility it is essential to maintain confidentiality. Teaching assistants may sometimes find that they are placed in a position where they are made aware of personal details concerning a pupil or family. Although background and school records are available to those within the school, it is not appropriate to discuss them with outsiders.

Be sensitive to pupils' needs

Whether an individual or classroom assistant, it is important to be able to judge how much support to give while still encouraging pupils' independence. Pupils need to be sure about what they have been asked to do and may need help organising their thoughts or strategies, but it is the pupil who must do the work and not the assistant.

Have good listening skills

A teaching assistant needs to be able to listen to others and have a sympathetic nature. This is an important quality for your interactions, both with pupils and other adults.

Be willing to undertake training for personal development

In any school there will always be occasions on which teaching assistants are invited or required to undergo training and these opportunities should be used where possible. You may also find that your role changes due to movement between classes or changing year groups. You need to be flexible and willing to rise to different expectations.

Be firm but fair with pupils

Children always quickly realise if an adult is not able to set fair boundaries of behaviour. Adults should always make sure that when they start working with pupils they make these boundaries clear.

Enjoy working with pupils and have a sense of humour

Teaching assistants need to be able to see the funny side of working with pupils, and humour is often a very useful asset!

When you have gone through and discussed your job description, review any previous targets and state whether or not they have been achieved. This may provoke further discussion or form a starting point for setting new targets, for example if you have started a course that has not yet been completed.

How to develop and set targets

When thinking about areas for development, it may help to divide up your knowledge and experience as follows:

- knowledge and experience of the curriculum
- knowledge and experience of behaviour management
- knowledge and experience of ICT
- knowledge and experience of relevant or new legislation
- knowledge and experience of health and safety
- knowledge and experience of working with or managing others
- knowledge and experience of record keeping
- knowledge and experience of special educational (ASL) needs.

You then need to think about your level of confidence in each of these areas so that you can begin to see areas of strength and those that may need further development. You will need guidance in order to turn these into targets.

Case study K9

Setting professional development targets

Eamonn, a Level 2 teaching assistant, has been asked to look at the areas above before his appraisal meeting and give himself a score, where 1 is very confident and 5 is not at all confident. He has looked through them and noted that his biggest areas for development are knowledge and experience of the curriculum and working with or managing others. He is also aware that ICT is not an area of strength.

- How will this help Eamonn and his line manager to set targets?
- What should he do if as an inexperienced assistant he feels he needs to develop in most of these areas?

Your line manager should be able to work with you to set personal development targets which are SMART, as in the following table.

SMART targets

Specific	You must make sure your target says exactly what is required.
Measurable	You should ensure that you will be able to measure whether the target has been achieved.
Achievable	The target should not be inaccessible or too difficult.
Realistic	You should ensure that you will have access to the training or resources that may be required.
Time-bound	There should be a limit to the time you have available to achieve your target. This is because otherwise you may continually put it off to a later date!

When thinking about targets you should not usually set more than three or four so that they will be achievable. Also ensure that you check between appraisal meetings to

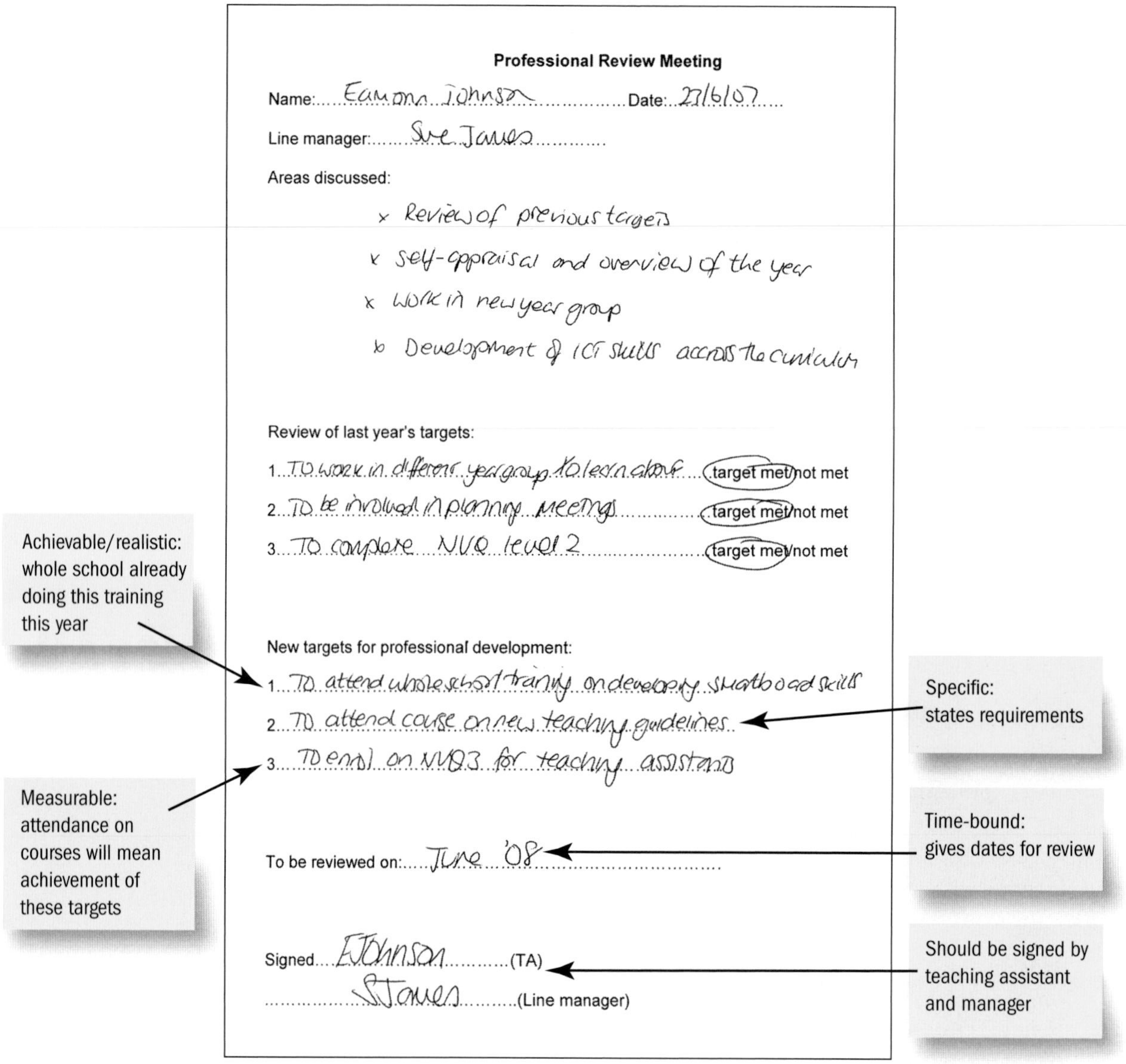

Professional Review Meeting

Name: Eamonn Johnson   Date: 27/6/07

Line manager: Sue James

Areas discussed:

- × Review of previous targets
- × Self-appraisal and overview of the year
- × Work in new year group
- b Development of ICT skills across the curriculum

Review of last year's targets:

1. To work in different year group to learn about ... (target met)/not met
2. To be involved in planning meetings ... (target met)/not met
3. To complete NVQ level 2 ... (target met)/not met

Achievable/realistic: whole school already doing this training this year →

New targets for professional development:

1. To attend whole school training on developing smartboard skills
2. To attend course on new teaching guidelines ← **Specific:** states requirements
3. To enrol on NVQ3 for teaching assistants

Measurable: attendance on courses will mean achievement of these targets →

To be reviewed on: June '08 ← **Time-bound:** gives dates for review

Signed EJohnson (TA) ← **Should be signed by teaching assistant and manager**
SJames (Line manager)

▲ Figure 22.7 Make sure your review meeting produces SMART targets

make sure that you are on course to meet your targets. There is little point in setting them if you have the meeting and then put the paperwork away again until next year!

You may find that because of the school development plan there are already training programmes planned over the next 12 months, for example on the use of the smartboard in the classroom and that you will be attending this anyway. This will therefore form one of your targets. You may also like to think about training courses that it would be useful to attend.

Availability and range of training and development opportunities in the local area and how to access these

You can usually find out through your school the different courses and development opportunities that are available. You may find that the school invites people from different outside agencies to speak to staff about particular subject areas during staff meetings, and these may be optional for support staff. Your line manager or supervisor should be able to give you information about training and help you to decide on the best courses and meetings to attend. The SENCo (ASL teacher) may be able to give you details about specific special educational (ASL) needs courses, such as those run by the Sensory Support Service, or the Behaviour Management Unit. If you have difficulty finding help, the local authority should publish details of courses run for teachers and support staff. You may also be able to contact the local borough council for information about professional training for assistants as this is undergoing a period of national change.

Most local authorities offer induction training for teaching assistants, which has been devised by the DCSF and is aimed at those who are completely new to the role. It is fairly comprehensive and covers areas such as behaviour, literacy and numeracy and special educational (ASL) needs. These courses should be free of charge to teaching assistants in local schools. The borough council's education department should have a member of staff responsible for support staff training, who will also be able to advise you.

Over the last few years there have been many developments in the qualifications available and you may find this confusing. Always check to make sure that these are validated by an awarding body and that they are nationally recognised. The centre will be able to tell you the name of the awarding body that checks the assessment of the course. (This may, e.g. be CACHE, EDEXCEL, OCR or City and Guilds). The Training and Development Agency for Schools website, www.tda.gov.uk, gives recommendations and guidance for most support staff qualifications and what the different levels mean.

It is important that you choose a qualification at the right level, as it will be useful to you when approaching employers to show them what level you are working at. If the course requires an interview, the centre should be able to advise you.

If you can, ask others who have been on training courses so that you can find out which most appeal or are most useful to you. Some courses may be full- or part-time and, depending on your hours at school, you may have to ask your headteacher for time out in order to study. Alternatively, some centres may offer evening classes so that you can attend outside school hours.

Always keep a record of all the qualifications you have gained and courses you have attended. You may or may not have certificates for all of these, but if you have one it is a good record of your professional development and is useful for you to have at hand if you need to update your CV or attend an interview.

Models of performance that apply to teaching assistants

Teaching assistants should be aware of models of performance and **best practice benchmarks**, which will have an impact on their training needs for professional qualifications. The National Occupational Standards for Teaching Assistants offer guidance on the wider aspects of competent performance. They also form the basis for the National Association of Professional Teaching Assistants (NAPTA) Profiles which some schools are asking their teaching assistants to complete (see www.napta.org.uk). The NVQ and SVQ Levels 2 and 3 are also based on the National Occupational Standards. Other models of performance

> **🛈 Key term**
> **Best practice benchmarks** – widely agreed as providing the most advanced, up-to-date thinking and practice against which you can measure what you are doing; not minimum standards; benchmarks can be statutory, regulatory or based on other requirements or research

that are accessible to teaching assistants include local and national guidelines for codes of practice, provided by government bodies such as the DCSF and Ofsted. These are often available in school or through the DCSF and Ofsted websites.

Assistants should also be aware that they can access expert advice and working practices by observing practitioners within both the school and the local authority. You may need to ask your line manager if you can watch experienced assistants at work in the school, or whether you can speak to local support service staff about any particular needs you may have.

K10 Portfolio activity

Accessing opportunities for professional development

You need to find out how to access training in your local area. If you do not know already, ask your line manager what opportunities exist in your school for support staff development. Write a reflective account showing how you would access any opportunities and whether these are tied into your targets for development.

Other development opportunities that may exist in school

If you are employed by the school as a teaching assistant on a permanent contract, you may find that you are able to have some say in choosing to work in an area of particular interest. For example, if you have always been in Years 7, 8 and 9 (S1, 2 and 3), but would like to find out more about working with the Year 10 (S4) work-related learning groups, you may be able to request a change through discussion with your supervisor or at appraisal. You may also find that you have always worked with the same teacher and would benefit from seeing how other teachers work. It is always worth asking about particular areas of interest so that your supervisor is aware of them.

On a wider ranging note, you would benefit from being part of any local cluster groups or other networks for teaching assistants. These may be formed from a group of local schools and meet regularly to discuss practice or just to give moral support. You may be surprised at how much valuable information and support can be gained from these meetings. Your school should be able to give you information about getting involved in local groups.

Keys to good practice

Areas for development

✓ Make sure you are aware of when and where courses for support staff are run.
✓ Look out for opportunities for development as they become available and ask about them.
✓ Read information boards and magazines in your school.
✓ Speak to your line manager or the class teacher about particular areas of interest.
✓ Join any local secondary school cluster groups or networks.

Importance of integrating new information and learning to meet best practice, quality schemes or regulatory requirements

Working with new information will be a constant part of your work in school. You need to know where different information is held in school and where to find it. As well as being given a great deal of day-to-day information, you always need to be proactively seeking out new information as it becomes available. This may be within the class itself, for example specific information on pupils, or in the wider school context and beyond.

Schools also need to bear new information in mind, update policies as information becomes available and inform staff. Your school may do this through teaching assistant meetings, general staff meetings or year group meetings. Make sure that your school has systems in place to keep you up to date and inform you about any new information. If you feel that you are not kept up to date as a matter of course, you need to raise this with your line manager.

The following diagram shows potential sources of new information. Those sources shaded in will give ongoing day-to-day information and those shaded in will offer wider information that may affect your practice.

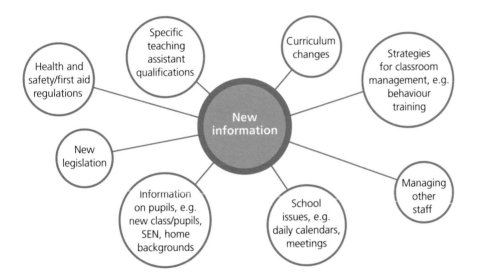

◀ Figure 22.8 How many sources of new information can you think of?

Health and safety/first aid regulations
Health and safety is an area that is always important but especially so in schools. Any changes need to be introduced immediately and will have an impact on you, for example, changes in the way the Criminal Record Bureau checks employees or the way in which first aid is administered. If new regulations affect all staff, they are usually easy to remember, but if they affect something with which you only come into contact periodically, you may need to remind yourself. Be aware of your school's health and safety policy and know the identity of your school's health and safety representative. All staff in schools have responsibilities for health and safety and you should not think of it as an issue that only affects someone else.

Curriculum changes
You need to be able to integrate new information regarding the curriculum into your practice. Examples of this might be the new Citizenship curriculum or the new

emphasis on work-related learning for those at risk of exclusion. Make sure you ask for some kind of training or development opportunities if you are expected to integrate them into your practice to ensure that you are implementing them correctly.

You need to have a chance to discuss new information with others, whether this is within the school or at outside training events organised by your local authority. This will help you to form ideas about how the changes will affect you in practice. For up-to-date information on the curriculum at all stages go to www.qca.org.uk.

New legislation

Legislation around schools and childcare is constantly being updated. One of the biggest areas of legislative change for schools in recent years has been the implementation of the Children Act 2004, and the Every Child Matters Framework (see also Unit 38). This has had a huge impact on both schools and the wider community. As part of this legislation, schools are required to work with other agencies to offer wrap-around care for children. This has meant that many support staff have been involved in the development of schemes such as the Extended Schools programme. Knowing about and understanding new legislation is vital for all those who work with children.

Specific teaching assistant qualifications

The current National Framework outlines different levels of professional qualifications for teaching assistants. You may also be interested in gaining HLTA status, which although not a qualification is a recognition of the level of your experience.

If you attend a training programme you will be encouraged to reflect on your practice and how you approach your work with pupils. It is also important that you are shown how to integrate any new information or training you are given into your practice.

K11 Case study

Taking on extra responsibilities

Martin has just gained HLTA status in a large five-form-entry inner-city secondary school. He has had his annual appraisal meeting with his line manager, who has asked him to take on responsibility for managing the other teaching assistants and ensuring they have regular meetings.

- How will this be important for Martin's own professional development?
- How will it benefit the school?
- What questions might you ask if you were Martin?

Strategies for classroom management

You could pick up new information on classroom management in different ways. In the course of your work and through experience you may gather information that you can integrate into your practice or you might have been on a course that suggests that you try a new approach. Your school may amend one of its policies and ask all staff to put the new policy into practice, in which case you should have been told exactly what you need to do. Examples of different strategies for classroom management might be:

- **Behaviour** – how you supervise pupils with both positive and negative behaviour
- **Managing groups or individuals** – maintaining good relationships with pupils with whom you are working
- **Equal opportunities and inclusion** – making sure you involve all pupils in the learning process
- **Special educational (ASL) needs** – ensuring you know the best ways of supporting any pupils who have special educational (ASL) needs.

For your portfolio... K9

If your school does not usually carry out a professional appraisal for teaching assistants, you may like to use the example form below in your portfolio.

The appraisal meeting as a whole should cover much of the performance criteria for this unit *if all the criteria are discussed*, although check with your assessor to make sure that your awarding body will accept this. If your assessor can be present at your appraisal interview and witness it, this is even better evidence for your portfolio, although that can be difficult to arrange.

Professional Review Meeting

Name: …………………………………..   Date: ………………….

Line manager: ……………………………………..

Areas discussed:

Review of last year's targets:

1 ……………………………………………….. target met/not met

2 ……………………………………………….. target met/not met

3 ……………………………………………...….target met/not met

New targets for professional development:

1 ………………………………………………………………………….

2 ………………………………………………………………………….

3 …………………………………………………………………….…...

To be reviewed on: …………………………………………..

Signed: ………………………………. (Teaching assistant)

…………………………………….. (Line manager)

▲ Figure 22.9 Blank review form for you to use

Examples of target-setting

- Some NVQ candidates choose to have one of their targets as completion of their award by a set date.
- Include any INSET training that your school will offer during the next 12 months, for example whole school training on the Primary National Strategy. In this way you are including something you will be doing anyway rather than setting additional work for yourself.
- Include any training you have requested specifically for yourself, for example a sign language course or a qualification to upgrade your Maths or English skills.

Remember that targets will all need to be SMART. If your line manager has written a target that is not clearly achievable within the timescale, or which is not clear, it is important that you point this out.

If you are having any difficulty in setting a meeting in your school, speak to your assessor. You may be able to set and review some targets of your own through your college course.

Sources of further information

Learning Support Magazine (for teaching assistants in Primary schools)

The Times Educational Supplement

Websites

www.napta.org.uk/resources/ttsacaps.pdf

www.ofsted.gov.uk

www.qca.org.uk

www.tda.gov.uk/support/careerdevframework.aspx (for National Occupational Standards for Teaching Assistants)

www.teachernet.gov.uk/teachingassistants

23 Plan, deliver and evaluate teaching and learning activities under the direction of a teacher

This unit is for teaching assistants or cover staff who may plan, deliver and evaluate learning activities under the direction or guidance of a teacher. This means that you may be asked to plan and carry out short-term activities independently for individuals or groups of pupils with whom you are working. These activities may take place in any learning environment, including educational visits and extended school provision.

If you are asked to do this, you should be working with a teacher and not be asked to deliver whole class activities. Teaching assistants and cover staff should be planning and delivering teaching and learning activities to complement, reinforce or extend the teaching and learning planned and delivered by the teacher. The evaluation process should involve your monitoring pupil progress as well as your own contribution to the learning activity. You will also need to be able to reflect on your experiences and show how they will influence your future planning and delivery.

Many of the knowledge points overlap with mandatory Unit 18 and have been omitted from the text in this section. You will therefore be able to cross reference these in your portfolio rather than repeat the same evidence. However, you will need to adjust the evidence to ensure that it shows your involvement in planning and evaluating, rather than supporting the teacher's own plans. Your assessor will be able to help you to make sure that your evidence covers the knowledge points in both units.

What you need to know and understand

For this unit, you will need to know and understand:

- The nature, extent and boundaries of your role in planning and delivering teaching and learning activities, and its relationship to the role of the teacher and others in the school

- *The importance of having high expectations of all pupils with whom you work* (See also Unit 18, page 32)

- *The relevant school curriculum and age-related expectations of pupils in the subject/curriculum area and age range of the pupils with whom you are working* (See also Unit 18, page 33)

- *The teaching and learning objectives of the learning activity and the place of these in the teacher's overall teaching programme* (See also Unit 18, page 34)

- How to take account of pupils' experiences, interests, aptitudes and preferences in planning personalised learning

- *The key factors that can affect the way pupils learn including age, gender, and physical, intellectual, linguistic, social, cultural and emotional development* (See also Unit 18, page 34)

- *How social organisation and relationships, such as pupil grouping and the way adults interact and respond to pupils, may affect learning* (See also Unit 18, page 36)

- Strategies for gathering information on pupil learning and progress, and how to plan for and use these in teaching and learning activities

- How to select and prepare teaching and learning resources for the learning activity to meet the needs of the pupils involved

- How to establish and maintain a purposeful learning environment and promote good behaviour

- The importance and methods of establishing rapport and respectful, trusting relationships with pupils

- How to select and use teaching and learning methods to support, motivate and interest all pupils with whom you are working

- School policies for inclusion and equality of opportunity and the implication of these for how you plan, deliver and evaluate teaching and learning activities

- *How to monitor the pupils' response to teaching and learning activities* (See also Unit 18, page 42)

- *When and how to modify teaching and learning activities* (See also Unit 18, page 43)

- *How to monitor and promote pupil participation and progress* (See also Unit 18, page 43)

- *The importance of working within your own sphere of competence and when you should refer to others* (See also Unit 18, page 45)

- How to reflect on and learn from experience

- How to evaluate teaching and learning activities and outcomes

- The school procedures for maintaining records and sharing information

Nature of your role in planning and delivering teaching and learning activities

As part of your role, you may be involved in developing different types of planning. Although the learning objectives will be given to you by the teacher and you will need to plan towards these, you may have some flexibility around planning and delivery if you are working with particular groups of pupils. The **plans** may be for one lesson or could be for a series of lessons that are linked together. You will need to work within the school's planning framework or structure, which will be divided into long-, medium- and short-term plans. By looking at these you will be able to see how your work with the pupils fits in.

Key term

Plans – These may relate to a single lesson or span a number of lessons, e.g. project plans, schemes of work; plans will be recorded in writing and agreed by the teacher before putting them into action

Long-, medium- and short-term planning

Stage of planning	Purpose	Content
Long term (curriculum framework)	Shows coverage of the subject and provides breadth	Summary of subject content
Medium term (termly or half-termly)	Provides a framework for all subjects	Shows overview of activities and/or topics. Links to National Curriculum for Key Stages 3 and 4 (In Scotland, 5–14 Curriculum)
Short term	Provides a plan for the week's lessons, which can be broken down by day	Should include: • learning intentions • activities • organisation/differentiation • provision for special educational (ASL) needs • use of other adults • rough time allocations • space for notes

It could be that the teacher plans for the long- and medium term, and that you are involved in short-term or daily plans, or plans for individual sessions. You should be given learning objectives so that you know what pupils will expected to have achieved by the end of the session.

Others in the school will be involved in monitoring the delivery of different subjects and may ask to look at plans or discuss them with you. It is likely that these subject co-ordinators or managers will also observe you delivering sessions at some point for moderation purposes.

Portfolio activity K1

Planning within the whole school framework

Using an example of a plan you have devised to work on with pupils in your class, show how what you have done fits in with the whole school framework. You can then put this evidence in your portfolio.

(For Keys to Good Practice when planning, see Unit 24, page 160.)

How to take account of pupils' experiences, interests, aptitudes and preferences in planning personalised learning

When planning, we should always take account of pupils' experiences and interests. Learning needs to be relevant to pupils in order to engage them and keep them motivated: we need to be able to relate what we are doing to their experiences in order to ensure that what they are learning makes sense to them.

When thinking about personalised learning, we need to consider pupils' personal and social as well as academic needs. In this way we are considering all aspects of the child – this links into the **Every Child Matters Framework**. (See also Unit 38, page 245.) 'Personalised learning' ('Individualised learning') is a term applied to a learning culture that recognises the individual needs of all pupils. We are moving towards a model that transfers the responsibility for learning away from the teacher and towards the learner. Teachers, support staff and individual learners need to know what must be fixed and what can be tailored to meet learners' likes, wants and needs.

Key term

Every Child Matters Framework – key government initiative relating to the importance of a multi-agency approach to children's services

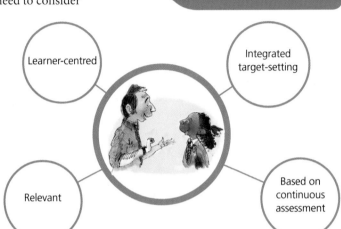

▲ Figure 23.1 Planning personalised learning

Learner-centred learning

'Personalisation' is a term very much linked to 'customisation' in the business world. In the same way that businesses need to think about customers' needs when devising products, learners' needs should be considered when we are planning how we are going to teach them. Learner-centeredness means that the active participation of the learner is crucial to the teaching and learning experience.

In the past, teaching has been about presenting information in a set way without thinking about the best ways in which individuals learn. Based on what we now know about different learning styles (see Unit 18, page 39), teaching and learning should be offered in ways that suit the needs of all learners.

Pupils come to the classroom with different needs and at different stages in the learning journey – some will have had positive and others negative learning experiences. They will all have different needs and abilities. This makes planning activities more challenging, but it also gives teachers opportunities to be creative and pupils the chance to learn how to learn.

Thinking point

How much do you consider pupils' aptitudes and interests when planning? For example, if they learn best by working on practical tasks, how are these integrated into the curriculum?

Relevant learning

For pupils to remain motivated and stay engaged in what they are doing, they need to understand the relevance and purpose of the activity. You may have witnessed first hand or remember times during your own learning experiences when you lost interest in what the teacher was saying as it did not seem relevant. To engage pupils we need to show them how what we are doing is going to be useful to them.

Learning based on continuous assessment

Pupils need to learn how to learn. That is, they should be able to find different ways of attaining the learning objective without a fear of 'getting it wrong'. Once pupils have become used to looking at their learning against the learning objectives, they can start to assess whether they have achieved. This is done first of all through **peer assessment** and later leads to **self-assessment**; (however, see also Unit 30 on assessment).

Integrated target-setting

Target-setting should be part of the teaching and learning process, as we are looking at how to help pupils to achieve. Schools will now integrate target-setting into pupils' work, in particular in Literacy and Numeracy (Language and Maths), so that pupils are aware of what they are working towards and be able to evaluate their learning.

Experiences, interests, aptitudes and preferences

When planning, all those concerned need to take account of pupils' experiences and preferences. As well as knowing your pupils well in order to plan effectively, you also need to have some knowledge of any special educational (Additional Support for Learning (ASL)) or medical needs.

Key terms

Peer assessment – a process by which pupils assess one another's learning

Self-assessment – pupils are able to assess their own learning

Case study K5

Planning to incorporate pupils' experiences and preferences

You have been asked to work with a group of Year 7 (S1) pupils on a French departmental project about visiting a French town, before their day trip to Calais. The project will take place over six weeks and the pupils will be required to make and set up a French market as a display to show others in the school.

This is what you know about the six pupils in your group:

- Jack has average ability and enjoys working with others
- Toni is very quiet but very creative and excellent at Art; she also has average ability for her age
- Jamal has a tendency to lose focus very quickly; you think that he is a kinaesthetic learner who works best when he is moving around and engaged in 'active' learning
- Shirley has excellent numeracy skills, although she lacks confidence with writing
- Eleni speaks English as an additional language but has above-average ability; she has been in school for two terms and goes for additional sessions to help with her understanding of language
- Ricky is immature and small for his age; he has an unsettled home background and often comes to school hungry and looking tired; he tries hard in school and has been particularly interested in this topic.

Show how you could plan and deliver a series of lessons, which would incorporate what you know about the pupils.

Strategies for gathering information on pupil learning and progress, and how to plan for and use these in teaching and learning activities

Key term

Teaching and learning activities – the teaching and learning activities for individual pupils or groups of pupils developed and delivered by the practitioner working within a framework set by the teacher

If you are asked to plan and deliver work with pupils, you should have some information about each individual's learning. This may be:

- in school records (previous evaluations of learning, reports or paperwork such as Individual Education Plans or records of assessment)
- written or verbal information passed on by the teacher and/or other staff
- from your own observation or knowledge of the pupil/s.

You should have access to school records about pupils' learning and be able to refer to paper or electronic records. This will give you details about pupils' educational background and will be particularly useful if you do not know the pupils well. Many classrooms now have a class file, which other adults such as teaching assistants can refer to so that they have access to information on pupils.

You may also gather information more informally through your own observations or discussions with other staff. Without realising it you will pick up information in different ways all the time that you are in the class with pupils.

K8 Case study

Planning to meet pupils' different learning needs

You are working in a Year 7 (S1) Maths class. Following their transfer from primary school in September you have seen the pupils' transfer reports, which were completed at the end of Year 6 (P5), and you have picked out information on their understanding of number bonds, in particular decimal number bonds. You have been asked to plan for a group of four pupils, who you have been told are of mixed ability. You have also observed that one of them can be quite emotional sometimes and gets upset if he doesn't understand the task.

Your learning objective is for the pupils to understand which decimal pairs make a whole number.

- How would you use the information you have to help you to plan the activity?
- How might you plan this session so that all the pupils are able to achieve?
- Would it be more difficult to plan bearing in mind the different needs of the pupils?

How to select and prepare teaching and learning resources for the learning activity to meet the needs of the pupils involved

If your plan is adequate and you have thought about resources beforehand, you should know exactly what is needed when you prepare for the activity. Think about individual pupils and how they learn best when you are deciding what resources might be useful.

One advantage of planning in advance is that you can think about additional resources that you might have to buy or gather from outside school. This may be straightforward, for example if you have been asked to use some artefacts to help you to discuss and find out about a religious festival and you know that these are always kept in the RE resources cupboard. However, if you have to think about and make or find resources to use, more preparation will be required.

When working with pupils who have particular needs, you may need to seek advice from specialist teachers or to borrow helpful equipment or resources.

Case study K9

Planning for pupils with particular needs

Maria is working with a group of pupils including Aaliyah, who is visually impaired. She has to find some resources on Ladakh in India because the class is looking at it in Geography in the following week. Maria has planned for her group to find India on a world map, but is concerned about Aaliyah. She speaks to the sensory support teacher to seek advice and ask about resources. She is told that they have a special Braille globe, which Maria can borrow so that Aaliyah can work on the activity with her peers.

- Give three reasons why the globe will help Aaliyah.
- Where might you seek advice if you needed additional resources to meet the needs of different children?

How to establish and maintain a purposeful learning environment and promote good behaviour

In order to establish and maintain a purposeful learning environment, you need to develop positive expectations of pupils and encourage them to take responsibilities for their environment. They should respect the classroom or other learning environments in the school and take ownership of them, for example through picking up litter or looking out for lost property. All members of the school community should have high expectations of the learning environment. If it is tidy and

▼ Figure 23.2 Displays encourage pupils to take pride in their learning environment

well organised, pupils will learn to take pride in their school surroundings. Having a purposeful learning environment means that the school should be conducive to learning, with clear, well-labelled displays, a welcoming atmosphere, and clear behaviour boundaries of which all pupils are aware. (See also Managing behaviour in Unit 19.)

Keys to good practice

Establishing and maintaining a purposeful learning environment

✓ Resources and facilities should be accessible for all pupils, including those with special educational (ASL) needs.

✓ The environment should be welcoming and contain clearly defined areas for different activities.

✓ Storage areas should be tidy and clearly labelled.

✓ Items hazardous to children should be stored safely.

✓ Displays and information should be at a height that all pupils can read them!

K10 Portfolio activity

Promoting good behaviour through expectations

Write a reflective account to show how you promote good behaviour through your expectations of pupils in your school and through the strategies you use.

Importance and methods of establishing rapport and respectful, trusting relationships with pupils

Once you have established high expectations and firm boundaries during your work with pupils, you will find that they will respect and trust you much more and this is a sound basis for your work with them. Pupils like to have boundaries of expected behaviour as long as it is clear what they are and you discuss with them what will happen if they do not adhere to them – and then stick to them.

There are a number of boundaries that you will need to establish with pupils.

Rights

Most pupils will be receptive to a discussion about the rights of all individuals. It is worth taking time at the beginning of each new academic year, when they have a new teacher, to establish what these rights are and to discuss and draw up a list of them with pupils. For example, pupils should know that all individuals have the right to be in school. Other examples might be:

- we all have a right to learn
- we all have a right to feel safe
- we all have a right to respect from others.

Responsibilities

These lead on from rights and all pupils should know how responsibilities need to be implemented. They need to be in place so that pupils are aware of them. For example:

- we are responsible for our learning
- we are responsible for keeping our school tidy
- we are responsible for being kind to others.

Rules

Once pupils understand the importance of rights and responsibilities, they will need to draw up a set of rules to work to, with an adult. In your class it is likely that pupils already have a set of rules, which tie in with the whole school policy. When you are working with individuals or groups it is good practice to go through expectations with pupils at the start so that they are clear on what they need to do when working with you. In this way there will be no misunderstandings when it comes to what they should and should not do.

Consequences

This then leads on to consequences. Pupils should be aware of the consequences of both good and poor behaviour. All staff should work together to ensure that there is a cohesive approach, and a set of rewards and sanctions on which everyone is clear.

Establishing rapport can take time as pupils also need to get to know you. It is always better to start out with firm boundaries and then show pupils your more relaxed side later on than vice versa. Trust and respect should not be left to chance. Once you have shown that you are clear on acceptable and non-acceptable behaviour and are fair in implementing consequences, trust and respect will follow.

Case study K11

Dealing with potentially disruptive behaviour

Kiria has been asked to plan and deliver a single session with a group of Year 7 (S1) girls. She has not worked with them before as a group and does not know them very well, but has been asked to do this at short notice. At the beginning of the session, Kiria notices that Kerry, one of the girls, is chewing some gum and is very distracted. She knows that Kerry is referred to by other staff as 'difficult' and chooses to pretend that she has not seen what is happening.

As the lesson progresses, Kerry starts to distract the others. She makes loud sighing noises and chats to them and it is clear that she will disrupt the learning process.

- What should Kiria have done at the beginning of the session?
- Can she rectify the situation? How?
- Why is it important that Kiria gets this first session 'right' with this group?

How to select and use teaching and learning methods to support, motivate and interest all pupils

When delivering sessions you need to ensure that the teaching and learning methods you have selected support and motivate all pupils. This means that there should be a

Figure 23.3 How would you adapt your teaching methods to support a range of different learning needs?

variety of delivery methods according to the needs of individual pupils. Some learners need to have more practical tasks in order to stimulate and motivate them, whereas others find that they work well researching through books or the Internet. As a general rule it is best to devise sessions that incorporate different methods of teaching and learning so that you will be able to meet the needs of all pupils.

K12 Case study

Tailoring learning to pupils' strengths

Using the information below, think about how you could tailor the rest of the lesson to the strengths of the four pupils in the group.

Learning objective: To be able to identify the main parts of the digestive system and understand their function (Year 8)	
Teaching and learning methods	
General intro	Use diagrams and whole class discussion to explain functions of parts of system. Ask pupils to assemble the names of the system in the correct order and identify the individual role they play in helping the body digest food.
Pupils	
Jack	Enjoys practical activities; lower ability
Shola	Very creative; lively
Suzanne	Good general ability and focus
Warren	Difficult to engage in learning; finds written work hard

School policies for inclusion and equality of opportunity and the implication of these for how you plan, deliver and evaluate teaching and learning activities

Your school's equal opportunities or inclusion policy will give you guidelines to which you should refer if you are concerned about ensuring pupil access when planning and carrying out learning activities. All schools have a duty to allow opportunities for all pupils to reach their potential. In its curriculum guidance QCA (the Qualifications and Curriculum Authority)(Learning and Teaching Scotland (LTS)) refers to the importance of equal opportunities for all. Ofsted also places responsibilities on inspectors to look at how far schools are 'socially inclusive' and ensure that all pupils have equal access. You need to look at your plan from the perspective of all the pupils with whom you are working to be sure that they are able to carry out your planned tasks. In other words, this is another aspect of personalised learning.

Portfolio activity K13

Incorporating equal opportunities

Using your school's equal opportunities or inclusion policy, highlight or write down any guidelines for planning learning activities. Include how the curriculum, resources and general organisation of the school reflect this.

How to reflect on and learn from experience

Always reflect on what you have done with pupils, not only in order to evaluate what they have learned, but also to consider the way in which you have managed different activities. You may find that sometimes you are not as satisfied as others with the outcome and this may be for a variety of reasons. It may be that there were unforeseen circumstances which meant that the session did not go as planned, as sometimes happens in school, or the task was inappropriate for the needs of the different pupils. Do not be disheartened about this – it happens to everyone – but consider why it happened so that you can learn from the experience.

A good way of doing this is to ask yourself the following questions at the end of an activity:

- How did it go?
- What was I pleased with?
- What didn't go as well as I had planned?
- What would I change if I had to do the activity again?

This will then help you to move on and evaluate what you have done with pupils.

(Reflection is also covered in Unit 22.)

How to evaluate teaching and learning activities and outcomes

The importance of clear learning objectives

If you are asked to take part in the **evaluation** of teaching and learning activities and outcomes, it is important that you look back to the learning objectives. We cannot measure what pupils have learned without knowing what we are measuring against. Learning objectives need to be clear for this to be possible, which means:

- learners must understand what they mean
- they must be achievable
- we must be able to assess pupils against them.

> **Key term**
>
> **Evaluation** – an assessment of how well teaching and learning activities achieved their objectives

Lesson objectives

Look at the following lesson objectives. Will you be able to measure against them? Try using the following words in front of them: 'At the end of the lesson we will be able…'

- to understand the changes in atmospheric pressure
- to form whole numbers using decimal number bonds
- to cut and paste from the Internet
- to convert decimals to fractions
- to identify synonyms in a poem
- to understand the use of the present tense in Spanish
- to identify different cloud formations.

If we do not think carefully about learning objectives at the planning stage, it will not always be possible to define whether pupils have achieved them.

Measuring success criteria

You should also have an idea about the success criteria when evaluating pupils' learning. Pupils may not meet the learning objective, but they could have a real enthusiasm for the subject and have participated fully in all aspects of the lesson – you will need to record this somewhere. Also look at the resources you have used and whether these were successful.

Keys to good practice

Evaluation

- ✓ Have pupils met the learning objectives?
- ✓ Have they participated fully in the session?
- ✓ Have they understood the vocabulary or terminology used?
- ✓ Were the resources you used appropriate for the session?
- ✓ Were you 'in control' of the session and did the pupils respond well to you?
- ✓ How could you have improved what you did?
- ✓ What will you do now?

Evaluating learning sessions

Using a reflective account or your own school's evaluation forms, give an example of an evaluation you have carried out on a session you planned yourself. Make sure you show whether the pupils with whom you were working achieved the learning objectives.

School procedures for maintaining records and sharing information (see also Unit 55)

Teaching assistants may be involved in several different forms of record keeping (see Unit 55). For the purpose of this unit, the kinds of records you will be maintaining will be those concerned with planning and assessment, and pupil progress and achievement. It is likely that your school will have an assessment, recording and reporting policy, which should give you guidelines when maintaining records. These may be around:

- keeping information secure
- ensuring records are filled in correctly (accurate and relevant)
- how information is used following assessments
- child protection procedures.

As well as school policies, you need to be aware of issues such as confidentiality and data protection. Always ensure that you do not share pupil information with anyone who does not have a genuine need to know it. People with whom it might be appropriate to share information could include other staff or professionals who have direct contact with the pupil. Under the Data Protection Act, information should only be used for the purpose for which it was gathered.

It may be that the only records you are asked to fill in are on the plans themselves so that you can feed back to the teacher. Always make sure that you discuss with the teacher how they want you to do this.

Portfolio activity K20

Contributing to records

Write an account of the kinds of records you have contributed to as part of your role. If you can, refer to your school's assessment, recording and reporting policy to show how you have followed your school's guidelines. You may include records of information you have had to fill in as part of the record-keeping process. Always remove any pupils' names if using this kind of evidence, for confidentiality reasons. You can then use this as evidence in your portfolio alongside your reflective account.

P1 (1.1)
P2 (1.1)
P4 (1.2)
P7 (1.2)
P1 (1.3)
P2 (1.3)
P5 (1.3)
P6 (1.3)
K18
K19

For your portfolio...

This unit is for those who plan, deliver and evaluate teaching and learning activities for individual pupils or groups of pupils under the teacher's guidance or instructions. Plan, carry out and evaluate a learning activity with an individual pupil or group of pupils, showing how what you did fitted in with the teacher's overall planning structure. You will also need to show that you have taken into account the information about different pupils that was available to you and how you fed back to the teacher, including your evaluation. Ask the teacher to sign the evidence to show that it took place; it will then cover some areas of performance as well as knowledge.

24 Contribute to the Planning and Evaluation of Teaching and Learning Activities

This unit is for teaching assistants who contribute to the planning and evaluation of teaching and learning activities, but who are not independently responsible for planning. If you are undertaking this unit, you should be taking part in planning meetings with the teacher on a regular basis as well as discussing pupil progress and evaluating the work you have done with pupils.

The teaching and learning activities you carry out may be for individual pupils or groups of pupils, or may be whole class activities, and carried out in any learning environment including school visits. You should be able to show how you contribute to meetings with teachers or others in the school in order to discuss your contribution to the planning and evaluation process.

If you elect to do this unit, some of the knowledge points overlap with mandatory Unit 18 and so these have been omitted from the text in this section. You will therefore be able to cross-reference these in your portfolio rather than repeat the same evidence. However, you will need to adjust or add to the evidence slightly to ensure that it shows your involvement in planning and evaluating, rather than supporting the teacher's own plans. Your assessor will be able to help you to make sure that your evidence covers the knowledge points in both units. You will find page references to the appropriate knowledge headings.

What you need to know and understand

For this unit, you will need to know and understand:

- The relationship between your own role and the role of the teacher within the learning environment

- The role and responsibilities of yourself and others in planning, implementing and evaluating teaching and learning activities

- Your role and responsibilities for supporting pupils' learning and the implications of this for the sort of support you can provide

- *The school policies for inclusion and equality of opportunity, and the implication of these for how you work with pupils* (See also Unit 18, page 37)

- *The relevant school curriculum and age-related expectations of pupils in the subject/curriculum area and age range of the pupils with whom you are working* (See also Unit 18, page 33)

- How children learn and the implications of this for planning teaching and learning activities

- Any particular learning needs and learning styles of the pupils concerned and how these may affect the planned teaching and learning activities

- The value of different learning contexts (e.g. indoors, outdoors, visits)

- The principles underlying effective communication, planning and collaboration

- Your experience and expertise in relation to supporting learning activities and how this relates to the planned activities

- Your strengths and weaknesses in relation to supporting different types of learning

- The importance of effective time management and how to achieve this

- How to give feedback in a constructive manner and in a way that ensures that working relationships are maintained

Relationship between your own role and the role of the teacher within the learning environment

The relationship between your role and that of the teacher should be clearly defined so that you can each carry out your duties effectively. Although you are working as an adult in the classroom, what you do within the learning environment should be managed and led by the teacher. It is the teacher who has overall responsibility for pupils' learning and will need to report back to others, such as parents and governors, about pupils' progress. Your role will be in supporting what the teacher does: the two roles should therefore complement one another.

Some of the duties around planning and implementing learning activities of the teacher and the teaching assistant

Role of teacher	Role of teaching assistant
• To be responsible for planning and preparing to the National Curriculum • To teach pupils according to their educational needs • To assess, record and report on the development, progress and attainment of pupils • To take responsibility for all other adults within the learning environment • To communicate and consult with the parents of pupils • To communicate and co-operate with persons or bodies outside the school • To participate in meetings arranged for any of the above purposes • Usually to undertake tutorial duties as outlined in the job description	• To plan and prepare work alongside the teacher • To support learning activities effectively as directed by the teacher • To assess/evaluate pupils' work as directed by the teacher • To report any problems or queries to the teacher • To give feedback to the teacher following planned activities • To act as co-tutors alongside teaching staff

Role and responsibilities of yourself and others in planning, implementing and evaluating teaching and learning activities

In your role as a teaching assistant, you may be asked to help with the **planning** of learning activities in the learning environment. Although the class teacher will have completed long-term plans for the class, you may be asked to work with the teacher and others in the year group to discuss and plan activities for the week so that you are aware in advance of what you are required to do. You will need to work together to ensure that the work you are covering fits in with the activities and topics planned for the term.

Depending on your role, you may be invited to come to medium- or short-term planning meetings so that you have some idea of topics or themes before planning takes place. At this planning stage, you should have an opportunity to give suggestions, as well as informing the teacher of any difficulties you anticipate when considering the needs of the pupils. Your role and the role of the teacher should be one of a partnership, where there are clear roles and responsibilities for working together to support the pupils. You may also be involved in planning a series of activities to be carried out over several sessions. This could be with the same group, if the pupils need to work on a particular idea, or with different pupils on a similar, perhaps differentiated, task. As you become more experienced or if you are working with a pupil who has special educational (Additional Support for Learning (ASL)) needs, you may add some of your own ideas during the sessions so that the pupil or pupils build on work done each time.

Ideally, you should be given this opportunity to input some of your own ideas into class activities when they are at the planning stage. This is because you may have your own areas of expertise or ideas, which may help the teacher to formulate activities for pupils. This is especially true for assistants who support individual pupils with special needs, as there will be some activities in which these pupils need more structured tasks. You should also be aware of your own areas of weakness. For example, if you

 Key term

Planning – deciding with the teacher what you will do, when, how and with which pupils, to ensure that planned teaching and learning activities are implemented effectively

Medium-term Planning Sheet Week 6				
Topic: Year 8 – Approriate sources of historical information		**Week beginning:**		
Activities	**Learning objectives**	**Learning outcomes**	**Comments**	
• Sort a collection of historical accounts into a set of categories. • Talk about characteristics of each set, e.g. uses sound, has moving images, is a still shot, a verbal account, etc. • Describe and evaluate the differences between two sources, e.g. graphic, colourful, eye-catching, dull, primary evidence, secondary evidence, objective, subjective, biased, etc.	**History: 4a–b, 5b** • Identify, select and use a range of appropriate sources of information (e.g. oral accounts, documents, printed sources, the media, artefacts, pictures, photographs, music, museums, buildings and ICT-based sources) as a basis for independent historical enquiries • Evaluate the sources used, select and record information relevant to the enquiry and reach conclusions • How choice of form, layout and presentation contribute to the effect, e.g. example, font, caption, illustration in printed text, sequencing, framing, soundtrack in moving image text **English (speaking and listening): 2a** • Concentrate on and recall the main features of a talk, reading, radio or television programme	• Sort accounts into the following sets: - oral accounts - printed sources - media artefacts - pictures - photos. • Explain why they have grouped accounts in a particular way. • Explain the main features of source of information and its effect.		
• Summarise what two information sources say explicitly. • Highlight words/phrases indicating different purposes, e.g. to explain, persuade, amuse or argue a case.	**English (speaking and listening): 2b, 2c, 2f** • Identify the major elements of what is being said both explicitly and implicitly • Distinguish features of presentation where a speaker aims to explain, persuade, amuse or argue a case • Ask questions and give relevant and helpful comments	• Answer questions on the explicit content of the two sources. • List words/phrases that can be used to explain, persuade, amuse or argue a case.		
• Given the words/phrases previously highlighted, identify the implicit purposes of the two sources of information, e.g. are they trying to persuade readers to buy a product?	**English (reading): 1a, 1b, 1c** • To extract meaning beyond the literal, explaining how the choice of language and style affects implied and explicit meanings • To analyse and discuss alternative interpretations, ambiguity and allusion • How ideas, values and emotions are explored and portrayed	• Provide an evaluation of the implicit purposes of the sources of information.		
• Using an Internet search engine to locate three sources of secondary evidence which are objective accounts of a recent historical event.	**ICT: 1b** • How to obtain information well matched to purpose by selecting appropriate sources, using and refining search methods and questioning the plausibility and value of the information found	• Use the Internet to search for sources of information.		
• Discuss why they are objective accounts.	**English (printed and ICT-based information texts): 4c** • Sift the relevant from the irrelevant and distinguish between fact and opinion, bias and objectivity	• Explain why the sources chosen are factual and objective.		

▲ Figure 24.1 Example of a planning sheet

know that you will find it difficult to take a group of pupils for an Art activity on printing because you have not done this for a long time, then say so. You should feel comfortable with what you are doing because it is important to be confident when carrying out the activity. If you anticipate any other difficulties in carrying out the plan, which the teacher has not foreseen, you should also point these out.

Following the session, both you and the class teacher should reflect on the effectiveness of the teaching and learning activities and their success in relation both to the learning objectives and also to other **success measures**.

For effective **evaluation**, you will need to look at whether the pupils you were working with were able to meet the learning objective through their task. If the majority of pupils achieved the objectives but one or two found certain **difficulties**, it would be appropriate to record by exception, for example: 'This group were all able to complete the task and had a good understanding, although George and Bayram could not understand the representation of the symbols for potassium (K) and hydrogen (H) in the periodic table of elements'. Similarly, if a pupil completes the task quickly and is more able than the rest of the group, this should also be recorded. (See also page 166 on feedback.)

You may also be involved in meetings or discussions with others in the year group during which you talk about topics or long-term plans for the year and whether you should repeat the same ideas the following year.

▼ Figure 24.2 Planning an activity gives you the opportunity to contribute your ideas

🛈 Key terms

Success measures – the criteria against which the teaching and learning activities are evaluated; they could relate to:
- the impact on individual or groups of pupils
- coverage of the curriculum
- individual learning targets

Evaluation – an assessment of how well the teaching and learning activities achieved their objectives

Difficulties – potential barriers and hindrances to implementing the planned teaching and learning activities; they could relate to:
- learning materials (e.g. cost, availability, quality)
- time (e.g. timetable restrictions, your contractual hours)
- learning environment/ setting (e.g. space, facilities, potential distractions or disruptions)
- your role and expertise (e.g. your job description and requirements for supporting particular pupils, your subject knowledge)

Portfolio activity

Inputting into medium- or short-term plans

Annotate and highlight a medium- or short-term plan that you have devised, alongside others, to show the input of both yourself and others in your team. You should also show how you have evaluated the effectiveness of the plan.

Your role and responsibilities for supporting pupils' learning and the implications of this for the sort of support you can provide

As your role is ultimately one of learning support, you should be aware of the extent and boundaries of what you are required to do within the learning environment. You will have a job description, which should set out the requirements of your role. If you are asked to cover areas that you are uncomfortable with or do not feel experienced enough to do, you should always speak to your line manager.

Case study

Working within role boundaries

Katy is working in a Year 10 (S4) English class. She works alongside the teacher and is involved in planning learning activities on a regular basis. The teacher is off sick and at short notice the cover supervisor asked Katy if she would mind taking the class for period 3 because she is very experienced. She has copies of the plans for the week and knows what the teacher was going to do. She has taken the class before but only for short periods and is quite anxious about taking the class now.

- Is this part of Katy's role?
- Should she say anything about taking the whole class?
- What should she say if she was asked to do this on a regular basis?

Keys to good practice

Planning learning activities

✓ Ensure you understand the teaching and learning objectives.
✓ Contribute your own ideas to planning sessions.
✓ Include any of your own strengths.
✓ Work within the boundaries of your role.
✓ Make sure you have time for what you need to do with pupils.
✓ Be aware of relevant curriculum policies and guidelines.

How children learn and the implications of this for planning teaching and learning activities

Theories of learning

There have been several theories put forward by educationalists and psychologists about how children learn and are influenced as they develop. (There are other, external influences on children's learning, discussed in Unit 18 on page 34, which also have a direct effect on how children learn.) The two main ideas about how children's learning takes place are behaviourist theory and cognitive theory. By looking at these we are able to focus on different aspects of children's learning and consider how best to support them in a school setting.

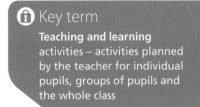

(i) Key term

Teaching and learning activities – activities planned by the teacher for individual pupils, groups of pupils and the whole class

Behaviourist theory

This theory was first put forward by Burrhus Frank Skinner (1904–94). It states that as individuals we will repeat experiences that are enjoyable and avoid those which are not. This is as relevant for learning experiences as for behaviour itself. For example, a pupil who learns that it is enjoyable to work with construction toys will want to repeat the experience and do it again. If a pupil is praised for working at a particular task, this may also reinforce their desire to repeat the experience. Skinner stated that good experiences are *positive reinforcement*. Many educationalists use the strategy of positive reinforcement when working with children, for example, by praising and encouraging them and by giving them tasks that they can carry out successfully.

We can ensure that pupils are gaining positive experiences when working by giving them:

- praise and encouragement
- enjoyable tasks
- manageable tasks.

You will need to be able to respond to pupils' reactions to tasks as sometimes they find it difficult to become motivated and lose enthusiasm quickly. It is important to recognise when pupils are not enjoying tasks and find out what may be the cause, so that you can encourage and motivate them. As you get to know pupils, it will be more apparent when they are not 'themselves' or are unable to focus on what they are doing. When pupils are not responding to a task, you should address them individually and try to find out the cause.

There may be a variety of reasons why a pupil is not motivated:

- pupil does not understand the requirements of the task
- pupil is unable to complete the task as it is too difficult
- pupil finds the task too easy
- pupil is not able to focus on the task due to individual reasons, such as illness or anxiety.

Once the cause has been established, you may need to work closely with the pupil or speak to the teacher about the problem to decide the best way forward. Where the task is too easy or too difficult, it may be possible to put the pupil in another group and restructure their work for later. Pupils whose work is not enjoyable or manageable are unlikely to want to repeat the experience.

Cognitive development theory

A second theory of learning is that put forward by Jean Piaget (1896–1980) and is based on the cognitive model. This states that a child needs to pass through different stages of a learning process. He stated that children pass through stages of learning which are broadly related to their age and that they cannot move from one stage to another until they are ready.

This theory has been criticised because all children learn and develop at different paces and it is hard to say at exactly what age particular skills will develop. However, it is accepted that children have individual learning needs and requirements.

Piaget's stages of learning

Age	Stage of learning	Characteristics
0–2 years	Sensory motor	Babies are starting to find out about the world around them and are discovering what things around them can do.
2–6 years	Pre-operational	Children are starting to develop thought processes and are using symbolic play. They find it easier to learn when they can see and use practical examples.
6–11 years	Concrete operational	Children are able to think on a more logical level. They can use more abstract concepts, e.g. a box can represent a car, but still may need concrete objects to work with.
12 years and over	Formal operational	Children no longer need concrete objects as they should be able to think abstractly. Children should also be able to formulate hypothesis. They will therefore be able to reason about what might be as well as what is.

It is important to recognise that children's learning will be based on their own individual experiences and that they will pass through learning stages, but that the age at which they reach them is not fixed.

When looking at the planning of pupils' work, all staff should remember the variety of needs that exist within each classroom. Some pupils will learn and develop at a different rate and this will have an effect on how their work is approached. School staff need to be able to cater for a range of abilities, while all the time challenging and motivating pupils to do their best. Unit 18 looks in detail at the key factors that affect the way pupils learn and develop, and gives some ideas about how this will affect planning and differentiation within the classroom.

There will be a spread of attainment that pupils at any age will be expected to achieve, but it is important to take into account those pupils who fall outside this expected level. This will usually be those pupils on the Special Needs Register, and teachers should plan differentiated work for them in line with their Individual Education Plan (IEP) targets. (See also Units 38–42 on special educational (ASL) needs and Unit 18 on equal opportunities and inclusion). Those pupils who are more able should also have opportunities to extend their knowledge (see Unit 34). Teachers will often cater for these pupils by planning similar activities but with extension work.

As can be seen from the lesson plan in the next case study, the teacher has planned for varying abilities while carrying the same theme through the lesson.

Case study K6

Evaluating theoretical basis of lesson plan

Look at the following lesson plan.

Lesson objective	At the end of this lesson, pupils will be able to use the French present tense for the regular 'er' verb 'regarder' (to watch).
Most pupils will be able to:	Recognise the verb 'regarder' in the present tense in written text
A few pupils will be able to:	Use the verb 'regarder' in the present tense independently
Introduction	Introduction to how the verb 'regarder' sounds in the present tense. Pupils listen to and then sing along to a short song 'Qu'est-ce que tu aimes regarder?' (What do you like to watch?).
Main focus of lesson	
More able group (8 pupils)	Pupils circulate in class asking the question 'Qu'est-ce que tu regardes lundi soir ? (What do you watch on Monday evenings?). Pupils record results, then write sentences to describe the results for: themselves, a female friend, a male friend, all the girls, all the boys.
Middle two groups (12 pupils)	Simpson's worksheet. Lisa Simpson completed a survey on what the following people like to watch on different days of the week: herself, Bart, Marge, the Simpson family, all the boys in her school, all the girls in her school. Pupils fill in missing gaps in sentences with correct part of the verb, e.g. 'Marge regarde Dr Who' (Marge watches Dr Who).
Less able group (6 pupils)	As above, except pupils are provided with three options and must circle the correct answer, e.g. 'Marge regardez/regardons/regarde Dr Who'.
SEN group (4 pupils)	Mix and match activity. Pupils cut out verbs and pronouns from a printed sheet to match correct pairs of verbs and pronouns.
Plenary	Whole class game based on the show 'Who wants to be a millionaire?'. Pupils are given increasingly harder sentences to complete using the correct form of the verb 'regarder'.

- How does the plan make an allowance for what you know about different theories of learning and learning styles?
- How has the teacher built flexibility into the plan?
- Do you think that this will be an effective plan? Why?

Any particular learning needs and learning styles of pupils and how these may affect the planned teaching and learning activities

See Unit 40, pages 269 and 271 on personalisation and planning for the individual needs of pupils. You can also use the case study on page 163 for this knowledge base.

Value of different learning contexts (e.g. indoors, outdoors, visits)

Teaching and learning activities should take place in a variety of environments in order to engage pupils and in particular to cater for different learning styles. Pupils should develop an awareness that learning takes place in all environments and not just in the classroom. By giving them opportunities in a variety of contexts we are encouraging them to apply what they are learning to different situations.

K8 Case study

Learning in different environments

You are taking a group of pupils on a trip to the Natural History Museum. Pupils have been given a 'find out about' list and will also be watching a 3-D film on evolution, which is to take place in the afternoon.

Give three ways in which the visit will benefit pupils and enhance their learning experience.

Principles underlying effective communication, planning and collaboration

Schools should provide a variety of opportunities for teachers and support staff to share information about the school and its pupils. It is important to make these times available because many support staff work part-time or work in several classes but only with one pupil. You need to have a chance to share ideas and experiences with others so that you do not feel isolated or out of touch with what is happening. Such opportunities could include:

- regular meetings for teaching assistants
- sharing information about the school
- teaching assistants working together to support classes or individuals
- notice boards and year group meetings.

These meetings and opportunities for discussion do not need to be long, but are an important part of the effective communication process that should take place in the school. If these kinds of opportunities are not given to staff for communicating with one another, they will find it much more difficult to work with one another and use time efficiently.

Your experience and expertise in relation to supporting learning activities and how this relates to the planned activities

As a practitioner working at this level, you will be able to use your experience to support learning activities. For example, it is likely that you will know that some pupils work best when they are not together and you will separate them at the beginning of the activity. You will also be able to look at the planned activities and be able to apply your own expertise as to how you can best carry them out. If you have been involved in planning, you will have been able to suggest to the teacher how you can use your own knowledge and skills to the benefit of the pupils.

Case study (K10)

Supporting learning activities with your experience and expertise

Lucy is working in a Year 9 (S3) Citizenship class with Josh, who has social and emotional needs. She regularly supports group activities and plans with the class teacher so that she can input into what she does both with Josh and the others in the group. In a week's time the teacher is planning to do some work on Chinese New Year. As Lucy's husband is Chinese, she has some items at home, which she suggests she can bring in to show the class and to start a discussion. She suggests that the pupils can then look at the items in groups and, following the pupils' work, they could be used for part of a display. The teacher then asks Lucy whether she has any other suggestions or if she can ask her husband about his experience of traditional celebrations.

- Why is it important to discuss plans beforehand as much as possible?
- How will Lucy's involvement enhance the pupils' experience?

Your strengths and weaknesses in relation to supporting different types of learning

In secondary schools, teachers and support staff have to work in many different subjects and situations, and everyone will be more competent in some than others. You are not teaching just the subjects of the National Curriculum, but also social skills, how to relate to others, how to be part of a school, and so on. You are likely to feel more confident in some areas than others, and this is natural. However, if you are asked to do something you are unsure or unclear how to approach, you should always speak to the teacher about it at the planning stage.

Importance of effective time management and how to achieve this

You will need to make sure that you are fully aware of the time available when implementing learning activities. There are many parts of the school day during which time is restricted and this needs to be considered, especially if there is a large group of pupils to work with on an individual basis. If the work seems unrealistically lengthy for the time allocated, you should not try to complete it all and rush the pupils to finish. This will make them feel that their work is less valued. Although time is limited in school, whenever possible teaching assistants should try not to communicate this to pupils when they are working on a task. If there is an unavoidable limit on time, you should give the pupils an opportunity to return to the task later if possible. Similarly, if pupils have completed their activity, you may need to give them alternatives or an extension activity. This will ensure that they are not waiting for further instructions rather than using their time effectively.

K12 Case study

Working within time limitations

You are working long term on some additional Literacy support activities with a group of Year 7 (S1) pupils. You are carrying out the activities as specified in the lesson plans, but regularly find that you run out of time to complete them. As a result, both you and the group are feeling disheartened with the process.

- How could you devise a more effective way of working so that you and the pupils have a more satisfying learning experience?
- Why is it important that time does not become an issue when working with pupils?

How to give feedback in a constructive manner and in a way that ensures that working relationships are maintained

Finding time to give feedback to teachers can be very difficult. There is often little time in school to sit down and discuss pupils' work with teachers. Some teachers and teaching assistants will discuss the lessons' activities in the staffroom on a daily basis. Another way in which feedback can be given if there is not time for verbal discussion is through the use of feedback forms. If these are planned and set out correctly, you will be able to show whether pupils have achieved learning objectives, how they responded to specific activities and how much support they needed.

? Thinking point

Discuss in groups what has happened in your experience when pupils have too much or not enough time to complete an activity and how you have dealt with this.

You may need to be tactful when feeding back to teachers about learning activities. There may be a number of reasons why an activity has not gone well. However, if it is clearly due to planning or the pupils have not found the task engaging, you may have to suggest this to the teacher. Depending on the personality and how well you get along with one another this may or may not present problems. If you have a relationship that allows you both to give suggestions to one another and discuss any issues as they arise, you will find it easier. Sometimes, however, if you are more experienced than the teacher or they are not used to working with other adults, it may be difficult.

Teacher/TA Feedback Sheet

Class: Year 7

To be filled in by teacher:
Teacher's name:
TA's name:

Brief description of activity

Revision of Year 6 work on plotting different points and shapes using co-ordinates on x and y axes.
Follow up to revise reflecting shapes.

How session is linked to medium-term plans

Departmental schemes of work – Revision of work on shape carried out in Year 6

TA's role

To check understanding of how to plot co-ordinates.

Important vocabulary

axis, perimeter, shape, diagonal, co-ordinate, edge, corner
names of shapes

Key learning points

To be able to plot points using co-ordinates.
To identify and reflect shapes.

For use during group work:

Pupils	D	H	Feedback/Assessment

D = Can do task
H = Help required to complete task

▲ **Figure 24.3** Example of a feedback sheet

The most important thing to remember is that even if you know you are right it is better to give your feedback in the form of suggestions.

K13 Case study

Giving constructive feedback

Serena has carried out a Science activity with a group of Year 10 (S4) pupils that has not gone well. She knows that this is because of the pupils' needs and although she has attempted to adapt the activity to accommodate these, it has proved a difficult session. At the end of the lesson the teacher asks her how it went.

- How could Serena give feedback to the teacher in a constructive manner?
- What could she do if the teacher reacted badly to her feedback?

K1 K3 K7 all performance criteria

For your portfolio

For this unit you will need to show how you plan and evaluate learning activities alongside the teacher. If your assessor can come to a planning meeting and observe you working together or speak to the teacher with whom you work, this will be an ideal opportunity to gather evidence for much of the performance criteria for this unit.

If this is not possible, you should be able to put actual plans to which you have contributed in your portfolio and annotate them to show your contribution and evaluations. If your class teacher can then write a witness testimony to confirm your involvement, this will also cover some of your performance criteria.

28 Support Teaching and Learning in a Curriculum Area

As a teaching assistant in a secondary school you may be asked to support a whole range of subjects across the curriculum and different age groups. This can seem daunting if you do not feel that you have the appropriate knowledge and skills within some curriculum areas. For this reason, some schools may ask you to provide support only within the curriculum area that you, and they, consider to be your strength. For example, a teaching assistant competent and confident in the use of Maths may be assigned to provide support only within the Maths department. Whichever is the case in your school, do not be discouraged if you are asked to support a curriculum area that you feel weak in. Although supporting a subject area in which you lack knowledge and skills may feel challenging, see it as an opportunity for self-development. You can work to improve your own subject knowledge in a variety of ways and in doing so you will see how your confidence will grow.

You may already have some experience of much of what is required from you in this unit. By the end of the unit you should have an in-depth knowledge of the curriculum and you will have worked to acquire new knowledge and skills, which should help increase your confidence.

What you need to know and understand

For this unit, you will need to know and understand:

- The relevant school curriculum and age-related expectations of pupils in the subject/ curriculum area and age range of the pupils with whom you are working
- How the subject/curriculum area contributes to the overall education of the pupils, including cross-curricular learning
- The purpose and benefits of developing your own subject knowledge for yourself and for others
- How to monitor, reflect on and evaluate your own subject knowledge and skills
- How to keep your subject knowledge and skills up to date given other pressures on your time and resources
- How to access information, resources and development opportunities to improve your subject knowledge and skills
- How to use your subject knowledge and skills to support teaching and learning, including developing and evaluating teaching and learning materials
- The importance of confirming the teaching and learning materials required
- Why it is important to establish realistic deadlines for providing information and materials
- How to deal with competing demands for information and materials
- The typical areas of interest of different people within the subject/curriculum area
- The kinds of requests for information and materials that lie outside of your own ability or responsibility to meet
- The importance of working within the boundaries of your role and competence and when you should refer to others
- What information and materials already exist within the subject/curriculum area and how to access and/or adapt these if appropriate
- Relevant sources of information and materials for the subject/curriculum area and the age range of the pupils
- How to research information efficiently and accurately
- Why you should maintain a record of sources of information that you have used and how to do so
- How to select and prepare teaching and learning materials to meet the needs of the pupils involved
- How to organise information for different audiences, e.g. teachers, pupils of different ages and abilities
- How to identify and develop culturally and linguistically appropriate teaching and learning materials
- The school or department's procedures for maintaining records of the information and materials obtained and developed

Curriculum and age-related expectations of pupils in the subject/curriculum area and age range

As a teaching assistant supporting pupils with a range of needs, you may work with pupils who are not achieving the expected **curriculum** outcomes for their age group. These pupils may have specific individual learning targets in Individual Education Plans (IEPs) or set by the subject teacher. Nonetheless, it is important for you to have an awareness of the age-related expectations, as set out in the **National Curriculum**, so that you can see how much the pupils you support are under-achieving compared with the age-related targets.

Information on age-related expectations (in terms of **attainment targets**, as well as **National Curriculum levels**) can be sought in a variety of locations including:

General
- Subject-specific National Curriculum and **programmes of study**
- departmental **schemes of work**
- daily lesson plans
- examination boards' criteria
- average Key Stage 3 SATs results and Key Stage 4 GCSE results

Special needs schools
- **P scales**
- annual reviews
- IEPs.

Disapplication of the National Curriculum at Key Stage 4
If at any time you feel that it is not appropriate for the pupils you support to work towards the age-related expectations in certain curriculum areas, then you must discuss this with the teacher so that other, more attainable targets can be set. Also remember that headteachers, if they deem necessary, may decide to disapply some areas of the National Curriculum at Key Stage 4 in order to meet particular pupil needs. However, with the changes introduced in 2006 following the White Paper, *14–19: Opportunity and Excellence*, the National Curriculum has been designed to suit more individual needs and some areas (e.g. Science) can no longer be disapplied.

Changes to the National Curriculum and age-related expectations
You also have to bear in mind that the National Curriculum is constantly being revised, updated and changed. It is important that you keep abreast with these changes. Most of the changes will appear in your school's **development** or **improvement plan** and there will be implications for you as part of the staff team. Ensure that you obtain a copy to remain aware of proposed changes. Also keep your eye on governmental white papers.

Key terms

Curriculum – all of the courses/subjects of study offered by schools. The National Occupational Standards for Teaching Assistants refer to curriculum areas covered in this unit as 'all forms of organised learning' apart from 'the specialist technical functions carried out by technicians, librarians and ICT professionals'. These 'specialist technical' areas are given separate units in the National Occupational Standards

National Curriculum – proposed statutory and non-statutory courses/subjects of study for all those in state schools

National Curriculum levels and **attainment targets** – these establish what pupils should know, understand and be able to do and to which level

Programmes of study – set out the content, knowledge and skills to be taught to enable children to achieve the attainments targets

Schemes of work – outline how a department intends to impart the content, knowledge and skills to achieve the attainment targets

P scales – 8 differentiated performance criteria for pupils with special educational (Additional Support for Learning (ASL)) needs working below level 1 on the National Curriculum

Development/improvement plan – outlines the school's targets and intentions to incorporate new legislation and working practices

Portfolio activity

Keeping up to date with the National Curriculum and targets

Familiarise yourself with the attainment targets, P-level data and National Curriculum levels for each of the subjects you support. Keep copies of the attainment targets, P-level data and National Curriculum level descriptors. Obtain copies of assessment grades for the pupils you support.

How the subject/curriculum contributes to the overall education of the pupils, including cross-curricular learning

The National Curriculum handbook outlines the importance of cross-curricular learning and sets out the areas for learning that should be cross-curricular. These are:

- promotion of spiritual, moral, social and cultural development
- promotion of Personal, Social and Health Education (PSHE)
- promotion of skills such as key skills and thinking skills
- promotion of other aspects of the school curriculum, e.g. education for sustainable development
- use of language (reading, writing, speaking, listening)
- use of information technology.

Some schools may give certain members of staff the responsibility to ensure **broad cross-curricular learning**. **Lesson cross-curricular development** remains the responsibility of the teacher and teaching assistant.

> **Key terms**
>
> **Broad cross-curricular learning** – skills are developed across a range of curriculum areas, e.g. by doing a project
>
> **Lesson cross-curricular development** – when different skills are embedded into the lessons, e.g. the interactive nature of speaking, listening, reading and writing such as decoding (reading) and encoding (spelling and writing) in all subjects

Benefits of cross-curricular learning

Lesson cross-curricular learning allows for the development of a range of skills, for example, completing surveys on traffic pollution for Geography may develop Numeracy skills, if pupils are asked to calculate percentages or look at averages. In this way pupils are learning to apply what they have learned in Maths in other subjects and areas of life. Embedding skills in cross-curricular learning in this way allows pupils to see how subjects relate to each other rather than existing as separate entities that are unrelated and irrelevant. The practice and application of skills in this way allows for constant re-capping and builds up experience in the use of the skills.

Broad cross-curricular learning can do all of the above and more. Among the many skills promoted by project work are the development of team work and organisation skills through collaborative learning. Cross-departmental learning allows for flexibility over the curriculum and can make learning interesting, varied and fun.

Implementing lesson and broad cross-curricular learning

The English department has teamed up with the Drama, Art and ICT departments to complete a Year 10 (S4) cross-curricular project on the theme of violence in the book, *Of Mice and Men* by John Steinbeck. You have been asked to attend the planning meeting.

- Which ideas could you suggest for lesson cross-curricular learning? Include an evaluation of the proposed benefits of the activities you suggest.
- Which ideas could you suggest for broad cross-curricular learning? Include an evaluation of the proposed advantages of the tasks you suggest.

The purpose and benefits of developing your subject knowledge for yourself and others

Developing your own subject knowledge will better equip you to support teaching and learning within the curriculum area. Increased subject knowledge will improve your own confidence levels and may allow you to obtain higher-level teaching assistant (HLTA) status in the specific subject area (the post of higher-level teaching assistant does not exist in Scotland). Once you have gained new skills you may be asked to contribute to staff development activities. Some teaching assistants are now being asked to provide training for other teaching assistants during team meetings or INSET days. Others are being asked to mentor new or less experienced teaching assistants or provide **extra-curricular activities**, such as football clubs.

> **🔒 Key term**
>
> **Extra-curricular activities** – activities offered outside of the usual curriculum subjects, e.g. after-school cricket club, lunchtime chess club

How to monitor, reflect on, evaluate and improve your subject knowledge and skills

Before you can decide what skills need to be developed, you need to highlight your strengths and weaknesses. One way you can do this is by seeking **constructive feedback** from teachers and others with whom you work on a regular basis. Another way is through **appraisal** or **performance management review**.

> **🔒 Key terms**
>
> **Constructive feedback** – feedback that is specific, highlights strengths and sets targets for development
>
> **Appraisal** or **performance management** review – meeting with a line manager to discuss job role, strengths and areas for development and training needs

Seeking and using feedback from teachers and others with whom you work

Constructive feedback should not feel like criticism, but should be viewed positively as it allows you to develop. Bear in mind that not only you, but everyone working within the education sector has to meet targets. Moreover, learn to accept positive feedback with grace, as you deserve it! If you receive little feedback, do not be worried about asking those with whom you are working how you are doing. You could even seek feedback from pupils.

Feedback can be given in a variety of ways, for example, through verbal or written means and either formally or informally.

Informal feedback

- Take note of comments that are made in passing, such as reference to your appropriate and clear use of language providing effective guidance and instruction: 'Sir, you really break it down for me. I understand it because you speak like me.'
- Similar comments may also be made by other members of staff.

Formal feedback

- Comments about teaching assistants may appear in Ofsted reports.
- References to teaching assistants may be made in internal inspections.
- Feedback paperwork on observations of your practice is an excellent source.
- Appraisal and meetings with line managers will also provide you with appropriate advice and guidance.

Keys to good practice

Effective use of feedback

✓ Be a reflective practitioner. Use self-assessment on a regular basis to evaluate your support strategies, resources and tasks.

✓ Use feedback to help understand what good performance is, as you may have a misunderstanding of what is expected from you.

✓ Use positive feedback to help motivate and develop your confidence.

✓ Use feedback to help close the gap between current and desired performance by setting new targets.

✓ Use feedback to promote dialogue between yourself and significant others about learning.

✓ Ask for suggested solutions on how to overcome your weaknesses.

✓ Prioritise your areas for improvement.

Appraisal and performance management review process

Your school should have a performance management review or appraisal process for teaching assistants. You may be asked to go through a self-assessment process before meeting with a line manger to discuss your progress. The National Association for Professional Teaching Assistants (NAPTA) has an online 'Professional Development Review', which measures competence against the National Occupational Standards for Teaching Assistants, the NVQ/SVQ units at both Levels 2 and 3, the **National Workloads Agreements 22 tasks** and the professional standards for **HLTA**. If your school does not have a self-appraisal process, you may wish to consider the following before your review:

- your job description and how it matches your current responsibilities
- your competencies against the National Occupational Standards

> **ⓘ Key terms**
>
> **National Workloads Agreements 22 tasks** – an agreement between government, employers and schools to help raise standards and tackle workloads
>
> **HTLA** – higher-level teaching assistants act as specialist assistants for a specific subject or department

- your competencies against the areas to be covered in the National Curriculum for the subject/s you support
- your strengths
- your areas for development
- possible solutions to overcome your weaknesses.

Once you have completed your self-appraisal, you may be observed in the classroom. You will then meet with your line manager to discuss your strengths and areas for development in relation to both your self-appraisal and the observation. Targets for development should be set together, with a date for review to ascertain whether you have achieved the targets and which new objectives should be set.

Case study K4 K5 K6

Evaluating and improving your subject knowledge and skills

At the beginning of the school year you were asked to support teaching and learning in Science for years 7, 8 and 9 (S1, 2 and 3). The idea was for you to become the school's Science HLTA. Before the term began you were asked to highlight your strengths and weakness according to the content, knowledge and skills pupils in Years 7, 8 and 9 (S1, 2 and 3) are expected to acquire.

- What curriculum or school documents would you refer to while evaluating your strengths and weaknesses?
- What strategies could you use to evaluate your strengths and weaknesses?
- How could you seek feedback from others on their perceptions of your strengths and weaknesses?
- What activities could you do to help yourself develop?

Finding time to develop your subject knowledge

The added task of ensuring that you keep up to date with your curriculum knowledge and skills may seem impossible with the many other commitments you may have. It is therefore important for you to find time- and cost-effective ways to develop your practice. For example, could you take younger family members to the local library for a beneficial learning experience while you do some research? Could you use any time in lieu for extra duties to research or read newspaper articles? Could you listen to the news in the car on the way home from work?

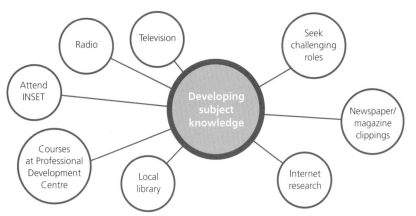

◀ **Figure 28.1** Methods of subject development

Accessing information, resources and development opportunities

The ways in which you access information, resources and development opportunities will really depend on the systems and materials available at your school and your own personal preferences. For example, there is usually a member of staff who co-ordinates staff training and development opportunities and it is important for you to approach them for advice and guidance. Ensure that you know how much training you are entitled to annually and bear in mind that unfortunately school budgets place limitations on the amount of training available. The sections that follow outline time- and cost-effective ways you can help yourself develop, source information and work collaboratively with others.

Working with others to improve your subject knowledge and skills

Working collaboratively with others will allow you to observe, discuss options and exchange ideas with experienced practitioners. Others can also learn from your strengths and skills. Working collaboratively will allow for informal training in creative ways that may help save money and time spent on development opportunities and resource creation.

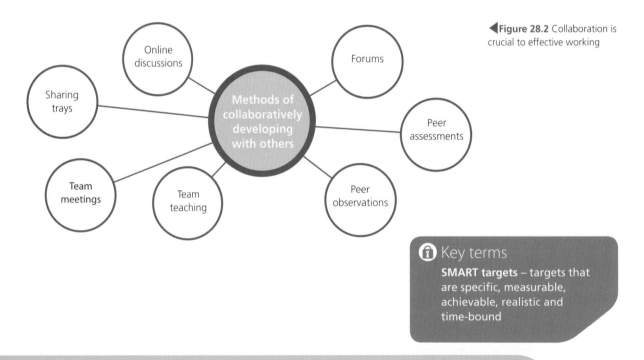

◀ **Figure 28.2** Collaboration is crucial to effective working

> **ⓘ Key terms**
>
> **SMART targets** – targets that are specific, measurable, achievable, realistic and time-bound

---

K4 K5 K6

Portfolio activity

Improving your subject knowledge and skills

Obtain copies of the National Curriculum, programmes of study and exam board criteria for the specific subjects you support. Make a list of the areas you feel competent supporting and those for which you feel you need to retrain. For example, you may have a firm grasp of all areas covered by the Maths National Curriculum for Key Stage 3 but not for Key Stage 4. Set yourself **SMART targets** on an action plan outlining how you intend to develop professionally. Discuss how you will pass on your newly acquired knowledge and skills to other members of staff.

How to use your subject knowledge and skills to support teaching and learning, including developing and evaluating teaching and learning materials

Having in-depth knowledge of the expected content, knowledge and skills within a subject will allow you to answer pupils' questions appropriately. However, if at any time you are unable to answer their questions, be prepared to offer solutions or sources of help other than 'Ask the teacher'. How can you encourage independence other than through the use of open-ended questioning to draw out pupils' ideas? Is there a reference book? Do you know a good website? Can you help the pupil run an Internet search? Will the answer be in a dictionary or encyclopaedia? Can another pupil help? The possibilities are endless!

Before developing new teaching and learning materials for curriculum areas, research the existing departmental stock. This will save valuable time, energy, materials and money by not reproducing something that already exists. Departments may have the subject-specific resources clearly organised in labelled boxes, trays or areas so that they can be easily be retrieved. If this is not the case, is this something that you could help organise? It may take some time, but it will be worthwhile in the long term.

Once you have a clear idea of the existing curriculum resources, you need to be aware of the process for booking or accessing them. Some departments may require staff to book resources, sign them out before using them and, if appropriate, sign them in on their return. This is a good way to keep track of stock.

Once you have accessed the resources, you can then decide how they can be adapted to suit the needs of the pupils you are supporting. For example, a visually impaired pupil may need text magnified or a dyslexic pupil may find it easier reading text on coloured paper. If in doubt, seek advice from your Special Educational Needs Co-ordinator (SENCo) (ASL teacher), who can best advise you on ways to adapt materials and resources.

Keys to good practice
Developing and evaluating your own resources

✓ When developing resources, consider the learning outcomes. After using a resource, evaluate if it helped pupils achieve the expected learning intention.
✓ Structure and present materials to suit pupil needs.
✓ Reuse resources that have been used in other subjects so that pupils have the necessary skills to use them, thus saving time and allowing you to focus more time on the outcome of the task.
✓ Search first. Has someone else completed material before that can simply be modified? However, do consider any copyright issues. Can you download resources from the Internet? Visit sites that are copyright free.
✓ Consider the resources' broad and lesson cross-curricular learning possibilities.
✓ If someone has developed the resource and used it before have they given any feedback or is an evaluation available?
✓ Examine other resources to compare them with what you are developing.
✓ Make your resource reusable.

Importance of confirming the teaching and learning materials required and establishing realistic deadlines for providing information and materials

Once you have searched the existing materials, ruled out the option of adapting them and decided to develop your own resources, it is necessary to consider various issues. First and foremost, remember that you are working under the direction of the teacher so you should discuss your ideas with them. The teacher will also indicate whether the resources will be effective for measuring achievement against the lesson objectives. The following sources will also provide ideas for learning materials which you can later confirm with the teacher:

- National Curriculum and programmes of study
- departmental schemes of work
- daily lesson plans from previous years.

Setting a deadline to confirm the resources before a session will give you the time to ascertain if they are suitable for use with the pupils you are supporting or whether they need to be adapted. For example, a pupil with cerebral palsy may find it easier to use a larger mouse during ICT due to difficulties with fine motor skills. You must be assertive when setting realistic deadlines for resource preparation. You may have more experience about the pupils' exact needs and you need to ensure teachers are aware how much time is needed to prepare learning materials.

Once you have decided on appropriate resources, you should familiarise yourself with their use in order that you can effectively support access to the curriculum area. For example, you may need to refresh your memory on how to use the digital camera for an ICT lesson. This is another reason why it is important to establish appropriate deadlines so that you give yourself adequate time to test and acquaint yourself with resources.

K8 K9 Case study

Confirming materials required and establishing realistic deadlines

Your school is campaigning for the local council to provide a school bus and has decided a broad cross-curricular project could be completed by Year 10 (S4) pupils. A travel survey will be completed as well as a public survey on opinions. Some pupils will contact local schools with mini-buses to gauge both pupil and staff opinion about the use of a mini-bus. The data collection is to be discussed during Citizenship. Percentages and data-handling will be covered in Maths. The school also wants to take a multi-media approach and produce a video campaign during ICT. All Year 10 (S4) pupils will take part and there are a range of cognitive learning needs such as dyslexia, etc.

- Why is it important to confirm the materials to be used with the teacher?
- Why is it important to establish realistic deadlines for providing information and materials?

Advance preparation will also allow you to consider any health and safety issues that may arise, for example from the use of Design Technology resources. You may have to prepare additional resources such as goggles to ensure health and safety.

Finally, you may wish to consider how certain resources could affect group dynamics, for example how an active experiment can over-excite pupils or highlight difficulties in sharing. In considering the potential group dynamics in advance, you can consider the strategies you will use to manage groups effectively should any problems arise.

How to deal with competing demands for information and materials

As departments must remain within their agreed annual financial budgets there may only be a limited supply of resources for the relevant curriculum area. It is therefore useless for you to draw up a wish list for unattainable resources and materials. Instead, you must work with what is available within the boundaries of your department. Also bear in mind that existing resources do not last forever. Constant use will take its toll and you should consider how resources can be protected to minimise the unintentional damage from daily wear and tear.

Added pressures are caused if departmental resources are lost or pupils forget to bring back books and equipment they have taken home. Unfortunately intentional damage may also be caused to materials by pupils with 'tags' and other graffiti.

Keys to good practice
Overcoming limitations on resources
✓ Have a tracking system to ensure that all the resources given out are given back. Should each resource have a number? Can items be signed in and out?
✓ Understand and sympathise with any limitations on resources caused by minimal departmental budgets.
✓ Have strategies to protect existing resources, for example laminate handouts or cover text books.
✓ Have sanction systems in place to deter consistent loss or intentional damage to resources.
✓ Could you carry a toolbox with you? For example, a Maths toolbox might contain a pairs of compasses, ruler, pencils, protractors, number squares, etc.
✓ Can you make copies of materials (bearing in mind any copyright restrictions)?
✓ Can you make resources that can be reused?
✓ Can resources be recycled, for example displays from the previous year?

Typical areas of interest of different people within the subject/curriculum area

As well as HLTAs and specialist technicians, you may be able to turn to different members of staff within the department for different types of support. For example, in PE there may be different specialists for rugby, hockey and/or gymnastics. In

Science there will be specialists in biology, chemistry and physics. In the Languages department there will be different modern foreign language specialists and there may also be specialists in other community languages. Even two members of staff who both specialise in literature may have different areas of specialist knowledge; one may focus on Shakespeare and the other on war poetry. It is therefore important that you turn to the appropriate person for the specialist knowledge you seek.

What to do should information and materials requested lie outside your area of responsibility or ability

If at any time you are unsure of how to use equipment or resources, you may need to turn to other staff members for help. For example, you may not know how to use the digital camera or some of the ICT software programs used by pupils. In such cases the subject teacher could be your first point of contact, although remember that some departments, such as Science or Design Technology, may have their own technicians with specialist knowledge about equipment or resources. Other schools may have HLTAs who are specialists in certain areas such as ICT and can offer you the support you need. Failing this, you may also be able to organise some informal training with the subject co-ordinator.

The above sources of support also apply with regard to the use of any equipment, resources or materials that lie outside your area of responsibility, such as first aid materials or chemicals used in Science.

It is important not to use equipment, resources or materials that you are not confident with or do not have the authority to use. Also bear in mind that some, especially equipment such as Design Technology drills, may necessitate health and safety training before you can use them.

K7
K12
K13

Case study

Working within the boundaries of your competence

You have been asked to prepare the Science classroom for a Year 9 (S3) experiment on the chemical reactions that take place when fuel burns. Pupils are to work together to burn items containing hydrogen and carbon. The teacher has asked you to prepare materials such as wax, wood, ethanol and a range of foods. You are confident in the preparation of Bunsen burners and fuel containers and you have enough old candles to bring in from home. However, there is little wood and you have not heard of ethanol. Moreover, one pupil is on the autistic spectrum and, although exceptionally bright, doesn't work well collaboratively.

- What materials should you go ahead and prepare?
- Who can you turn to for help with the materials that are missing or that you do not feel competent using?
- If a member of staff is not available, what other sources of help can you use?
- Who could you turn to for help on how best to support the pupil with special needs?

How to research subject-specific information and materials relevant to the age range you work with

With the new personalisation agenda, following the Every Child Matters framework, more emphasis is being placed on personalising the educational experience of each pupil to ensure conducive learning experiences for all. To be inclusive all information and materials should take into account the learning needs of the pupils, the best format in which to present the information and the pupils' linguistic and cultural backgrounds. To achieve all of this it is necessary to be efficient and systematic when researching relevant subject-specific information.

Researching relevant information efficiently and accurately

The way you research information about a curriculum area will depend on the resources available to you and your personal preferences. However, to research efficiently, ensure you use the appropriate source for the type of information you seek. For example, the radio or daily newspapers will not be the best source of information for the collection of evidence about past events. It is also important to understand that some sources contain bias and stereotypes. To ensure valid, reliable and accurate sources of information, you also need to be able to differentiate between fact and opinion. You also need to decide when it is appropriate to use **primary** or **secondary sources of information**.

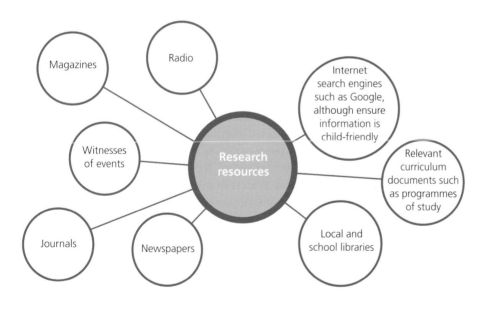

◄**Figure 28.3** Information can be obtained from a range of resources

Why you should maintain a record of sources of information and how to do so

When searching for information that may be referred to later, it is important to record the sources in order to ensure the information:

- is at an appropriate level for the target age group
- is appropriate for pupils with different learning needs and styles

- is deemed safe and has been approved for use by the school
- is culturally and linguistically appropriate
- is reliable and trustworthy, providing the objective facts (or is it full of bias, opinion and subjective information?)
- can easily be located again to save valuable time
- readily accessible to information if you are concerned about plagiarism.

Sources of information can be recorded in different ways on paper or electronically. They could be included at the end of a piece of work or kept on a logging or alphabetical filing system.

How to select and prepare teaching and learning materials to meet the needs of the pupils involved

When selecting and preparing learning materials for one pupil or a group with specific learning needs, any IEPs will suggest strategies and resources to use. You can also speak to the SENCo (ASL teacher), who will be able to inform you of suitable resource options. You will need to consider preferred learning styles, for example a pupil who is a visual learner may benefit from using a DVD. You may also consider the social and emotional needs of pupils, for example to establish whether a pupil would benefit from a collaborative learning experience such as a game. Finally, in order for learning materials to provide concrete learning experiences, they should also be culturally and linguistically relevant to the audience.

How to organise information for different audiences

The way you organise or present information will depend on the intended audience. For pupils, information must be age appropriate and appeal in terms of language, ability, knowledge and skills. Information presented in the subjunctive tense to a Year 7 (S1) French class that is just beginning to master the present tense will be meaningless. A Year 8 (S2) English class will probably find information in *The Guardian* much more difficult to process than information in a teen magazine. The older pupils are, the more complex the information and its presentation can be, whereas younger pupils need information to be simpler in content and structure. However, also be aware that some pupils, whether gifted or with special needs, will respond better to information that is presented in a way that suits their particular learning needs rather than in the same way as for their peers. Subject teachers and curriculum documents will be able to provide you with guidance.

At times you may be asked to present information to adults, for example, during a staff meeting or training sessions. Do not assume that organising and presenting information for adults will be an easier task. To present the information effectively you still need to consider different learning styles, preferences and needs just as you do for pupils.

Remember that different learning styles can go beyond the simplistic view of visual, auditory, kinaesthetic and tactile. For example, some pupils learn more effectively in team activities in collaboration with others. Others may learn better if they are given time to reflect on their own first. Some pupils may be linguistically intelligent or prefer a mathematical approach. So think about the specific needs of the pupils you work with and discuss these with the teacher before deciding how to present information.

You will need to find sources of information and resources to suit the different learning styles. Visual learners will prefer images, diagrams, charts; audio learners will need lectures, story tapes and radio extracts; and kinaesthetic learners will need to

gather the information through their own experience or experiments. Most learners probably fall into more than one category and you should also consider multi-sensory approaches and sources of information such as video materials, web conferences and DVDs.

▲ **Figure 28.4** Information can be presented by and to children in a number of ways

K18 K19

Portfolio activity

Presenting information for pupils with special educational (ASL) needs

Think about a curriculum area you currently work in and prepare a collection of information and materials for a specific topic, for example on monarchs for a Year 7 (S1) History project. Outline how to best present the information to pupils with particular special educational (ASL) needs such as:

- visual impairment
- hearing impairment
- dyslexia
- low phonological awareness.

How to identify and develop culturally and linguistically appropriate teaching and learning materials

Make sure you know about the cultural and linguistic backgrounds of the pupils you support. Try to develop a repertoire of basic words and phrases such as 'hello', 'how are you', 'goodbye' in the relevant languages. Make sure you are aware of any cultural stereotypes and bias, so that you can deal with them if they occur.

Making materials culturally and linguistically relevant does not mean including less content or making it less challenging; all culturally and linguistically relevant material needs to be as rich as any other. Listen carefully to pupils and be sensitive to their perspectives, norms, values and preferences. Involve them in selecting their own culturally appropriate resources. If you are unable to involve them, there may be other sources within the school or wider community you can turn to for help.

Culturally and linguistically relevant material will enhance self-concept and motivation to learn and ensure that pupils have their own local context and real-life examples to turn to when attempting to understand theoretical or difficult abstract concepts. Multicultural resources make individuals feel valued.

Keys to good practice
Selecting and developing materials to meet objectives

✓ Start with simple activities and move to more complex tasks.
✓ Start with general examples and move to more specific areas.
✓ Use previously learned knowledge to move from the known to the unknown.
✓ Decide how materials will assess learning against objectives.
✓ What level of cognitive skills or question types are necessary to achieve the learning objectives?
✓ Link specific parts of the activity to specific objectives.
✓ Consider optimum presentation in the form of text, images, graphic and multimedia elements.

School/departmental procedures for maintaining records of the information and materials obtained and developed

Your school may have a departmental resource room that has clearly labelled resources and materials. It may also have a signing-in and out system to keep track of who is using resources and where they are being used. Some departments store resources in alphabetical order or in topic locations, such as items for special educational (ASL) needs or culturally and linguistically relevant resources. There may be a sharing tray for ideas and resources that have been developed by other members of staff. Departmental schemes of work and daily lesson plans will also record the types of materials used.

Having stock control methods in place will not only make it easier to locate resources, but it will also make internal stock audits more manageable. If such a system does not exist, perhaps you could suggest introducing a new system.

For your portfolio...

K1
K2
K3
K4
K5
K6
K7

Obtain a range of schemes of work from the different subjects you support.
Highlight and annotate the following points:

- examples of age-related expectations, noting whether or not pupils you support are achieving these targets or not
- examples of how cross-curricular opportunities have been built into the schemes of work
- areas you feel most confident supporting
- areas you need further training in
- areas you would feel confident delivering staff training in.

This portfolio activity can cover a range of performance criteria depending on your answers to the task.

Websites

www.classroom-assistant.net

www.curriculumonline.gov.uk

www.dfes.gov.uk

www.learningsupport.co.uk

www.napta.org.uk

www.qca.org.uk/14-19

www.rlo-cetl.ac.uk

www.tda.gov.uk

www.teachernet.gov.uk

30 Contribute to Assessment for Learning

Assessment for learning informs and promotes the achievement of all pupils as it encourages them to take responsibility for their own learning. The process involves explaining learning outcomes to pupils, giving them feedback on their progress and enabling them to develop their self-assessment skills so that they are ultimately able to reflect on and recognise their achievements.

As part of this process, first of all you need to know the kinds of strategies that teachers use to inform assessment. You will then need to show how you involve pupils in checking and reviewing their progress and enable them to apply self-assessment strategies to check their learning as they work.

What you need to know and understand

For this unit you will need to know and understand:

- The teacher's responsibility for assessing pupil achievement and your role in supporting this

- The difference between formative and summative assessment

- *The basic principles of how children and young people learn* (See Unit 24, page 161)

- The inter-relationship between motivation and self-esteem, effective learning and progress, and assessment for learning

- *The relevant school curriculum and age-related expectations of pupils in the subject/curriculum area and age range of the pupils with whom you are working* (See Unit 18, page 33)

- The importance of having high expectations of pupils and how this is demonstrated through your practice

- The importance of believing that every pupil can improve in comparison with previous achievements and the implications of this for how you support pupils' learning

- The strategies and techniques for supporting assessment for learning which are within your role and sphere of competence

- The importance of working within the boundaries of your role and competence and when you should refer to others

- How to communicate clearly and objectively with pupils about their learning goals and achievements

- How to encourage pupils to keep in mind their learning goals and to assess their own progress to meeting these as they proceed

- How to support pupils in becoming active learners who can take increasing responsibility for their own progress

- How to review and reflect on pupils' performance and progress

- How to provide constructive feedback to pupils

- How to help pupils to review their learning strategies and achievements and plan future learning

- *The importance of active listening and how to do this* (See Unit 18, page 47)

- Self-assessment techniques and how to support pupils in developing these

- How to promote the skills of collaboration in peer assessment

- How assessment for learning contributes to planning for future learning carried out by:
  - the teacher
  - the pupils
  - yourself

- How to reflect on and learn from experience

Teacher's responsibility for assessing pupil achievement and your role in supporting this

One of the main responsibilities of the class teacher is to monitor and assess pupil achievement. They need to know how all pupils in their class are progressing and be able to report back to parents and other staff. Assessment is an ongoing process, which takes different forms, and in your role as a teaching assistant you need to be able to support teachers with the process.

Teachers plan lessons and schemes of work, which should set out clear **learning objectives** so that learner progress can be measured. The pupils and adults in the class will need to be clear about what the learning objectives are and it is good practice for teachers to set out and display them at the start of each session. In this way you can share with the pupils what they are going to learn as well as having a clear understanding of the objectives you are supporting.

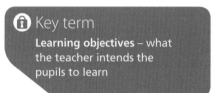

🔒 Key term

Learning objectives – what the teacher intends the pupils to learn

The difference between formative and summative assessment

As learning takes place you will need to measure pupil learning against these objectives using ongoing methods of assessment. These are known as formative assessment methods and can be used to check the learning in any lesson.

Formative assessment strategies

Using open-ended questions
This encourages pupils to put their ideas forward without being led by adults, for example 'Tell me how you are going to…'

Observing pupils
We gather much of our knowledge of how pupils are achieving through watching them work and noticing the kinds of strategies they use to work things out or what they find more difficult. This can take place on a daily basis or can be carried out more formally through direct observations.

Listening to how pupils describe their work and their reasoning
Through doing this, we are hearing about the methods that pupils use.

Checking pupils' understanding
You can do this by questioning pupils about their learning and asking them what they know.

Engaging pupils in reviewing progress
This should take place at the end of each session when pupils should be encouraged to think about what they have learned, measure it against the learning objectives and think about how they might apply this knowledge in the future.

Summative assessment

This is the other main form of assessment that teachers use to check learning. It occurs at the end of a term or scheme of work when it is important to know what pupils have achieved at a particular time. It could take the form of end of key stage SATs or an end of year school report, and informs various people about the level of a pupil's work. It could really be called assessment *of* learning.

Inter-relationship between motivation and self-esteem, effective learning and progress, and assessment for learning

Research has shown that there is a clear relationship between being part of the process of assessment and pupil motivation. Pupils who are actively engaged with their progress feel empowered to improve their performance as they feel more ownership of their learning. This in turn develops their self-esteem and motivation. Pupils who feel that they are not part of the learning process are far more likely to become disengaged and consequently lose interest. Effective feedback also ensures that adults are supporting more able as well as less able pupils by giving them the tools to achieve to the best of their potential. Assessment for learning is a device to enable pupils to understand the aim of what they are doing, what they need to do to reach that aim and where they are in relation to it.

K4 Case study

Encouraging motivation

Adam is in Year 11 (S5) and is a lively and happy boy. For some time, however, he has been finding school work challenging and has become less willing to participate, particularly in Maths lessons. When you have talked to him about it and tried to encourage him to carry on with his work, his response has been, 'I can't, Miss, I'm rubbish at Maths'.

- Outline how you could help Adam to regain his confidence and present some ideas you could work on with the class teacher.
- Why is it particularly important that you monitor Adam's progress in this case?

Importance of having high expectations of pupils and how this is demonstrated through your practice

As adults we should always have high expectations of pupils and communicate this to them. Pupils need to be encouraged to have pride in their achievements and be positive about their learning. If we fail to notice the efforts and achievements of pupils, they will lose their enthusiasm for learning. Research shows that if we expect more from pupils they will be more likely to be able to raise their attainment. Assessment for learning also supports the encouragement of high expectation by emphasising the achievement of pupils rather than focusing on what they can't do.

Having high expectations of pupils

Alice and Stephen are teaching assistants in two different Year 10 (S4) Art classes.

In Alice's class the teacher is often out of the classroom due to illness and other responsibilities in the school. There has been a series of supply teachers, which means that Alice is the only one who has got to know the pupils. Although she has tried to praise them as much as possible for their achievements, she has begun to feel that she is fighting a losing battle as the class are so unsettled. In Stephen's class, there is an enthusiastic teacher. He regularly praises pupils and gives them feedback on their learning, and his belief that all his pupils will do well is infectious.

One day, the teaching assistants have to swap and when they meet up at break they discuss the difference between the classes.

- Explain how the respective classes have been affected by the different circumstances.
- Why is it important for Alice's class that the school recognise and address what is happening?
- What would you do if you were in Alice's situation?

Importance of believing that every pupil can improve in comparison with previous achievements and the implications of this for how you support pupils' learning

An important aspect of assessment for learning is that pupils' progress is measured against their own previous achievements rather than compared to those of others. Pupils' learning should be set at a level that ensures that they are building on what they learn. This means that they should be starting from a point of previous understanding and then extending their learning to take in new information. Pupils benefit from discussing previous learning experiences to consolidate what they know and reinforce their understanding before moving on to take in new concepts and ideas. You need to encourage and motivate pupils, in particular if they are finding it difficult to understand or there are other factors impacting on their learning (see Unit 23, page 144 for examples). It is important that you show pupils that you believe in them and are able to support them as they start from what they know.

If you have pupils with low self-esteem and who prefer a particular style of learning, for example, audiovisual, you may need to adapt or modify what they have been asked to do in order to help them.

Case study

Supporting pupils to improve on previous achievements

Alex is working with a group that has been doing some sketches outside. She has been looking with them at how they should approach their work and Ros, in particular, has needed additional support because she tends to rush and then become frustrated. Alex has enlisted the help of Ben, one of Ros' friends, to help her think about what she needs to remember before starting the task. Alex has told Ros that if she thinks before rushing, she will be able to improve on her previous achievements and this might help her to feel happier about her work.

- How might this approach help Ros?
- Do you think it is beneficial to ask Ben to help?

Strategies and techniques for supporting assessment for learning which are within the boundaries of your role and competence, and when to refer to others

When supporting assessment for learning, you need to use a range of techniques and be aware of how they enhance the process, as well as know which are within your role and when to refer to others. You need to be able to use these techniques effectively when communicating with pupils so that they are able to reflect and build on their achievements.

As in all situations when supporting assessment for learning, you should be aware of when you should refer to others. If a pupil is having difficulties, which you are unable to resolve, you should always refer to the teacher. (For more on this, see Unit 18, page 45).

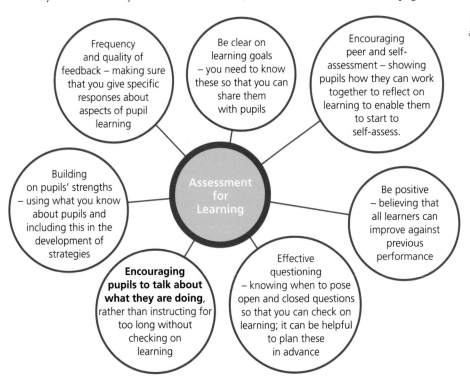

◀ Figure 30.1 Supporting assessment for learning

Techniques to support assessment

Mary is working with a group of pupils who have been looking at descriptive language in their writing. They are all working towards the learning objective to use a variety of descriptive words in creative writing. Mary has ensured that they all understand what they need to do.

- What kinds of strategies can Mary use to support the pupils as they work?
- What could Mary do if one of the pupils says that he is unable to think of any more ways to make his writing more descriptive?
- How could Mary extend the task if one of the pupils says that he has finished?

How to communicate clearly and objectively with pupils about their learning goals and achievements and to help them assess their own progress

When starting a new activity with pupils, you need to make sure that they are aware not only of the learning objective of the task but also that they keep in mind any additional personal **learning goals**. For example, pupils may have individual subject targets, which they are aware will be reviewed regularly with them in order to check their progress. They should also know the **success criteria** for the task, in other words the steps which they need to pass through to achieve their objectives. In addition, pupils with special educational (Additional Support for Learning) needs will have targets on their Individual Education Plans, which will also be reviewed on a regular basis and checked during learning if they are relevant to the task. This helps pupils with self-assessment as they are able to check whether they are meeting their individual targets.

> **🔒 Key terms**
>
> **Learning goals** – personalised learning targets for individual pupils, which relate to learning objectives and take account of the past achievements and current learning needs of the pupil
>
> **Success criteria** – summary of the key points that pupils need to understand as steps to success in achieving the learning objectives

Encouraging pupils to keep their goals in mind

In Maths in Year 8 (S2), Cheryl is supporting a group of pupils who have the same number targets for the term. Today they are working together to solve problems using travelling times and distance. The learning objective is to be able to choose and use appropriate operations to solve word problems. In addition, the pupils' specific number target is to be able to recall their times tables.

In order for the activity to meet the success criteria, the group need to think about the steps they must take to achieve the task successfully, as well as bearing in mind their own learning goals.

- How can Cheryl communicate clearly to the group what they have to do?
- What sort of encouragement could she give to ensure that pupils bear in mind both their targets and the learning objective?
- Could this task also be appropriate for pupils with different abilities?

How to support pupils in becoming active learners who can take increasing responsibility for their own progress

At the start of any activity, pupils need to be clear about what they are going to learn and how they will be assessed. For assessment for learning to be effective, pupils need to know *what* they are learning, *why* they are learning it and *how* assessment will take place. Pupils should discuss these with you at the start of each session and will need you to give them specific criteria against which their learning will be measured. As pupils take on more responsibility for their learning, they will find it easier to look at learning criteria to see whether these have been met. A simple example of this might be a literacy activity in which pupils are revising how to use semicolons and then filling in gaps in sentences to check their knowledge:

What pupils are learning	Where semicolons need to be applied
Why they are learning it	To enable them to use the correct form of written English
How assessment will take place	Teacher and teaching assistant will check that pupils are using semicolons correctly and consistently in their written work

K12 Portfolio activity

Supporting responsibility for own learning

Using examples from your own experience, describe how you have supported pupils to enable them to take on more responsibility for their own learning and become more active learners.

How to review and reflect on pupils' performance and progress

In order to help you to review pupil's progress, it may be helpful for you to follow a checklist like this.

- Ensure pupils understand the learning objectives and any individual learning goals.
- Tell pupils what they have to do and whether they need to hand work in.
- Inform pupils how they will be assessed and ensure they understand.
- Give examples of work produced by other learners if possible so that pupils can see how the assessment criteria are applied.
- Provide individual support and oral feedback as pupils are working.
- Ensure there are opportunities for either peer or self-assessment.
- Assess pupils' work when complete.
- Provide written feedback.

You do not need to use all the points above, but they are indicators for you to make sure you have not missed any of the opportunities to support assessment for learning.

Supporting pupils through learning activities

Using the list above as a guide, reflect on how you have supported either an individual or a group of pupils through a learning activity.

How to provide constructive feedback to pupils

For assessment for learning to be effective, it is essential that pupils receive constructive feedback from adults that focuses on their strengths, as well as support and guidance through any difficulties they may have. You need to give feedback that:

- gives information that focuses on performance
- is delivered positively
- is not personal, but based on facts.

There are different types of feedback to give pupils during and following learning activities.

- **Affirmation feedback** – this should be delivered as soon as possible, for example, 'Well done, you remembered to include all the points we discussed!' This type of feedback helps to motivate pupils.
- **Developmental feedback** – this kind of feedback suggests what to do next time, for example, 'Nathan, try to remember to get all the equipment you need before starting the activity.'

Both types of feedback can be written or oral, but to be effective it should be given as promptly as possible. If feedback is given too long after an activity has been completed, pupils find it harder to apply it to their learning. This may be particularly true in the case of marking, which should be done as soon as possible after an activity is completed, if possible with the pupil present.

> **? Thinking point**
> Think about and discuss in groups feedback you remember receiving when you were at school. Possibly you received feedback that focused on negative rather than positive points. What effect did this have on you as a learner?

Keys to good practice

Providing feedback

✓ Remain non-judgemental.
✓ Focus on strengths.
✓ Work through one thing at a time.
✓ Give constructive advice where needed and guidance on how a pupil can improve.
✓ Make sure feedback is directly linked to what has been observed or written.
✓ End positively.

Case study

Providing constructive feedback

You have been working with a group of pupils who are finding a task quite difficult. You have tried praising them for the work they have done so far, but they are continuing to struggle and you are concerned that they might not want to continue.

- What kind of feedback should you be giving the group?
- Outline the steps you might go through to encourage them back on task.

How to help pupils to review their learning strategies and achievements and plan future learning

It is good practice at the end of any session for adults to review with pupils what they have learned, but this can be harder for you to do in some learning situations than in others. This may be due to time, but might also be due to the way in which the activity was presented to pupils. Where possible, you encourage pupils to measure their achievements against the learning objectives and think about how they might approach their learning in the future based on this. For example, this might be part of the plenary at the end of lessons, where pupils are asked to think about their learning and apply it to different situations. This may be part of a whole class discussion or pupils may work in groups on reviewing their learning as a matter of course. In design activities, pupils are usually asked to review their learning and think about how they might approach the task differently if they did it again. However, not all activities lend themselves to review so easily.

Case study

Helping pupils review their achievements and plan future learning

Think about the following activities:

- a walk to look at building materials in the local environment and evaluate whether they are the most effective for the buildings selected
- making biscuits with a group of pupils
- a group project on the Roman invasion
- a series of Maths investigations around data handling.

What challenges might there be to pupils reviewing these activities? How could you build in a way of supporting pupils through the review process and plan for future learning?

Self-assessment techniques and how to support pupils in developing these

When supporting pupils during self-assessment, you need to structure learning activities so that their purpose and outcomes are very clear. The younger the child, the more you may need to do this. However, if pupils understand *why* they are doing something, it is far more likely that they will want to learn. Pupils will need to look at simple specific criteria to start with so that they can measure their learning against this. Self-assessment for younger children is more difficult and it will be better for them to start with peer assessment to encourage them to think about learning aims. Older pupils will also benefit from using peer assessment as a starting point (see below).

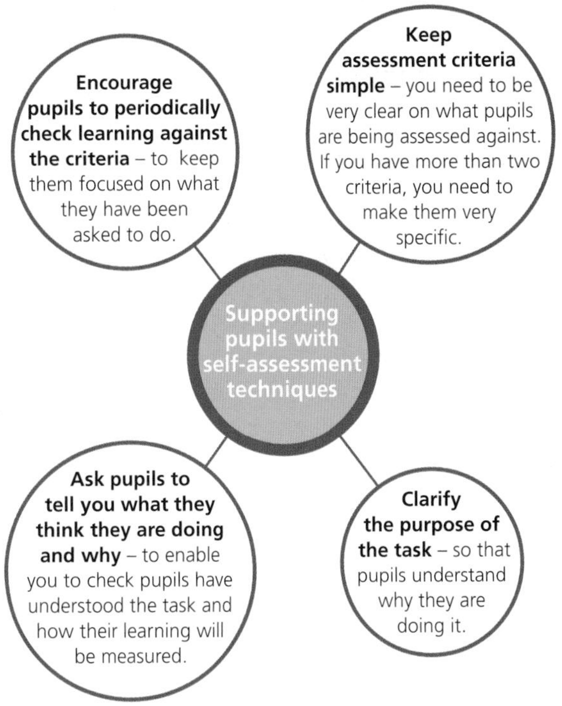

How to promote the skills of collaboration in peer assessment

Pupils will build up their assessment techniques through working with adults and their peers so that they can ultimately begin to assess their own learning against learning outcomes and to look more objectively at their achievements. Peer assessment is not supposed to compare pupils' achievements or cause them to grade one another according to their performance. For this reason it is very important that pupils are clear on what they will be assessed against. They should look at one another's work and notice how it relates to the assessment criteria. They can discuss what they have been asked to do and how their work reflects this. This starts to bring their attention to what teachers are looking for when measuring achievement.

Through looking at the work of others, they may be able to see more easily how assessment criteria can be used to measure learning.

Encourage pupils to periodically check learning against the criteria – to keep them focused on what they have been asked to do.

Keep assessment criteria simple – you need to be very clear on what pupils are being assessed against. If you have more than two criteria, you need to make them very specific.

Supporting pupils with self-assessment techniques

Ask pupils to tell you what they think they are doing and why – to enable you to check pupils have understood the task and how their learning will be measured.

Clarify the purpose of the task – so that pupils understand why they are doing it.

▲ Figure 30.2 Pupils need to develop their self-assessment skills

Case study

K17
K18

You have been asked to work with a Year 7 (S1) Art class and support them as they critically evaluate their own work against a list of assessment criteria. They are working on a series of activities to look at the local environment and record sketches of details in building, such as patterns, textures and other details. The assessment criteria have been defined as:

1. choose six interesting features of the local environment and record them in your sketch book
2. look at proportions, lines and shapes, and draw attention to these
3. show two ways in which light has affected the different features.

- How would you start pupils off so that they were not asked to self-evaluate straightaway?
- How could this start as a peer assessment and then move on to a self-assessment activity?
- How would you ensure that you did not emphasise pupils' weaknesses and damage their self esteem?

How assessment for learning contributes to planning for future learning

Assessment for learning must by definition contribute to future planning for all who are involved in the learning process. As such, it is a valuable tool and it means that all concerned learn from the experience.

- **For the teacher** – Effective assessment for learning enables them over time to pass on the responsibility for managing their own learning to the pupil so that they become more actively involved in the process.
- **For the pupil** – The process informs pupils about how they approach learning and tackle areas they need to work on. They can consider areas for improvement by looking at assessment criteria and develop their ability to self-assess. Their increased awareness of how to learn will develop their confidence and help them to recognise when to ask for support.
- **For you** – Assessment for learning will inform how you approach pupil questioning based on what you have discovered about how they learn. You may need to pace the progress of learners depending on their needs so that less able pupils are given opportunities to revisit areas of uncertainty.

How to reflect on and learn from experience

You need to be able to reflect on your own learning and experience when supporting pupil learning so that you can adjust your approach if necessary. You should think about the following areas and how they went:

- how you questioned pupils
- how you gave feedback to pupils
- how you supported both peer and self-assessment.

You may also need to discuss the pupils' responses to the process with the teacher as some will have found it easier to manage than others. Depending on the ages and needs of the pupils, the use of peer or self-assessment may need to be amended.

K1, K6, K7, K8, K10, K11, K12, K13, K14, K15, K16, K17, K18

For your portfolio...

In order to gather evidence for this unit, it would be helpful if your assessor could witness you planning and carrying out an assessment for learning lesson in which you are encouraging pupils to look at their progress against learning objectives and their own personal targets. If you can also encourage pupils to review their work, this will enable you to gather evidence for much of the performance criteria, K1, K6–8, K10–16 and possibly K17 or K18.

Websites

www.qca.org.uk – the QCA website has plenty of information and references around assessment for learning and suggestions for further reading

www.teachers.tv/video/3311 – Teachers' TV

34 Support Gifted and Talented Pupils

As part of your teaching assistant role, you may be required to support gifted and talented pupils. This may be through the support you give to individuals within the class or through work with groups from different year groups. You will need to work with others to develop learning programmes for these pupils to increase their opportunities and ensure that they are challenged within the class. You may also be asked to support gifted and talented pupils who have additional needs such as behavioural difficulties or speech and language disorders as they also need to have access to learning programmes that enrich and extend their learning. Professionals both within and outside the school will be able to help with the identification and support you provide for such pupils.

What you need to know and understand

For this unit, you will need to know and understand:

- The nature and boundaries of your role in supporting gifted and talented pupils, and its relationship to the role of the teacher and others in the school

- The importance of having high expectations of pupils with whom you work and how this is demonstrated through your practice

- The relevant school curriculum and age-related expectations of pupils, including learning objectives for older aged pupils than the age of those with whom you work

- School policies for inclusion and equality of opportunity and the implication of these for how you support gifted and talented pupils

- The role of others in planning and delivery of learning programmes for gifted and talented pupils and the particular benefits and strengths which each brings to the process

- The purpose of clarifying your own role and that of others in meeting the needs of gifted and talented pupils

- The principles underlying effective communication, planning and collaboration

- The benefits of acting as a co-learner rather than supporter or 'teacher' of gifted and talented pupils and how to do this

- The resources (people, equipment and materials, including ICT) that are available to enrich learning for gifted and talented pupils and how to make effective use of these

- The importance of starting pupils on a task at an appropriate level of difficulty, using challenging questions to deepen thinking, and extending and opening up tasks

- Strategies for challenging and motivating gifted and talented pupils to work in more depth, in a broader range of contexts and at a faster pace

- How to negotiate learning objectives with pupils

- The importance of independent learning for gifted and talented pupils and how to encourage and support this in pupils

- How to help pupils to reflect on their learning strategies and achievements and plan future learning

- The opportunities for learning outside of the classroom, school and school day to enable pupils to develop their particular gifts or talents and how to support pupils in accessing these

Nature and boundaries of your role in supporting gifted and talented pupils, and its relationship to the role of the teacher and others in the school

The **Gifted** and **Talented** Programme was introduced in 1999 to ensure that schools were doing as much as possible to identify and provide for those pupils who are working at a higher level than their peers. The 2005 White Paper *Better Schools For All* also reinforced the idea that all children, whatever their needs, should be given personalised support in order to maximise their achievements. It aims to reach the top 5–10 per cent of pupils in schools and to encourage the development of their skills and talents. You should understand the difference between the terms 'gifted' and 'talented' if you are asked to work with these pupils.

Your role when supporting gifted and talented pupils in school must be to enable them to achieve to the best of their ability. Working alongside the teacher, plan to use strategies that enable these pupils to develop the skills they have. If possible when you are planning, it would also be useful to have the input of the school's Gifted and Talented (G&T) Co-ordinator who may be able to give you additional suggestions. You may be asked to carry out learning activities with these pupils in different ways.

Working within the class environment

This is the ideal way of working with gifted and talented pupils as it does not single them out. Also, by keeping them with their peers, you will encourage others to develop their own skills.

Taking small groups to work outside the class

This is usually done by a specialist teacher and groups may contain pupils from several classes or year groups. However, you may be asked to work with pupils to give them more focused opportunities to work with others who have also been identified as higher achievers. In this situation you should be given activities to carry out and not have to devise them yourself.

Recognising gifted and talented pupils

You may feel that you are working with pupils who are gifted and talented, but who have not yet been recognised. This is possible because although the school should be

▼ **Figure 34.1** Do you know any children who are gifted and talented?

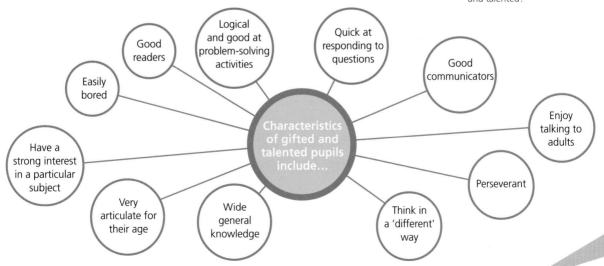

- Good readers
- Logical and good at problem-solving activities
- Quick at responding to questions
- Good communicators
- Easily bored
- Enjoy talking to adults
- Have a strong interest in a particular subject
- **Characteristics of gifted and talented pupils include...**
- Perseverant
- Very articulate for their age
- Wide general knowledge
- Think in a 'different' way

constantly looking out for these pupils, their abilities may become more apparent as they move through the school.

Pupils will not show all of the characteristics in the diagram, but just one or two may be indicators that a pupil is particularly able. If you suspect that a pupil in your class is showing some of these indicators, take note of some examples you have noticed and then either speak to the class teacher or the school's G&T Co-ordinator.

Importance of having high expectations of pupils

There should be a climate of high expectation in schools. All staff should have high expectations of pupils and demonstrate this by challenging and encouraging them to develop higher level thinking skills where possible (see page 206). All pupils, not just the gifted and talented, should be told that they can achieve at a high level (See also Unit 18, page 32). In this way pupils will be encouraged to develop their self-esteem and self-belief. Opportunities for pupils to work and experiment should be part of the curriculum so those who find written work more challenging are able to use their knowledge and skills in different ways. It is also particularly important that gifted or talented but disadvantaged pupils are encouraged so that their aspirations are raised.

K2 Case study

Encouraging pupils to achieve at a high level

Immi has had long periods of illness and spent a lot of time in hospital. She has recently started in Form 8R after missing the first two months. As the teaching assistant who supports Form 8R as a co-tutor, you say to the tutor that you are sure that Immi will find the work difficult because she has missed so much school. Her Year 7 (S1) tutor says that she has never been good at writing or Maths and seems easily distracted. However, even after a few days with Immi, you realise that she is a particularly good reader who is articulate and keen to talk about activities she has done in class. She enjoys activities that are practical and enable her to work logically and tells you that she is a member of the school chess club. You ask the Maths teacher whether you can carry out some problem-solving activities with Immi to challenge her and find that she scores highly even though she did not achieve particularly well in her Key Stage 2 SATS.

- Why do you think Immi's potential has not been picked up before?
- How could you encourage and challenge Immi and help to enrich her learning experience?

Relevant school curriculum and age-related expectations of pupils, including learning objectives for older aged pupils than the age of those with whom you work

Whatever age or ability of pupils you are supporting, you need to know the relevant school curriculum and the level at which pupils should be working (see also Unit 18, page 33). In this way you can identify those pupils whose abilities and interests are beyond those normally expected of the age range. It may also be helpful to have some idea of the way in which the curriculum develops so that you can draw on further ideas to help you with planning. The National Curriculum programmes of study, for example, give ideas for progression within different activities, which are useful when supporting Literacy and Mathematics. However, bear in mind that academically gifted pupils should be challenged by broadening and enriching their learning experience as much as possible before taking them to the next level.

School policies for inclusion and equality of opportunity and the implication of these for how you support gifted and talented pupils

Your school equal opportunities or inclusion policy will give details of expectations when supporting gifted and talented pupils. Equal opportunities are the right of every child and it is important that schools make provision for those pupils who have particular talents and abilities.

Pupils who speak English as an additional language or have special educational (Additional Support for Learning (ASL)) needs may also be identified as being gifted and talented, and should be supported appropriately. They may need to access support through different means than other pupils especially if they are gifted and talented in their home language.

> **?** Thinking point…
>
> The school has a 'gifted and talented register', which is updated regularly and staff, parents and pupils are aware of this. One aim is that the register should be amended on a regular basis as pupils develop their skills and abilities. Think about pupils who might have been put on the register and then removed from it later.
> • What might the school say to their parents?
> • How might these pupils be affected?

▼ **Figure 34.2** Gifted and talented pupils should work with their classmates as much as possible

Portfolio activity

Investigating policies that support gifted and talented pupils

Using your school's equal opportunities policy or a policy document, find out about and record what provision your school makes for gifted and talented pupils. If you are unable to obtain a copy or do not have a G&T Co-ordinator in your school, ask your headteacher for information about your school's gifted and talented cluster group and how local schools support one another.

Role of others in planning and delivery of learning programmes for gifted and talented pupils and the particular benefits and strengths which each brings to the process

When planning to support their needs, the first person you should get to know is the gifted and talented pupil. Through speaking to them and discussing their interests, you will develop a picture of what they are like and what motivates them. You may also need to work with their parents so that you can discuss with them any specific issues concerning the pupil. They will know their child best and may be able to give you information that will help you.

The staff members you should go to include your school's G&T Co-ordinator. Their role is to keep an up-to-date list of those pupils who demonstrate through testing, teacher observation or enthusiasm and willingness to learn that they are working at a higher level than their peers. This co-ordinator will be used to working with gifted and talented pupils and devising extension activities alongside other staff. They will therefore be skilled at helping you to find ways to broaden and enrich the activities you are carrying out with pupils. Your school's Special Educational Needs Co-ordinator (SENCo)(ASL teacher) may also be able to help as they should have experience in managing gifted and talented programmes within school. Previous class teachers are also likely to be a source of help as they may be able to tell you what has interested pupils in the past and the kind of work that has stimulated them.

Purpose of clarifying your own role and that of others in meeting the needs of gifted and talented pupils

When working with these pupils you need to be sure that you know how much and how often support should be in place, and whether you are working to specific targets that will be monitored. You need to clarify, either through the class teacher or the G&T Co-ordinator, how your work with pupils will meet their needs most effectively. You should also know how often you can speak to others in order to check on pupil progress and seek additional support if needed.

Clarifying the role

Warren has been asked by his class teacher to work with two gifted and talented pupils in a Year 10 (S4) Drama class. He is new to the class and has not worked with the pupils before. The teacher has set aside some time for general planning with Warren to help him think of ways in which he can best support the pupils' needs.

- What kinds of questions should Warren be asking the class teacher in order to clarify his role?
- How else could he gather information in order to help with the planning process?

Principles underlying effective communication, planning and collaboration

Planning with teachers is always important for support staff, but when working with gifted and talented pupils you need to be able to identify how you will broaden and enrich their learning experiences. If you have not targeted these pupils before, ask for specific support from school staff. Through effective communication with others, you will be able to draw on their experiences and also talk through your own ideas.

Using effective communication

Joan has been asked to support Rajif in Year 11 (S5), who is preparing to go to a further education college. He is particularly able academically and the G&T Co-ordinator is working alongside Joan to set up contacts in his new college.

- Why should the school and college work together in this instance?
- Why is it important to have opportunities to discuss your approach with others?

Benefits of acting as a co-learner rather than supporter or 'teacher' of gifted and talented pupils and how to do this

When you are working with gifted and talented pupils and setting projects or tasks that require them to devise their own objectives and strategies, you will be acting as a co-learner rather than a facilitator. Pupils will be taking responsibility for their own learning and devising their own methods, which they will then be investigating.

You may also feel that the pupil you are supporting is more knowledgeable than you – it is perfectly acceptable to say 'Let's try to find out together' if you do not know the answer yourself. Your role in this situation will be more about targeting questions to encourage them to think about their learning and develop their own ideas. It may be more appropriate to use language such as 'What are we trying to find out?' or 'What can we do to help us?' rather than using the term 'you', so that the process is seen as a shared experience. Pupils will also benefit from the feeling of learning being a process of discovery, rather than something adults know already and they have to find out.

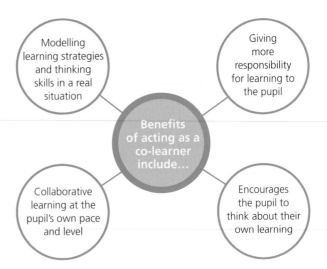

Modelling learning strategies and thinking skills in a real situation

Giving more responsibility for learning to the pupil

Benefits of acting as a co-learner include…

Collaborative learning at the pupil's own pace and level

Encourages the pupil to think about their own learning

▲ Figure 34.3 As a teaching assistant you may act as a co-learner to a gifted and talented child

Resources that are available to enrich learning for gifted and talented pupils and how to make effective use of these

Your school's G&T Co-ordinator and your local authority should be able to give you information about the resources and equipment that are available in your local area. You may also be able to find out about others through research or your own contacts. There are a number of useful websites offering activities and ideas for additional resources (see page 211).

You may be able to use equipment and resources that are used by older pupils if these are appropriate to support the work you are doing.

(see page 211).

K9 # Case study

Making effective use of additional resources

Jez is in Year 9 (S3) and is a talented sportsman. He is particularly good at tennis. As a member of your local tennis club you have a number of contacts and are aware that there is a professional there who gives coaching.

- What could you do to help Jez and who could you approach in school to help you?
- How could you find out about any additional support for Jez?

Importance of starting pupils on a task at an appropriate level of difficulty, using challenging questions to deepen thinking, and extending and opening up tasks

All pupils need to be given tasks that give them opportunities to deepen their thinking. In 1956 Benjamin Bloom, alongside a group of psychologists, devised a classification of levels (taxonomy) by which intelligent thought can be measured. These range from simple recall of knowledge at the lowest level to the gradual development of more complex and abstract ideas leading to evaluation.

The tasks you carry out with pupils should be based on a mixture of activities that enable lower achievers to succeed in the more accessible areas, while those who are able to think at a higher level are also challenged.

Pupils who are academically gifted should be given opportunities to think about how they can apply what they know to different situations. Pupils who are only ever asked to recall knowledge or answer comprehension questions are not being challenged to develop these skills. In your school, you should be able to see the range of ways in which problems and investigations reflect the series of higher level thinking skills using Bloom's criteria.

Bloom's taxonomy

Look at the questions and statements below and try to place them on the appropriate level in Bloom's taxonomy.

- How old are you?
- Have you any brothers and sisters?
- When is your mum's birthday?
- Tell me the way to the nearest shops.
- How would you work out the difference in age between you and your grandmother or grandfather?
- Give me instructions about how to boil an egg.
- Explain the reasons why you enjoy your favourite hobby.
- If you could change anything about school, what would it be?
- Design a menu that incorporates all your favourite foods.

In order to work out the appropriate level of questioning for a pupil or group, in the first instance always refer to the class teacher. You may also like to give pupils more challenging questions if they respond very easily to the simpler question structures to see whether they rise to the challenge.

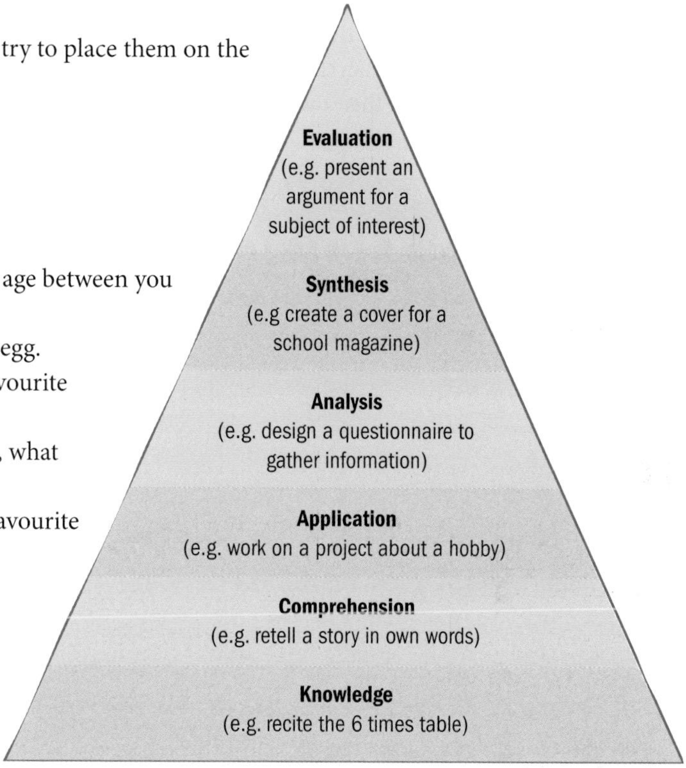

Evaluation (e.g. present an argument for a subject of interest)

Synthesis (e.g create a cover for a school magazine)

Analysis (e.g. design a questionnaire to gather information)

Application (e.g. work on a project about a hobby)

Comprehension (e.g. retell a story in own words)

Knowledge (e.g. recite the 6 times table)

▲ **Figure 34.4** There are many more examples and applications for Bloom's taxonomy on the Internet

Portfolio activity K10

Opening up tasks for more able pupils

Using examples from your school or the work you have done with pupils, show how the questioning which has been used has opened up the task for more able pupils. Give examples and show how pupils have benefited from deeper questioning.

Strategies for challenging and motivating gifted and talented pupils

If you are supporting gifted and talented pupils within the class, you need to be able to give them more challenging tasks, which are based on the same activities which are being carried out by the other pupils. The kinds of strategies you use will need to stretch them and deepen their learning experiences. They should be able to work on more open-ended tasks, which will give them opportunities to do the following:

- **Work in more depth** – Your group or pupil will need to have learning experiences that encourage them to think more and question why things happen, for example 'What might have made the Romans such ambitious and skilled builders?'
- **Work in a broader range of contexts** – Pupils should be encouraged to apply what they have learned to different contexts, for example to consider what would happen if different materials were used to make everyday objects.
- **Work at a faster pace** – As these pupils often have a greater understanding of new concepts and ideas than their peers, they need to have an environment that enables them to work at their own pace without standing out from others.

Keys to good practice
Suggestions for supporting gifted and talented pupils

✓ Speak to parents and offer suggestions about the kinds of activities they can do with their children.
✓ Question pupils in a way that deepens their thinking.
✓ Encourage pupils to find out a word or fact of the week and give them opportunities to feed back to others.
✓ Encourage them to try out new activities and experiences as well as focusing on their specific talents.
✓ Give them access to a range of games, logic puzzles or quizzes and ask them to devise their own.
✓ Talk to them about the importance of making mistakes and how they can learn from them.

K11 Case study
Using strategies for challenging gifted pupils

You are working with Hoi Ming in Year 11 (S5), who is particularly gifted. She always works quickly and quietly through her classwork and her behaviour is not a cause for concern. However the English teacher has said to you that he would like to set tougher challenges for her as he does not feel that she is given enough opportunities to develop and extend her thinking.

- How might you and the teacher devise activities for Hoi Ming that will motivate her?
- Is it necessary to give Hoi Ming different activities from the rest of the class?

How to negotiate learning objectives with pupils and promote independent learning

It is important for all pupils to be encouraged in their independence, and for gifted and talented pupils this means that they need to have opportunities to identify how they will measure their own learning (see also Unit 30, page 193). Where possible, encourage gifted and talented pupils to try to negotiate a learning objective around the work they are doing and then measure how this will be achieved. By setting their own criteria for measuring their learning, pupils are enabled to take more responsibility. An example of this might be a Science activity on freezing and melting materials. Pupils could be asked what they want to find out, for example at what temperature ice begins to melt. They could then devise a learning objective around this, for example 'To discover in which part of the classroom ice will start to melt first.' Following this pupils' success criteria might read:

- set up an investigation related to freezing or melting
- make the test fair (e.g. it starts at the same time and involves the same amount of ice)
- check the ice at the same time intervals
- select an appropriate unit of measurement (e.g. degrees Centigrade for temperature)
- record the findings in a suitable format.

Case study K12 K13

Negotiating learning objectives with pupils

Class 7F were asked to decide on a local traffic issue that they would like to investigate as part of a Geography project. They discussed a range of ideas and eventually narrowed these down to the problems that were caused by parking outside the school.

- What kinds of strategies could you use with pupils to encourage them to develop a series of stages for the project and to negotiate learning objectives?
- How could the pupils work together and use different activities to work through the project?

How to help pupils to reflect on their learning strategies and achievements and plan future learning

When you carry out learning activities with gifted and talented pupils, encourage them to think about their learning and whether the objectives were met. You might do this as a matter of routine at the end of each session, making sure that you ask them specific questions about how they arrived at their conclusions and how this might affect their learning in the future. You could also encourage them to discuss with each other the way in which they arrived at a particular conclusion so that they can evaluate different ways of tackling tasks. If working with a group, you could ask them to tell the rest of the class or school about the task and invite questions about the strategies they used or ask others to give them feedback.

Gifted and talented pupils may struggle with the concept of 'getting it wrong' sometimes. They may be so used to achieving that when tasks are more challenging or they are having difficulty, they become frustrated. This is another reason for setting them appropriate challenges. It is very important that these pupils understand the importance of learning through making mistakes and finding out that they may not always be the most able.

K14 Case study

Helping pupils reflect on their learning strategies

Each week Beth takes a group of four Year 8 (S2) pupils for investigation and problem-solving sessions during Maths. Today the group have been asked to find how many different ways they can fit 12 people into a bus with 24 seats. They then have to think of alternative seat layouts based on the size of the bus to see whether they would be able to fit more passengers in. At the end of the session, the pupils talk about how they have approached the task.

- How could Beth question the pupils to encourage them to reflect on the strategies they have used?
- How could she ask them how this might affect their approach to this kind of task in the future?

Opportunities for learning outside of the classroom, school and school day to enable pupils to develop their particular gifts or talents and how to support pupils in accessing these

Gifted and talented pupils should be given opportunities to develop their skills not only within the school but also through contact and liaison with outside organisations. If a pupil has a particular talent in Art, Sport or Music and does not have any outside encouragement, it is important that the school both investigates and suggests to parents how this might be accessed. It is particularly important that pupils from disadvantaged backgrounds are given some additional support to encourage them to participate in activities outside school. Some schools may have extended provision that gives pupils opportunities to develop their particular skills, while others might have access through their local cluster groups. Increasingly schools are working alongside local authorities to develop summer schools.

Case study K15

Supporting pupils' access to learning outside school

Becky is a talented musician. She has joined the school music club and always stays behind as long as possible following the sessions to talk to the teacher. She does not have any external contacts with musicians, but on talking to her you know that she would like to develop her skills further.

- How could you support Becky in getting access to further training?
- Where might you go in order to do this?

For your portfolio...

K1
K2
K5
K6
K9
K10
K11

Plan a series of activities to use with all pupils in the class based on a current topic which you are carrying out in your year group. Think specifically about the kinds of questions you might work on in order to encourage all pupils to achieve at the appropriate level. Explain what your role would be in these activities and how you would challenge and motivate pupils who are gifted and talented. Include any additional resources that you need to obtain in order to carry out the activities.

Websites

www.geoffpetty.com/downloads.html – Geoff Petty's Teaching Today website has plenty of useful information for teaching strategies.

www.gridclub.com – This website is a fun, cross-curricular online learning tool.

www.londongt.org/homepages/index.php – London Gifted and Talented site.

www.nagc.org – National Association for Gifted Children

www.nagty.ac.uk – National Academy for Gifted and Talented Youth

www.nc.uk.net/gt – The National Curriculum online has information about the identification of gifted and talented pupils.

www.standards.dfes.gov.uk/giftedandtalented

www.standards.dfes.gov.uk/primaryframeworks/ – The National Primary Framework also gives ideas for gifted and talented pupils.

www.teachers.tv/video/2518 – This has lots of information, suggestions, and videos to support the learning of gifted and talented pupils.

35 Support Bilingual/ Multilingual Pupils

This unit is for staff who support bilingual and multilingual pupils in the target language (English or Welsh) and looks at the way in which children develop their language skills. Pupils from bilingual and multilingual backgrounds will need more support in the classroom when developing these skills. Teaching assistants will need to be aware of the way in which all children process language and the importance for bilingual and multilingual pupils of retaining their identity through valuing and promoting their home language. In this unit, you will identify strategies for promoting pupils' development in speaking and listening, reading and writing in the target language. You will need to build on the pupils' experience when developing their skills in the target language and encourage them to develop as independent learners.

Unit 36, 'Provide bilingual/multilingual support for teaching and learning' is for bilingual/multilingual teaching assistants who provide support for pupils and families, and who use the pupils' first language to assess their abilities. Many of the knowledge points for Unit 36 overlap with those for Unit 35 and in these cases are included in this chapter to cover the requirements of both units. In order to work on Unit 36, you will need to look at the two chapters together. However, as part of your NVQ, you should only choose one unit or the other for your portfolio, depending on your role.

What you need to know and understand

For this unit, you need to know and understand:

- The school's policy and procedures for supporting bilingual/multilingual pupils

- The school's policies and practices for inclusion, equality of opportunity, multiculturalism and anti-racism

- The process and stages of language acquisition and the factors that promote or hinder language development

- How to obtain and interpret information about a pupil's language and educational background, capabilities and skills, and language support needs (see also Unit 36 for assessment)

- Strategies suitable for supporting pupils in developing their speaking/talking, reading and writing skills in the target language and how these relate to specific learning activities across the curriculum

- The interactive use of speaking/talking, listening, reading and writing to promote language development in pupils

- How to plan and evaluate learning activities to support development of the target language

- How aspects of culture, religion, upbringing, home and family circumstances and emotional health could affect the pupils' learning in the classroom and how to respond to these

- How to use praise and constructive feedback to promote pupils' learning and language development

- The role of self-esteem in developing communication and self-expression and how to promote the self-esteem of pupils through the support you provide

- The importance of valuing and promoting cultural diversity, pupils' home language and the benefits of bilingualism/multilingualism, and how to do this

- The curriculum plans and learning programmes developed by the teachers with whom you work when supporting bilingual/multilingual pupils

- How to provide appropriate support for bilingual/multilingual pupils according to their age, emotional needs, abilities and learning needs

- How to identify and develop culturally and linguistically appropriate teaching and learning resources to provide effective access to the curriculum

- The sorts of problems that might occur in providing support for bilingual/multilingual pupils and how to respond to these

- How to monitor, assess and feed back information on pupils' participation and progress across the curriculum to relevant people within the school

School's policy and procedures for supporting bilingual/multilingual pupils

According to government statistics, English is now spoken as a second language by one in eight pupils in primary schools. Over 200 languages are spoken by pupils attending British schools. When supporting **bilingual/multilingual pupils**, all staff need to think about how they can promote the development of the target language while valuing the child's home language and culture. This is particularly important if there is only one bilingual/multilingual pupil learning the target language in the class. The school should have its own policies and practices for how pupils with English as an additional language are supported. The different strategies that the school has in place may include:

Key Term

Bilingual/multilingual pupils – Pupils who need to develop a second or additional language to access the curriculum

- policies to promote positive images and role models
- policies and practices on inclusion, equal opportunities and multiculturalism
- identifying bilingual/multilingual pupils, for example, if there is a small group, photos in the staff room so that all staff are aware
- providing opportunities for pupils to develop their language skills
- having established school and class routines
- finding opportunities to talk with parents of bilingual children and encourage links with the school
- celebrating linguistic and cultural diversity.

Many schools now also have a governor and/or teacher in the school who has overall responsibility for **EAL** pupils. The role of the teacher would be to advise other staff on the strategies that might be the most effective.

Key Term

EAL – English as an additional language

Portfolio activity
Units 35 & 36, K1

Identifying your school's policies
Find out which of your school's policies are relevant to pupils from bilingual/multilingual backgrounds. How are bilingual/multilingual pupils and their families supported within the school community?

School's policies and practices for inclusion, equality of opportunity, multiculturalism and anti-racism

You should know how your school's inclusion and/or equal opportunities policies (covered in Unit 18, page 37) relate to the needs of bilingual and multilingual pupils. Along with the policies for multiculturalism and anti-racism, they will give you guidelines for working with bilingual and multilingual pupils. For example, many schools now greet pupils or take the register in different languages at the beginning of the day to raise awareness of the different languages that may be spoken in the school.

Multicultural and anti-racism policies will outline the different ways in which the school recognises and celebrates different languages and cultures. Depending on the location and intake of your school, you may have a very high or low number of these pupils and the policies will take account of this.

The process and stages of language acquisition and the factors that promote or hinder language development

In order to build a picture of how we learn language, it is important to consider the two stages linguists consider all children pass through. These are known as the pre-linguistic and the linguistic stages.

The pre-linguistic stage is during the first 12 months, when babies begin to learn basic communication skills. During this time they start to attract the attention of adults and repeat back the different sounds they hear. This is true of any language, but, although babies world wide are born with the potential to make the same sounds, by the age of 12 months they can only repeat back the sounds that they hear around them.

The linguistic stage is when babies start to use the words that they hear and learn how to make sentences. Children develop this stage gradually over the next few years so that by the age of about 5, they are fluent in their home language. Children who learn more than one language may learn to speak slightly more slowly as they absorb different language systems. This should not, however, affect their overall language development.

The table below shows the stages of language development in children. Adults need to support children through all these stages in order to encourage and promote language development. At each stage, the role of the adult may be different. For example, a baby needs positive recognition of their attempts to communicate through eye contact and speech. A 5- or 6-year-old child may need adults to help them to extend their

Stages of language development in children

Age	Stage of development
0–6 months	Babies try to communicate through crying, starting to smile and babbling. They start to establish eye contact with adults.
6–18 months	Babies start to speak their first words. They start to use gestures to indicate what they mean. At this stage, they are able to recognise and respond to pictures of familiar objects.
18 months–3 years	Children start to develop their vocabulary rapidly and make up their own sentences. At this stage, children enjoy simple and repetitive rhymes and stories.
3–8 years	Children start to use more and more vocabulary and the structure of their language becomes more complex. As they develop their language skills, they are able to use language in a variety of situations.
8 + years	Children continue to develop the complexity of their language skills and their confidence in the use of language should begin to flourish. The attainment targets in the English National Curriculum set out the specific language skills expected of pupils at the different Key Stages.

vocabulary through the use of open-ended questions or 'what if?' strategies. Where children's language progresses more slowly through these stages, there may be other factors involved, such as:

- learning more than one language
- a communication difficulty such as autism
- a speech difficulty such as a stutter
- lack of stimulation from others
- a hearing impairment.

Theories of language acquisition

There have been several theories about how children learn or acquire language. In the early part of the twentieth century there were a number of theories with the same broad idea that children acquire language by learning a word together with the thing it means or stands for and that through interacting with adults they begin to develop sounds that have meaning and gain a positive response. This is called the associationist theory.

Noam Chomsky, an American linguist working in the 1960s, claimed that we are all born with an innate knowledge of the system of language, or a 'Language Acquisition Device'. In this way, a child can learn whatever language it needs and decode the accompanying grammar. This theory helps to explain why children apply grammatical rules wrongly sometimes because, although they have heard examples of the rules, they have not yet learned the exceptions. An example of this might be: 'I bringed my drink'.

John Macnamara, working in the 1970s, proposed that children are able to learn language because they have an ability to make sense of situations. This means that a child understands the intention of a situation and respond accordingly. For example, if a child sees an adult beckoning towards them and holding out their hand, they know that the adult's intention is for the child to come towards them. This will be the case even if the child does not understand the words that the adult is saying.

▼ **Figure 35.1** Language can develop in a range of situations

Although there have been many theories about how children develop language, there are still no definite answers. Adults who work in educational settings need to be aware of the ways we can help all children to develop their language skills and build on their present knowledge.

Opportunities for developing language

Pupils from all backgrounds, whether they are learning one or more languages, need to be given opportunities to develop their language skills in a variety of different ways. If pupils come to school only speaking their home language and need to develop their English, they need to have more support in order to do this. However, also remember that it is normal to have a 'silent phase' in learning a new langugage when the learner is 'tuning in' to new sounds and vocabulary. It is important not to push pupils to speak before they are ready.

Keys to good practice
Creating opportunities for developing language

✓ Create a secure and happy environment where the pupil and their families feel valued and part of the school.
✓ Raise cultural awareness in school for all pupils.
✓ Reinforce language learning by using resources such as dual-language texts.
✓ Reinforce language learning by giving immediate verbal and non-verbal feedback and praise.
✓ Give pupils time to think about questions before they respond.
✓ Create more opportunities for speaking and listening, such as paired conversations with other pupils.

How to obtain and interpret information about a pupil's language and educational background, capabilities and skills, and language support needs

Where pupils have come from a different background, culture or language from others in the class, entering school may be a difficult experience for them, particularly if they have not been in an educational environment before. They may find it hard due to lack of confidence or self-esteem, and staff need to be aware of their needs. Sometimes bilingual assistants are employed, especially where there is a large number of pupils who speak English or Welsh as a second language (see also Unit 36). Usually the school has systems in place when pupils enter school so that they are aware of those who speak the target language as a second language. Parents are asked to fill in forms before the child enters school and home visits can sometimes be a valuable way of gathering information.

The different backgrounds and skills of individual pupils influence their learning and the development of the target language. It can be very difficult to assess the needs of bilingual pupils and staff need to find out whatever they can about each pupil when they first enter school in order to support them fully. This may involve carrying out specific assessments or observations.

Educational backgrounds

When a pupil first enters school, there may be records from the primary school that give some indication of progress to date in the target language. If your school is the first contact the pupil has had with the target language, the school needs to devise some educational targets for them to work on so that they can begin to develop their language skills. It is important to gain as much information as possible from the child's previous school if they have transferred. That school is required to send records of assessment and attainment, but these may take some time to come through, and the class teachers may need to contact the previous school, particularly if there is an area of concern. There may also have been other agencies, such as speech therapists, involved with the child's development and records from these professionals will be useful in finding out more.

Where pupils have come from very different educational backgrounds from others in the class, they may take more time to settle into school, for example if they have come from an area where there are many bilingual pupils to one where there are very few or from an area where learning styles are different.

Home backgrounds

These may be varied and will have the greatest influence on the pupil. Those whose home backgrounds have been traumatic, such as refugees, may have had wide and varied educational experiences. The school needs to obtain as much information as possible about the pupil's background and if possible seek the help of an interpreter so that discussions can take place directly with the parents.

The experiences that a child has had may also affect their behaviour, for example being non-responsive. It may be difficult to obtain information from home and this can cause problems, such as sickness notes or forms not being completed and returned to school. Pupils who come from backgrounds with a different culture or religion from the majority of others in the school may feel isolated and it is important for them that the school values cultural diversity. Staff also need to be aware of religious issues that can affect pupil's learning, such as fasting during Ramadan. Issues of health and physical development may also need to be discussed with other professionals and these checks should be included in the pupil's records.

Language backgrounds

Pupils who come into school with English or Welsh as a second language or those who are multilingual may find settling into school difficult due to the development of their language skills in the target language or due to a combination of factors. If staff know that the pupil has never been exposed to the target language before, this knowledge can help them to devise their educational plan. However, pupils who come into school at 12 years old need a different level of support from those who come into school at 15 years old. The school needs to ensure that each pupil has an education plan that takes individual learning needs into account, including appropriate targets.

Case study

Gathering information on language and emotional support needs

You have been asked to work with Jose, a Spanish pupil who has just come into school in Year 9 (S3). This is his second English school and he does speak some English.

- How would you go about gathering information on his language support needs?
- What emotional support might Jose need?

Strategies suitable for supporting pupils in developing their speaking, reading and writing skills in the target language and the interactive use of these across the curriculum

Speaking and listening skills

These skills clearly need to be developed in EAL pupils and you may find that you are working with individuals or small groups to facilitate this. With Year 7 (S1) pupils the approach may be different from with Year 11 (S5) pupils, but the strategies should be the same and should apply across the curriculum.

Opportunities to talk

Pupils need to be given as much opportunity as possible to talk and discuss ideas with others. At a younger age this may include opportunities such as role play, whereas older pupils may enjoy discussions.

Physical cues and gestures

Physical cues and gestures such as thumbs up, thumbs down enable pupils to make sense of a situation more quickly.

Songs and rhymes

Pupils develop concepts of pattern and rhyme in language through learning rhymes and songs. These are also an enjoyable way of developing language skills, as well as being part of a group. You may also be able to introduce rhymes and songs in other languages for all the pupils to learn and so develop their cultural awareness.

Games

These opportunities are useful as they help pupils to socialise with others as well as practise their language skills.

Practical examples

These can be used to help pupils when they are being given instructions, for example showing a model of what they will do in group work.

Discussions with a partner

This may help EAL pupils gain confidence before telling their ideas to the class. They should work with a variety of pupils to provide good language models.

Appropriate vocabulary

Staff need to think about the language they use with bilingual and multilingual pupils to ensure that it is appropriate to their age and level of understanding. If the teacher is talking to the class and has used language that is difficult to understand, you may need to clarify what has been said for particular pupils.

Purposeful listening

If pupils have come into school with very limited experience of the target language, you may be asked to work with them on specific areas of language. For example, the teacher may be focusing on positional words to ensure that pupils understand words such as *behind*, *above*, *below*, *next to* and so on. You may need to work with pictures or other resources to help pupils develop their understanding of these words.

Purpose of the activity

Explain the purpose of the activity because pupils should be aware of why they are undertaking a particular activity and what they are going to learn from it.

Reading and writing skills

Pupils who are learning to speak English or Welsh as an additional language need to have opportunities to read and listen to books in the target language so that they can associate their developing verbal and written skills with the printed page. Bilingual pupils will also benefit from working with the rest of the class during English lessons. They will be able to share texts with the whole class and smaller groups, although teachers may need to use additional strategies so that they maximise learning opportunities. These should be clear to teaching assistants so that they can support pupils by reinforcing the skills being taught. Such strategies may include:

- using repetitive texts
- revising the previous weeks' work to build confidence
- using pictures more in order to point out individual words
- making sure the lesson is paced to give bilingual pupils time to read the text
- grouping EAL pupils according to their actual ability rather than their understanding or knowledge of English
- pairing EAL pupils with another pupil or an adult to work on shared writing activities
- displaying and referring to a selection of vocabulary that is relevant to topic
- giving praise and encouragement wherever possible
- using computer programs to help with reading.

Pupils who are learning to read English or Welsh may need to decipher the meaning of some words with adult support. They may also need more support during guided reading sessions, but should benefit from these as they will be able to model good practice from other pupils. As with all pupils, they need to experience a wide variety of texts, both fiction and non-fiction, in order to maximise their vocabulary. It may be that a pupil is able to read and understand more than has been expected: in this case, staff should always continue to extend their vocabulary by discussing the text further.

After consultation with the class teacher, you may find that you need to adapt and modify the learning resources that the pupils are using, to help them access the curriculum more fully. You may also need to explain and reinforce vocabulary that is used in the classroom, for example during a topic. Often, the types of resources that benefit bilingual pupils will also be useful for others in the class or group.

Unit 35, K5 / Unit 36, K8 — Case study

Grouping EAL pupils

You are the only teaching assistant in a Citizenship class of Year 7 (S1) pupils. The class includes eight EAL pupils, who are grouped together for all subjects. You are usually asked to sit with them and support their language skills.

- What do you think about this strategy for supporting EAL pupils?
- Do you think pupils should be grouped in this way for all curriculum subjects? Give your reasons and outline any alternatives.

How to plan, deliver and evaluate learning activities to support development of the target language

Pupils entering school with English or Welsh as an additional language may come from a wide range of backgrounds and experiences of the target language. They may:

- be completely new to written and spoken English
- have learned English or Welsh as a foreign language
- appear to be quite fluent, but have some gaps in their understanding
- be unfamiliar with the Roman alphabet
- have no previous experience of school.

If you are working with bilingual and multilingual pupils and are asked to plan and evaluate learning activities to support their language development, you should have some guidance from other professionals as well as a clear idea about the pupils' needs (see also Curriculum plans developed by teachers, page 226). Pupils should have structured activities embedded into the curriculum in order to support their language development, but these will depend on their individual needs. As language is the basis for all learning, it is important that you plan carefully to ensure that you give pupils full access to the curriculum.

You need to make sure that you plan for different types of talk, which should include working in pairs, individual and group work, and sharing whole class activities such as stories. Understanding of key words should be checked and reinforced, and effective questioning used in order to assess pupils' knowledge.

It is important to remember that there is a difference between the social language in which pupils may be starting to gain fluency and classroom language. This is because in social situations the meaning of what is being communicated is often backed up by visual cues. Classroom language is frequently more abstract and it can be difficult for pupils to tune in to the kinds of functional language required in some learning situations, for example for hypothesising, evaluating, predicting, inferring. It is likely that there will be less visual demonstration to support learning: you need to make sure that planning takes account of this so that you can give practical support to pupils.

Portfolio activity

Unit 35, K7
Unit 36, K11

Evaluating activities for supporting development of English

If you regularly plan and evaluate work that you carry out with bilingual pupils, give examples of the kinds of activities you have used to support their development of English. Evaluate these activities and how successful they have been by answering the following questions.

● What went well during the activity?
● What did not go as well as expected?
● How did you manage to bridge the gap between social and classroom language?

How aspects of culture, religion, upbringing, home and family circumstances and emotional health could affect the pupils' learning in the classroom and how to respond to these

As with any other pupils, bilingual pupils come from a variety of backgrounds and circumstances. As you get to know them you will find out about their individuality and the kinds of adjustments they are having to make. The primary needs of all pupils, especially those who speak English as an additional language, is that they feel safe, settled, valued (that their work or language is represented in the classroom) and have a sense of belonging.

◄Figure 35.2 What can affect pupils' learning?

Bilingual pupils may have to make significant adjustments to life in a new country. They will often have found it a real 'culture shock' and have great anxiety, not only about communicating with others, but also in adapting to their new environment. However, it may also be an advantage to them to be in a structured and secure environment if they have experienced trauma or an unsettled period. The kinds of effects could be that the pupil:

- becomes withdrawn
- is frustrated by being unable to communicate and displays behaviour problems
- is anxious and reluctant to participate in class activities.

All of these effects make it difficult for pupils to participate in classroom activities. You need to make sure that you develop as many strategies as possible for pupils who need emotional support.

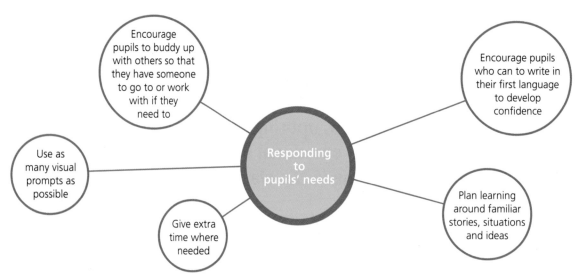

▲ **Figure 35.3** Strategies to support pupils

How to use praise and constructive feedback to promote pupils' learning and language development

As with all situations, effective use of praise is very important when working with EAL pupils (see also Unit 18, page 42). You need to provide encouragement and support to bilingual and multilingual pupils as they will be insecure in the target language. Through the use of a positive learning environment and opportunities for them to develop relationships with others, you will encourage and support their learning. Examples of this might be:

- repeating what the teacher is saying
- explaining what has been said
- rehearsing with them before they respond
- acting as their talk partner
- encouraging them through smiles, nods, gestures and body language.

When giving pupils feedback in learning situations and repeating back words or phrases to them, you may need to 'remodel' language or extend their responses. For example, if they use language incorrectly, such as 'I go to the shops last weekend', you could respond 'You went to the shops last weekend? What did you buy?' rather than specifically pointing out an error.

Role of self-esteem in developing communication and self-expression and how to promote the self-esteem of pupils through the support you provide

It is very important for all pupils that staff in school are aware of their home language and culture. This is because pupils' self-esteem is affected by their perception of how others see them and their confidence when using language. It is especially important for everyone to pronounce the pupils' names correctly. If their parents do not speak English, this may be a pupil's first experience of having to communicate with others in a language other than their own. It is important for the pupil to be able to communicate in school and, although children usually pick up language reasonably quickly, this can be a difficult time for them. If you notice that any pupil is finding it hard to make friends, it is important to discuss this with the class teachers and tutor. You may also be able to help pupils to socialise with others through the introduction of specific group activities during the tutor period.

Case study K10

Helping a pupil to socialise

Sobiga is a new pupil in your tutor group and does not speak any English. Although she has made friends and is involved in class activities, you have noticed that at play- and lunchtimes she is often on her own.

- What kind of support does Sobiga need and why?
- List three strategies that you could use to help her to develop her self-esteem.

The importance of valuing and promoting cultural diversity, pupils' home language and the benefits of bilingualism/multilingualism, and how to do this

It is very important for bilingual pupils that their home language and heritage is recognised in school. Pupils need to know that their culture and status is valued as this helps them to feel settled and secure, factors which contribute to their being able to develop skills in a new language. Pupils need to want to learn; if they feel isolated or anxious, it is more likely that this will be difficult for them. If you are a bilingual teaching assistant, you can encourage pupils to speak their home language in school. If you have two or more pupils in the class who speak the same language, encourage them to use it together – by discussing things in one language, it will help the development of the target language.

Cultural awareness has become more important as schools recognise the value of bilingual pupils' experiences and knowledge. The status of other languages should be recognised in school through assemblies, displays, school trips and cultural events. Personal, social and health education (PSHE) activities may also focus on the importance of valuing individuals and celebrating diversity.

▲ Figure 35.4 Cultural awareness in the classroom is very important

Curriculum plans and learning programmes developed by the teachers with whom you work when supporting bilingual/multilingual pupils

Bilingual pupils should be integrated into whole class teaching and learning programmes alongside their peers as much as possible. Adults need to support them to develop their social and academic skills, and through involvement with others and access to the school curriculum, they will have the ideal base from which to develop these skills. The curriculum plans developed by the teacher will give opportunities for bilingual pupils to practise speaking and listening skills in the target language, and additional strategies or opportunities should be outlined in the plans.

Unit 35, K12
Unit 36, K10

Portfolio activity

Differentiating work

Using a daily or weekly plan, show how work is differentiated for bilingual pupils in your class. Highlight examples of the kinds of activities or specific vocabulary that you focus on with these pupils.

How to provide appropriate support for bilingual/multilingual pupils according to their age, emotional needs, abilities and learning needs

Pupils may feel differently about the experience of learning an additional language for a variety of reasons. You need to know how these different factors might affect your support of their learning.

Age

A pupil's age may make a difference to how they learn language. Older pupils may find it more challenging due to the demands of the curriculum and the fact that they need to learn to speak, read and write in English in order to access it. They may also be self-conscious and as a result less likely to attempt to speak. A younger child may be more relaxed and less anxious about acquiring language. Research has shown that the younger the child, the easier it is for them to learn additional languages. For children to attempt to initiate language, they need to feel relaxed and confident that their contributions will be valued.

Emotional needs

See pages 223–4 and 225.

Abilities and learning needs

You need to remember that a pupil's ability to speak additional languages is not a reflection of their overall abilities. Although speaking two or more languages is a gift and should be celebrated, all pupils can be of higher or lower than average ability overall. However, it may take longer to determine if there are any additional needs and this is another reason why it is important to monitor pupils' development in the target language.

Case study

Unit 35, K13
Unit 36, K13

Supporting pupils of mixed ability

You are working with a group of three Year 7 (S1) pupils, who all speak Gujarati. Although they have the language in common, their needs are all different. Ahmed speaks very little English and has just come to this country. Mahir has lived here all his life, but has always spoken Gujarati at home and needs extra support with his English. He is of average ability. Marian is bilingual and able in her work, but is very anxious and reluctant to speak English, although she is able to.

- Would you approach the support you give these pupils differently even if you had to group them together?
- How could you balance the needs of the pupils while supporting them effectively?

How to identify and develop culturally and linguistically appropriate teaching and learning resources to provide effective access to the curriculum

If you are responsible for supporting EAL pupils in your school, you should have access to appropriate **resources**. You may already have some in school and your school or local authority can put you in touch with sources of additional materials. The Internet is also an excellent resource, although you may need to have time to look for appropriate sites and programs to use (see the end of the chapter for a list of websites). You may also be asked to produce resources, especially if you are bilingual yourself, in order to support pupil learning. These might include displays or word banks for pupils, as well as dual language texts. If you find additional resources, always check with the teacher before using them with pupils.

Key terms

Resources – Teaching and learning resources to provide effective access to the curriculum, including written materials, videos, bilingual and pictorial dictionaries, bilingual software

---

Unit 35, K14
Unit 36, K12

Portfolio activity

Recording the kinds of resources used

Complete a table like the one below to show the kinds of resources you have used with or produced for bilingual and multilingual pupils.

Type of resource	Source
Bilingual reading program for computer	Local EAL advisory teacher

---

The sorts of problems that might occur in providing support for bilingual/multilingual pupils and how to respond to these

There may be a number of problems that occur when supporting bilingual/multilingual pupils. If a group or individual is finding a particular activity too challenging, the teaching assistant may need to modify or change the plan to accommodate this, as it may not always be possible to speak immediately to the teacher. However, it is important that the teacher is informed as soon as possible in order to inform future planning. Some pupils may take a long time to become confident in a second language and it will be apparent that they understand much more than they are able to say. This is not unusual and staff must not push pupils into talking before they are ready. The most important thing to do is to encourage and praise pupils wherever possible, repeating back to them so that they develop a positive view of themselves.

It can take longer to detect a specific learning difficulty if a pupil is bilingual. This is because staff may feel that the pupil is finding school more difficult just because of their development of the target language. If a teaching assistant finds that a particular pupil is not able to manage the tasks set and is not progressing, they should always speak to the class teacher.

Other problems could include inadequate or unsuitable resources and disruptions within the learning environment, as outlined in Unit 31.

Keys to good practice

Supporting bilingual and multilingual pupils

✓ Group bilingual/multilingual pupils with pupils of similar ability.
✓ Involve them in purposeful talk as much as possible.
✓ Allow pupils more time to think about what they are going to say.
✓ Use strategies that develop self-esteem and confidence.
✓ Provide visual and physical supports to help understanding.
✓ Model language using other pupils.

Case study
Unit 35, K14
Unit 36, K17

Supporting bilingual and multilingual pupils

Outline how you would deal with the following:

- a bilingual pupil who refuses to speak
- a dispute based on a misunderstanding between the parent of a bilingual pupil and the school
- a bilingual pupil with whom others in the class do not mix
- a group of pupils from the same community who are reluctant to communicate in English or Welsh.

How to monitor, assess and feed back information on pupils' participation and progress across the curriculum to relevant people

When working with bilingual and multilingual pupils, you need to provide frequent feedback to others on their progress. In a secondary school, the other professionals you need to report to are the class teachers, tutors and possibly the Special Educational Needs Co-ordinator (SENCo)(Additional Support for Learning (ASL) teacher) and EAL teachers who may visit the school. You should have opportunities to contribute to meetings and/or paperwork such as IEPs (Individual Education Plan) concerning the pupils with whom you are working. It is important that there is a 'joined-up' approach by all those who are working with bilingual pupils so that their progress can be measured.

Case study

Monitoring pupils' progress

You are often asked to work with Hulya in Year 9 (S3) English, who has been in school since Year 7 (S1) and is a Turkish speaker. Although her English is good, there are some gaps in her understanding. The teacher does not see the need for Hulya to have an IEP and, although you are asked to work with her, you do not have any specific areas to work on or guidance as to what to do with her. You feed back to the teacher informally about Hulya when you have the time.

- Is there anything else that you could do to monitor Hulya's progress more effectively?
- What would you do if the class teacher was unwilling to help you to plan specific activities to help Hulya?

K5
K6
K8

For your portfolio...

You are working in Year 8 (S2) with Cassie, who has moved to this country from Latvia. She is an able pupil although she has not found it easy to settle and often talks about her country. Her father has recently lost his job and she has a younger sister who is disabled. She has been in school for a year and speaks reasonable English, although it is clear that she has gaps in her knowledge and understanding. She has a language support plan in place and you work with her for 15 minutes a day during tutorial to focus on different aspects of her language skills while integrating these into the curriculum.

- How might Cassie be affected by her background and circumstances?
- What kinds of strategies and activities might you use to support Cassie?
- How could you integrate these into curriculum plans?

To gather additional evidence for this unit, you may wish to speak to your assessor about the pupil or pupils with whom you work and the kinds of strategies you have used to help support their learning and how these relate to the teacher's plans. You can set up a professional discussion to do this.

Websites

www.becta.org.uk – Becta community languages website.

www.dfes.gov.uk – The standards site has information under EAL learners, the QCA and Teachernet (type in 'EAL' under 'search').

www.freeenglish.com – A website with resources for those learning English.

www.naldic.org.uk – This organisation, National Association for Language Development in the Curriculum, aims to raise attainment of EAL learners.

36 Provide Bilingual/ Multilingual Support for Teaching and Learning

This unit is for teaching assistants who use the pupil's first language to support teaching and learning in schools. If you speak another language you may be asked to use this knowledge to help assess pupil's educational abilities and support needs. You may also be involved in providing support for families and liaising with them in order to promote pupil participation. Through your role in school it is likely that you will develop a knowledge of the kinds of external support and programmes that are available to families, in particular through local community support groups.

Unit 35, 'Support bilingual and multilingual pupils' is for teaching assistants who provide support for bilingual pupils in the target language. Many of the knowledge points for Unit 35 overlap with those for this unit; the knowledge points listed below in italic print have been included in Unit 35 to cover the requirements of both units. In order to work on Unit 36, you will need to look at the two chapters together. However, as part of your NVQ, you should only choose one unit or the other for your portfolio, depending on your role.

What you need to know and understand

For this unit, you need to know and understand:

- *The school's policy and procedures for supporting bilingual/multilingual pupils and their families* (see also Unit 35, page 215)

- *The school's policies and practices for inclusion, equality of opportunity, multiculturalism and anti-racism* (see also Unit 35, page 215)

- How to communicate effectively and sensitively with pupils and their families

- *The process and stages of language acquisition and the factors that promote or hinder language development* (see also Unit 35, page 216)

- How to obtain and interpret information about a pupil's language and educational background, capabilities and skills and language support needs (see also Unit 35)

- When to refer pupils for specialist assessment and the school procedures for arranging this

- How to provide feedback to pupils, families and colleagues on the pupil's learning needs and ways of addressing these

- *The interactive use of listening, speaking, reading and writing to promote language development in pupils* (see also Unit 35, page 220)

- *Strategies suitable for supporting pupils in developing their listening, speaking, reading and writing skills in the target language and how these relate to specific learning activities across the curriculum* (see also Unit 35, page 220)

- *The curriculum plans and learning programmes developed by the teachers with whom you work when supporting bilingual/multilingual pupils* (see also Unit 35, page 226)

- *How to plan, deliver and evaluate learning activities to support pupils' language and learning development* (see also Unit 35, page 222)

- *How to identify and develop culturally and linguistically appropriate teaching and learning materials* (see also Unit 35, page 228)

- *How to provide appropriate support for bilingual/multilingual pupils according to their age, emotional needs, abilities and learning needs* (see also Unit 35, page 227)

- *How aspects of culture, religion, upbringing, home and family circumstances and emotional health could affect the pupils' learning and how to respond to these* (see also Unit 35, page 223)

- *How to use praise and constructive feedback to promote pupils' learning and language development* (see also Unit 35, page 224)

- *The role of self-esteem in developing communication and self-expression and how to promote the self-esteem of pupils through the support you provide* (see also Unit 35, page 225)

- *The sorts of problems that might occur in providing support for bilingual/multilingual pupils and how to respond to these* (see also Unit 35, page 228)

- *How to monitor, assess and feed back information on pupils' participation and progress across the curriculum to relevant people within the school* (see also Unit 35, page 229)

- Why it is important to work with families to identify their communication needs and how you can do this

- *The importance of valuing and promoting cultural diversity, pupils' home language and the benefits of bilingualism/multilingualism, and how to do this* (see also Unit 35, page 225)

- Methods that can be used to communicate with families whose first or preferred language is different from that used in the school

- How to recognise communication differences and difficulties, and identify the possible reasons for these

- Why it is important to evaluate the effectiveness of communication, and strategies you can use to do this

- Ways in which you could adapt communication methods and the support you provide in order to improve the effectiveness of communication between families and the school

How to communicate effectively and sensitively with pupils and their families

Working with families

If you are a bilingual teaching assistant working in a school with a high percentage of bilingual learners, it is likely that you will be involved in providing support and information to **families**. You should have opportunities to liaise with the named governor or teacher in the school who is responsible for advising teachers about EAL learners. There should also be systems in place to enable you to pass information to parents and carers and for them to pass information to the school.

Parents or carers of bilingual pupils may sometimes speak very little, if any, English themselves. In this situation the school needs to devise additional strategies to encourage their involvement and understanding (see also communicating with families on page 238). It is important that parents and carers feel able to approach the school and share information in order to maximise the opportunities to communicate. However, remember that if you are passing information between school and families, that is all you should be doing. Be careful not to include your own opinions or ideas about what should be happening on either side without consulting with other staff first.

You may be communicating with pupils and families who are refugees or have come from situations where they have experienced trauma. In this case, seek outside support from your local authority to ensure that you are offering as much help and advice as possible, and, as a bilingual speaker, you will be well placed to offer the information. Pupils who have had unsettled backgrounds may take longer to settle into school, and communication and language development may be affected.

> **ⓘ Key term**
>
> **Families** – This includes parents, carers and extended and chosen families who contribute significantly to the well-being of individual pupils and who may or may not have legal responsibility

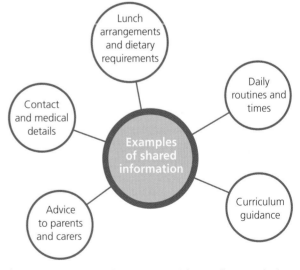

▲ **Figure 36.1** Shared information is crucial to good communication

Working with pupils

Working with bilingual learners and families, you need to be sensitive not only to language but also to different cultural needs. As a bilingual speaker you may already be aware of these, but it is likely that you will discover other needs in the course of your work. These kinds of issues may be around dress or diet, but may also be to do with religious or cultural customs with which you may not be familiar. The school's policies will welcome pupils and families from all cultures and you need to make sure that you follow these.

K3 Case study

Being aware of all learning and cultural needs

Soraya is Tamil and, as well as speaking an additional language, she has global learning delay. She came into school with a Statement of Special Educational Needs (Co-ordinated Support Plan) in Year 7 (S1) and you have been supporting her since then as you also speak her language. You are aware that her mother also has some learning needs and that neither parent speaks any English. Soraya is now in Year 10 (S4) and although she is making some progress, she is still a cause for concern and you are about to be involved in the review meeting with Soraya and her parents.

- Devise a list of questions which you might want to go through with the Special Educational Needs Co-ordinator (SENCo)(Additional Support for Learning (ASL) teacher) prior to the meeting.
- What kinds of issues might you be aware of at the meeting?
- Why might you need to be sensitive in what you say to Soraya and her parents?

How to obtain and interpret information about a pupil's language and educational background, capabilities and skills and language support needs

As well as seeking information from parents and other schools about pupil background and their home language, you may also be asked to assess and observe their level of English and to monitor their progress. You need to take into account their level of fluency in their home language as this is also important.

QCA have also produced guidance, *A language in common: assessing English as an additional language,* on how to assess pupils who are in the early stages of learning English. This is so that there is some standardisation in how bilingual pupils are assessed, although individual local authorities may have produced their own versions. It enables teachers to track pupil progress in speaking and listening, reading and writing. The guidance comprises detailed descriptors for features of English language use up to level 1 of the National Curriculum. It can be found at www.qca.org.uk/3359.html.

Following assessment, staff can build up a profile of each pupil. This can then be amended as more information is gathered and pupil levels in speaking and listening, reading and writing can be added.

Name:	Adelina Haliti
Date:	25/09/06
Boy/girl:	Girl
Date of birth:	28/08/1995
Year group:	7
Date arrived in UK:	30/06/2006
Date admitted to school:	6/7/2006
Languages spoken:	Albanian
Languages pupil can read:	Albanian
Languages pupil can write:	Albanian
Previous school in UK:	–
Previous school elsewhere:	–
Community school:	–

▲ **Figure 36.2** Example of a pupil profile – preliminary statement. Taken from Primary Induction Training for Teaching Assistants: Inclusion (TDA, 2006)

When and how to refer pupils for specialist assessment and the school procedures for arranging this

Most pupils, over a period of time, will be able to understand and communicate in an additional language. It is quite common for pupils to pick up English or Welsh as an additional language quickly when they start a new school as they have another language to relate it to. They may need support in order to develop their spoken and written English/Welsh language skills, but as these develop the support should be required less.

Case study K6

Referring pupils for specialist assessment

Nadia has been in an English school since Year 7 (S1), although she had always spoken Russian at home. However her English language acquisition has been very slow and despite being in the school environment for two years she is making little progress. You can speak Russian and know that she has difficulty in linking English and Russian words despite quite a lot of focused work with targeted language activities. You have spoken to her and she has said that she finds school very difficult and often doesn't understand.

- Outline the process you would have to go through in order to start to refer Nadia for specialist assessment.

However, in some cases, speaking English/Welsh as an additional language may hide additional language needs. As a bilingual teaching assistant, you will be able to tell if pupils are proficient in their own language or not and this can help to assess whether there is a language disorder or learning delay. In this situation, always speak to your class teacher and SENCo (ASL teacher), who will need to refer the pupil for specialist assessment, either to an Educational Psychologist or Speech and Language Therapist.

How to provide feedback to pupils, families and colleagues on the pupil's learning needs and ways of addressing these

Providing feedback to pupils and their families

As a bilingual assistant it is likely that you will be involved in providing feedback to pupils and their families about pupil progress. Pupils should always be fully involved in the procedure. The best way in which to do this is to set aside regular intervals with pupils to discuss their work and to think about any additional support they might need.

The most commonly used method of tracking pupil progress is by target setting and monitoring. This will enable pupils, staff and parents to see the focus of the work that is being done in school and to assess how successfully it is being implemented. You may be invited to annual review days and other events in order to support teachers and other staff in passing on information to parents.

If you are asked to speak to parents you should have an opportunity to speak to teachers beforehand so that you know what information they need to have passed on and how they would like you to structure what you say.

Providing feedback to colleagues

If you provide regular support to bilingual pupils you need to give feedback to colleagues, particularly if pupils speak very little English. Colleagues need you to pass

▼ Figure 36.3 Feedback should fully involve the pupil

Figure 36.4 Example of a language support plan

Language support plan: Spring term 2008

Name: Jamilla Khan   **Year:** 7   **Date:** 15 January 2008

Targets:

1. To familiarise Jamilla with the school and routines, and start to learn school vocabulary
2. To know 10 initial sounds and 5 core words from the Key Stage 3 National Strategy

Support: Daily during tutorial time with Mrs Evans (assistant) Individual and group work

Review: End of Spring term 2008

Signed: _____   _____
            (teacher)   (parent)

---

on information about pupils' development in English and also their knowledge and use of their home language, which may reflect their confidence in using language generally. A pupil who has a working knowledge of one language already understands the purpose of language and the process involved, and is more likely to be able to apply it to another language. The feedback you give to colleagues may be written or verbal depending on the school policy, but it is best to keep a record of some kind so that the information is available to others if required at a later date.

Case study K7

Providing feedback on pupil's learning needs

David has just entered school in Year 8 (S2). He comes from Switzerland and has never been to school before. He speaks German, French and a little English. You speak German and have been asked to talk to him and to assess his level of English. The teacher has said that David's parents are coming in to school to discuss how they can help him to settle and have asked whether there is anything specific they can do at home. You have carried out an assessment on David, which has shown that he listens well in class and is starting to use English, but prefers working in smaller groups where he feels more comfortable. He enjoys reading and has been looking at some dual language textbooks that you have in school. He is at Level 1 threshold in speaking and listening and Step 2 in reading and writing.

- What sort of advice might you and the teacher give to David and his parents?
- How could you reassure them if they were concerned about his progress?

Why it is important to work with families to identify their communication needs and how you can do this

If you are supporting pupils whose first language is not English, you need to have as many opportunities as possible to communicate with parents and families. It is also important that you and the school are able to work with the families from the outset to distinguish what their needs might be. This may start informally or, in schools with a high percentage of EAL pupils, may be approached in a more structured way. Families of bilingual children may have complex needs as well as communication issues and the school may be one of the first points of contact for them to access additional support and become established in local communities. Through school events, community projects and extended schools programmes, parents should be encouraged to be included in a variety of ways.

Methods that can be used to communicate with families whose first or preferred language is different from that used in school

When pupils first enter school, there should be procedures in place to ensure that school documents are available for parents and families whose first language is not that used in school. Schools also need to gather as much written information as possible on pupil and family background, including medical history and any prior schooling. You may also be involved in gathering oral information. As a bilingual teaching assistant, your experience and expertise will be invaluable in helping to make a link between home and school. In cases where bilingual support is not available within school, it may be necessary to have translators or interpreters involved.

How to recognise communication differences and difficulties, and identify the possible reasons for these

There may be a number of reasons why difficulties arise when communicating with parents or pupils.

Cultural differences
Although you may speak the language, there may be differences in areas of culture which mean that communication is hindered.

Reluctance
There may be a reluctance on the part of the family to become involved in school life. This may be due to anxiety about what it involves and how the system differs from their previous experience.

Special educational (ASL) needs
If, over a period of time, parents or pupils find communication difficult, this may indicate that they have special educational (ASL) needs.

If it is clear that communication is being hindered, think about ways of changing your approach to meet the needs of pupils and their families.

Why it is important to evaluate the effectiveness of communication, and how to adapt the support you provide

If your communication methods are not effective for whatever reason and you find that some families are unable or reluctant to liaise with the school, you may need to adapt the support provided. As in all school practice, you need to identify any issues, evaluate how effective your methods are and think about whether any amendments or improvements may be necessary. Examples of adapting what you do may be:

- through providing additional opportunities for parents to come into school. These may be through specific events and support networks for bilingual parents, particularly if they are reluctant or unsure about approaching the school. You may also invite parents into school to speak to pupils about cultural issues, such as different festivals.
- being able to translate important letters that go home or provide alternative support so that families can access the information.

For your portfolio...

K20
K21
K23
K24

Write a reflective account to show the kinds of events and opportunities your school has to encourage communication with families of bilingual and multilingual pupils. Have there been measurable benefits? Why do you think these kinds of events are important?

If you have had to adapt the way in which you communicate with families, outline how you have done this.

As with Unit 35, rather than writing this down as a reflective account you may wish to have a professional discussion with your assessor to show how you provide bilingual support for teaching and learning. Plan this so that you can decide which of the knowledge points you want to cover. Your assessor may also wish to speak to the parents, teacher or others with whom you work.

Websites (see also Unit 35)

www.continyou.org.uk – This is an organisation that supports inclusion and lifelong learning.

www.naldic.org.uk – (National Association for Language Development in the Curriculum) has a large amount of material, articles and suggestions on issues surrounding bilingual pupils.

www.qca.org/qca_5739.aspx – for *A language in common – assessing English as an additional language*, 2000

www.teachernet.gov.uk – for further ideas for supporting EAL pupils

38 Support children with disabilities or special educational needs and their families

Working with pupils who have special educational (Additional Support for Learning (ASL)) needs or disabilities will require you to have skills in a number of areas. You will need to be able to relate well to a variety of different people, including parents, carers and other professionals. You may have a high level of responsibility for working with these pupils and need to work in partnership both with the pupil and with others who support them, both at home and to provide educational provision.

You will need to show how the needs of the pupil(s) impact on the support you provide both to them and their families, and how you adapt what you do to support them. You will have to identify the resources available to you and access any training as it becomes available.

What you need to know and understand

- The possible impact of having a child or young person with a disability or special educational needs within a family and the varied responses of carers, siblings, and the wider family

- Legislation, regulations and codes of practice affecting provision for disabled children and children with special educational needs within your home country

- Assessment and intervention frameworks for children with special educational needs

- The rights of all children and young people to participation and equality of access and how this affects provision

- Specialist local and national support and information that is available for you and for the children/young people and families

- Partnerships with parents and families are at the heart of provision as they know most about their child

- There are 'expert parents' with wide-ranging and in-depth knowledge of their child and the disability or special educational need who can offer support to others

- How integration/inclusion works in your setting and local area and the reasons for its benefits or otherwise

- Details about particular disabilities or special educational needs as they affect the children/young people in your care and your ability to provide a high-quality service

- The expected pattern of development for the children/young people for whom you are responsible

- *The possible effects of communication difficulties and attention deficits* (See Unit 22, K5 and K6)

- The purpose and use of Alternative and Augmentative Communication and assisting children/young people through use of all available senses and experiences

- Planning for each child/young person's individual requirements according to their age, needs, gender and abilities

- How to adapt your practice to meet the needs of all the children/young people for whom you are responsible, according to their age, needs and abilities

- What specialist aids and equipment are relevant and available for the children/young people you work with and how to use these safely

- The importance of early recognition and intervention to prevent learning or other difficulties from developing

- Awareness of, and ability to use, specialist terminology in the interest of the children/young people with whom you work, while ensuring that use of such terminology does not act as a barrier to communication

Possible impact of having a child with a disability or special educational needs within a family and the varied responses of carers, siblings, and the wider family

What does special educational (ASL) needs mean?

Special educational (ASL) needs are defined in the Code of Practice 2001 as the child having

- 'a significantly greater difficulty in learning than the majority of children the same age'
- 'a disability which prevents or hinders them from making use of educational facilities of a kind generally provided for children of the same age'.

If you are working with pupils who have special educational (ASL) needs and disabilities as part of your role within school, you need to have an awareness of how their needs affect those closest to them. However, the situations you will encounter will differ as pupils may have special educational (ASL) needs during different periods in their schooling. For example, a pupil may have learning needs and require support for a short period during their school career but over time cease to need help. A pupil with a disability may also require varying degrees of support from the school and local services at different times.

If a pupil has always had a disability or special educational (ASL) needs throughout their time in school, the family will have had time to become used to the fact that they may need additional support. However the daily pressures of caring for their child may mean that they become tired or find their child's needs difficult to manage on a day-to-day basis. Parents and carers have varied responses because each child and situation is different and needs to be treated accordingly.

Parents may feel angry or isolated when their child's needs are first identified or may not want their child to go for assessments because they do not want them to be 'labelled'. They may need to have access to specialist support groups and organisations, which are available to families of pupils who have special educational (ASL) needs or disabilities (see the end of this unit for examples).

Case study K1

Supporting siblings of pupils with a disability or special educational (ASL) needs

Polly in Year 9 (S3) has Down's Syndrome. Her brother is in the class you support in Year 7 (S1). You are on playground duty and notice that he is on his own and looks unhappy. When you ask him what has happened, he tells you that some pupils in his class are teasing him about Polly and the fact that she is 'different'. He tells you that he wants to stand up for her but doesn't want to be teased.

- What can you and the school do in this situation to support Polly and her family?
- Can you prevent this kind of behaviour from happening?

Legislation, regulations and codes of practice affecting provision for disabled children and children with special educational needs within your home country

There have been many changes to legislation in the UK over recent years, which have affected educational provision for children who have disabilities or special educational (ASL) needs. A very brief history is listed below.

Education Act (Handicapped Children) 1970

Until this time, children with special educational (ASL) needs were looked after by the health service. This act transferred the responsibility for their education to the local authority and as a result many special schools were built.

The Warnock Report 1978

This was a report rather than an act of legislation, but it had an impact on subsequent Acts of parliament as it was a study of the needs of special educational (ASL) needs children. It introduced a number of suggestions as to how children with these needs should be supported – through access to the curriculum, changes to the curriculum and changes to the environment. It influenced the Special Educational Needs (SEN) Code of Practice 2001 through its focus on inclusion.

Education Act 1981

This was based on the findings of the Warnock Report and gave additional legal responsibilities to local authorities as well as power to parents.

Education Reform Act 1988

This introduced the National Curriculum into all schools in England and Wales. Although this meant that all schools had to teach the same basic curriculum, it allowed schools to change or modify what was taught for special educational (ASL) needs pupils if the basic curriculum was not appropriate for them.

Children Act 1989

This requires that the welfare of the child must be considered at all times and their rights and wishes should be taken into consideration.

Education Act 1993

This required that a Code of Practice be introduced for guidance on the identification and provision of special educational (ASL) needs. The role of the (Special Educational Needs Co-ordinator (SENCo)(ASL teacher) was introduced in schools and parents were able to challenge local authorities about providing for special educational (ASL) needs pupils.

Disability Discrimination Act 1995

This made it illegal for services, such as shops and employers, to discriminate against disabled people.

Carers and Disabled Children Act 2001

This was the first act that recognised the needs of carers as well as those of children.

SENDA and Special Educational Needs Code of Practice 2001

The Special Educational Needs and Disability Act (SENDA) strengthens the rights of parents and special educational (ASL) needs children to a mainstream education. (In Scotland, the Education (Additional Support for Learning)(Scotland) Act 2004 provides detailed information about the rights of a child with additional support needs to a Co-ordinated Support Plan and all the necessary information for a candidate in Scotland undertaking the SVQ3 for Classroom Assistants.)

Every Child Matters 2005

This was put into place to ensure that all organisations and agencies involved with children between the ages of birth and 19 years should work together to ensure that children have the support needed to be healthy, stay safe, enjoy and achieve, make a positive contribution and achieve economic well-being. The acronym SHEEP can help you remember this:

Stay safe   **H**ealthy   **E**njoy and achieve   **E**conomic well-being   **P**ositive contribution

Portfolio activity K2

Identifying legislative provision for special educational (ASL) needs pupils

Choose one area of legislation and show in more detail how it has affected provision for special educational (ASL) needs pupils.

Assessment and intervention frameworks for children with special educational needs

Special educational (ASL) needs pupils are assessed through a specific process. Assessment and identification of special educational (ASL) needs may occur in the Early Years or the Primary phase before they start Secondary school. However, there are times when pupils enter Year 7 (S1) with unidentified special educational (ASL) needs and are not assessed until they are in the Secondary phase. There are usually three stages to assessment.

School Action

At this stage, the school will put additional strategies in place if it the pupil is finding it hard to keep up with their peers. This will usually take the form of educational targets on an IEP (Individual Education Plan).

School Action Plus

If the pupil has been on School Action for some time and is still behind their peers, they may be moved onto School Action Plus. This means that the school will consult outside agencies for further assessments, advice or strategies for supporting the pupil's needs.

Statement of Special Educational Needs (Co-ordinated Support Plan)

This means that the pupil will be assessed as to whether they need a Statement of Special Educational Needs (Co-ordinated Support Plan) and additional support in school. The school will need to gather all the paperwork from professionals who have worked with the pupil, in addition to providing evidence of the strategies they have used.

If a pupil has serious special educational (ASL) needs or disabilities, they may have been assessed before entering school or nursery and issued with a statement (co-ordinated support plan) then.

The rights of all children to participation and equality of access and how this affects provision

All children, whatever their needs and abilities, have an equal right to education and learning. Equal opportunities should include not only access to provision but also to facilities within and outside the school setting. Schools and other organisations offering educational provision must by law ensure that all pupils have access to a broad and balanced curriculum.

Provision in schools may be affected by any of the barriers opposite if the school does not take active steps to make sure that they do not occur. It is important that schools:

- have high expectations of pupils and develop their attitudes of self-belief through appropriate challenges
- celebrate and value diversity, rather than fear it
- are aware that all pupils have more in common than is different
- encourage the participation of all pupils in the curriculum and social life of the school
- work to include all pupils in the main activities of the class wherever possible.

> **ⓘ Key term**
>
> **Equality of access** – ensuring that discriminatory barriers to access are removed and that information about provision is accessible to all families in the community

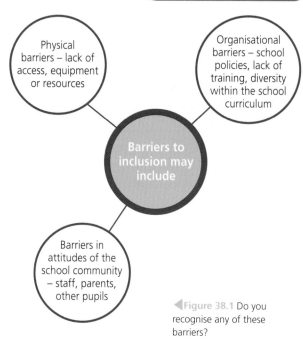

◄Figure 38.1 Do you recognise any of these barriers?

Specialist local and national support and information that is available for you and for the children and families

You will need to have access to additional support for the pupils you are working alongside, as will their parents and carers. This may be available through services within your local authority or NHS trust, but may also come from independent research into particular conditions or impairments. You may need to have training if you have not worked with these pupils before or need to ask your SENCo (ASL teacher) where local support might be available. For example, if you work with pupils on the autistic spectrum, it is likely that your local authority will have information and support for schools. It will also be able to refer you to any local or national support groups. (See also the websites at the end of the unit.)

▲ Figure 38.2 All pupils have the right to inclusion and equality of access

Portfolio activity K5

Using specialist support

If you have supported a pupil who has specific needs, show how you have sought additional support and what has been available locally and nationally.

Partnerships with parents and families and how 'expert parents' can support others

Many parents who have children with disabilities or special educational (ASL) needs have become experts on the particular need or condition. They may have researched in detail what support is available and have access to special groups or other sources of help. With their experience of the difficulties as carers, they will also be in a good position to offer sympathy and support to other families in similar circumstances. Partnerships with parents and families are crucial to the process of working with special educational (ASL) needs pupils. Schools will also need to ensure that they are as supportive as possible through clear communication and discussion with parents.

Case study

Offering support through partnership

You are working with Ben in Year 9 (S3), who is in a wheelchair due to spina bifida. Your school is fully accessible and Ben is fully integrated into his class. By chance Helen, who also has spina bifida, is just starting school in Year 7 (S1) and her parents are anxious about her settling in and having access to all the school facilities.

● Give three ways in which the school could help Helen and her parents and support the settling-in process.

How integration/inclusion works in your setting and local area and the reasons for its benefits or otherwise

You will need to speak to your assessor about your inclusion or equal opportunities policy (see also Unit 18, page 37) and identify the way in which pupils who have special educational (ASL) needs and disabilities are integrated into school. If this is not possible, write a reflective account to cover how inclusion works in your own experience of your school and local area. The benefits of inclusion should be clear – that all pupils are entitled to be educated together and are able to access the same education without any form of discrimination or **barriers to participation**.

 Key term

Barriers to participation – anything that prevents the pupil participating fully in activities and experiences offered by the school

Details about particular disabilities or special educational needs as they affect the children in your care and your ability to provide a high-quality service

For this knowledge point you need to identify the details of particular disabilities or special educational (ASL) needs of pupils with whom you work, and discuss how you have managed them with the support that is available to you. You need to show how you have worked with others in the school and local authority to provide a high-quality service to these pupils. To do this, speak to your assessor and if possible ask a teacher or someone you have worked with to provide a witness testimony.

The expected pattern of development for the children for whom you are responsible

You need to know how the pupil(s) you are supporting differ(s) from their peers in their expected pattern of development. If you work with pupils of a particular age range, it will be easier for you to identify whether they are fitting the normal pattern of development for their age. (See Unit 19 for stages of physical development and Unit 27 for stages of intellectual development.)

Purpose and use of Alternative and Augmentative Communication and assisting pupils through use of all available senses and experiences

As part of your role in supporting teaching and learning in the classroom, you should be aware of the need for pupils who have communication difficulties to have specialist resources or equipment. You may need to have additional training in their use, for example to support a pupil using communication technology such as PaceBlade.

🛈 Key term

Alternative and Augmentative communication (AAC) – any device, system or method of communication that helps individuals with communication difficulties to communicate more easily

Case study K12

Providing support without AAC

Tilak has recently arrived in your school and is on the autistic spectrum. His specialist autism teacher has told the school that he needs to have access to a Picture Exchange Communication System (PECS) in order to communicate. You have not worked with one before and will have training, but this is not available for two months.

● Where would you seek help in the meantime to support Tilak effectively?

Planning and adapting your practice for each child's individual requirements according to their age, needs, gender and abilities

Lesson plans should always include differentiated activities for pupils who have additional educational needs. If you plan alongside the teacher, you may be able to make suggestions at this stage for the pupils you support. Any additional training you may have had around the needs of the pupil may give you ideas about the kinds of activities and resources that will be beneficial.

However, you may still need to adapt work if the pupil is finding it challenging. You will need to monitor pupil participation and intervene if necessary so that they are able to achieve the learning objective.

Portfolio activity K13 K14

Planning and adapting lessons plans

Using a plan you devised alongside the teacher, show how you planned for the needs of different pupils in your class, including those with special educational (ASL) needs. If you had to adapt the plan during the lesson to make it more accessible to pupils, annotate it to show this.

What specialist aids and equipment are relevant and available for the pupils you work with and how to use these safely

If you work with specialist equipment, you need to be able show this to your assessor and explain how it is used. For example, a pupil with cerebral palsy may be required to use a standing frame for some of the day. In this instance you should talk through its use and your role in setting it up safely for the pupil. If you are unable to show your assessor, you need to have a professional discussion with them or write about what is involved.

Importance of early recognition and intervention to prevent learning or other difficulties from developing

Early recognition is important because it means that parents, carers and staff have the maximum available information in order to support the pupil. Early Years settings are now able to request assessments for young children if it is felt that intervention is required before they reach school age. Doctors and health service professionals may also be involved in preparing reports and recommendations to support such assessments.

K16 Case study

Recognising learning difficulties early

Barney is in Year 7 (S1). He is a bright and happy pupil, but you have concerns because he does not often communicate with adults or his peers and is often 'in his own little world'. You decide to watch him and notice that he is often unaware when people are talking to him.

- What would be your course of action?
- Why would it be important that you discussed your concerns?

Awareness of, and ability to use, specialist terminology in the interest of the children with whom you work, while ensuring that use of such terminology does not act as a barrier to communication

When communicating with pupils, parents and other professionals, you need to have an awareness of the kinds of terminology that may be useful. This may be educational jargon or specialist terminology that you may come across in the course of your work. You should also be aware that pupils, parents and carers may not use specialist terminology and so you must ensure that they are clear on points that arise in meetings or during discussions.

Identifying specialist special educational (ASL) needs terminology

As part of a class session, work alongside others in your group to formulate a list of the kinds of terminology with which you might come into contact when working with special educational (ASL) needs pupils.

For your portfolio...

K6
K7
K9
K10
K11
K12
K13
K14
K15
K17

The most useful way of gathering knowledge-based evidence for this and all the special educational (ASL) needs units is to have a professional discussion with your assessor. Decide beforehand what you would like to cover so that you are ready to answer, but make sure you are able to talk about the particular needs of a pupil you support and your role in relation to this. An example of a plan for discussion might be:

- look through and talk about the pupil's IEP, and discuss their needs (K9, K10, K11)
- describe the relationship between the school and the pupil's parents, and the specific support needed (K6, K7)
- explain how you plan to support the pupil's individual needs and the use of any terminology or equipment (K12, K13, K14, K15, K17).

Further reading

There are a number of magazines and periodicals available for school staff who support special educational (ASL) needs pupils, such as *Special Children* and *Special! Magazine*. You should also keep up to date by reading the *Times Educational Supplement* and checking websites such as those listed below.

Websites

www.bbc.co.uk/health – advice on a range of conditions and illnesses

www.cafamily.org.uk – national charity for families of disabled children

www.direct.gov.uk – go to 'Special educational needs' for advice and support

www.everychildmatters.gov.uk

www.parentpartnership.org.uk – National Parent Partnership Network, supporting parents and children

www.specialfamilies.org – as above

www.surestart.gov.uk – national charity for families and children

39 Support Pupils with Communication and Interaction Needs

This unit is for teaching assistants who are working with pupils who have speech and language delay, impairments or disorders. You may also support pupils who have specific learning difficulties such as dyslexia or dyspraxia (also known as Developmental Co-ordination Disorder (DCD)), or those who are on the autistic spectrum. Pupils may have communication needs due to a sensory or physical impairment. Children with these difficulties may also have moderate, severe or profound learning needs.

Pupils who have communication and interaction needs need to have support in a variety of ways; this may take the form of developing social relationships, organising their language for learning or supporting them in using alternative means of communication. You will need to show how you work with others to develop pupils' communication and language skills.

What you need to know and understand

For this unit, you will need to know and understand:

- *The school's policy on inclusive education and equality of opportunity and your role and responsibility in relation to this* (See Unit 18, K7, page 37 and Unit 23, K13, page 151)

- The school's policy and procedures for supporting pupils with communication and interaction needs

- The school's language and behaviour policies and how these impact on your work with pupils with communication and interaction needs

- The roles and responsibilities of others, both within and external to the school, who contribute to the support of pupils with communication and interaction needs

- The characteristics of the communication impairments and disorders of the pupils with whom you work, and the implications for language and communication development, social interaction and learning

- The differences between normal communication and the specific or more unusual patterns of communication demonstrated by pupils with significant developmental delay, impairment or those having some form of communication or language disorder

- The interaction between delayed language acquisition, cognitive development and sensory deficit

- The specific language, communication and interaction needs of the pupil(s) with whom you work

- Any individual education plans and/or behaviour support plans for the pupils with whom you work

- Strategies to enhance and promote non-verbal communication

- Visual and auditory teaching approaches that can enhance communicative and social interactions

- How to adapt the general and technical vocabulary used by the teacher(s) in order to match the needs of pupils with communication difficulties

- Physical and emotional factors which impact on a pupil's ability to engage in oral communication and ways of overcoming or minimising the effects of these

- The role of communication and self-expression in developing self-esteem

- How to use praise and constructive feedback to promote communication which is appropriate to the situation

- The communication methods used by the pupils with whom you work, how to use these, and how to support and promote the pupil's ability to use these effectively

- Aspects of culture, upbringing and home circumstances that could affect a pupil's ability to communicate with others, e.g. the different interpretations of signs and gestures

- The school procedures for recording and sharing information

School's policy and procedures for supporting pupils with communication and interaction needs

Although the school may not have a policy specifically written for these pupils, the procedures and guidelines for working with them should be incorporated into the school's special educational (Additional Support for Learning (ASL)) needs and inclusion policies. Teaching assistants need to be familiar with these as they will outline the school's commitment to supporting all pupils. Pupils with communication and interaction difficulties will have a range of needs and staff should have access to specialist support from outside agencies.

Specialist support from outside agencies
- **Speech and language unit** – will give support to pupils with a range of difficulties, from minor speech impairment to more complex language disorders
- **Sensory support service** – deals with difficulties such as permanent sensory or physical impairment, including auditory and visual problems
- **Complex communications service** – will diagnose and advise on disorders such as those in the autistic spectrum

Portfolio activity K2

Identifying guidance for support in school policies

Copy and highlight or annotate the appropriate pages in your school's special educational (ASL) needs and/or inclusion policies (you do not need to include the whole policy) to show guidance for supporting pupils with communication and interaction needs.

School's language and behaviour policies and how these impact on your work with pupils with communication and interaction needs

You need to be familiar with these policies and show how they impact on your work with pupils who have communication and interaction needs. They will both be particularly relevant as the behaviour of these pupils may be affected by their communication needs.

Your school's language policy may come under the literacy policy as it involves speaking and listening, and will give you guidelines as well as outline the kinds of strategies and sanctions your school follows.

The behaviour policy may not have specific advice about these pupils, but should give you more general information about how to deal with specific behaviour issues. You also need so show that you know what level of behaviour you can deal with as a teaching assistant and when you need to refer to other staff such as the class teacher or Special Educational Needs Co-ordinator (SENCo)(ASL) teacher).

K3 Case study

Recognising how school policies impact on your work

Jai is supporting William in Year 10 (S4), who has Asperger's Syndrome. She has worked with him since Year 7 (S1) and knows him well. This morning a supply teacher is covering the double English class, and William is uneasy because he has not met the teacher before. As the morning progresses, William becomes more disruptive, calling out and requiring Jai to calm him down on several occasions. Eventually she has to remove him from the class and speak to him about his behaviour.

- How would the school's behaviour and language policies impact on how Jai manages the situation?
- Give an example of how your work with pupils who have communication and interaction needs has been influenced by school policy.

Roles and responsibilities of others, both within and external to the school, who contribute to the support of pupils with communication and interaction needs

There will be a number of other professionals with whom you may come into contact if you are supporting pupils with communication and interaction needs. These will depend on the specific needs of the pupil but may include the following.

- **Class teacher** – The teacher is responsible for all pupils in the class and you need to work with them to ensure that the pupil's needs are met.
- **SENCo (ASL teacher)** – The SENCo (ASL teacher) is the school's main point of contact for other professionals who come into school.
- **Support staff** – You may work alongside other support staff to manage the needs of these pupils.
- **Speech and language therapist** – The therapist will have contact with the school and may come in to discuss pupils' speech and language targets with you.
- **Educational psychologist** – You may be involved in discussions with the educational psychologist around assessment of pupils' needs.
- **Autism advisory teacher** – This advisory teacher may come into school to advise staff on the kinds of strategies to use when working with autistic pupils.

- **Sensory support teacher** – This advisory teacher will work with staff who support pupils with communication difficulties due to sensory impairment, such as deafness or visual impairment.

Characteristics of the communication impairments and disorders of the pupils with whom you work, and the implications for language and communication development, social interaction and learning

You need to know the characteristics of the pupils you support so that you can work with them effectively. Discuss with your assessor their specific needs and how you support them so that this can be marked off in your portfolio. Examples of the kinds of communication impairments and disorders you may encounter are given below.

Speech and language delay and disorders

These may be varied and range from problems such as a stutter to more complicated disorders where pupils have difficulties in processing their language. Some children may require frequent speech and language therapy input to help them develop their communication skills.

Sensory impairment

Children with a permanent sensory or physical impairment, such as deafness or deaf/blindness, are at a disadvantage when communicating and they may not have the benefit of additional cues such as body language. They may need to have access to alternative means of communication such as sign systems, Braille or specialist equipment.

Specific learning difficulties

These may not be obvious straightaway when a child enters school and it can take a while for them to become apparent. Children with these kinds of difficulties may have slower language processing skills or have difficulty following instructions. They may also have a limited understanding of non-verbal communication and find concentrating or organisational skills difficult. As a result, their communication skills will be poorer than those of other children.

Autistic spectrum disorder (ASD)

Autistic children have a developmental disability which affects the way they relate to others. This may vary in its severity – some autistic children just seem distracted, while others display quite disruptive behaviour such as frequent interruptions. They find it difficult to empathise with other children and to play imaginatively, and may react inappropriately in some social situations. Autistic children need varying degrees of support in these areas.

Moderate, severe or profound learning difficulties

These children have a more general learning difficulty which will affect many areas, including their communication with others. Teaching assistants need to respond to the pupils' level of language to encourage them to interact with others, while drawing on advice and support from other professionals.

Quite often, children will have communication difficulties in more than one of these areas; for example, there may be an autistic pupil who also has input from the speech and language unit. In all of these cases, pupils need support to enable them to interact constructively with others.

K5

Portfolio activity

Reflecting on the support you give

Write a short reflective account or talk to your assessor about the kinds of difficulties faced by the pupil(s) you support with communication and interaction needs.

Differences between normal communication and the patterns of communication demonstrated by pupils with developmental delay, impairment or some form of communication or language disorder

Most children follow a similar pattern of language development. (See Unit 35, K3, page 216.)

Where the development of language is delayed, this may be due to a number of different factors, which may be isolated or work in combination. Pupils who have communication impairments or disorders may also have very different needs. For example, a pupil who has a physical factor such as a cleft palate affecting their speech will need different support from a pupil who has a speech and language disorder such as oral dyspraxia (also known as DCD).

Children who have ASD will have difficulties with what is known as the 'triad of impairments', in other words social interaction, social communication and imagination. The way in which children are affected will vary, for example, in social situations some children with ASD may not be at all interested in playing with other children, while others may wish to join in but not show appropriate behaviour.

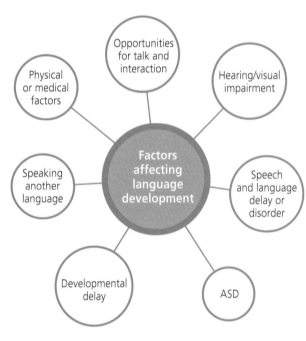

▲ Figure 39.1 Several factors may delay language development

Interaction between delayed language acquisition, cognitive development and sensory deficit

Language is crucial to learning as it is linked to our thoughts. It enables us to store information in an organised way. If pupils have difficulties in communicating with others due to one of the factors listed above, they will be working at a disadvantage because they are less able to organise their thought processes and express themselves.

As pupils grow older and the curriculum becomes more demanding, the use of rational and abstract thought becomes more important. The earlier the diagnosis of delayed language acquisition, the easier it is for professionals and others to target the pupil's needs so that they are able to give support.

Pupils with language delay may also find it harder to form relationships with others. As a result they may become both frustrated, leading to possible behaviour problems, and isolated.

Case study K7

Supporting pupils in the classroom

Douglas in Year 11 (S5) has a visual impairment, which means that he often finds it difficult to pick up on non-verbal methods of communication. He is aware of this and other pupils in the class know that when communicating with him they will sometimes need to give alternative cues.

- How else could you help Douglas in a classroom situation?
- Why is it important that others in the class are made aware of his needs?

Specific language, communication and interaction needs of the pupil(s) with whom you work

As each pupil has different needs, part of your role is to get to know them and find out their individual needs. You may be sent on specific training, for example if you are supporting a pupil with ADS, or you may need to do some research and find out about the pupil's needs yourself. Most local authorities offer training, and additional support is also available through schools, which will receive details of courses and have access to specialist teachers (see also K5).

Any individual education plans and/or behaviour support plans for the pupils with whom you work

You should be aware of what is included in the individual education plan (IEP) for the pupil(s) you support and you need to include a copy of this in your portfolio. This should include their communication targets and your role in relation to this should be highlighted. Remember to remove pupils' names from any paperwork. If your school prefers you not to document this, you can show the IEP to your assessor and talk through the targets and your role in supporting the pupil.

Strategies to enhance and promote non-verbal communication

A great deal of our communication with others is expressed non-verbally. It is important for children that they are able to recognise and respond to non-verbal signals from others. Children who are on the autistic spectrum, for example, may

Figure 39.2 Communication involves more than speech

well have difficulty in recognising and interpreting non-verbal signs. It is likely that if you are working with a pupil who has communication and interaction needs, you will be using different non-verbal strategies to support them. By using this form of communication you will be giving pupils an additional aid to understanding. The kinds of strategies you could use might be:

- **Using gestures** – This could be something as simple as a 'thumbs up' or beckoning the pupil to come over.
- **Pointing to objects** – You can help pupils to understand by giving concrete examples of what you are discussing and encouraging them to point to different objects in a similar way.
- **Using facial expressions** – A smile or nod can show approval, while you can also indicate excitement, disapproval, happiness and other emotions.
- **Using body language** – You can show that you are giving the pupil your attention through the way in which you sit or stand.
- **Specific signs and gestures** – If you suspect that a pupil has not understood a particular sign or gesture, ask them if they have, and if not, explain in a different way.

In order to enhance the non-verbal communication you use with pupils, you should also make sure that you interact with them verbally at the same time where possible. They may then be encouraged to use similar methods of non-verbal communication themselves.

Visual and auditory teaching approaches that can enhance communicative and social interactions

A number of visual and auditory approaches can be used to enhance communication and will give additional support to pupils.

- **Pictures** can be used to initiate or supplement conversation as they are a good starting point. The pupil can select a picture if they need to communicate something or show adults what they want to say.

- **Games** are often used successfully to initiate speech and involve pupils in social interactions with others.
- **Signs** are used to support pupils who are unable to communicate verbally. However, they should not be used exclusively by these pupils, as other pupils will enjoy learning the signs and teaching them to one another.
- **Story tapes, CDs, computer programmes and interactive whiteboards** are useful means of stimulating pupils' communication skills.
- **Modelling language** is important as it gives pupils the chance to hear the correct use of language.
- **Songs and rhymes** are another excellent way of reinforcing language.

Case study K10 K11

Encouraging pupil communication

Cassie in Year 7 (S1) has been in school for two terms, but does not speak at all to adults. She interacts verbally with her peers and both you and the class teacher speak to her as to other pupils, but her only responses have been to nod or shake her head.

- What strategies might you use to encourage Cassie to communicate, both verbally and non-verbally?
- How could you work with others to support Cassie in school?

How to adapt the general and technical vocabulary used by the teacher in order to match the needs of pupils with communication difficulties

Pupils with communication and interaction needs may need support when listening to the teacher in order to fully access the curriculum. This may mean that you have to check that they understand what has been said by the teacher. You can do this by asking them to repeat back to you what they understand and by talking to them as they work about what they are doing. If you are signing for pupils, make sure that you give them opportunities to show that they understand what has been said.

Physical and emotional factors which impact on a pupil's ability to engage in oral communication and ways of overcoming or minimising the effects of these

Pupils who have difficulty with oral communication may have a physical condition that makes it difficult for them to speak. A stammer or other speech impairment can often resolve itself if it is handled in a sensitive way. However, pupils who are pressurised or anxious about speaking are more likely to have persistent problems. It is important that the school, as well as parents, ensure that they do not put pressure on the pupil and allow them to take their time.

Case study

Overcoming the effects of barriers to oral communication

Matthew in Year 9 (S3) has a speech impediment, which he is usually able to overcome, although it is more apparent when he is tired. He has been working with a speech therapist, who has told the school that he should not be put under pressure when speaking. The tutor group is working on an assembly and Matthew has said that he would like to be one of the readers as he does not want his stammer to exclude him. His parents feel this is not a good idea as they are worried he will have difficulties.

- What could you do to support Matthew in this situation?
- What could the school say to his parents if he was adamant that he wanted to take part?

Role of communication and self expression in developing self-esteem (see also Unit 30)

Communicating with others is an important aspect in the development of self-esteem. As we grow up, we interact with others, which in turn reinforces our understanding of who we are and how we fit into our own families and the wider community. It is important for children as they develop that they have opportunities to socialise and work with others and to feel part of different situations. Pupils who have communication and interaction needs need to have support and encouragement and should be included in all activities with other pupils.

? Thinking point

Living without effective communication

How might you feel if you were unable to communicate effectively with others?

How to use praise and constructive feedback to promote communication which is appropriate to the situation

It is always important to praise and give feedback to pupils as they are working. All pupils will be motivated and encouraged to learn through positive interaction with adults. You can praise and feed back through verbal or non-verbal means, although as a teaching assistant you may have more opportunities than teachers to notice and acknowledge pupil progress verbally. Your assessor should see you doing this as part of your work with the pupil(s) you support, so this evidence can be covered by direct observation.

Communication methods used by the pupils with whom you work, how to use these, and how to support and promote the pupil's ability to use these effectively

It is likely that if you are supporting pupils with communication and interaction needs you will be working alongside other professionals who will be able to guide you.

You may also have had specific training, for example in the use of Makaton or other communication methods. You should also be guided by others as to the nature and extent of the support you give pupils so that it is effective, for example through the way you set up individual targets for pupils (see also Unit 21, page 114).

(see also Unit 21, page 114).

Case study K16

Supporting a pupil without an IEP

You have been asked to use Picture Exchange Communication Systems (PECS) with Anton, a Year 8 (S2) pupil on the autistic spectrum. He is new to the school and although you have used the system before it was a while ago with a much older pupil. The class teacher has asked you to work with him on a daily basis using PECS in order to develop his language skills, although you have not been given any specific language targets because he does not have an IEP yet.

- Will you be able to use the system effectively?
- What could you do in order to support Anton more meaningfully?

Aspects of culture, upbringing and home circumstances that could affect a pupil's ability to communicate with others, e.g. the different interpretations of signs and gestures

Pupils' backgrounds will have an impact on their communication patterns. This may be due to home expectations, for example in many families, children and adults do not sit down to eat together, which is one of the main opportunities for communication. One of the most important ways in which children learn to communicate is through opportunities to have language modelled and reinforced by adults. Children who do not have regular conversations with adults have less chance to listen, respond and pick up new vocabulary.

You should also be aware that different cultures may have a range of responses to the kinds of communication methods commonplace in the UK. A common or acceptable gesture or facial expression may be rude or even offensive to some cultures. For example, many Asian and African cultures avoid using eye contact as a sign of respect, whereas in Europe or North America this may imply a lack of attention and be seen as impolite.

School procedures for recording and sharing information

Your school will need to keep records and documentation to show how it has tracked the progress of pupils with special educational (ASL) needs. It is likely that your SENCo (ASL teacher) will have a system and templates for recording information on pupils, which you may be required to use for record-keeping purposes. Make sure that you follow any procedures required by the school when record-keeping and that you maintain confidentiality.

For your portfolio...

The most useful way of gathering knowledge-based evidence for this and all the special educational (ASL) needs units is to have a professional discussion with your assessor. Decide beforehand what you would like to cover so that you are ready to answer, but make sure your are able to talk about the particular needs of a pupil you support and your role in relation to this. An example of a plan for discussion might be:

- look through and talk about the pupil's IEP, and discuss their needs (K5, K8, K9, K16)
- describe the relationship between the school and the pupil's parents, and the specific support needed (K4, K17)
- explain how you plan to support the pupil's individual needs and the use of any terminology or equipment (K12).

Further reading (see also Unit 21)

Tassoni, Penny (2003) *Supporting Special Needs – Understanding Inclusion in the Early Years* (Oxford; Heinemann)

Websites

www.makaton.org – Makaton information

www.nas.org.uk – National Autistic Society

www.pecs.org.uk – PECS information

40 Support Pupils with Cognition and Learning Needs

This unit is for those who support pupils with moderate, severe or profound learning difficulties, specific learning difficulties or features of autistic spectrum disorder (ASD).

These pupils may also have sensory, physical and/or behavioural difficulties.

You may be working in a mainstream or special school.

What you need to know and understand

For this unit, you need to know and understand:

- *The school's policy on inclusive education and equality of opportunity and your role and responsibility in relation to this* (See Unit 18, K7, page 37 and Unit 23, K13, page 151)

- *The relevant school curriculum and age-related expectations of pupils in the subject/curriculum area and age range of the pupils with whom you are working* (See Unit 18, K3, page 33)

- *The teaching and learning objectives of the learning activity and the place of these in the teacher's overall teaching programme* (See Unit 18, K4, page 34)

- The cognition and learning needs of the pupil(s) with whom you work and the implications of these for supporting different types of learning activities

- How cognitive difficulties impact upon the development of language and communication, and vice versa, and how this affects learning

- The significant differences between global learning difficulties which can affect all aspects of a pupil's learning, and specific learning difficulties, e.g. dyslexia, dyspraxia, specific language impairment, which can exist as an anomaly in the overall pattern of a pupil's abilities

- The individual education plans for the pupil(s) with whom you work

- How to adapt and modify teaching and pupil materials so that pupils with cognition and learning needs are given every opportunity to understand concepts and ideas

- The importance of active learning for pupils with cognition and learning difficulties and how to promote this

- The impact of any medication used by the pupils with whom you work on their cognitive and physical abilities, behaviour and emotional responsiveness

- How to adapt or modify planned activities for pupils who are making extremely slow progress

- The sorts of problems that might occur when supporting pupils with cognition and learning difficulties and how to deal with these

- The range of cognitive skills necessary for effective learning and the effects of single or multiple disabilities on functions such as perception, memory and information processing

- Strategies for challenging and motivating pupils with learning difficulties to learn

- *The importance of active listening and how to do this* (See Unit 18, K15, page 47)

- The importance of and methods for helping pupils with cognition and learning needs to review their learning strategies and achievements and plan future learning

- *The school procedures for recording and sharing information* (See Unit 39, K18, page 263)

Cognition and learning needs of the pupil(s) with whom you work and the implications of these for supporting different types of learning activities

For effective learning to take place, pupils need to have developed a range of cognitive skills for processing and storing information. When children have cognitive difficulties, there will be an impact on the development of these skills. Pupils may therefore need help in the following areas.

- **Language, memory and reasoning skills** – Children who have cognitive and learning difficulties take longer to develop language skills. This in turn affects their learning, as they are less able to store and process information.
- **Sequencing and organisational skills** – Pupils may need help and support when organising themselves because they may find it difficult to follow sequences of ideas.
- **Understanding of numbers** – The abstract concepts of arithmetic may be difficult for these pupils to grasp and they will need practical help with numbers.
- **Problem-solving and concept development** – Understanding new ideas may take more time for these pupils and they may need you to give one-to-one support.
- **Improving gross and fine motor competencies** – These physical aspects of children's development may be affected and pupils may need regular practice or therapy.

You should talk to your assessor about the needs of the pupil(s) you support and how this affects different learning activities (see the portfolio activity on page 274).

How cognitive difficulties impact upon the development of language and communication, and vice versa, and how this affects learning

Cognitive difficulties impact on children's language and communication skills because the development of thought and language is interrelated. As children begin to understand language, they start by learning words to describe objects in the world around them. As their language development becomes more sophisticated, they begin to reason, process and store information. If a child has a language delay or disorder, their cognitive development may be affected as a result. They will also be restricted in the way they express their own ideas, which can cause frustration (see also Unit 39, K18, page 263).

Case study

Recognising how language needs impact on cognitive development

Max is in Year 10 (S4) and has a learning difficulty, which affects his ability to process language. He has a limited vocabulary and is unable to talk through his ideas effectively in class. When playing with his peers he is able to make himself understood, although he tends to play with the same three or four friends.

- How might Max's language needs impact on his cognitive development?
- Where might you seek additional help to enable you to devise some strategies to support Max?

Significant differences between global and specific learning difficulties

If you work with pupils with cognition and learning difficulties, you need to help them to develop learning strategies and begin to take responsibility for their own learning. You should agree areas and levels of support with the class teacher, following advice from outside agencies and specialists. Pupils who demonstrate features of cognitive and learning difficulties may have some of the following special educational (Additional Support for Learning (ASL)) needs:

- moderate, severe or profound learning difficulties (global learning difficulties)
- specific learning difficulties (e.g. dyslexia, dyspraxia, specific language impairment)
- autistic spectrum disorder (ASD).

Moderate, severe or profound learning difficulties

Pupils who have these difficulties are said to have a global learning difficulty, which means that all aspects of their learning can be affected. They may need help not only in the learning environment but in all areas of school and should have individual learning programmes.

Specific learning difficulties

Pupils with specific learning difficulties, such as dyslexia and dyspraxia (also known as Developmental Co-ordination Disorder (DCD)), may have problems with abstract ideas. They often find it difficult to organise themselves in the classroom and need to have input in these areas, for example thinking through what they are going to do before they start. Specific learning difficulties may only affect one area of a pupil's development as opposed to global learning difficulties, which affect all.

ASD

Pupils who have been diagnosed as having ASD may need support in learning activities as they find it difficult to think in an abstract way or pick up inferences.

They may also rely on routines and set patterns, and find it very difficult if these are changed for any reason. Autistic children may become obsessive about routine and react strongly to loud noises, which can mean that they disturb other children.

Any Individual Education Plans for the pupil(s) with whom you work

You should be aware of what is included in the individual education plan (IEP) for the pupil(s) you support and you need to include a copy of this in your portfolio. This should include their communication targets and your role in relation to this should be highlighted. Remember to remove pupils' names from any paperwork. If your school prefers you not to document this, you can show the IEP to your assessor and talk through the targets and your role in supporting the pupil.

How to adapt and modify teaching and pupil materials so that pupils with cognition and learning needs are given every opportunity to understand concepts and ideas

For learning to take place successfully, pupils need to have the necessary language and cognitive skills. Pupils who have difficulty with concepts and ideas will have problems in the areas of storing, processing and applying information (see also K11, page 271). They may therefore need support in any or all of these areas.

Storing information
In order to store new information, we need to concentrate on what we are doing. This means that pupils who are distracted or cannot make sense of the task are not able to take in what is being said. If more abstract ideas and concepts are hard for them, you will need to involve their senses in a way that will hold their attention.

Processing information
Pupils with cognition and learning needs may need to have more time to process information. They may also need you to talk through ideas with them as it may help them to vocalise their thoughts.

Applying information
This means applying what they know already in a different context or situation. Pupils with cognition and learning needs may need support in this area as they may not be able to see similarities between what they are doing and relate it to other situations.

As part of your role when supporting pupils with cognition and learning needs, you need to be able to modify and adapt materials to ensure that the curriculum is accessible to them. You may need to work with others creatively to develop appropriate materials for such pupils to help them store, process or apply information.

Case study

Modifying teaching materials

Faizana supports Suzanne, a Year 7 (S1) pupil, who has a Statement of Special Educational Needs (Co-ordinated Support Plan). In Maths today the class are completing revision on the relationship between multiplication and division, and focusing on their 5, 6, 7, 8, 9 and 10 times tables. They will be having a mental Maths test and then using worksheets, computer websites, such as the BBC bite-size revision site, and assessing one another in pairs. Suzanne has been working on her 5 and 10 times tables, but has not yet started to use the others.

- Suggest ways in which you might modify what other pupils have been asked to do in order to make the lesson more accessible to Suzanne.
- Show how you would use a step-by-step approach and check on Suzanne's learning.

Importance of active learning for pupils with cognition and learning difficulties and how to promote this

You need to support pupils with cognition and learning difficulties by acting in an enabling role, rather than by encouraging them to become dependent on your support. This is known as active learning and means that all staff should provide opportunities for pupils to develop skills such as decision-making, problem-solving and exercising choice. It is also important to think about other pupils in the class or group and how they can work together. You need to give positive reinforcement and praise to encourage all pupils when working with them on tasks and projects, to give them a feeling of achievement and to sustain their interest.

Case study

Supporting active learning

Keith has ASD and is in Year 11 (S5). He finds the demands of the curriculum difficult, especially if he is required to sit still for long periods of time, and prefers working on his own. You are in his class, although he does not have individual support. This morning Keith is working on a writing task in which he has to think about and structure a story introduction. He has started well, but has started to lose interest and keeps getting out of his chair to sharpen his pencil and delay his writing.

- Why do you think that Keith is having difficulties with this task?
- What could you do to support him in this situation?

Impact of any medication used by the pupils with whom you work on their cognitive and physical abilities, behaviour and emotional responsiveness

You should bear in mind that if pupils with whom you work are on medication this may affect their ability to focus, as well as their physical abilities or behaviour. This is because medication can slow down how children react in different situations or affect their emotions. An example of this is medication to control epilepsy, which can make children drowsy. A change in effect may also take place if a pupil increases dosage of a drug or starts to take a different type of medication. Schools should be aware if pupils are on medication and ensure that parents inform them if any changes are made, so that those working with the pupil can be notified.

Case study K10

Recognising the impact of medication

Kayleigh is on medication to control Attention deficit hyperactivity disorder (ADHD). She has to go to the school office at lunchtime to take her medication and the school signs a book to record when the medication is administered. She is in Year 8 (S2) and has been on her medication for 3 years.

You work in Kayleigh's class and notice that she has recently seemed very detached and you often catch her daydreaming or 'in her own world'.

● Do you think that Kayleigh's behaviour is a cause for concern?
● If you are working with any pupils on medication, identify how this might affect them.

How to adapt or modify planned activities for pupils who are making extremely slow progress

If you are working in a mainstream school with pupils who have cognition and learning needs, it is likely that you will need to adapt or modify planned activities at some stage to enable them to achieve (see also K8). You should have some direction from the teacher through the way in which work is differentiated, but you may also have to modify work further if pupils are still having difficulties. As you get to know pupils you will be able to tell whether planned activities will be challenging for them and be able to discuss this with the teacher, ideally at the planning stage. Modifying or adapting work may also mean taking pupils back over concepts they have already worked on in the past, in order to build up their confidence before taking them further.

Modifying or adapting work also covers additional strategies you may need to use with pupils, such as:

● changing the pace of the activity
● removing any distractions that may prevent pupils from being able to concentrate

- not giving pupils too many things to do at once or providing them with too much information (for example, 'come in and take a worksheet, put your bags under your desk, get out your books and sit down' will be too much for some)
- repeating information or instructions if necessary.

Sorts of problems that might occur when supporting pupils with cognition and learning difficulties and how to deal with these

You may find that you experience problems when supporting pupils with these difficulties. These may be related to a range of issues around the learning environment, the resources or the pupils' ability to learn.

Learning environment

Both you and pupils need to be comfortable in the learning environment. For example, you may have difficulties if you are trying to work with an autistic pupil and there are loud noises disturbing you from outside.

Resources you need

Difficulties may arise due to insufficient or inappropriate resources for the pupils you are supporting.

Pupils' ability to learn

As these pupils have cognition and learning difficulties and you may not always be able to speak to the class teacher, you need to be able to adapt to unexpected changes in activities and to modify what you have been asked to do. If you know the pupil well, and are aware of other areas targeted in their IEP, you may need to change the focus of the activity to another of greater benefit. Where possible, however, you should always aim towards the intended learning outcomes of the activity.

Range of cognitive skills necessary for effective learning and the effects of single or multiple disabilities on functions such as perception, memory and information processing

For effective learning to take place, pupils need to have a range of cognitive skills. If one or more of these are impaired, their ability to process and store information will be hampered and they will require additional support (see also K8).

- **Language skills** – Pupils need to have an appropriate level of language skills to enable them to work at the same level as their peers.
- **Self-help skills** – Pupils need to be able to organise and settle themselves so that they are 'learner ready'.
- **Motivation** – Pupils need to understand the purpose of what they are doing. Tasks should appear relevant and be geared towards the pupil's abilities and interests.
- **Concentration** – Pupils who have difficulties in concentrating are less able to take on information and store ideas.

You need to know and understand how pupils with whom you work are affected by their disabilities so that you can best support their specific needs.

Supporting cognitive skill development

Fran works in a special needs school with a number of pupils who have severe and profound learning difficulties. She spends the first half an hour of each day in greeting pupils in her class and organising timetables with them. Although she works with different pupils every day, she is aware of all their needs as the classes are small. Many of the pupils are unable to concentrate on tasks for very long. Fran and the other teaching assistants spend a long time talking to the pupils individually, encouraging them to talk about what they are doing and to relate it to their own experiences.

- What are Fran and the other adults in the school doing in order to prepare and support these pupils in the learning environment?
- How does their support impact on the cognitive skills the pupils need to develop?

Strategies for challenging and motivating pupils with learning difficulties to learn

If you are working with pupils who have learning difficulties, you need to be able to help them to sequence and structure their learning so that they begin to develop independence skills. For example, an autistic pupil will need to be aware of the routines and timetables of the classroom and will benefit from a visual timetable to show what is going to happen. It may be helpful to give the pupil the responsibility for changing the timetable daily along with another pupil. This will also help to develop their social and communication skills.

The timetable may or may not need to have the actual time of day, but will give the pupil an idea of what to expect. It will also be helpful if there is a change in routine, for example a visitor to the school. The timetable may also benefit other pupils in the class.

Pupils with cognitive and learning difficulties may benefit from 'chaining' activities to help them with their organisational skills. This involves encouraging the pupil to think about the next step when working through a series of actions. For example, if the pupil needs to organise themselves to start an activity, you need to talk them through the next step to encourage them to think ahead. This will help the pupil to start to develop these types of skills independently.

Pupils who have severe, complex or profound learning needs need to have a specialised level of support. You should work alongside teachers and other professionals to devise individual programmes, which recognise and take account of pupils' needs. They should be working towards targets, which have been shared with them where possible to enable them to experience a sense of achievement, which will in turn motivate them further.

Importance of and methods for helping pupils with cognition and learning needs to review their learning strategies and achievements and plan future learning.

It is important for all pupils to be able to review their learning strategies and start to plan for future learning. At the beginning of teaching session, pupils with cognition and learning needs in particular will benefit from revisiting what they have done before and reviewing the strategies they have used successfully. This will give them the chance to return to activities that have helped them to understand and work on different concepts. Teaching sessions should include a review of what has been covered and give opportunities for pupils to think about how they might work on a similar task in the future.

K16

Case study

Supporting learning strategy review and future learning planning

Sajida, a learning support assistant in a mainstream school, has been working with Ita, who has global learning delay. Ita is in Year 9 (S3) and is considerably behind her peers. She has support in school during the mornings.

Ita has particular difficulties with Maths concepts and Sajida is working alongside her with one other pupil on a regular basis to help her to develop her confidence. Although both pupils are working with the rest of the class during the introduction and the plenary part of the Maths lesson, Sajida also needs to give them additional support at these times.

- What can Sajida do to help both pupils to review their learning strategies?
- How will this help them to plan for future learning?

K4
K7
K2
K3
K11
K14

For your portfolio...

The most useful way of gathering knowledge-based evidence for this and all the special educational (ASL) needs units is to have a professional discussion with your assessor. Decide beforehand what you would like to cover so that you are ready to answer, but make sure your are able to talk about the particular needs of a pupil you support and your role in relation to this. An example of a plan for discussion might be:

- look through and talk about the pupil's IEP, and discuss their needs
- explain how you plan to support the pupil's individual needs.

41 Support Pupils with Behavioural, Emotional and Social Development Needs

This unit is for teaching assistants supporting pupils who have Statements of Special Educational Needs (Co-ordinated Support Plans) or individual support due to behavioural, emotional and social development needs. These pupils may also have personality disorders or challenging behaviour that arises from having complex special educational (Additional Support for Learning (ASL)) needs.

(In Scotland, the term for behavioural, emotional and social development needs is social, emotional and behavioural difficulties (SEBD).)

What you need to know and understand

For this unit, you need to know and understand:

- *The school's policy on inclusive education and equality of opportunity and your role and responsibility in relation to this* (See Unit 18, K7, page 37 and Unit 23, K13, page 151)

- The school policies and procedures relating to the behavioural, emotional and social development of pupils

- *The roles and responsibilities of others, both within and external to the school, who contribute to the support of pupils with behavioural, emotional and social development needs* (See Unit 19, K13, page 65)

- *The impact of any medication taken by pupils with whom you work on their cognitive and physical abilities, behaviour and emotional responsiveness* (See Unit 40, K10, page 271)

- The impact of any negative or traumatic home experiences of the pupils with whom you work on their behaviour and emotional responsiveness

- Any individual education plans and behaviour support plans for pupils with whom you work

- How pupil grouping and teaching and learning contexts affect the behaviour of the pupils with whom you work

- Intervention strategies appropriate for pupils with behavioural, emotional and social development needs

- The importance of modelling the behaviour you want to see and the implications of this for your own behaviour

- How to encourage and foster pupils' skills of self-monitoring and self-control

- *The importance of recognising and rewarding positive behaviour and how to do this* (See Unit 19, K8, page 62)

- *The sorts of behaviour patterns that might indicate problems such as medical problems, child abuse, substance abuse, or bullying, and who you should report these to* (See Unit 3, K17 and K18, pages 21 and 23)

- How to manage conflict, including negotiation skills and a range of diffusion and de-escalation strategies, positive handling and recovery strategies

- How and when to use physical restraint to prevent harm to pupils, yourself or others

- The sorts of behaviour or discipline problems that you should refer to others and to whom these should be referred (See K3 above)

- Levels of co-operation that can be expected of pupils at different ages and stages of development

- *Aspects of culture, upbringing, home circumstances, and physical and emotional health of pupils that could affect their ability to relate to others and how to deal with these* (See Unit 19, K17, page 68)

- Factors which influence the responses of pupils, parents/carers, teachers and others to pupils with limited social or interpersonal skills

- The factors within and outside school which influence the responsiveness to others of pupils with limited social or interpersonal skills

- How any psychological and psychiatric disorders affecting the pupils with whom you work may impact on the way in which they relate to others

- The effects of specific types of verbal behaviour, e.g. proximity, tone and gesture, and non-verbal behaviour, e.g. body language, personal space, on pupils' emotional and behavioural responses, and how positive examples of these can improve pupils' self-esteem and social response

- School policies and practices for dealing with conflicts and inappropriate behaviour

- Strategies for rebuilding damaged emotional relationships between adults and pupils, and between pupils and their peers

- *The importance of active listening skills and how these should be used to promote pupils' self-esteem* (See Unit 18, K17, page 47)

- The factors which affect the development of self-esteem

- How classroom and group dynamics can contribute to, accentuate or reinforce good/poor self-image

- Strategies that can be used to encourage and support pupils in decision-making

- When it is appropriate to give responsibility to pupils, why this is important and how family/cultural expectations of this may vary

- Stereotypical assumptions about pupils' self-reliance relative to gender, cultural background and special educational (ASL) needs and how these can limit pupils' development

- *Expected levels of self-reliance and social behaviour at different ages and developmental stages* (See Unit 19, K6, page 58)

- The importance of positive reinforcement for effort and achievement and how to provide this

- The relationship between pupil self-esteem, self-management and learning

- *The school procedures for recording and sharing information* (See Unit 39, K18, page 263 and Unit 55)

▼ Figure 41.1 Do you know what your school's behavioural and social development policies are?

School policies and procedures relating to the behavioural, emotional and social development of pupils

It is likely that your school will have a number of policies relating to pupils' behavioural and social development. You need to know what the school guidelines are and how your role relates to these. The kinds of policies of which you need to be aware are listed in more detail on Unit 19, K18, page 70.

Impact of negative or traumatic home experiences of the pupils with whom you work on their behaviour and emotional responsiveness (see also K25)

Children who have emotional and behaviour problems may be experiencing a difficult time or have had traumatic experiences at other times in their lives. For children's emotional needs to be met, they need to feel loved and secure. Children who have behavioural problems often feel less valued and may have low self-esteem as a result. In order for children to learn, their self-esteem needs to be developed, as negative opinions of themselves will damage their ability to learn. Their behaviour is often a way of seeking attention and to these children even negative attention is better than none at all. Such children need to start to feel valued again and gain positive experiences from their time in school. It is important for staff to find out as much as they can about a child's background so they can work with parents and help the child in school.

Any Individual Education Plans and behaviour support plans for pupils with whom you work

Pupils who have targets for behaviour will usually have a **behaviour support plan** or **Individual Education Plan (IEP)** in place so that they and all staff working with them are aware of their areas for development. You should be aware of what is included in the IEP for the pupil(s) you support and you need to include a copy of this in your portfolio. This should include their behaviour targets and your role in relation to this should be highlighted. Remember to remove pupils' names from any paperwork. If your school prefers you not to document this, you can show the IEP to your assessor and talk through the targets and your role in supporting the pupil. For an example of a behaviour support plan, see Unit 19, page 71.

Key terms

Behaviour support plan – statements setting out arrangements for the education of pupils with behavioural difficulties

Individual Education Plan (IEP) – targets and planned implementation strategies for pupils with special educational (ASL) needs

How pupil grouping and teaching and learning contexts affect the behaviour of the pupils with whom you work

In cases where pupils have difficulties with behaviour or social development, it is very important that they are grouped in a way which supports rather than distracts them in teaching and learning situations. You need to be aware of triggers, for example working with a particular pupil or group, or being in situations with fewer boundaries, such as outside or on school trips. As you get to know pupils you will be able to identify how they are affected by different contexts.

Minimising the adverse effects of certain contexts

Emil is 12 years old and is in a unit for pupils with social and emotional development needs attached to a mainstream school. You have just started to work at the unit and do not know him well, but are aware that he has a traumatic home life and low self-esteem and finds it hard to relate positively to adults.

You have been asked to take Emil and another pupil to the local shops as part of their work on general life skills. They have been asked to buy ingredients for the class to make biscuits. While you are walking to the shops, Emil becomes agitated, although he will not tell you why and threatens to run off as he is quite close to home.

- Do you think you should have been asked to take Emil off site?
- Is there anything you could have done before setting out that would have made it less likely for Emil to react in this way?
- What might you do in this situation both when you are out and on your return to school?

Intervention strategies appropriate for pupils with behavioural, emotional and social development needs

The kinds of intervention strategies you are able to use with pupils will to a certain extent depend on school policies and guidelines. You need to know what strategies and sanctions are available to you and whether you need to contact teachers or other staff before proceeding in some situations.

As with all pupils, those with behavioural, emotional and social development needs need adults to be proactive rather than reactive in their approach. In other words, it is important that pupils are aware of guidelines for their behaviour and the consequences of their actions. They also need to be given opportunities to develop relationships with others and treat them with respect.

▲ Figure 41.2 Strategies for intervention in schools

How to encourage and foster pupils' skills of self-monitoring and self-control

The pupils with whom you are working may need to be taught or reminded how to control their feelings. If they start to feel that they might react to a situation, they should know how to deal with their feelings. Younger pupils will generally find it harder to demonstrate self-control and even older pupils with behavioural difficulties may need support. The British Association for Anger Management (see the website at the end of this unit) gives tips and guidelines, including calming strategies, rules of anger management and steps to tackle anger.

How to manage conflict, including negotiation skills and a range of diffusion and de-escalation strategies, positive handling and recovery strategies

You may find that you have to deal with situations of conflict when managing challenging behaviour. This may involve verbal or physical aggression or abuse in the form of racist or sexist remarks. If you have not been in these sorts of situations before, you need to be prepared for them and ensure you protect your own safety and that of others. You should also make sure that you are clear on agreed school policy through discussion with others in the school. You should work to an agreed procedure and know what this is in advance.

When dealing with conflict situations, it is important to remain composed and to encourage pupils to tell you what has happened. This may involve moving away from one pupil while you speak to another, to enable them to calm down. You may also need to rebuild damaged relationships between the two parties following areas of conflict, which may involve negotiations and discussions with both sides. Increasingly, schools are using the model of restorative justice, which encourages both parties to sit down together and talk about what has happened.

The situations you could find yourself in may escalate due to the needs of the pupils with whom you are working. They may find it more difficult to control their feelings than others or sometimes display aggressive behaviour. Medication can also affect the way in which these pupils behave.

How and when to use physical restraint to prevent harm to pupils, yourself or others

Physical restraint should only be used in circumstances where pupils are likely to cause harm to others or themselves. You should always seek help as soon as possible in this situation, by sending another pupil for assistance if necessary. If you are on your own with the pupil, if possible try to move to another area where there is another adult who can act as a witness. Your school should have a policy or guidance for dealing with pupil restraint but if not, there will be local authority guidelines and all staff should be aware of these.

K14 Case study

Deciding when to use physical restraint

Lucas is in Year 7 (S1) and has been displaying some behaviour problems. He has recently been pushing, pinching and throwing things at those around him when he thinks no one is looking. However pupils have been calling out because he is hurting them and it is becoming increasingly difficult for him to remain in these whole class situations. When you have spoken to him about his behaviour, he says that he doesn't like the other pupils.

- Would you use physical restraint if he continues to do this?
- How else might you resolve this issue?
- What might be the next steps?

Levels of co-operation that can be expected of pupils at different ages and stages of development

Depending on the age and stage of the pupils you are supporting, you need to be aware of what to expect in terms of co-operation and how you should respond. Pupils at secondary school should be able to sit still and listen for longer periods than younger pupils. However to maximise concentration, passive listening periods should be interspersed with interactive learning opportunities and active tasks. In order to help pupils develop their social relationships, you need to be aware of the different stages of social development that can be expected of the pupils with whom you are working. (See also Unit 19, K6, page 58.)

Factors which influence the responses of pupils, parents/carers, teachers and others to pupils with limited social or interpersonal skills

If you work with pupils who have limited social or interpersonal skills, you need to be aware of the responses of others with whom they come into contact. People may have negative preconceptions about pupils' behaviour, emotional and social development difficulties, or they may be influenced by the comments of others. You should be careful to ensure that any negative comments are challenged and to promote a climate of equal opportunity.

The kinds of factors that influence the responses of others include:

- **Social factors** – These may exist both within and outside school. It may seem the 'norm' to talk about these pupils in a negative way or make assumptions about what they can and cannot do.
- **Peer pressure** – Other pupils may develop responses to these pupils based on the reactions of their peers. Opportunities for social integration are important so that pupils are not ignorant about those within their class or peer group who have behaviour, emotional and social development needs.
- **Previous experiences of pupils with these needs** – While it is human nature to compare experiences, you need to be careful not to make assumptions about what one pupil can do in comparison with another. All pupils will have different backgrounds and strengths.

Case study K18

Recognising influencing factors

You are working in a Year 10 (S4) tutor group and a new pupil is coming to the class. The pupil is coming from a pupil referral unit for those with behavioural needs and you have been asked to support her transition into school. At a meeting to discuss how the school will accommodate her, the class teacher says to you, 'I really don't know how we are going to manage. We had a pupil with her needs when I was working in Year 8 (S2) and it was very hard to engage him in anything.'

- How is this teacher being influenced and how might this affect you?
- Would you challenge the teacher's views?
- What would be a more appropriate approach?

Factors within and outside school which influence the responsiveness to others of pupils with limited social or interpersonal skills

Pupils who have limited social or interpersonal skills are influenced by their own backgrounds and level of need. This means that they may not be used to recognising the responses of others or are unaware of expected patterns of behaviour. They may need to be supported in how they should respond to others and taught how their own responses will affect how others see them.

The kinds of factors that influence pupils' responses to others include:

- **Degree of parental or carer involvement** – If a pupil has had limited social experiences outside school and does not have regular meaningful interactions with others, this will influence the development of their social skills. If parents or carers work with the school to support the development of these skills, the pupil is more likely to make progress.
- **Nature of pupil's needs** – The pupil may have a condition or impairment that makes communication difficult and as a result does not find it easy to relate to others.
- **Influence of outside professionals** – As teachers and other professionals work with these pupils, they should be more able to make progress and develop their social skills.

K19 Case study

Supporting pupils' responsiveness to others

Jessica is in Year 11 (S5) and has limited interpersonal skills. She has been on a behaviour support plan since starting school and works with a teaching assistant and group of other pupils for a short time each day to develop her social skills. The activities include games and group activities, discussions about others' feelings and learning to manage their own feelings.

- How might these kinds of activities benefit Jessica?
- Why is it important that Jessica's parents try to work on the same kinds of activities with her?
- Can you think of any other factors that will help Jessica?

How any psychological and psychiatric disorders affecting the pupils with whom you work may impact on the way they relate to others

If pupils with whom you work have psychological or psychiatric disorders, it is likely that they need to have additional support in relating to others. You may not have been aware of the disorder, but it could become apparent while you are working with the pupil(s). Recent research has shown that children are more likely to have these kinds of disorders if they have parents with similar conditions or if they are looked after by children (source: Tamsin Ford, Institute of Psychiatry, Kings College London).

These pupils need to have specific support and you should be given some guidance either through your Special Educational Needs Co-ordinator (SENCo)(ASL) teacher) or an educational psychologist.

Effects of specific types of verbal and non-verbal behaviour on pupils' emotional and behavioural responses, and how positive examples of these can improve pupils' self-esteem and social response

Pupils who have social and emotional development needs need to have as much positive intervention as possible to develop their self-esteem. In your work in the classroom you may be well placed to give different forms of encouragement to these pupils. For example, you may notice a pupil who is behaving well and be able to give a 'thumbs up' or other positive form of encouragement while the teacher is talking to the class. Drawing close to a pupil who is working hard and smiling or nodding may make a real difference. Remember that you may be more likely to have time to notice when these pupils are making a particular effort and should make sure that you give regular positive attention where possible.

School policies and practices for dealing with conflicts and inappropriate behaviour

As explained on page 279, you need to be clear on how to deal with conflict and **inappropriate behaviour** before it occurs so that you have a planned response. All staff should be up to date and ready to manage situations of conflict if they are working with pupils whose behaviour may be unpredictable (see also K2 and K13 and Unit 19, K11, page 64).

> ### ⓘ Key term
>
> **Inappropriate behaviour** – behaviour which conflicts with the accepted values and beliefs of the school and society. Inappropriate behaviour may be demonstrated through speech, writing, non-verbal behaviour or physical abuse

Strategies for rebuilding damaged emotional relationships between adults and pupils, and between pupils and their peers

Where relationships between adults and pupils, or pupils and peers, have broken down, it may be necessary to involve outside agencies or to set up meetings between the parties to enable them to discuss what has happened. This will give both sides opportunities to put forward their reasons for behaving in the way they did. If you are caught in the middle of an argument or difficult situation, it is always a good idea to remove one of the parties to give both sides an opportunity to calm down. You should always encourage negotiation where possible and ask pupils to talk about how they are feeling.

Factors which affect the development of self-esteem

An individual's self-esteem is affected by a number of factors, which can build up over time. If a child is given regular positive attention, opportunities to try new experiences and has a stable and loving home background, it is more likely that they will grow up to be confident individuals. A child who has low self-esteem is more likely to have had limited experiences and fewer opportunities to develop self-help skills.

K25 Case study

Identifying low self-esteem

Marlon and Antony are both in Year 9 (S2). Marlon is from a single-parent family. His mother is currently retraining as a beauty therapist. He has a large extended family, including older cousins at the school. He enjoys football and has recently been made school captain. Marlon is outgoing and has lots of friends.

Antony is from a large family with wealthy parents. He is brought to school every day with his brothers and sisters and attends breakfast and after-school clubs. He is very quiet and does not seem to enjoy school.

- Which of these two pupils do you think might have low self-esteem?
- What kinds of factors might contribute to this?

How classroom and group dynamics can contribute to, accentuate or reinforce good/poor self-image

Classroom and group dynamics can contribute to or reinforce the development of self-image as the pupil will spend a good deal of time in these situations. If they often hear that they are good or poor at something they will start to believe that it is true. This is often called 'a self-fulfilling prophecy'. Most classrooms have pupils who are known to have reputations for good or poor behaviour. If the expectation of behaviour does not encourage pupils to take pride in their achievements, they will be less likely to want to participate.

K26 Case study

Reinforcing good self-image

Sam is in Year 7 (S1) and you are working with her on an activity. She lacks motivation and has poor attention, and after a while she asks you if she has to complete all of the exercise she is working on as she is finding it difficult. However, you notice that she has managed the task well and has worked through the English activity without asking for any help. You tell her to work to the bottom of the page and then show you what she has done but she replies, 'English is difficult, I can't spell and this is the group for thickos, everyone in the class says so'.

- How could you respond to what Sam has said?
- What could you and the class teacher do to make the group feel more positive about their English skills?

Strategies that can be used to encourage and support pupils in decision-making

As children become more mature, they can be given tasks that require them to make their own decisions and choices. They will need to be given guidance as to how they can think the process through to help them to do this.

When it is appropriate to give responsibility to pupils, why this is important and how family/cultural expectations of this may vary

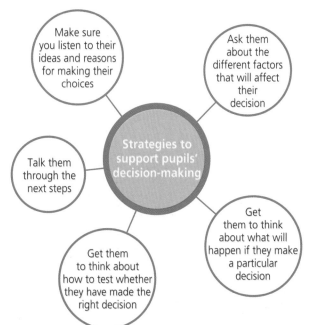

▲ **Figure 41.3** Strategies to support pupils decision-making

Self-help skills emerge as children start to develop their own independence and make their own choices when working. You may find that some pupils have been given more responsibility for their own actions at home, whereas others may have had everything done for them. However, it is important that pupils learn to take responsibilty for their own work and develop different skills. These may include:

- **Independent learning** – finding out and learning things for themselves through their work
- **Decision-making** – thinking about the next step and being responsible for their actions
- **Problem-solving** – being able to think things through using their learning skills
- **Self-expression** – being able to express what they feel
- **Exercising choice** – making their own choices about what they are going to do
- **General life skills** – being able to help themselves and others.

When you are supporting teaching and learning, pupils will ask you for your help with tasks that they may be able to do unassisted. For example, special educational (ASL) needs pupils may ask you to scribe for them just because they lack motivation rather than because the task is too difficult. You may need to break tasks down into smaller and more manageable steps, or talk pupils through them. As they become older, pupils may need help with organising themselves and planning their work, but you should be able to encourage them to be independent wherever possible. Your expectations should always be for pupils to succeed at what they are doing and they should be encouraged and praised as much as possible. In this way, they will continue to attempt to be independent. For example, sometimes you might start something off for a pupil to encourage them to continue it.

Stereotypical assumptions about pupils' self-reliance and how these can limit pupils' development (see also Unit 19, K16)

Stereotyping of any kind can have a negative effect. You should make sure that you do not make stereotypical assumptions about pupils' self-reliance for any reason such as gender, disability or cultural background. You may not be aware that you are doing it, but by mentioning these issues, pupils' self-esteem and motivation can be easily damaged. You should also make sure that if you hear any pupils making comments about others in negative terms, you speak to them straightaway.

K29 Case study

Being aware of the effect of stereotypical assumptions

You are working with a group of Year 8 (S2) pupils when you hear Isla talking to another pupil about her twin brother and the school trip to France the following week. She says that he always needs his mum to get everything ready for him in the morning because boys are not as good at being organised and that she hopes she will not have to do everything for him while they are away.

- How could Isla's comments be limiting to her brother's development if she speaks about him like this on a regular basis?
- What might you say to Isla in this situation?

Importance of positive reinforcement for effort and achievement and how to provide this (see also K11)

Pupils need to be given plenty of positive reinforcement for effort as well as for achievement. Schools may do this in a number of ways, including merit marks, certificates or special assemblies as well as through verbal praise. Although you should always notice and praise what pupils have achieved, their efforts should also be acknowledged. Pupils may sometimes work very hard, but then compare their work with that of others and feel that they have not done as well. Teaching assistants will often be in a position to notice and recognise pupils' efforts and achievements and, where appropriate, comment on their observations to teachers.

K31 Portfolio activity

Reinforcing positive efforts and achievements

Outline some of the ways in which your school reinforces the positive efforts and achievements of pupils.

Relationship between pupil self-esteem, self-management and learning

As already discussed, the level of pupils' self-esteem will be directly related to how they perceive themselves – their self-image. (See also Social and emotional development in Unit 19, page 58.)

Children who are developing normally show levels of independence and self-reliance at about the stages defined in the table of social and emotional development (see page 58). It is important for adults to help children to build up their self-image and self-esteem through giving them tasks that are achievable for their age and stage of development. Children's self-image will be based largely on adults' reactions to what they do, which will in turn help them to gain a positive view of themselves. It is vital that pupils develop a good self-image, to give them greater confidence in their abilities and enable them to fulfil their academic potential.

For your portfolio...

**K3
K6
K7
K8
K9
K11
K15
K20
K21
K24
K27**

The most useful way of gathering knowledge-based evidence for this and all the special educational (ASL) needs units is to have a professional discussion with your assessor. Decide beforehand what you would like to cover so that you are ready to answer, but make sure you are able to talk about the particular needs of a pupil you support and your role in relation to this. An example of a plan for discussion might be:

- look through and talk about the pupil's IEP, and discuss their needs (K6)
- explain how you plan to support the pupil's individual needs and the use of any terminology or equipment (K3, K15, K20)
- discuss how any strategies you use with these pupils will support their behaviour (K6, K7, K8, K9, K11, K21, K24, K27).

Websites

www.angermanage.co.uk/keepcool.html – British Association of Anger Management (BAAM)

www.iop.kcl.ac.uk – Institute of Psychiatry

42 Support Pupils with Sensory and/or Physical Needs

This unit is for those who provide support for pupils who have degrees of hearing, visual and/or physical impairment. This may be in a special needs school or mainstream setting. If you are supporting pupils who have needs in these areas, you will need to show how you enable them to maximise learning in individual, group and class activities.

What you need to know and understand

For this unit you will need to know and understand:

- *The school's policy on inclusive education and equality of opportunity and your role and responsibility in relation to this* (See Unit 18, K7, page 37 and Unit 23, K13, page 151)

- The basic principles of current disability discrimination, equality and rights legislation, regulation and codes of practice

- The roles and responsibilities of others, both within and external to the school, who contribute to the support of pupils with sensory and/or physical needs

- The effect of a primary disability on pupils' social, emotional and physical development

- How to select and use teaching and learning materials in an appropriate medium, e.g. tactile diagrams, Braille, computer software, symbols and subtitled video material

- The physical management of pupils, including suitable lifting techniques, appropriate seating, lighting and acoustic conditioning

- The sorts of specialist equipment and technology used by the pupils with whom you work, and how it helps overcome or reduce the impact of sensory or physical impairment

- How to help pupils to contribute to the management of their own specialist equipment

- The impact of chronic illness, pain and fatigue on learning

- *The impact of any medication taken by the pupils with whom you work on their cognitive and physical abilities, behaviour and emotional responsiveness* (See Unit 40, K10, page 271)

- The effect of long-standing or progressive conditions on the emotions, learning, behaviour and quality of life of pupils

- The importance of praise and encouragement in helping pupils to experience achievement and independence and how to use these effectively

- How to make optimal use of residual sensory and physical functions

- The range of physical, motor and/or sensory disabilities of the pupils with whom you work and the sorts of structured activities needed to help them overcome or reduce the impact of these

- How to provide a structured activity within a group setting

- The need for responsiveness and flexibility in implementing structured activities for pupils with sensory and/or physical needs

- Techniques for positive reinforcement, how it should be used and its effects on pupils

- The need and methods for adaptive responses to the pupil's behaviour and achievements

- A pupil's need for independence, control, challenge and sense of achievement

- The importance of valuing a pupil and how to communicate this

- When it is appropriate to intervene in a pupil's activity and how to do this with sensitivity and respect for the pupil

- The importance of responding to and interacting with the pupil, including communicating plans and intentions to the pupil, in an appropriate way

- *The school procedures for recording and sharing information* (See Unit 39, K18, page 263)

Basic principles of current disability discrimination, equality and rights legislation, regulation and codes of practice

If you are supporting pupils with sensory and/or physical impairment, it is important that you should have an awareness of disability and equal rights legislation and codes of practice. For a detailed list of current legislation and codes of practice, see Unit 38, K2, page 244.

Roles and responsibilities of others, both within and external to the school, who contribute to the support of pupils with sensory and/or physical needs

As well as the class teacher, there will be others both within and outside school who contribute to the support of pupils with sensory or physical impairment. You may also have access to written information and reports from the following sources.

- The school's **SENCo** (Special Educational Needs Co-ordinator)(Additional Support for Learning (ASL) teacher) will be available to support the class teacher and teaching assistant in the development of IEPs (Individual Education Plans).
- **Specialist teachers** – these professionals may be available from the local Sensory Support Service to offer advice and equipment and to visit the pupil from time to time.
- **Physiotherapists/occupational therapists** – may be able to visit the school, or pupils may have to go on a waiting list before they can be seen. These therapists will develop individual programmes for pupils to use at home, with advice for activities they can work on in school.
- **Other professionals** – these may be inside or outside the school, but may have experience of dealing with children who have physical or sensory impairment.

You will also periodically need to provide these people with information about the pupil's progress and participation in learning activities, whether these are cognitive, creative or physical.

Portfolio activity

Identifying those who contribute to supporting pupils with sensory and/or physical needs

Using the list above as a guide, write down the help available within your school for yourself and other support staff who contribute to the learning needs of pupils with sensory and/or physical impairment.

Effect of a primary disability on pupils' social, emotional and physical development

Pupils with physical or sensory impairments may be less able to concentrate than their peers. They may find that they tire easily or become frustrated if they are unable to complete tasks as quickly or as well as they would hope to. One way of supporting these pupils is through the use of multi-sensory activities, which will help them to sustain their concentration. It is also important that adults are able to reassure pupils and give them encouragement to maintain their interest and enthusiasm. This can be done by praising them for their efforts and by giving them levels of assistance that are consistent with their abilities. If too much help is given, pupils will not experience a sense of achievement and independence, but if too little is given, they may become frustrated and lose interest. Inclusive education is important to ensure that these pupils do not lose confidence by being unable to participate in learning activities enjoyed by their peers.

Case study

Recognising the effects of disabilities on development

Bianca has albinism and as a result has a lack of pigment in her skin, hair and eyes, and has a visual impairment. She has a level of independence, but can get angry and frustrated with her condition and upset when she takes longer to complete tasks than her peers. She tells you that she does not like feeling 'different' from other pupils and wishes that she did not have to ask for help.

- How has Bianca's condition affected her physical, social and emotional development?
- What would you say to her in this situation?

How to select and use teaching and learning materials in an appropriate medium

You need to develop an awareness of the kind of teaching and learning materials appropriate for the needs of the pupil(s) you are supporting. These may be quite straightforward and easy to use or you may need to have further training, for example if you are expected to work with Braille. The list in the table below is not exhaustive, but gives some examples of what might be available to you.

Materials and potential uses

Tactile diagrams	These may be used for pupils with sensory impairment to support discussions and aid their understanding.
Braille	Your school may have learning materials already available or you may need to have training in order to prepare materials. If you are working in a special needs school, you may have access to additional resources to support different subject areas, such as Braille globes for geography.
Computer software	Pupils with physical or sensory support needs may be able to use a variety of technology and computer software to stimulate their learning. Computer software may be useful for both aural and visual stimulation, and also for developing the responses of pupils with physical impairment.
Symbols	Symbols may be used to support hearing-impaired pupils or those who have communication difficulties due to physical impairment.
Subtitled video material	This will be useful for hearing-impaired pupils.

When you start to work with a pupil who has a sensory or physical impairment, it is likely you will be given some information about the kinds of teaching and learning materials available to you. You may also get to know suitable materials through your work with pupils, but you should also keep a lookout for any new materials that become available. One way of doing this is through special needs catalogues and magazines, which you should be able to access through your SENCo (ASL teacher). You may also get information from outside professionals who come into school to support your work with these pupils or through training sessions run by your local authority.

If you have found your own materials outside school or through other contacts, make sure that you consult the SENCO (ASL teacher) or class teacher before using them in school.

Case study K5

Introducing new activities

Hannah is working with Jenna, a child in Year 7 (S1), who has difficulties with her fine motor skills and hand/eye co-ordination. She needs additional work each day in order to develop her muscle control and manipulative skills. Although Hannah has been given a list of activities to work on, including cake-making tasks, threading and puzzles, she would like to make the activities more varied and interesting for Jenna.

● How would Hannah go about developing more activities to work on?
● Would she need to speak to other staff before introducing any new activities?

Physical management of pupils, including suitable lifting techniques, appropriate seating, lighting and acoustic conditioning

If you are supporting pupils with sensory or physical development needs, it is likely that you will have additional help and advice through other professionals, such as specialist teachers or physiotherapists, to help with physical management. These pupils are likely to need adjustments to be made to the learning environment to enable them to have full access to the curriculum. For example, a pupil who has a physical impairment may need to have a special seat or wheelchair appropriately positioned in the classroom. Pupils with visual impairments may be sensitive to lighting or unable to face windows due to the glare. Pupils with hearing impairments may need to be positioned to enable them to hear more clearly or to lip-read. Make sure that you are aware of measures you can take to help pupils with physical needs to access the curriculum more fully.

Unless you are working in a special needs school, it is unlikely that you will be required to lift pupils, but if you are asked to do, so it is important that you receive appropriate training. (See also Unit 3, page 7.)

(See also Unit 3, page 7.)

K6 Portfolio activity

Identifying the adaptations needed for physical management of pupils

Either show your assessor how the learning environment has been adapted or describe what considerations need to be taken into account in order to manage the pupil(s) you support who have a physical impairment.

Sorts of specialist equipment and technology used by the pupils with whom you work, and how it helps overcome or reduce the impact of sensory or physical impairment

You need to know the kinds of **specialist equipment** and technology that are designed to help children overcome or reduce the impact of their sensory or physical impairment, and to select and use the ones that are appropriate for helping the pupil with whom you are working.

You may be given advice and equipment from outside agencies, which go into schools to acquaint staff with the kinds of equipment available. These may include Brailling machines, which enable trained support workers to prepare materials in Braille form; auditory aids such as microphones or hearing loops, which may need to be professionally installed; or other technical equipment that is on the market to support these pupils. The school may also be visited by professionals such as the

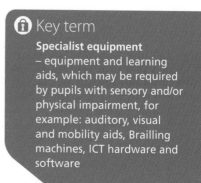

ⓘ Key term

Specialist equipment – equipment and learning aids, which may be required by pupils with sensory and/or physical impairment, for example: auditory, visual and mobility aids, Brailling machines, ICT hardware and software

local institute for the blind, which may give advice on equipment that could be used in school or suggest ways the enviroment could be adapted.

Some equipment, such as sloping desks to help pupils who have difficulties with handwriting or specialist ICT software, may already be available in school. You should have support from your SENCo (ASL teacher) and class teacher so that you are able to access this, use any specialist equipment and attend any training that becomes available.

Portfolio activity K7

Recognising the benefits of using specialist equipment or technology

Show or describe to your assessor during a school visit or write a written account of the types of specialist equipment or technology that is used by the pupil(s) who you support. What impact does the equipment have on the pupil(s) and how does it help them to overcome or reduce the impact of their impairment on their learning?

How to help pupils to contribute to the management of their own specialist equipment

Pupils may be accustomed to using particular pieces of equipment and so may also be able to show you or others how to use it. Ideally, they will become used to managing some of it; for example, if they use a hearing aid, they may be able to change the battery independently. Pupils should be encouraged to be as independent as possible rather than rely on adults to manage equipment for them.

When supporting pupils, particularly if they are younger or if you are demonstrating or using equipment for the first time, make sure you go through procedures slowly with them and talk about what you are doing as you go so that they understand why you are doing it. You can then ask them to try to do it themselves. Depending on the equipment used, you may need to go through manuals with them or talk to them about how they might access further support if needed.

Impact of chronic illness, pain and fatigue on learning

If pupils have chronic illnesses or conditions which mean that they are in pain or tire easily, they will not be able to concentrate for as long as their peers and may well find learning more of a challenge. This may lead to frustration and other issues (such as being upset about their condition, reluctance to engage in structured activities such as physiotherapy or fear about the progressive nature of their condition), which may be challenging for you to manage in the learning environment. If pupils are affected by such factors, you should speak to other professionals about how to approach them.

Effect of long-standing or progressive conditions on the emotions, learning, behaviour and quality of life of pupils

As well as tiring easily, pupils who have sensory and/or physical impairment may also find that their emotions are affected by their condition. As their needs and personalities will vary, this may take different forms, but you will need to speak to others about how to approach a pupil whose condition is affecting their behaviour.

K9 K19

Case study

Supporting pupils' development

Reece has Duchenne Muscular Dystrophy and is in a mainstream secondary school. When he started in Year 7 (S1), he was able to walk independently, but his condition is progressive and he will eventually need to be permanently in a wheelchair. His physiotherapist comes in each week to talk to you and you have close contact with his parents. He is presently in Year 8 (S2) and is using a walking frame to move around the school, which means that his progress is slower than other pupils'. In the classroom, he is able but not enthusiastic about learning. He mixes with other pupils well and they are patient with him. However, he often says that he wishes he was able to join in with them more, particularly at playtimes.

- How is Reece's condition affecting different areas of his development?
- What could you do to support him and improve his quality of life while he is at school?

▲ **Figure 42.1** Does your school promote inclusion?

Importance of praise and encouragement in helping pupils to experience achievement and independence and how to use these effectively

All pupils need to be praised and encouraged during their learning in order to develop their confidence and self-esteem, and also to help sustain their concentration. Pupils with physical impairments may find it harder to experience achievement and independence, and as you get to know them you should acknowledge when they are trying hard and making particular effort. The way in which you do this may be verbal if you are sitting close to them or you may be able to make non-verbal gestures, such as a smile or thumbs up, if you are unable to speak to them. You should also tell the class teacher and others who work with the pupil if they have worked particularly hard or made progress. It is very important to be positive with pupils, in particular if the effects of their condition mean that they can become disheartened easily.

How to make optimal use of residual sensory and physical functions

You need to work alongside other professionals so that you can devise a programme of activities for pupils which builds on their strengths in other areas. Depending on their needs, pupils should have access to a range of sensory activities that enable them to play as full a part in the curriculum as possible. You should always make sure that you speak to others before introducing new activities.

Portfolio activity K13

Maximising the use of sensory and physical functions

How might you use other senses and physical functions to support the learning of a pupil who:

- is hearing impaired
- is visually impaired
- has cystic spina bifida and limited mobility?

Range of physical, motor and/or sensory disabilities of the pupils with whom you work and the sorts of structured activities needed to help them overcome or reduce the impact of these

The range of physical impairments you support will depend on the setting in which you work. If you are employed in a special needs school, you may be working with different pupils every day, who each have their own programmes and timetables to enable them to develop in different areas. In a mainstream school, the pupil will work alongside other pupils for most of the time, but may need to come out of class on a daily basis for other sessions, such as physiotherapy, with an adult.

Each pupil should have an IEP, outlining time-bound targets on which they are working at any time. Their programme of activities will then take these targets into consideration.

You should show or discuss with your assessor the profile of the pupil(s) with whom you work and how activities are structured to support their specific needs. (See 'For your portfolio' at end of this unit.)

How to provide a structured activity within a group setting

Depending on the needs of others within the group, you may be able to structure activities for the benefit of all pupils. For example, if the pupil you support needs to develop their fine motor skills through additional activities and there are other pupils with similar needs, they may be able to work together. You can do this through sitting close to your pupil while monitoring the progress of others.

Need for responsiveness and flexibility in implementing structured activities for pupils with sensory and/or physical needs

If pupils with sensory or physical impairment are finding an activity more challenging than anticipated, it is important that you respond to this accordingly (see also K21 below). Because you know the pupil and their needs, you will be able to tell if the task is inappropriate or the pupil is unlikely to complete it for a short-term reason such as being upset. You may need to modify the task so that it is more achievable. Alternatively, if the pupil does well and completes the task quickly, you may be able to extend the activity or take the pupil to the next stage. You should make sure that you respond appropriately to the pupil and the situation; if you are not sure how to do this, it is worth discussing with the teacher at the planning stage so that you are prepared.

Pupil's need for independence, control, challenge and sense of achievement

All pupils need to experience a degree of independence. Without this they will not have a sense of control and achievement, which is crucial to effective learning. Pupils should be given opportunities to face challenges in their learning, develop their own ideas, and have ownership of what they are doing. Your role is to act as an enabler so that, through appropriate tasks and effective questioning, pupils can reach learning objectives.

Importance of valuing a pupil and how to communicate this

When supporting any pupil, not only those who have special educational (ASL) needs, you should show that you value them by demonstrating active listening and responding appropriately to what they are doing and saying. You should always communicate and discuss plans and intentions with pupils so that they feel more involved in the learning experience and understand what will be happening. This may take the form of a visual timetable that all pupils use or there might be a sign on each table outlining the activity and learning objective. It is important to take pupils' ideas and concerns seriously and to respond appropriately so that they feel able to talk about any worries they may have.

Pupils will be aware if you do not appear interested in their activities or are insincere when speaking to them. This will mean that any praise or positive reinforcement will not have the desired effect. If adults do not show respect for children, it is unlikely that they will be able to show it themselves.

When it is appropriate to intervene in a pupil's activity and how to do this with sensitivity and respect for the pupil

If you are working with a pupil who is finding an activity difficult to complete due to their physical or sensory impairment, it may be necessary for you to intervene. Although this is not ideal and tasks should be set so that they are attainable, pupils may occasionally be unable to continue. You may need to talk to them about this and ask whether it would help if you were to intervene. You should always speak to them first and talk them through your suggestions.

Case study
K16
K18
K21

Intervening in activities

You are working in a Drama lesson with John, a Year 8 (S2) pupil, who has poor spatial skills and co-ordination. He has dyspraxia and one of his targets is to work on throwing and catching. His group has suggested a role play, which unfortunately involves an obstacle course and throwing a ball through a hoop. Before showing the role play to the rest of the class, John becomes upset and says that he will not be able to do it.

- What would you say to John?
- When and why should you intervene in this case?
- Can you think of some suggestions you could make in order to maintain John's self-esteem and enable him to complete the activity?

K3
K4
K5
K7
K8
K9
K11
K14
K15
K18

For your portfolio...

The most useful way of gathering knowledge-based evidence for this and all the special educational (ASL) needs units, apart from being observed with the pupil you support, is to have a professional discussion with your assessor. You should decide beforehand what you would like to cover so that you are ready to answer, but should be able to talk about the particular needs of the pupil you support and your role in relation to this. An example of a plan for discussion might be:

- look through and talk about the pupil's IEP and discuss their needs and targets
- talk about the effects of the pupil's disability on their development and how this influences the support you give them (K4, K9, K11, K18)
- explain how you support the pupil's individual needs, the input of other professionals and the use of any specialist terminology or equipment (K3, K5, K7, K8, K14, K15).

References

McNamara, S. and Moreton, G. (1993) *Teaching Special Needs* (David Fulton)

QCA (2001) *Planning, Teaching and Assessing the Curriculum for Pupils with Learning Difficulties* (available from www.nc.uk.net/ld/ and giving general guidance plus individual guides for each National Curriculum subject)

Tassoni, P. (2003) *Supporting Special Needs – Understanding Inclusion in the Early Years* (Oxford; Heinemann)

Websites

www.dfes.gov.uk/sen

www.inclusion.ngfl.gov.uk/

www.nasen.org.uk – National Association for Special Educational Needs

47 Enable Young People to be Active Citizens

This unit is suitable for those who support pupils during Citizenship lessons or activities that are based within the community. It looks at how you can help pupils develop their understanding of the issues within their community through investigation. It also looks at how to empower pupils to have a voice and to present their ideas and opinions to members of their communities.

What you need to know and understand

For this unit, you will need to consider:

- Different types of communities

- Internal and wider issues affecting young people in their communities

- Roles, rights and responsibilities of individuals and groups in relation to communities and society

- Legal requirements, equal opportunities and anti-discriminatory practice

- The way in which special interest groups such as young people interact with other special interest groups within the community

- Decision-making processes in various communities

- Why it is important to build young people's confidence in their ability to influence the situations in which they operate

- How to assist young people to develop and use a range of influencing skills

- Assertiveness and confidence-building techniques

- Why it is important to encourage young people to develop and present their views and needs themselves

- A range of methods for developing a presentation or business case

- A range of sources of information (e.g. grant application guidelines, needs analyses, own and organisational objectives) which could be used when developing presentations or business cases

- What kinds of skills young people may be able to contribute in preparing presentations or business cases

- The aims, objectives and values of the young people and those of the decision-makers

- How to enable young people to make effective presentations

- How to work with young people to build their negotiation skills

- How to review the outcomes of presentations

With the introduction of the National Curriculum subject **Citizenship** at Key Stages 3 and 4, schools have a responsibility to develop not only the educational skills but the personal and social aptitudes of their pupils. The Citizenship **programme of study** contains the following three strands, which enable young people to be active citizens within their community:

- social and moral responsibility
- community involvement
- political literacy.

 Key terms

Citizenship – the subject that looks at the status, roles, rights and responsibilities of young people as active citizens within their community.

Programme of study – sets out the content, knowledge and skills to be taught to enable pupils to achieve the attainments targets

The Citizenship curriculum also provides pupils with the potential tools to achieve the following outcomes outlined in the recently introduced Every Child Matters framework:

- succeed in and enjoy life
- recognise and manage risks and stay safe
- be aware of how to stay healthy
- take part in society and develop relationships
- participate in working life.

Giving pupils social and moral responsibility, involving them in the community, developing their political literacy, allowing them to participate in working life, society and helping them to develop relationships will provide them with the necessary skills to become fully active citizens.

Different types of communities

It is not easy to define the term 'community' as so many competing theories and definitions exist. For example, some believe a community to be based on a geographical area or place; physical features such as a river or mountain range make it clear where the community boundaries begin and end. However, Cohen (1985) believed that community boundaries are not always as obvious as physical features, but suggests that they exist in the minds of those who are part of the community. Frazer (1999) agrees and stipulates that communities could be approached or defined in terms of values, for example, a religious community. Hoggett (1997) goes on to define a community in terms of a group of people who share a common characteristic, for example, linguistic or ethnic similarities. Moreover, online and virtual communities have now also emerged.

'Britain – A Diverse Society', a unit at Key Stage 3 in the Citizenship curriculum, requires pupils to look at and respect their own identity and the different national, cultural, regional, religious and ethnic identities of other communities.

Portfolio activity K1

Identifying relevant communities

Make a list of all the possible communities the pupils you support could be considered a part of. Ensure you include geographical communities as well as those based on values and common characteristics. Describe the main features of the communities you list.

Internal and wider issues affecting young people in their communities

There are many issues affecting young people in their communities today. You only have to open a local, national or international newspaper or watch the news to be reminded of this fact on a daily basis. Unfortunately, communities can sometimes be plagued by both **intra-community** problems and **inter-community** problems. Some problems affect many communities and others are specific to a particular community.

The Citizenship curriculum focuses on a variety of internal and wider issues affecting communities

Key Stage 3	• crime • human rights • how the law protects animals – a local-to-global study • government, elections and voting • debating a global issue • how we deal with conflict
Key Stage 4	• challenging racism and discrimination • how and why laws are made • how the economy functions • business and enterprise • taking part – planning a community event • consumer rights and responsibilities

There are many agencies, bodies and laws that have been, and are constantly being, introduced to help overcome detrimental community issues. For example, anti-social behaviour orders (ASBOs) have been introduced to try and curb violent, destructive and abusive behaviour. The probation and police services are also trying to introduce preventative measures for anti-social behaviour such as recreation facilities, youth provision and educational visits to schools. Anti-bullying Week also forms part of the Citizenship curriculum nationwide and many schools use this as a tool to highlight the concerns around bullying within communities.

> **🛈 Key terms**
>
> **intra-community** – affecting the community from within, e.g. internal conflicts such as a civil war
>
> **inter-community** – affecting two or more communities, e.g. war between two or more different communities

K2 K3 Portfolio activity

Considering community issues and how they are dealt with

Chose a community with which the pupils you support can be identified. Write a reflective account to highlight any inter/intra-community issues affecting that community. You may wish to include past as well as present issues. Outline the agencies, bodies, legislation introduced/to be introduced or strategies used/to be used to help resolve the issues.

Roles, rights and responsibilities of individuals and groups, including legal requirements

Communities and their members have many different roles, rights and responsibilities. The majority of rights and responsibilities that apply to all sections of society are outlined in **public Acts of Parliament**. In contrast, the rights and responsibilities conferred in **private Acts of Parliament** are applicable only to specific groups, such as particular local authorities or companies.

There are also other types of 'law', which are shaped by the morals and values (e.g. family, cultural and religious values) commonly held within specific communities.

ⓘ Key terms

Public Acts of Parliament – legislation enforced by parliament, which changes the general law and applies to all sections of society

Private Acts of Parliament – legislation, also known as local and personal Acts, enforced by parliament and applicable to specific groups within society

Examples of the roles, rights and responsibilities assigned by different acts

Act	Examples of roles, rights and responsibilities
Violent Crime Reduction Act 2006	• local police authority must ensure the welfare of community members in alcohol disorder zones • if a pupil is suspected of carrying a knife only the headteacher (or a member of staff designated by the headteacher), of the same sex, in the presence of another member of staff of the same sex, can carry out a search; only outer clothing can be removed
Disability Discrimination Act 2005	• individuals with disabilities have the right to equality between disabled persons and other persons, to be treated with positive attitudes and to be encouraged to participate in public life
Education Act 2005	• the school governing body can take responsibility for the training and development of the school workforce
Human Rights Act 1998	• all humans have the right to freedom of expression, thought, conscience and religion

The Citizenship course intends to build an awareness of the roles, rights and responsibilities of individuals within the community through various units of study

Key Stage 3	• human rights • how the law protects animals • celebrating human rights
Key Stage 4	• human rights • consumer rights and responsibilities • rights and responsibilities of the world of work

Equal opportunities and anti-discriminatory practice

Enforcing equal opportunities and making sure that practices do not discriminate helps community members to feel valued and accepted, and tends to give them a sense of belonging and responsibility towards the community. Discrimination, such as racial discrimination, may lead to individuals becoming segregated and isolated from the community and to tensions and conflict within society.

Groups have been established by the government to ensure equal opportunities and anti-discriminatory practice. For example, the Commission for Equality and Human Rights – www.cehr.org.uk.

The Commission for Equality and Human Rights replaced the following legislation in October 2007:

- Equal Opportunities Commission which dealt with sex discrimination
- Commission for Racial Equality
- Disability Rights Commission

The websites of the above commissions have now been amalgamated into www.equalityhumanrights.com

The Department for Communities and Local Government (DCLG) (http://www.communities.gov.uk/) has overall responsibility to carry out regular **discrimination law reviews** to ensure current anti-discriminatory legislation is up to date.

> **Key term**
>
> **Discrimination law reviews** – analyse how efficient the current equality legislation is and bring current frameworks up to date and in line with European legislation

K3 K4 Case study

Recognising the importance of anti-discriminatory practice

You have been asked to support a Year 10 (S4) Citizenship class to prepare a campaign for the human rights of those with disabilities within their own communities. You have been asked to give pupils a short five-minute presentation on the importance of anti-discriminatory practice.

- Which legislation or guidance will you ask the pupils to refer to?
- What information will you give on the importance of anti-discriminatory practice?
- What rights, roles and responsibilities of those with disabilities will you expect the pupils to include in their campaign?

K3 K4 Portfolio activity

Identifying legislation relevant to citizens' roles and responsibilities

Research the legislation that outlines the roles and responsibilities of community members as required by the Citizenship curriculum for the key stage/s you support. Pay particular attention to equal opportunities and anti-discriminatory practice.

The way in which young people interact with others in the community

There are many different ways that young people interact with others within their community. Speaking and listening are used on a daily basis to interact, although different linguistic nuances, dialects, slang come into play depending on which

▲ Figure 47.1 Terminology used by secondary pupils can sometimes seem like a foreign language to adults

community the young person identifies with. Written language, for example in the form of campaign posters, also communicates with others. This also varies from one community to another, for example, Chinese and Japanese alphabets use symbols to represent ideas, whereas most European alphabets use letters to represent speech sounds.

Also bear in mind that the way in which young people interact depends on who they are interacting with. For interacting with their peers, they have their own 'text talk' (e.g. 'lol' for 'laugh out loud'), street talk (e.g. 'phat' for something that is good) and chat room and instant messenger talk (e.g. 'MOS' for 'mother over shoulder'). This can sometimes seem like a foreign language to adults, and pupils are unlikely to interact in this way with their headteacher.

It is also important to consider non-verbal forms of interaction such as gestures and other forms of body language. Group members may have a preferred gesture to greet each other, such as a kiss on the cheek or a specific type of handshake.

It is also amazing how young people take all the constant rapid development of online communication methods in their stride and regularly use a vast range of virtual communication.

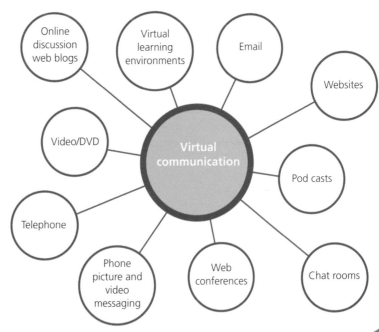

▲ Figure 47.2 There are many methods for communicating with young people

Case study

Supporting work on acceptable and unacceptable interaction

There has been a recent spurt of violent gang-style interaction within your community, a community you share with the majority of the pupils at your school. The media have suggested that the violence is a result of racism between two sub-groups in the community. The headteacher asks you to support a group of Year 11 (S4) Drama pupils to prepare an assembly on acceptable and unacceptable methods of interaction.

- How could the pupils demonstrate that violence is an unacceptable form of communication?
- How could the message of acceptable forms of interaction be portrayed?
- Which units of the Citizenship curriculum could you revisit and why?

Decision-making processes in various communities

Democratic communities, such as Britain today, allow certain members of the community to elect people to represent them. In principle, decisions are reached after the pros and cons of issues have been discussed, either at national or local level. Some communities elect sub-committees, which evaluate issues and fine tune decisions on behalf of the wider community. Such sub-committees, for example school governing bodies, usually include individuals most affected by the decisions taken, as well as neutral members.

In other communities, decisions are taken in different ways; for example they may be based on religious faiths and beliefs. In dictatorships, decisions are made by one person and all members of the community are expected to accept the dictator's decisions without question, for example, in the Franco era in Spain and in Hitler's Germany. Youth sub-communities may make decisions according to an 'unwritten' code and fall easy prey to peer pressure, where a few dominant members of the group have the power to sway decisions.

Pupils at your school will have some background knowledge of different communities and their politics (and hence how they make decisions) through their study of history. You may be able to help them draw information from this knowledge when discussing different decision-making processes.

Citizenship units that focus on the different types of decision-making process within the British and European communities

Key Stage 3	• local democracy • governments, elections and voting • developing skills of democratic participation
Key Stage 4	• how and why laws are made • Europe – who decides

Evaluating decision-making processes

List the communities or sub-groups which you are part of in your school, for example, you may be a member of the inclusion team or a school governor. Write a reflective account about a time when your 'community' or sub-group was required to make a decision. Produce a flow chart of the steps taken in the decision-making process. Evaluate the decision-making process and suggest alternatives.

Building young people's abilities to influence situations

To empower pupils to voice their opinions and ideas to others within their communities or to other communities you need to help them develop a range of skills. For example, you need to build their confidence and assertiveness, and look at the skills needed to influence and present ideas and opinions.

You also need to help them understand that their own aims, objectives and values may differ considerably from those of the people they are trying to influence. That is why it is important for them to be assertive and have the confidence to voice their opinions if they differ from those of the decision-maker. However, pupils must also respect the opinions of others and accept that they have a right to them. Nonetheless, a strong and effectively presented case or presentation may lead two parties with different values to at least compromise.

The importance of building young people's confidence and assertiveness to develop and present their views and needs themselves

With confidence comes the ability to become involved in social situations as the citizen of a community. Moreover, confident young people tend to be more charismatic and popular, and may find it easier to overcome life's challenges. Confidence and assertiveness can lead to good mental health and eliminate poor self-attitudes, ensuring pupils learn how to value their own views and opinions. With confidence, they can find the strength to motivate themselves. If they can neither value their own opinions nor motivate themselves, how can they be expected to present their views and have a voice?

Assertive presentation of views is the middle ground between aggressive and passive communication. Aggressive pupils will believe that they can express all their ideas and opinions at the expense of others' rights. Aggressive pupils will behave as if the others' rights do not matter. Passive individuals take into account others' rights too much to the extent that they give up the opportunity to express their own ideas and opinions.

It is important to build assertive communication skills in your pupils as this will allow them to express themselves clearly and freely without conflict or feelings of guilt and regret. Unfortunately, however, media and societal pressures, and in particular peer pressure, can have detrimental effects on the self-esteem, confidence and assertiveness of individuals.

Keys to good practice

Confidence-building techniques

✓ Praise individuals for their successes and also for failed attempts.

✓ Be genuine in your praise in all four areas of learning (physical, intellectual, emotional and social).

✓ Provide constructive feedback.

✓ Actively listen to pupils to show that you value what they have to say.

✓ Engage in discussion with pupils to demonstrate that you find them interesting.

✓ Encourage the development of friendships to enhance social interaction.

✓ Allow choice. This encourages pupils to take more responsibility for what they are doing, which will motivate them to put more effort into tasks.

✓ Provide varied activities so that pupils can experiment and find out what they are good at.

Assertiveness-building techniques

✓ Teach pupils how to read and use body language appropriately, e.g. how finger pointing can be seen as aggressive and confrontational.

✓ Teach pupils the importance of tone and volume of voice, e.g. how talking in a low, quivery voice can convey a lack of confidence.

✓ Make sure pupils are aware of their rights and responsibilities. Not knowing them or having the wrong concept of them can lead to passive or aggressive behaviour.

✓ Provide role models of assertive communicators for pupils to follow.

✓ Develop pupils' self-awareness so they can exercise self-control, e.g. by not succumbing to peer pressure and by having the confidence to walk away from a confrontational situation.

✓ Teach pupils the importance of listening to develop an understanding of how not to violate others' rights and needs.

Case study

K7
K9
K10

Building pupils' confidence and assertiveness

You have been asked to run some emotional health sessions with a group of pupils who are either too passive or aggressive in their actions and modes of communication. One pupil lacks self-esteem and is very passive and withdrawn. Two others, who also lack self-esteem, give in to peer pressure very easily in order to feel accepted and use confrontational, aggressive behaviour such as inappropriate language and physical violence to gain a false sense of confidence.

● How could you encourage the withdrawn pupil to interact with other group members?

● Which activities could you complete to help those lacking in confidence to participate?

● What examples of appropriate behaviour and communication could you provide for the aggressive pupils? Who would you use as a role model?

● What activities could you provide to help pupils develop their self-awareness?

▲ Figure 47.3 Young people need to develop their communication skills

Assisting young people to develop and use a range of influencing and negotiating skills

Once you have worked on helping pupils develop their confidence and assertiveness, you will have given them the tools to begin to communicate their opinions in a non-aggressive and non-passive manner. Pupils will then need the tools to convince and influence others that their ideas are valuable and beneficial to the community.

To be able to influence others, pupils need to inspire and gain support from those concerned, persuade them and engage their imagination. Effective influencing skills require a good grasp of interpersonal communication, presentation and assertiveness techniques. Influencing is not about pushing and bullying but about communication and negotiation – the compromises people make and the way they listen to each other and find outcomes that suit each other.

Before the negotiation process starts, pupils should be clear about their objective/s so that they do not digress, loose the thread of their argument or include too many insignificant details. They should plan and research their ideas properly to ensure that they are informed, factual, objective and possibly backed up by existing evidence elsewhere.

In the first stages of negotiating, it is important for pupils to establish trust and rapport with those they are attempting to influence. When a good relationship has been developed, both parties will be more open, accepting and willing to listen to and respect each other.

During the negotiation process pupils should be clear in their arguments about how the outcome will benefit all parties. They need to be clear about what would be involved to achieve the desired outcome. It is also always advisable for pupils to have a plan B up their sleeves should plan A fall apart or be rejected. A good negotiating technique is to use open-ended questions, which ensures interactivity, makes the other party feel that their ideas are valued and builds an understanding of the other party's ideas.

It is important to know about the other party in other ways too, for example, who may be a source of resistance and why. If pupils understand the sources of resistance beforehand, they will be better equipped to deal with them when they arise. For example, for people who fear change failure may be among the many sources of resistance. Teach pupils that resistance or rejection should not demotivate them, but make them work harder to revise their objectives, arguments, and negotiation and influencing strategies.

Keys to good practice

Influencing skills

✓ Build confidence and assertiveness skills first.
✓ Ensure an appointment to negotiate so there is time to prepare arguments in advance.
✓ Give pupils a rich source of trust-building techniques, e.g. recognising the importance of being fair, not making idle promises, listening to each other's needs, sharing thoughts and feelings.
✓ Teach pupils about the importance of listening to and taking into consideration others' views.
✓ Allow pupils lots of practice at debate and discussion.
✓ Help pupils to create inspiring presentations to suit the audience.
✓ Help pupils to understand the importance of dynamic verbal (e.g. tone, volume) and body language.

Building young people's skills to develop, make and review an effective presentation or business case

There are many different aspects to consider when helping pupils to make effective presentations of their views and ideas, including the methods, sources of information and skills they use, as outlined in the following sections.

A range of methods for developing an effective presentation or business case

For pupils to develop an effective presentation or business case, first you need to help them to research so that they can present an informed proposal. Provide pupils with a wide variety of research methods (see K12, page 314). Once they have gathered their ideas, they can plan and capture all the different ideas collaboratively using methods such as spider diagrams, mind maps and note-taking.

▲ Figure 47.4 By working together young people can develop new ideas

Next, pupils need to sift through their ideas, select the most appropriate for their case and begin to structure their arguments and decide how the key points will link to each other.

Once the elements of the business case are clear, you may have to support pupils in deciding the best mode of communicating their presentation. They could use a variety of different approaches, for example, visual, auditory, kinaesthetic or multi-modal communication in the form of PowerPoint, OHP, handouts, images, materials, role play, video/DVD, etc. Help them to select the method(s) that best suits their audience. Whichever mode of delivery they choose, it is imperative that they discuss the optimum way to use it. For example, if they chose to use a presentation tool such as PowerPoint, ensure they discuss the best use of graphics, colour and text, etc.

Case study K11

Supporting the development of a presentation

You are supporting a group of Year 10 (S4) pupils to complete a presentation on their ideas about how to tackle car crime committed by young people in the community. You have been asked to monitor the presentation and help the pupils practise their delivery.

- According to the Key Stage 4 Citizenship unit, 'Crime – Young People and Car Crime', what content should be included in the presentation?
- How would you suggest the group capture their audience's attention?
- How could they make their presentation interactive to include the audience?
- How should they use their voices, eye contact and body language?

A range of sources of information to use when developing a presentation or business case

There are many sources that can be used for research purposes when developing a presentation or business case. A needs analysis may need to be completed to decide where to start the search for information. For example, if pupils have been asked to present the case for the application for a grant to help buy resources, it would make sense to have an idea of what resources were needed first. Help pupils to find the appropriate source for the type of information they seek. For example, current radio news broadcasts or daily newspapers will not be the best source of evidence about past events. Instead, pupils could access past issues of newspapers in the archives at the local library. It is also important for pupils to understand that some sources may contain bias and to differentiate between fact and opinion.

The skills young people may be able to contribute in preparing a presentation or business case

Although pupils need to be taught a broad range of skills for making effective presentations, some will find that certain skills come more naturally and others may have already developed skills that will make a significant contribution. Certainly, it is very important to consider the different learning styles and needs of the pupils who will present the case. For example, those with strong literacy skills may be selected to research newspapers or the Internet, whereas kinaesthetic learners may produce better research by actively conducting surveys. Certain group members may have clear and concise use of written language and could be the best candidates to prepare the text for a presentation. On the other hand, the group members who are very IT literate could take charge of creating an excellent PowerPoint presentation.

Finally, consider the different interactive styles of the pupils presenting the business case. Those who have a clear use of spoken language, are confident, assertive and dynamic could be selected to present the arguments to the audience. Your role is to help pupils audit their strengths and delegate responsibilities appropriately.

How to review the outcomes of presentations

The outcomes of a presentation may be exactly as hoped for or not, but pupils need to understand that reviewing their presentation and its outcomes is a positive exercise, which can be used to inform the creation of a stronger case. They need to realise that any compromises reached are a success not a failure. They also need to be taught how to cope with rejection, resistance or an unsuccessful outcome so that they do not become demotivated.

Reviews can be completed in a range of different ways. Pupils could complete individual self-evaluations or work collaboratively in groups to audit their strengths and weaknesses. They could seek their audience's opinions about the strengths and weaknesses of their presentation or observe other groups giving successful presentations to compare with their own. They should consider all aspects of their presentation, for example:

- the appropriateness of their objectives
- whether sufficient research was done
- if the arguments were suitably structured
- whether the presentation was adequately prepared
- the suitability of the delivery of the presentation for the audience.

For your portfolio...

K2
K8
K11
K13
K14
K15
K16
K17

Write a reflective account about a time when you have supported pupils developing a presentation or business case. Include the following points.

- Describe the different types of communities involved and the issues the pupils were attempting to resolve.
- Describe the aims, objectives and values of the pupils and how they differed from those of the decision-makers.
- Describe and evaluate the activities completed to help pupils develop their influencing and negotiating skills, confidence and assertiveness.
- Outline the sources of information the pupils used to prepare their presentation.
- Describe and evaluate the presentation methods used and the way the presentation was delivered.
- Explain how successful the presentation was and how you helped the pupils review the outcome of it.

References

Cohen, A.P. (1985) *The Symbolic Construction of Community* (London; Tavistock)

Frazer, E. (1999) *The Problem of Communitarian Politics. Unity and Conflict* (Oxford; Oxford University Press)

Hoggett, P. (1997) 'Contested communities' in P. Hoggett (ed.) *Contested Communities. Experiences, struggles, policies* (Bristol; Policy Press)

Websites

www.curriculumonline.gov.uk

www.everychildmatters.gov.uk

www.opsi.gov.uk/acts.htm

www.qca.org.uk

www.scottish.parliament.uk/home.htm

50 Facilitate Children and Young People's Learning and Development Through Mentoring

The role of the mentor has become a key part of the work of some support staff. Learning mentors are involved in helping to remove barriers to learning and raise pupil achievement in school. Working alongside the teacher, you will need to demonstrate how you mentor pupils in a formal or informal capacity. This will provide support for the learning process rather than for the teaching and assessment of pupils.

You will need to show how you work with other professionals to establish mentoring programmes that take into account the needs of different pupils and raise achievement. The knowledge points in this unit are quite long and complex, so you may need to demonstrate your knowledge for some of the points through a variety of means.

What you need to know and understand

For this unit, you will need to know and understand:

Working with individual children/young persons and groups

■ Strategies for effective communication and negotiation; how to give constructive feedback; what active listening is and what barriers to a child/young person's expression may exist

■ *Learning styles and methods – what these are and how they differ between children and young people, ways of identifying a child/young person's learning needs, styles and methods* (See Unit 18, K8, page 39)

■ How bias and stereotyping may occur within the learning and mentoring process; ways of combating them; impact of own attitudes, values and behaviour on work with children and young people and methods of monitoring that these are not adversely affecting work with children and young people

■ Methods for encouraging and maintaining a child/young person's motivation and self-esteem; ways to adapt approaches to meet the needs of the child/young person; problem-solving techniques such as lateral thinking, how to use them and how to encourage children and young people to develop these skills themselves

■ Children and young people's rights within the mentoring process (to confidentiality, to make decisions, etc.) and how to monitor that these are upheld

■ How to assist children and young people's decision-making in ways that promote the child/young person's autonomy; factors and pressures which impact on children and young people's ability to make informed decisions; the range of relevant sources of information which can be accessed to support and assist children and young people; factors which may affect ability to access information

■ Formats for action plans, how to make action plans SMART (Specific, Measurable, Achievable, Realistic, Time-bound); how prior achievements, experience and learning may influence current and future choices; methods of assessing realistic rates of progress and timescales for courses of action, how to encourage children and young people to review their plans in a way that encourages them to be realistic

■ Methods of reviewing and evaluating the effectiveness of mentoring, ways of effectively involving children and young people in the process

Working with children, young people and those who care for them

■ The specific legislation, guidelines of good practice, charters and service standards which relate to the work being undertaken and the impact of this on the work

Working to improve agency practice

■ The role of the school and its services and how they relate to other agencies and services in the children's sector

- Own role and responsibilities and from whom assistance and advice should be sought if you are unsure

- Any particular factors relating to the school's policies and practices which have affected the work undertaken

- *How you have applied the principles of equality, diversity and anti-discriminatory practice to your work* (See Unit 20, K6, page 84)

- Methods of evaluating your own competence, determining when further support and expertise are needed and the measures taken to improve your own competence in this area of work

- The options for working with children and young people which you considered and the reasoning processes you used in determining the most appropriate approach for the child/young person concerned

Strategies for effective communication and negotiation

In order to work as a mentor it is essential for you to have effective communication skills. It is important to be able to work with pupils to identify their learning and development needs, as well as offer pastoral support. You may have been on additional training such as the five-day DfES Learning Mentor Training Programme, which is run by local authorities to support your role and to give you guidelines on how you should approach your work with pupils. You should have some experience of working with pupils in a support role, as the role of the learning mentor is an extension of the role of the teaching assistant. (See also Unit 20, K15–20, pages 89–91 for the development of communication skills and strategies for effective communication.)

Negotiation

When negotiating with pupils, it is important to be clear on the behaviour or issue to be addressed. Depending on their age and stage, pupils also need to be encouraged to develop skills of negotiation for themselves. At the earliest stages this will be around developing their confidence and learning that their opinions and thoughts are valued. Older pupils need to be given opportunities to be involved in some aspects of what they do in school, for example arranging activities or setting limits on behaviour. However all pupils need to be aware that their involvement will be limited and that there are some things that they will not be able to change.

How to give constructive feedback

Constructive feedback is about how you offer support to pupils when they are working. Always ensure that the feedback you give is helpful rather than critical. In other words, the pupil should be left feeling that what they have done is worthwhile, even if they may still need to do more work on it. (See also Unit 18, K10–12, pages 42–3.)

How bias and stereotyping may occur within the learning and mentoring process and ways of combating them

You may find that you experience degrees of stereotyping when you are working with pupils. This could come either from pupils or adults and you need to handle it sensitively. Stereotyping means expecting particular characteristics of certain groups of people. For example, people might say that particular groups such as women, black people or gay people have particular characteristics. You may find that some pupils in any given group hold anti-social opinions or ideas. Biased opinions should be challenged immediately so that pupils do not think that bias is acceptable. The school environment should be one that welcomes all individuals equally and celebrates diversity.

Impact of your own attitudes, values and behaviour on your work with children

You need to make sure that any underlying attitudes and values you have do not impact on your work with pupils. This means having an awareness of how your own background and ideals may affect how you manage their learning (see also Unit 20, K6, page 84).

K3 # Portfolio activity

Dealing with bias and stereotyping sensitively

What would you do in each of these situations?

- Hanif, in the Year 7E (S1) class, has upset the Catholic pupils in his class by saying that God doesn't exist.
- Mrs Jones, an outspoken parent, has complained that Jake, who you are mentoring, has more one-to-one attention than her own child, who she says needs more support and does not like school.

How do you think your own attitudes and beliefs might influence how you respond? Might this affect how you work with Hanif or Mrs Jones' child?

Methods for encouraging and maintaining a child's motivation and self-esteem

A key part of your work as a learning mentor is to encourage and develop pupils' self-esteem. This is because the pupils who need this kind of pastoral support are often those who are the most vulnerable and disadvantaged, and who need additional time with adults and other pupils. The level of pupils' self-esteem and how they feel about themselves and school forms a key part of their ability to learn and make the most of the school environment. You may need to encourage pupils who are reluctant to come to school or who have had limited social experience.

You need to give your time and positive attention to the pupil(s) with whom you work; these are likely to be key ingredients in the support they need through the mentoring process.

▲ Figure 50.1 Methods for encouraging self-esteem

Influence of adults

Children are influenced in a positive or negative way by the interactions and messages they receive from adults. If children are continually told that they are no good or given very little attention, they do not develop a positive image of themselves. In turn, this can lead to a lack of confidence and a reluctance to participate in learning activities. Your role is to motivate pupils by giving them support and encouragement through the development of positive relationships so that they feel confident enough about themselves to be able to work effectively.

Self concept

Everyone has a self concept or an 'ideal self', which is an image of how they would like to be. Sometimes a child's 'ideal self' may be close to how they perceive themselves and at other times the self-image may be far removed from their ideal. If children experience success and gain approval, they are more likely to feel that they are closer to their ideal self.

Opportunities to be in control

Children need to be given plenty of opportunity to be in control of situations and to make decisions in a safe environment. As adults we can support this by making sure that activities give pupils opportunities to make choices in their learning and develop an awareness of risk.

Achievable tasks and goals

It is important that children are given tasks that they are able to achieve so that they can experience a feeling of accomplishment. You may need to monitor and adapt work that you do with a pupil to enable them to complete it.

Adapting approaches to meet the needs of the child

You may need to adapt what you are doing with a pupil in order to meet their particular needs, such as the social needs of an autistic child with an obsession. A mentor uses approaches that suit the child in order to develop their confidence and resilience.

Using problem-solving techniques such as lateral thinking

You need to be able to encourage pupils to develop their problem-solving skills in different areas, so that they learn to use these skills themselves. Pupils need to learn to work through tasks and problems in a structured way which enables them to think logically. Some find it helpful to draw mind maps and flow charts so they can look at a problem in a more visual way, while others prefer to talk problems through. If you can support pupils in identifying their preferred learning style and way of working, they can find the best ways in which to work. Lateral thinking skills also give pupils the opportunity to use their ideas and imaginations in different ways from the traditional 'question and answer' approaches that have historically been used in schools.

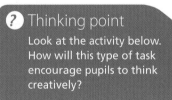

? Thinking point

Look at the activity below. How will this type of task encourage pupils to think creatively?

You are the Knave of Hearts and have been accused of stealing a tray of jam tarts. The King of Hearts is furious that you have stolen them as his wife the Queen had been baking them for his birthday. He has demanded that you are thrown in jail, but before you are sent there you have the opportunity of telling him the circumstances which led to your stealing the tarts. Present your case to him in the most convincing way.

Children and young people's rights within the mentoring process

Any pupils with whom you are working as part of the mentoring process are entitled to have their rights respected. Bear in mind that these rights form an important part of the expectations of the mentoring process and in particular, if you are working with a group, you may wish to establish ground rules with pupils from the outset.

The United Nations Convention on the Rights of the Child (UNCRC) was drawn up in 1989 and ratified by the UK in 1991. There are 54 articles; those that relate directly to relationships with children are identified below:

- **Article 2** – children have a right to protection from any form of discrimination
- **Article 3** – the best interests of the child are the primary consideration
- **Article 12** – children are entitled to express their views, which should be given consideration in keeping with the child's age and maturity
- **Article 28** – all children have an equal right to education.

You should also be aware that confidentiality is important. Pupils may not wish to discuss personal issues and you should not pressure them into doing so, even if it is relevant to the process. The only exception might be if there are child protection issues, which should be passed on to the appropriate professionals. Also remember that pupils and their families should not be discussed in any situation outside the school setting.

K5 Portfolio activity

Upholding the rights of pupils

Give examples of how you have upheld the rights of pupils during your work in the mentoring process.

How to assist children and young people's decision-making in ways that promote their autonomy

Assisting pupils with decision-making does not mean that you are giving them total control; rather it means that you are looking for ways in which to involve them. Pupils need to be encouraged to make decisions in a balanced way while thinking about the consequences of what they do and being responsible for their actions. As they learn to make decisions and take risks they will also be developing their own confidence and independence. If you are working with pupils to support decision-making you need to adapt your questioning so that you encourage them to look at the different ways their decisions will affect outcomes.

Factors and pressures that impact on children and young people's ability to make informed decisions

Pupils' ability to make decisions about their learning or be responsible for decision-making will relate to their own experiences and ages. Very young or immature children, who have not had much experience, may not understand how a particular decision could impact on what they do. Even very basic decisions such as choosing where they going to sit or taking opportunities to explore new equipment will help them to feel more confident. If pupils are always told what to do without any explanation or involvement they are more likely to challenge adults, which can cause a range of problems. However by encouraging them to make choices, even at a very basic level, you will be supporting their emotional well-being. Older pupils, who have been encouraged to make decisions and choices about matters that affect them, will be more willing to accept boundaries.

However, there may also be times when pupils' ability to make informed decisions is affected by circumstances, for example if their own needs have to be balanced with the needs of a group due to safety. Also remember that pupils will not be able to make informed decisions if they do not have all the relevant information available.

▲ Figure 50.2 Influences on a child's decision-making

Keys to good practice

Supporting decision-making

✓ Provide pupils with choices during activities and tasks, for example giving more open-ended activities.
✓ Encourage pupils through noticing their individual strengths and ideas.
✓ Discuss the effects of their decisions on others in the group if it is a shared activity.
✓ Make sure pupils have all the information required.

Range of relevant sources of information which can be accessed to support and assist children and young people

The mentoring process should be regulated through your local authority and it is likely that there will be a range of information to support and assist pupils in need. Learning mentors will support pupils with a variety of specific needs such as:

● supporting the transition from primary school
● bereavement or family break-ups
● practical help for families, such as interpreters and help with healthcare
● liaison with traveller families
● additional study support
● school attendance.

There will be a number of information and support groups locally but there are also national organisations that may be able to help. Check with your special educational

> **?** Thinking point…
> Think about the different ways in which your school encourages pupils to make their own choices and decisions.

needs co-ordinator (SENCo)(Additional Support for Learning (ASL) teacher) or inclusion manager to help you find the best sources of information for your particular needs.

Factors which may affect ability to access information

It may be difficult for you to access information if you have not been a learning mentor before or do not know the kind of support that is available. However, your school should be able to guide you as to the relevant sources of information available and provide links within your local authority. Make sure you also check relevant websites or publications, regularly as information may be regularly updated.

Formats for action plans, and how to make action plans SMART

You should make sure that you follow any agreed formats used by the school when devising action plans for pupils. In order to make them SMART (Specific, Measurable, Achievable, Realistic and Time-bound) you need to be careful that you look closely at the targets you are formulating. You should work through these with the pupil, discuss them as they are being set and ensure that the pupil understands what they mean. It is not advisable to set more than three or four targets because more may seem less achievable to the pupil. There should also be regular contact with the families or carers, to encourage positive family involvement in the pupil's learning. Work with pupils should generally be regular, short and focused, and aimed at giving them the opportunity to discuss issues and to work on targets in their action plan.

SMART action plans

- **Specific** – You must make sure that the target states clearly what is required.
- **Measurable** – You should ensure that you will be able to measure whether the target has been achieved and what level of confidentiality is required.
- **Achievable** – The target should not be inaccessible or too difficult for the pupil.
- **Realistic** – You should ensure that the pupil will be able to attain what is being set in the time available and that any others involved have been consulted.
- **Time-bound** – There should be a time limit set to achieve the target. This gives an opportunity to look again at the action plan and discuss the pupil's progress.

How prior achievements, experience and learning may influence current and future choices

Prior achievements, experience and learning will all have an influence on the ability of pupils to make decisions. If a pupil has limited experience of success and achievement, they may find it difficult to make informed decisions about their progress.

Methods of assessing realistic rates of progress and timescales for courses of action

You may wish to identify stages towards the goals being set. These will be helpful to the pupil as they will be able to see progress even within a short space of time. However the targets themselves should not be too ambitious.

Depending on the needs of your pupils, you should be able to set realistic timescales. If you are unsure about whether a pupil will be able to meet targets, perhaps because you do not know them well, it is advisable to start with less challenging targets or to work closely with the teacher.

How to encourage children and young people to review their plans in a way that encourages them to be realistic

When reviewing plans, you need to make sure that pupils are able to think about the progress they have made so far and discuss any difficulties they have faced, so they can apply this to setting future goals. Similarly, where they have been successful, they should be able to look at factors that have influenced this. Pupils should review their plans regularly with you to keep them motivated and also to check their progress. The plan is a working document and if circumstances change or it becomes apparent that the target is too ambitious, you should be able to amend it.

Portfolio activity K7

Setting targets with pupils

For the evidence section of your portfolio, include an annotated copy of an action plan. Highlight the targets you have worked on with pupils and annotate them to show how they relate to the pupils' prior learning and experiences. Show how you have made decisions about the rate of progress and the timescales selected.

Methods of reviewing and evaluating the effectiveness of mentoring, and involving children and young people in the process

When you are involved in mentoring programmes it is essential that there are systems in place to monitor and evaluate the quality and impact of work with pupils. These should include:

- careful planning of work and mentoring sessions
- reviews of work with individual pupils
- pupil, teacher and parent evaluations
- review of targets and priorities in the action plan
- monitoring of cohorts (by ethnicity, gender, EAL, etc.)
- monitoring of attendance, punctuality and exclusions
- performance Appraisal for learning mentors
- line manager observations of learning mentor work
- use of the DCSF learning mentor audit instrument (under review at the time of writing, but a useful tool for schools to measure the impact of mentoring; it is available through www.standards.dfes.gov.uk/learningmentors/downloads/moneval.doc.

However, the Every Child Matters initiative also highlights the importance of involving learners in the evaluation of work undertaken with them. This may take place through interviews or questionnaires, or through discussion following the process so that pupils have the chance to say what they think and mentors to act upon it.

Specific legislation, guidelines of good practice, charters and service standards which relate to the work being undertaken and the impact of this on the work

Learning mentors were originally devised as part of the government's Excellence in Cities Initiative in 2001. This was designed to improve inner city education through a range of measures, which also includes the Gifted and Talented Programme. As part of the initiative, learning mentors were recruited to support schools in raising standards, improving attendance and reducing exclusions.

The four core beliefs of the Excellence in Cities Initiative are:

- **High expectations of every individual** – to remove barriers to learning both inside and outside the school environment
- **Diversity** – to increase provision to all pupils and to take a more individualised approach
- **Networks** – to encourage the working together of schools to achieve more for pupils, families and communities
- **Extending opportunity** – to ensure that through collaboration the success of some schools can be repeated in those that do not have the same track record.

The Good Practice Guidelines for Learning Mentors sets out the purpose, expectations and guidelines for those in this role. The guidelines also invite recommendations from those running mentoring schemes in communities to feed back on the effectiveness of particular schemes (see also K10, below).

(See Unit 20, K2 page 81 for the relevant legislation.)

Role of the school and its services and how they relate to other agencies and services in the children's sector

The mentoring process should be regulated through your local authority and it is likely that there will be a link learning mentor who will be able to establish networks and share good practice between schools and other services, as well as directing schools to other local and national groups. The role of your school will be to set up the initial mentoring action plan after discussion with the pupil and their family and to involve other services where required.

At secondary level this list will be extended to other services such as Connexions and business support services. As outlined in the Every Child Matters guidelines, it is important that all agencies work together for the benefit of the pupil.

▲ Figure 50.3 Services the school may have to interact with

Identifying other local services

Find out about the services available in your local area.

Your own role and responsibilities and from whom assistance and advice should be sought if you are unsure

Your role as a learning mentor should be defined in your job description and will be an extension to the role of teaching assistant. However, the role extends to a more pastoral role, often outside the classroom, and may include work with families. The role of a learning mentor is to help with all aspects of school life, whether this is with learning, socialising or anger management. You need to speak to your line manager, who may be the SENCo (ASL teacher) or Inclusion Manager, regarding the kinds of activities you are to undertake with particular pupils and the time allocated. If you are asked to work with individuals or groups of pupils in a mentoring capacity, always make sure you have had discussions with other professionals so that you know what to expect and are aware of any issues that might arise.

Clarification of the learning mentor role, based on DfES Learning Mentor guidance (Source: *Haringey Primary Learning Mentor Guidance* document)

A learning mentor should...	A learning mentor should not...
<ul><li>act as a role model</li><li>be an active listener</li><li>challenge the assumptions that others have of pupils and that they have of themselves</li><li>observe pupils to assess their needs and devise supportive strategies</li><li>be involved in running after-school activities</li><li>work one to one with pupils</li><li>be an 'encourager'</li><li>form professional friendships with pupils</li><li>give guidance</li><li>negotiate targets</li><li>be a reliable, approachable, non-judgemental and realistic supporter of pupils, families and staff</li><li>run pupil drop-in sessions</li><li>work with small groups on anger management, self-esteem and emotional literacy etc.</li><li>support families</li><li>develop pupils' self-esteem</li><li>develop strategies to improve attendance and punctuality</li><li>support KS2/3 transfer</li><li>liaise with outside agencies to gain additional support for pupils and the school</li><li>support mentees in class as part of a structured programme of mentoring support</li></ul>	<ul><li>be involved in *counselling* (involving properly qualified professionals, formal referrals and parental consent) sessions with pupils</li><li>be a teaching assistant</li><li>be the person to whom a pupil is sent when naughty and/or sent out of class</li><li>be expected to support teachers in delivering Literacy and Numeracy lessons</li><li>co-ordinate and administer whole school attendance monitoring</li><li>be child protection co-ordinator</li><li>*teach* gifted and talented pupils</li></ul>

Portfolio activity

Identifying areas of your role as learning mentor

Include a copy of your job description. Highlight those areas that are specific to your role as a learning mentor and annotate them to show from whom you would seek assistance and advice when needed.

Any particular factors relating to the school's policies and practices which have affected the work undertaken

All school policies will affect your work, as they give guidelines for how to approach your work with pupils. However, you may need to check that you are following policy at different stages in the process, particularly if any issues arise. If you find out that school policy may affect what you do or how you approach specific work with pupils, you may need to adapt what you are doing to accommodate this.

Methods of evaluating your own competence

It may be difficult for you to assess your own competence when mentoring pupils as the process can be a slow one and any progress you make may well take considerable time. However, there should be opportunities for you to have an appraisal as part of your own professional development and this will enable you to consider, alongside your line manager, the effectiveness of your mentoring work with pupils. In preparation for your appraisal you should consider how your work with pupils has impacted on them and how you have coped with any difficulties as well as elements of your work you think have been particularly successful.

Options for working with children and young people which you considered and the reasoning processes you used in determining the most appropriate approach for the child/young person concerned

When you are asked to mentor a pupil or group of pupils it is likely that you will sit down with other staff in the school and discuss the different options available. These will be based on individual circumstances and the best interests of the pupil. You may also talk about the process with the pupil and consider how to best approach your work together as you set targets for the action plan.

Considering different options

Write down or tell your assessor about the different options you considered when deciding on the approach to use with your pupils.

For your portfolio...

K1
K2
K3
K4
K9
K13
K14

To gather evidence for this unit it would be useful for your assessor to observe you carrying out a mentoring session with an individual or group of pupils. You should talk through the process from the beginning, discussing how you have formulated action plans bearing in mind the needs of pupils, how you have reviewed them and in particular how they have been evaluated. You should show how you have applied principles of equality and anti-discriminatory practice to your work as well as any specific legislation or guidelines you had to follow.

References

DfES (2001) *Good Practice Guidelines for Learning Mentors* (ISBN 1841856169) also available online from the DfES website (see below) ; an excellent and very helpful document containing a number of references, case studies and websites for further reference

Websites

www.nmn.org.uk – National Mentoring Network

www.standards.dfes.gov.uk/learningmentors

www.teachers.tv – Enter 'Learning mentors' in the search for video and other links

www.users.globalnet.co.uk/~ebdstudy/strategy/behave.htm

55 Contribute to Maintaining Pupil Records

This unit is for teaching assistants who make a contribution to maintaining pupil records. It is about keeping up-to-date pupil records and also making sure that school systems are efficient and maintained effectively. You may be asked to complete a variety of different records including assessments, health records, pupil activity records and records of out-of-school activities. You should be clear on the requirements of the task and also ensure that you maintain confidentiality at all times. You must also make sure that you pass on any concerns you have regarding the information you are recording to the appropriate member of staff using the correct channels.

What you need to know and understand

For this unit you need to know and understand:

- The school's record-keeping policy, including confidentiality requirements

- The range, nature and purpose of pupil records kept by the school

- The roles and responsibilities within the school for maintaining pupil records

- That different types of information exist (e.g. confidential information, personal data and sensitive personal data) and appreciate the implications of those differences

- The sorts of information included in the different types of record that you contribute to and where this information can be found

- What information to record, how long to keep it, how to dispose of records correctly and when to feed back or follow up

- How to collate relevant information about pupils either by completing paperwork or using ICT skills

- The importance of updating records on a regular basis and the frequency of updating needed for the different types of record that you contribute to

- The importance of checking the validity and reliability of information and how to do this

- How to identify gaps in information and what action to take in relation to gaps in information

- The sorts of information which may indicate potential problems with individual pupils, e.g. frequent absences or late arrival at school and/or lessons

- How to assess the relevance and status of information (e.g. whether it is observation or opinion) and to pass it on when appropriate

- The importance of sharing information, how it can help and the dangers of not doing so

- Who to share information with and when

- The basic principles underpinning current legislation and the common law duty of confidentiality and any legislation which specifically restricts the disclosure of certain information

- That the Data Protection Act can be a tool to enable and encourage information sharing

- That consent is not always necessary to share information; even where information is confidential in nature, it may be shared without consent in certain circumstances (e.g. where the child is at risk of harm or there is a legal obligation to disclose)

- The difference between permissive statutory gateways (where a provision permits the sharing of information) and mandatory statutory gateways (where a provision places a duty upon a person to share information) and their implications for sharing information

- The record-keeping system(s) and procedures used within the school, including the storage and security of pupil records

- The importance of reviewing the effectiveness of the record-keeping system and how you contribute to this

School's record-keeping policy, including confidentiality requirements

All schools are required to have a policy on record keeping so that staff know the correct procedures to use. It may have a title such as 'Assessment, Recording and Reporting Policy' and will give information and guidelines about record keeping within the school. The system may be such that most of the school's records are kept on computer, so staff will need to be trained in how to use it. You may have opportunities for training with other staff and this will be important if you are to help them update records. Even if you are not expected to do this, it is useful to see how records are used and how information is kept within the school.

Schools should offer guidelines for the use of personal information and make sure that systems and documentation are secure and only restricted to appropriate staff. There may be a policy for the storage and security of pupil records within the school and you should be familiar with this if you are dealing with pupil records. (See also K15, page 343.)

> **ⓘ Key term**
>
> **Confidentiality** – only providing information or access to records to those who are authorised to have it

Portfolio activity K1 K19

Understanding the record-keeping policy and your role within it

Show that you know and understand your school policy for record keeping and your own role in relation to this, by doing one of the following.

- Annotate or highlight a copy of the policy to show that you understand your role in relation to it.
- Use a blank policy document form (see the Interactive Tutor Resource File for this course (Heinemann 2007)) and fill it in to record what is in your school's policy and how it affects you.
- Write a reflective account giving the guidelines for data protection within your school and naming some of the ways in which your school protects information and keeps it secure.

Range, nature and purpose of pupil records kept by the school

Teaching assistants may come into contact with a variety of different records when working in school. These may be kept in different parts of the school, for example, general **pupil records** may be in the school office or located in the classroom. Very often, records are kept on computer systems.

> **ⓘ Key term**
>
> **Pupil records** – the information about pupils that is recorded and stored by the school

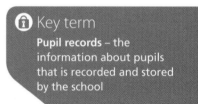

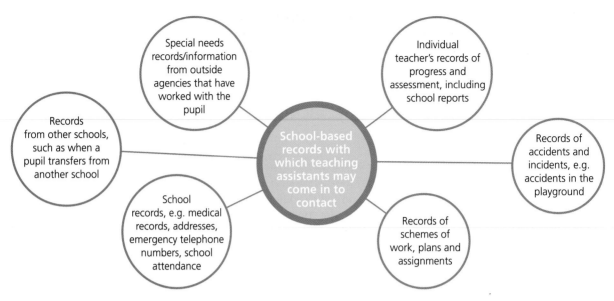

▲ Figure 55.1 Nature of records kept by the school

School records

All schools keep these records, which are particularly important on a day-to-day basis. In the case of medical records, the school may also keep lists of pupils who have particular conditions such as asthma, and keep inhalers in school so that they are accessible in an emergency. It is vital to keep these records, especially emergency telephone numbers, up to date and schools should have systems in place to remind parents about this. If school staff are asked to administer daily medication, such as Ritalin, records need to be kept of the number of tablets in school and the exact dosage given.

Where pupils are taking part in out-of-school activities, school records may need to be reviewed to ensure that staff have access to up-to-date emergency numbers. It is recommended that schools keep records of school attendance for five to seven years. Persistent absence by pupils without parents and carers giving a written reason are classified as unauthorised. A series of unauthorised absences by any one pupil may be noted by the educational welfare officer, who should visit the school regularly.

Individual teachers' records of progress and assessment

These records are kept in the classroom and will contain the teacher's individual comments and assessments when working with pupils. They are necessary to give a breakdown of each pupil's progress over a period of time and may be used to help with planning. They may also contain pupils' scores in any tests the teacher undertakes, such as the Key Stage SATS (Standardised Assessment Tasks) or mock GCSE (General Certificate of Secondary Education) scores. They will also include copies of pupils' school reports. Records of any national tests will also be collated and kept in the school's record system to help identify any areas for development.

Information from other agencies

Pupils with special needs are often the subject of a lot of paperwork. The Special Educational Needs Co-ordinator (SENCo)(Additional Support for Learning (ASL) teacher) will have their own systems for keeping this, so that information about the pupil is easily accessible when needed. The information contained in these records will usually be reports from professionals such as speech and language therapists, who will record their findings and pass the information to the school. Special Needs records will also contain information about what the school is doing to address an individual pupil's needs and their Individual Education Plans (IEPs).

Records of schemes of work, plans and assignments

These records will give a breakdown of the work being covered with pupils during the term. It may include schemes of work, broken down into subject areas, and topic-based activities to be carried out with pupils. This will give a record of what each pupil has learned.

Records from other schools

When a pupil transfers from another school, it will forward any records about the pupil's achievement. This will be useful for the class teachers as it will give an indication of the level reached and the results of any tests completed.

Records of accidents or incidents in school

There are times when you may be required to record details of an incident in school such as a pupil banging their head or acting aggressively towards another. The school will usually have an accident book, as there needs to be a record of any incidents, particularly if a pupil has been injured as a result. (See Unit 3, page 17 for an example of an accident record form.)

Records of out-of-school activities

When pupils go off the school site, the school needs to seek parental permission and keep the forms parents have signed as a record. This includes activities such as school trips.

Portfolio activity K2

Describing the kinds of records used

Either write a reflective account or have a professional discussion with your assessor to describe the different kinds of records used by your school. You should discuss the nature and purpose of each record to which you refer.

Roles and responsibilities within the school for maintaining pupil records

The different records held within the school will be the responsibility of different members of staff. Usually the majority of pupil records will be held with the class teacher, but others may need to have access to them. They will usually be stored in locked cupboards or filing cabinets in the classroom.

Headteachers, SENCos (ASL teachers) and subject managers need to have a knowledge of pupils' records as they have responsibilities to report to others. In the case of the headteacher, this may include reporting to governors and parents about the school's achievements. Subject managers need to report to the headteacher and staff about

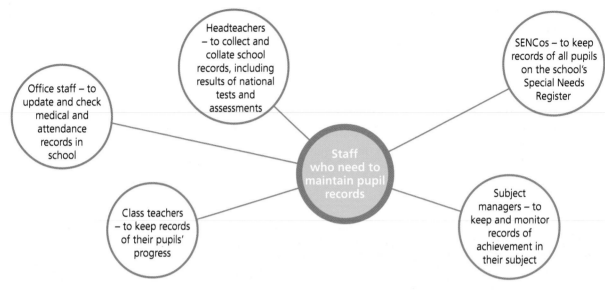

▲ **Figure 55.2** Staff responsibilities for record keeping

teaching and learning in their subject. They may also need to monitor and moderate work, as well as look at achievements and areas for development. SENCos (ASL teachers) need to keep detailed records to access concerns about specific pupils. Office or administrative staff may be asked to record information on computer systems or check that parents keep the school up to date with medical or other personal information.

K3

Portfolio activity

Identifying staff responsibilities for record keeping

Find out the responsibilities of the following staff in your school with regards to record keeping:

- office staff
- class teachers
- subject managers
- SENCo (ASL teacher).

Are any others responsible for pupil records?

That different types of information exist and appreciate the implications of those differences

You need to be aware that stored information on individual pupils may consist of different levels of confidentiality. All information held on pupils comes under data protection guidelines, but you can share some of this with colleagues as part of your day-to-day dealings with pupils. However, you may find that you are working with pupils who are a particular cause for concern. Unfortunately, sensitive issues regarding pupils do come to light – if you have any concerns or if a pupil confides in you, you may need to pass on sensitive information. This will usually be straight to the headteacher. You should *not* share this kind of information with others.

- **Personal data** – This includes names and addresses, medical or health records, dates of birth, etc. It needs to be kept secure.
- **Confidential information** – This consists of any professional recommendations or reports that should be shared only between parents or carers and professionals working with the pupil.
- **Sensitive personal data** – This may be to do with issues such as suspected child abuse or cases that may be going to court.

Case study K5

Reporting sensitive information

Jemma is working with Adam in Year 7 (S1), who has some learning difficulties. He has come into school and told her that his mum and dad had a big fight last night and his dad hurt him. He shows her the bruises. Jemma asks Adam to tell her exactly what happened, which he does. Jemma recognises that she must pass this information on to the Child Protection Officer in school, who is the headteacher.

- Should this kind of information be passed to anyone else in the school?
- If so, who would be responsible for doing this?

Sorts of information included in the different types of record that you contribute to and where this information can be found

The different types of record you contribute to will require that you fill in specific information and you will need to know where to go in order to find it. Usually your class teacher or the person who has asked you to fill in the record will give you the information you need, although you may need to go back and check with them if you are unsure. Generally speaking, class records of achievement or assessment, schemes of work and plans are more likely to be classroom-based, whereas personal data is more likely to be stored centrally in offices or on computers.

What information to record, how long to keep it, how to dispose of records correctly and when to feed back or follow up

Depending on the type of record, you need to be clear on exactly what you have been asked to record and file.

Most school records around pupil progress, including school reports and assessment records, need to be kept for the whole time the pupil is at the school. You may have to dispose of some records, such as information regarding past school trips. In this

▲ **Figure 55.3** You will need to keep records for a variety of purposes

situation, dispose of any information such as names and addresses by shredding or ensuring that personal details cannot be read. Files saved on computer should be deleted when they are no longer required, although remember that computer information is difficult to erase completely.

K6 Case study

Filing records and finding outstanding information

You have just started to work as a co-tutor teaching assistant in a Year 7 (S1) class and have been given all the forms that parents have been asked to fill in regarding their children. These include:

- medical forms and declarations
- family circumstances, siblings, religion, language spoken at home
- home–school agreement
- information from primary school
- special educational (ASL) needs information
- emergency telephone numbers.

You have been asked to check the forms and file them in paper record folders for each pupil. A number of records are incomplete as parents or previous schools have not returned all the information needed.

- What would you do when filing the information?
- How would you go about finding the outstanding information?

You may need to follow up information in records the school is already storing, for example health information or changes of address. If any problems arise, speak to the member of staff who has asked you to complete the record.

How to collate relevant information about pupils either by completing paperwork or using ICT skills

You may be asked to complete information about pupils in different ways. If you have to update or maintain paper-based records, you need to ensure that you do this on school premises so that confidentiality is less likely to be breached. When filling in records, do so methodically to ensure that you do not make any errors. Be careful about which line of information you are following on tables or charts as it can be easy to do this incorrectly.

Portfolio activity K8

Collating pupil information

Write a reflective account about the process you have followed when collating pupil information using paperwork or computers. You may wish to include a copy of the paper-based record, although make sure that you delete pupils' names.

Importance of updating records on a regular basis and the frequency of updating needed for the different types of record that you contribute to

You need to update information at the required intervals to ensure that records remain relevant for use by the school. However, you may not be responsible for when records are updated. If parents tell you about any changes, for example if they are moving house or changing doctor, you should remind them that the school will need to be aware of this for their records.

You should be aware of the frequency of updating required for different types of record. School plans or activity records may need to be updated on a daily basis as you complete work with pupils, in order to give feedback to the teacher. Records of assessment need to be completed as and when they occur; schools usually carry out some kind of assessment on pupils at least termly. Progress records or reports to parents will be completed by the teacher annually and you may be asked to pass on information to the teacher.

Importance of checking the validity and reliability of information and how to do this

While you are completing records, you should check that the information you have is valid and makes sense. Make sure that you read through information before filling it in and ensure that it has been completed or signed by the appropriate person. Check that any dates required are still valid and ensure that any discrepancies are dealt with straight away – you may not remember to come back to them later.

How to identify gaps in information and what action to take

If you find that there is some information missing for any reason, report this straight away so that it can be completed accurately.

Actions required for incomplete or missing information

Type of record	Action required
Pupil assessment	Go back to the teacher concerned and request the remaining details. If the pupil was absent for the assessment, you may be asked to take them for an assessment. Otherwise it may be possible to record the absence.
Activity record	These are the teacher's records in relation to work completed by pupils. If they are incomplete, you may need to ask the teacher for the reason and what action to take.
Pupil registers	Accurate pupil registers are a legal document. If they have not been completed, information should be sought from the class teacher or parent.
School trips	It is very important that the school gathers information prior to school trips such as parent or carer's contact details, any health issues such as allergies or medication and whether payment for the trip has been made. If any of these are missing, you should point this out as soon as you notice it.

The sorts of information which may indicate potential problems with individual pupils

If you feel that information you have gathered indicates that there may be potential problems with individual pupils, you need to report this as soon as you discover it. For example, you may notice that a pupil has regular patterns of absence and is always away on Mondays. Make sure that you refer this to the appropriate member of staff.

How to assess the relevance and status of information and pass it on when appropriate

You need to know how to recognise whether information you have recorded or passed on is relevant for the purpose for which it has been gathered. As you read it, assess whether what you have recorded is based on opinion or fact. Always ensure that you avoid writing down or passing on anything that could be based on opinion. In order to check against this, ask yourself the following questions.

- Did I see this happen?
- Is there evidence to back up the information?
- Could my own personal feelings or opinions be involved?

Collating information and obtaining outstanding information

Caleb has been asked to collate records concerning a week-long Year 8 (S2) trip to a local activity centre, which is to take place the following month. He has a large amount of information to gather and is using a spreadsheet to ensure he has the required record for each pupil, including contact numbers, parental consent forms, payment and so on. As he gathers the information, Caleb comes across the following:

- four pupils' parents have not signed consent forms, but have submitted the required payment
- one pupil's health form states that she is on medication for asthma, but that she will not need to have her inhaler with her
- one form has been completed by the pupil's grandparent and Caleb is concerned that some of the information is inaccurate
- one pupil's parents have not returned the forms and Caleb is aware that they speak English as an additional language.

What action should Caleb take regarding each of these issues?

The importance of sharing information with others, when to do it, how it can help and the dangers of not doing so

By contributing to the school's record-keeping process, you are effectively enabling members of staff to share information with one another. Efficient and timely record keeping is vital so that pupil assessment and progress can be monitored across year groups and between teachers, and reported to parents. Schools are always busy places, but it is important not to build up a backlog that will take a long time to clear. If information is passed on verbally and not recorded, it cannot be accessed again by those who need to see it.

Dealing with gaps in records

Kate is working in a large secondary school and often has to swap classes to cover for different staff when they are absent. She has been working in the school for several years and is frequently required to fill in records.

On this occasion, Kate has been asked to help to collate information on a pupil for whom the school is seeking additional support. She has been given the special educational (ASL) needs file and is going through reports and assessments relevant to the process of giving Statements of Special Educational Needs (Co-ordinated Support Plans). As she knows the pupil well and has worked with him on a number of occasions, she is aware that there are gaps in the paperwork. She knows that the pupil was referred some time ago for additional support that he did receive, but is unable to find any documentation to support this. She knows what happened and would be able to write a report herself if necessary.

- What is Kate's responsibility in this situation?
- Why is it important that all information on pupils is shared between professionals?

Basic principles underpinning current legislation and the common law duty of confidentiality

The basic principle of current legislation, and common law, around confidentiality is that any information held on individuals should be shared only with those who need to see it.

Data Protection Act 1998

The 1998 Act, replacing the 1984 Act, is the most specific with regard to restricting how we use information. It is designed to prevent data on individuals from being passed on to others without their consent. It sets standards for the acquisition, keeping, using or disposing of personal data and states that information should:

- be obtained fairly
- only be kept for as long as is necessary
- be relevant to requirements
- not be used in any way that is not compatible to its purpose.

The Act also means that individuals can request information that organisations hold on them.

Human Rights Act 1998

This allows UK citizens to assert their rights under the European Convention of Human Rights. It strengthens the rights of individuals and requires courts to bear in mind the fact that they have a right to private lives, which should be respected.

Children Act 2004

This Act was published alongside Every Child Matters, which focuses on the needs of children and families. It promotes children's services working together to minimise risks and promote children's welfare. Information needs to be shared between service providers, but the contact details of those working with the child, rather than the information about the child, should be stored on a main database.

That the Data Protection Act can be a tool to enable and encourage information sharing and when consent is needed

Although the main purpose of confidentiality legislation is to protect the individual's right to privacy, in some cases information may need to be shared without consent. The Data Protection Act is not intended to stop information being shared; it is often very important for different organisations to share information. As far as schools are concerned, information can legally be shared with other professionals who have a need to know it. In the case of children, parental consent needs to be given before information can be shared with other professionals. However, if there are any issues to indicate that the child is at risk from the parents or if there is a legal obligation placed on the school to disclose information, the relevant information can be disclosed.

Difference between permissive statutory gateways and mandatory statutory gateways and their implications for sharing information

You need to know the difference between permissive and mandatory statutory gateways, which are terms applied to public sector data-sharing protocols.

Permissive statutory gateways – This means that information may be shared between individuals or organisations. In the case of schools, information may need to be shared with outside agencies that also work with the child.

Mandatory statutory gateways – It is compulsory to share certain types of information with other specified people and agencies.

Record-keeping system(s) and procedures used within the school, including the storage and security of pupil records

You need to know your school's procedures for record keeping and where the records you are required to update are stored and kept secure. Your school will have a record-keeping policy, which should give you information about the systems and procedures you may be asked to use.

Importance of reviewing the effectiveness of the record-keeping system and how you contribute to this

As part of good practice, your school should review the record-keeping systems they use and you may be invited to contribute to meetings or give your opinion. If you keep any records, you may be able to suggest improvements to the systems.

Case study

Reviewing record-keeping systems

Luisa is a teaching assistant in a small village secondary school. Alongside the SENCo (ASL teacher), she is responsible for ensuring that the special educational (ASL) needs records are kept up to date and stored in the correct place. She has weekly meetings with the SENCo (ASL teacher) and two other teaching assistants. This week she has been on some training and raises the question of how the team store the information they have on pupils with special educational (ASL) needs.

● Why are meetings of this kind a good idea for support staff?
● How else might Luisa have put forward her ideas?

Maintaining school records

✓ Ensure you understand what you are asked to do.
✓ Make sure records are kept up to date and accurate.
✓ Ensure records are relevant.
✓ Maintain confidentiality and security.
✓ Report any problems or breaches of confidence to the appropriate person.

For your portfolio...

In order to show your competence in this unit, you need to show that you are aware of school policies and the type of records you are likely to be asked to contribute to (see K1 and K2). You may wish to submit examples of some of the records for which you have been responsible. However if you do this, you should remove any pupils' names for confidentiality reasons.

You may then either have a professional discussion with your assessor to answer areas of the knowledge base that are not covered by case studies or write a reflective account about your role with regard to record keeping and particular situations that you have dealt with. If you have been involved with any sensitive cases, you should not be specific when writing them down but should tell your assessor about them so that he/she can record that you acted appropriately.

Websites

www.opsi.gov.uk/acts/acts1998/19980042.htm – Human Rights Act

www.opsi.gov.uk/acts/acts1998/19980029.htm – Data Protection Act

www.dca.gov.uk – Department for Constitutional Affairs

57 Organise Cover for Absent Colleagues

Following the National Agreement on Raising Standards and Tackling Workload between government, employers and schools, it is expected that a number of administrative and clerical tasks will be completed by support staff to allow teachers to focus on teaching. Among these tasks, administering cover is having a particular impact on the roles of teaching assistants in schools.

New cover supervisor jobs are being introduced into some secondary schools and teaching assistants at NVQ/SVQ, Level 3 are moving into this new role. They are required to organise short-term cover on a daily basis for unexpected absences and absences known in advance. Teaching assistants who work as cover supervisors will sometimes have to cover classes themselves, as well as arrange for cover by supply teachers, cover staff employed on a full-time basis at the school and other teachers at the school. Cover supervisors will also be expected to provide the person covering with appropriate work and support throughout the day.

What you need to know and understand

For this unit, you will need to know and understand:

- The school's cover policy
- Legislation, regulations, guidelines and codes of practice relating to cover arrangements in schools
- The importance of confirming/clarifying the cover required with the appropriate person and how to do this effectively
- Which members of staff you should approach, and at what stage, to provide cover
- Why it is important to allocate cover work on a fair basis and how to do so
- The importance of making sure that the requirement to provide cover is not at the expense of other elements of an individual's job
- The limits and restrictions on the amount of cover that can normally be expected by different members of staff
- The difference in cover supervision and specified work and who within and outside the school you can call on to provide one and/or the other as required
- When and how supply staff would be called on to cover for absent colleagues and your role in arranging supply cover
- Who you should inform of any difficulties in organising cover
- Who you should approach for appropriate work for pupils who are being supervised
- Why it is important to brief people on the cover they have been allocated; what information they need; and how to provide this information
- The sorts of situations where those covering classes may require help and advice and how you should respond to these
- Effective ways of regularly and fairly checking the progress and quality of cover arrangements
- How to provide prompt and constructive feedback to those who contribute to cover arrangements
- The types of problems that may occur in providing cover and how to support people in dealing with these
- The importance of working within the boundaries of your role and competence and when you should refer to others
- The importance of consulting a wide range of interests, including pupils if appropriate, on the effectiveness of cover arrangements
- How to offer suggestions and ideas for improving cover arrangements in a constructive manner
- The importance of keeping accurate and complete records of cover requirements and arrangements made to meet these, and the school procedures for this

School's cover policy

Your school may have already drawn up a school policy for **administering cover**. However, if this is not the case, you may be able to obtain model policies from your local education authority. Cover policies will usually contain the following information:

- a definition of cover supervision
- how the policy links to the government initiatives that necessitate the production of the policy
- who the **cover supervisor** is
- the skills, knowledge and training necessary to take on the cover supervisor role
- appropriate use of cover supervision
- cover strategies outlining the number of days' notice required for known absences, who supervises the cover supervision (e.g. teacher, headteacher, subject co-ordinator), the advisable number of days before obtaining a fully qualified staff member to provide cover, etc.
- roles and responsibilities of key staff
- monitoring and policy/procedure review methods.

Key terms

Administering cover – the process of co-ordinating, organising and overseeing the lessons that need to be covered and the staff who cover them

Cover supervisor – the person employed to carry out the process of administering cover, who will also provide lesson cover when necessary and revert back to teaching assistant duties when no cover administration is required

Legislation, regulations, guidelines and codes of practice relating to cover arrangements in schools

Other guidelines on cover supervision can be obtained from the following sources:

- the Workforce Agreement Monitoring Group (WAMG), which monitors the remodelling of the school workforce following the National Agreement, has produced new regulations, guidelines and case studies; for further information, see www.tda.gov.uk/upload/resources/pdf/w/wamg_guidance_cover.pdf
- the School Teachers Pay and Conditions Document 2003 outlines acceptable conditions and pay for teachers; for further information, see www.teachernet.gov.uk/paydoc
- your school's insurance policy and the implications for cover (e.g. volunteers are not covered to supervise children)
- Education (Specified Work and Registration) (England) Regulations 2003 outline the rights and responsibilities of those completing specified work within the education sector; for further information, see www.opsi.gov.uk/si/si2003/20031663.htm
- your school's absence policy
- the Ofsted report, Schools' Use of Temporary Teachers (2002) also outlines good practice in the use of supply teachers (e.g. careful induction into the school); for further information, see www.ofsted.gov.uk/assets/3121.pdf
- The Part-time Workers' (Prevention of Less Favourable Treatment) Regulations 2000, which outlines the rights and responsibilities of those who work part time, means day-to-day supply teachers will have certain entitlements, as do other teachers, within the school (e.g. access to continuing professional development); for further information see: www.opsi.gov.uk/si/si2000/20001551.htm

Portfolio activity

Identifying the relevant provisions for cover in school

Obtain a copy of your school's cover policy or obtain a model policy from your local education authority. Also investigate all the other relevant legislation and guidance on cover supervision. Make notes for your portfolio and highlight any provisions that impact on your own role.

Importance of confirming/clarifying the cover required with the appropriate person and how to do this effectively

When deciding whether to call in a supply teacher or not, it is important to clarify the amount of time for which cover is needed and the tasks that need to be undertaken in the course of the cover. However, you may need to organise cover for many absentees in one day and, given the time constraints, it can be difficult to check the requirements with the different staff members involved. Although you may have known about some absences and been able to confirm the cover required well in advance, most cover will probably be required due to unforeseen absences. You therefore need to have in place some time-effective methods of organising cover and procedures for gathering the necessary information about the cover required.

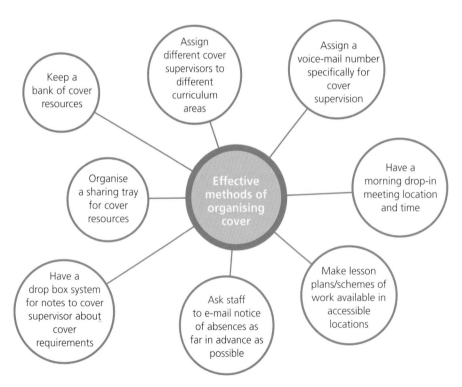

▲ **Figure 57.1** Organising procedures for cover makes the procedure far less disruptive for the school and pupils

Which members of staff you should approach, and at what stage, to provide cover

Sometimes you will be aware of the cover arrangements needed well in advance, for example for an end-of-year school trip organised at the beginning of the academic year. At other times you may only be given a month, a week or even one or two days' notice. Whenever possible, confirm cover requirements with the staff member who requires cover in advance. However, despite having a general idea about what needs to be covered from the scheme of work, teachers will probably not be able to give you more specific details until about a week before the lesson.

In the case of unforeseen absences, staff members should communicate the required cover before the school day begins. If, for some reason, the absent staff member is unable to contact you, you may be able to approach the following members of staff for information:

- head of department
- subject co-ordinator
- higher-level teaching assistant (HLTA) within a curriculum area
- other departmental teachers.

Why it is important to allocate cover work on a fair basis and how to do so

It is important that cover work is spread equally across the staff team and that the work each staff member provides is spread equally over the year. For example it would be unfair to allocate 38 hours of cover to one member of staff in one half term. Tensions can arise within teams if some members of staff feel that they are being called on to cover more than others. Keeping clear records of who has covered when and where will keep the allocation of cover work as fair as possible.

Importance of making sure that the requirement to provide cover is not at the expense of other elements of an individual's job

If cover is not allocated on a fair basis, staff members may not be able to carry out their regular roles and responsibilities effectively due to the extra pressure on their time. To make sure this does not happen, you must be aware of all their duties and any increases in pressure at particular times of year, and bear these in mind when organising cover. For example, a staff member who is a tutor, full-time teacher and provides weekly extra-curricular activities will be under more pressure than one who only teaches if they are given cover duties during their non-contact periods. Equally, the teacher of Years 7 and 8 (S1 and S2) will not have the same workload during SATs, GCSEs, mock exams and coursework preparation as the staff member who teaches Years 9, 10 and 11 (S3, S4 and S5). Try to allocate cover work to staff based on who has fewer other responsibilities at the time.

Limits and restrictions on the amount of cover that can normally be expected by different members of staff

The contractual limit of 38 hours' cover work per staff member per year must be adhered to. You will therefore need to clarify in advance the hours already covered by certain staff members so as to keep within these limits.

Knowing the cover requirements in advance will allow for you to consult the school and departmental yearly and termly planners. This is particularly useful at certain times of year; for example, in the summer term those teaching Year 10 and 11 (S4 and S5) classes do not need to teach because pupils are on experience placements and sitting GCSEs. This reduction in teaching hours is known as **gained time** and, although cover undertaken in this period must count towards the 38-hour limit, it allows some flexibility in arranging cover. For example, certain activities outlined in the School Teachers Pay and Conditions Document 2003 can be undertaken during gained time, including:

> **ⓘ Key term**
>
> **Gained time** – the hours teachers gain when usual teaching hours are not needed due to pupil examinations, work placements, trips, etc.

- developing and revising departmental and subject curriculum materials, schemes of work, lesson plans and policies in preparation for the new academic year, including identifying appropriate materials for use by supply staff and cover supervisors
- assisting colleagues in appropriate, planned team teaching activities
- taking groups of pupils to provide additional learning support
- supporting selected pupils with coursework
- undertaking planned activities with pupils transferring between year groups or from primary schools
- being released for continuing professional development.

(K3 K7) Case study

Planning around the annual limits for cover

Unfortunately, there is a stomach bug affecting many staff members and nine teachers have called in sick. There are also four members of staff on a training course and, although the course was booked a month ago, you were only told today. Moreover, two members of staff are on long-term sick leave. Although it is the summer term and Year 11 (S4) teachers have lost the vast majority of their teaching hours, nearly all members of staff have completed the contractual 38-hour annual limit for cover.

- Why is it important to have been told in advance about the cover requirements for the staff on training?
- How could you plan to use 'gained time' creatively?

Differences between cover supervision and specified work, and who can provide each

Cover supervision is not really considered to be **active teaching**. Instead, pupils are supervised while completing tasks prepared in advance. These tasks aim to provide continuity of the curriculum during the time of staff absence. Support staff, and teaching assistants provided through agencies, with the appropriate skills and training (to S/NVQ Level 3, HLTA and above) can provide cover supervision.

Specified work is carried out only by qualified teachers and active teaching should take place. Pre-planned materials should still be issued to ensure continuity. Qualified teachers in the school can be asked to carry out specified work, providing it falls within their 38-hour contractual limit per year. There are also many supply agencies providing cover teachers who are adequately qualified. Your headteacher (or the member of staff designated by the head-teacher) will usually decide when a qualified supply teacher should be called in. The key factors in making the decision to call in a supply teacher to complete specified work are:

- if continuity of learning can no longer be maintained through cover supervision
- if the length of time without a teacher is considered too long
- if the total proportion of curriculum coverage lost over a term is high.

The school may have a list of preferred agencies or supply teachers that they have built up a good relationship with. Some schools also employ **floating teachers**, who are exempt from the 38-hours-a-year restrictions, to provide cover lessons and specified work.

> **ⓘ Key terms**
>
> **Active teaching** – teaching that uses strategies to maximize learning through interaction
>
> **Floating teachers** – teachers employed by a school to carry out specified work on a full- or part-time basis, but not assigned to teach within a curriculum subject

Portfolio activity K8

Recognising the differences between cover supervision and specified work

Observe a session led by a cover supervisor and one led by a specified worker. Describe the differences in the teaching and learning support methods used for both sessions. You may find that cover staff are unsure of the differences between the cover supervision role and the specified worker role. Use your findings to produce a definition for each to include in both your portfolio and an information pack for cover teachers.

When and how supply staff would be called on to cover for absent colleagues and your role in arranging supply cover

Supply teachers are usually employed by outside agencies that specialise in educational placements. More often than not, they are qualified teachers who choose to work in temporary placements and carry out specified work. Agencies attempt to send supply teachers qualified in the curriculum area needing cover, although this is not always possible.

Your school's cover policy will outline the role of a supply teacher in detail and you may wish to give supply teachers this information on arrival. Bear in mind that their roles and responsibilities will also be outlined by the supply agency (e.g. see http://www.teachers-uk.co.uk/candidates/welcome/role.php) and you should be aware of the expectations of the agencies you use. In brief, supply teachers are expected to support pupils and teachers by ensuring continuity in curriculum coverage. Those on short-term supply (e.g. for a day or week) would not be expected to plan activities. However, those on long-term supply (e.g. a term) would be expected to take over all the regular duties of the absent staff member.

Who you should inform of any difficulties in organising cover

It may be wise to create in advance a flow diagram of the steps you intend to follow should you have difficulties in organising cover and you may wish to include this in the cover policy. If you do have difficulties in organising cover, try to find solutions yourself before burdening others with the responsibility.

It may be possible to share the pupils from the class requiring cover around other classes, in which case you could approach helpful teachers who may be willing to cater for slightly larger classes. Your headteacher will inform you of the maximum numbers of pupils allowed in a class. At other times, specialist teachers or teaching assistants may be happy to provide an extra-curricular activity such as a Drama or Sports lesson, instead of cover supervision. Again your headteacher will inform you if they are happy with this decision. In some schools it may be possible for pupils to be supervised while completing tasks in a self-directed learning place such as a library or ICT suite.

Always take into account the reason cover is required before using your judgement to decide who to inform about any difficulties. For example, if a known absence is due to a dental appointment, you could ask the staff member if a more suitable time is available. However, if the known absence is for a funeral, it is not advisable to burden the staff member with unnecessary worry at such a difficult time. Moreover, ensure your solutions to the cover difficulties do not fall outside contractual rights or guidelines proposed by legislation, policy and codes of practice.

K10 # Case study

Difficulties in organising cover

On a busy day with many absentees, you quickly realise it is going to be difficult to find cover for every class. There is a particular problem in finding cover for two Year 7 (S1) French classes (middle and lower ability) during period 2. You feel as if you have exhausted all possibilities. Not one teacher, cover teacher or supply teacher is available – even the floating supply and you yourself are covering during this period.

- List all the possible solutions you need to investigate before asking for help.
- Who could you turn to for help and what may they suggest?

Who you should approach for appropriate work for pupils who are being supervised

The best source of appropriate work is the class teacher because they know exactly what the pupils have or have not done, what they need to do next, their ability range, any special educational (Additional Support for Learning (ASL)) needs and the types of activities and teaching strategies that suit the learning styles and dynamics of the class.

However, if it is not possible to speak to the class teacher, you may be able to turn to other teachers in the same department, who teach similar content to similar age groups and will at least be able to advise you on tasks of the appropriate level. Other teachers in the school, who teach the class for other subjects, could provide you with valuable information about the special educational (ASL) needs and preferences of the pupils. For activities with suitable content on appropriate levels, you may also wish to approach the head of department, a specialist teaching assistant or a technician assigned to the relevant curriculum area.

If you are unable to speak to a relevant staff member, you will need to think of other ways to obtain information about appropriate teaching materials. You may have kept a bank of materials or set up a sharing tray system specifically for cover work, which could provide something suitable. Schemes of work will also outline suitable activities and materials, as will lesson plans on the same topic from the previous year.

It would also be wise to draw up a list of sources of information or people you can turn to for help should a similar problem arise in the future.

Portfolio activity K11

Evaluating the systems used for obtain cover work

Write a reflective account of the procedures followed in your school to obtain information about appropriate work for pupils who are being supervised. Describe the systems and evaluate their effectiveness. Suggest possible improvements to the way in which the information is obtained.

Why it is important to brief people on the cover they have been allocated; what information they need and how to provide it

The amount of time you have to brief the people allocated cover will be limited and, on some days, there may be so much cover supervision that you cannot brief everyone personally. Therefore a central system or location for cover staff to collect information and materials should be available. In the morning, prepare and disseminate a cover timetable for the day, indicating what subjects, year groups, periods and rooms need covering, as well as giving information about where suitable materials can be found. If possible, attach a brief lesson plan with appropriate resources, materials or worksheets to the timetable for those carrying out specified work. Those completing cover supervision will only need a list of instructions. A school proforma outlining cover requirements will ensure consistency of information.

It is also beneficial to have pre-prepared information on each class so that pupils can be effectively supported, especially for their special educational (ASL) or English as an additional language needs. A pre-prepared attendance register will allow teachers or specified workers to record attendance and lateness accurately. A seating plan can be used to ensure pupils sit in their usual places and so may help to manage behaviour.

Cover teachers from outside the school will also need additional information. You may wish to personally meet and greet cover staff from outside and introduce them to the subject team. You may also need to provide them with information such as:

- timings of the school day
- emergency procedures as required by health and safety legislation
- location of toilets, staff room and drinks
- warning, sanction and rewards systems
- information pack for supply teachers, to be returned at the end of the day
- information of how and where you can be contacted.

Sorts of problems and situations where those covering classes may require help and advice and how you should respond

Various problems, which commonly arise for those covering classes, are listed below, with suggestions for responding to or preventing them.

▼ Figure 57.2 Discussion and sharing of information can help support cover teachers

▲ Figure 57.3 To the rescue – a supply box can save the day

- **Not knowing pupils' names or having relationship with them** – A seating plan and attendance register will help with names and providing other information, for example of special educational (ASL) needs may make relationship development an easier process.
- **Work at inappropriate levels** – Information on prior attainment levels should ensure that work is pitched at the correct level and providing a bank of extension and gap-filler resources will also help.
- **Work completed too quickly** – A standardised protocol, such as having something to read, something to write or copy, something to draw and something for fun, will ensure activities last an hour.
- **Work requires a high level of subject knowledge** – A standardised protocol ensuring that the work can be completed by any adult should eliminate technical problems.
- **Work that pupils have done before** – Access to previous lesson plans and Schemes of work will ensure pupils do not repeat work.
- **Behaviour management** – Information on the warnings and sanction systems and who to turn to for support will help cover teachers manage behaviour.
- **Inexperienced teachers**, e.g. who usually work in primary settings – Using the same supply teacher on a regular basis or having a floating supply teacher in school will ensure cover staff who are experienced in the setting and a better pupil to teacher relationship.
- **Lack of resources and access to materials** – A supply box, which contains all the necessary materials and should be returned at the end of the school day, will help overcome resource problems.
- **Feeling unsupported** – Make cover teachers feel supported and valued by visiting them from time to time for updates.

Portfolio activity

Overcoming the problems in providing cover work

Write a reflective account of the different problems you have encountered during cover lessons. Describe how your school has attempted to overcome these problems. Suggest alternatives to the strategies used to attempt to solve the problems in your school.

Effective ways of regularly and fairly checking the progress and quality of cover arrangements

It is important to seek regular, prompt and constructive feedback from all those involved with cover arrangements, including:

- staff who need to be covered
- teachers in the school
- supply teachers who regularly come into school
- floating teachers in school
- your line manager
- pupils.

After collating feedback, you should evaluate the strengths and weaknesses of the cover arrangement systems and make suggestions for improvements. Remember you may also need to update the cover policy.

▲ **Figure 57.4** Feedback is crucial for self-development

How to provide prompt and constructive feedback to those who contribute to cover arrangements

The following methods can be used to provide and seek feedback from those who contribute to cover arrangements:

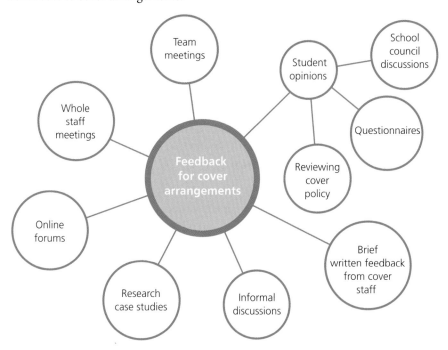

▲ Figure 57.5 There are many ways of supplying feedback for cover teachers

Importance of consulting a wide range of interests, including pupils if appropriate, on the effectiveness of cover arrangements

It is important to obtain information about the effectiveness of cover procedures so that strengths and weaknesses can be evaluated and suggestions for improvement carefully discussed. To make evaluations of effectiveness more valid, objective and reliable, you should consult more than one source of feedback.

Giving others the opportunity to voice their ideas helps them to feel they have some power to influence decisions and, as a result, staff members may take more care to follow the correct procedures for organising cover arrangements.

How to offer suggestions and ideas for improving cover arrangements in a constructive manner

Suggestions for improvement can be offered in a constructive manner by taking into account opinions, evaluations and ideas from a range of sources. This will ensure that suggestions for improvements are based on collective ideas. Discussions about areas for improvement should be kept professional and impersonal, with specific examples of practices or procedures that could be improved. Be open to feedback and keep targets SMART – specific, measurable, achievable, realistic and time-bound – so that staff stay motivated.

Importance of working within the boundaries of your role and competence and when you should refer to others

It is important to find solutions to problems yourself whenever possible. However, you should turn to the headteacher (or whoever they have designated) to help decide if the cover needed warrants a change from cover supervisor to a specified worker. You should also ask for advice if you are unable to find cover, having exhausted all the options you have the authority to implement. You should also turn to others more competent in the relevant subject area to provide you with ideas for activities or if a specialised problem or concern arises.

There will be times when you need to refer other issues that are beyond your responsibility (e.g. behaviour, health and safety or child protection issues) to others. Any concerns that you have about a supply teacher should also be passed on to the relevant school staff and supply agency.

For more information on your duties, working within your sphere of competence and who to call on for further support, study your job description, cover policy and other school policies that have implications for the support you provide (e.g. behaviour, child protection and grievance policies).

If you feel you need additional training to fulfil your everyday duties as a cover supervisor, seek advice on how best to develop your skills from your line manager or the member of staff who co-ordinates development opportunities. You will also need to think about who could take over your duties as cover supervisor should you need to be covered.

K17 Case study

Recognising when to refer to others

As a cover supervisor you are often called upon to help cover staff manage disruptive behaviour. You provide them with an information pack, which includes a brief summary of the school behaviour policy and strategies used to manage negative behaviour. However, you find that neither the cover staff nor you can deal with some situations and you have to call for assistance.

- What strategies could you try to implement to help manage difficult situations yourself?
- Who can you turn to for help within the school context?
- Where could you access information or training to help with managing challenging behaviour?

Importance of keeping accurate and complete records of cover requirements and arrangements made to meet these, and the school procedures for this

Keep complete, up-to-date and accurate records to ensure the smooth and efficient running of cover arrangements.

Keys to good practice

Record keeping

✓ Have ready access to special educational (ASL) needs records so that the information can be disseminated to cover staff, which will inform the task and resource development, as well as showing the best ways to support individual pupils.

✓ Keep records of prior attainment to provide information on the levels attained by pupils.

✓ By law, attendance and punctuality records must be accurate and sent to the relevant staff members.

✓ A record of the cover hours completed by staff members will ensure they do not cover more than the contractual limit per year.

✓ Yearly and termly planners will help with forward planning of cover during busy periods.

✓ Records of effective cover teachers and good supply agencies will ensure you select cover teachers best suited to your school and pupils.

✓ Records of feedback will help highlight strengths and areas for development during audits, internal and external inspections and review of cover arrangements.

✓ Records of all policies and legislation, and the implications for cover supervision will help ensure guidelines are adhered to.

Portfolio activity

K20

Evaluating record-keeping arrangements

Write a reflective account outlining the importance of keeping records of cover requirements. Include a description of the arrangements for record keeping at your school, evaluate their effectiveness and suggest ideas for improvement.

Websites

www.remodelling.org – information provided by the Training and Development Agency for Schools on the remodelling of the school workforce following the National Agreement on Raising Standards and Tackling Workload, which aims to give support staff responsibility over some areas traditionally managed by teaching staff

www.tda.gov.uk/upload/resources/pdf/c/cover_teachers_pay_cond.pdf – Time for Standards, School Teachers' Pay and Conditions Document

www.tda.gov.uk/upload/resources/pdf/t/timeforstandards_workforce.pdf – Time for Standards, Transforming the School Workforce: Cover strategies – Good Practice

www.tda.gov.uk/upload/resources/pdf/w/wamg_guidance_cover.pdf – cover supervision guidance provided by the Training and Development Agency for Schools

www.teachernet.gov.uk/paydoc/ – information provided by TeacherNet on the School Teachers Pay and Conditions Document 2003

www.teachernet.gov.uk/wholeschool/remodelling – information provided by TeacherNet on the remodelling of the school workforce following the National Agreement on Raising Standards and Tackling Workload

For your portfolio...

K1
K11
K12
K13
K14
K16
K20

1. Design an information pack for cover teachers at your school. Include all the information you consider necessary and relevant to your school, especially:

- brief summary of the relevant sections of the school cover policy
- who cover staff can approach for help with work should the cover supervisor not be available
- basic information such as school timings, fire procedures, cover supervisor's contact details, etc.
- brief outline of possible problems and actions cover staff can take to help resolve issues
- how the cover supervisor will provide and collect feedback from cover staff
- types of records and documentation cover staff may be given and why.

K4
K5
K6

2. Write a reflective account about a particularly busy week for cover, outlining the following:

- the members of staff you had to approach to organise cover and when you approached them
- how you ensured fair allocation of cover
- how you made sure the cover did not affect any other roles and responsibilities of staff members.

K7
K9

3. Obtain a copy of your school cover policy and highlight the following:

- what it states about the amount of cover allowed to be undertaken by different staff members
- when and how supply teachers should be called on for cover.

K15
K18
K19

4. Write a diary entry about a cover supervision meeting you have attended, outlining the following:

- how feedback was given and sought about the effectiveness of cover arrangements
- from whom feedback about cover arrangements was sought
- why it is important to obtain a variety of views
- which suggestions for improvements in cover arrangements were forwarded.

If possible, attach the minutes from the meeting.

62 Develop and Maintain Working Relationships with Other Practitioners

This unit looks at how you work with other professionals both within and outside school in order to support pupils effectively. In the course of your work you will need to show that you are able to develop and maintain working relationships with others. It is likely that you will be asked to attend meetings and both pass on and receive information, as well as show professionalism in all your dealings with others.

You may need to give advice and guidance to others in the course of your work, in particular if your school has parental or community volunteers. You should always do what you can to support the work of other practitioners and to learn through them so that you can support and develop your own working practice.

What you need to know and understand

For this unit, you will need to know and understand:

- How to establish and maintain effective working relationships with other practitioners

- Principles of effective communication and how to apply them in order to communicate effectively with other practitioners

- The importance of exchanging information and resources with other practitioners

- The school policy for confidentiality of information – who is entitled to pass on what information to whom

- The school's protocols and procedures for recording and sharing information

- Your role within the school and the limitations of your own competence and area of responsibility

- Your role within different group situations, including multi-agency working, and how you contribute to the overall group process

- The roles and responsibilities of staff in the school and other professionals in contact with school

- Your own and others' professional boundaries

- The importance of working within the school's values, beliefs and culture

- The importance of respecting the skills and expertise of other practitioners

- The value of sharing how you approach your role with other practitioners

- School policy and procedures for making and maintaining contact with professionals outside of the school setting

- How to judge when you should provide information and/or support yourself and when you should refer the situation to another practitioner

- The specialist support and advice that is available to you in the school and from other professionals in contact with the school

How to establish and maintain effective working relationships

When you are working with other practitioners, you need to be able to work in an environment of mutual support and openness. In school surroundings, you will not be able to work independently of others, nor would it be practicable to do so.

The support you will be required to give others will be on several levels (which you can remember with the acronym PIPE):

- **Practical** – You may be working with others who are unfamiliar with the classroom or school surroundings and need to have help or advice with finding or using equipment and resources.
- **Professional** – You may be in a position to support or help others with issues such as planning, or you may be asked whether others can observe your work with pupils or discuss your work with them.
- **Informative** – You may need to give support to those who do not have information about particular issues. Alternatively, you may be asked to prepare and write reports about particular pupils.
- **Emotional** – It is important to support others through day-to-day events and retain a sense of humour!

The school should also support and encourage good lines of communication between all staff as this is one of the most effective ways of maintaining effective working relationships. Where poor communication occurs between staff this is likely to create uneasiness and occasionally gossip, which can be very damaging.

Case study K1

Developing effective working relationships

Mel has just started a new job in a secondary school. She has been introduced to all the staff at the first whole school staff meeting and has been given a staff list and a detailed whole school staff information pack. This gives details of formal events in school and staff responsibilities. There is also a list on the support staff notice board of events that are more informal and open to all staff.

- Why do you think that this might be good practice?
- How might it help Mel to develop effective relationships with other staff?

Keys to good practice

Establishing and maintaining effective working relationships

✓ Remain professional in the school environment and when communicating with other practitioners in contact with the school.
✓ Treat others with respect.
✓ Notice the efforts and achievements of others.
✓ Give practical support where needed.
✓ Avoid talking about others in a negative way such as gossiping.

Principles of effective communication and how to apply them in order to communicate effectively with other practitioners

For the principles of effective communication, see Unit 21, page 105. Although in this situation you may not be working in a team, you need to follow the same principles; you should think about how the way you communicate with other individuals might affect your work with them.

Importance of exchanging information and resources with other practitioners

You should always think about how any information or resources you receive may be useful to other practitioners with whom you are working. Education is an area that changes regularly and new resources and ideas are often implemented. You should also make sure that you keep up to date with any new information that is available to help you with pupils you support.

If you are more experienced than others, you may also need to give advice or guidance, in particular if for some reason others have not received important information. (See Unit 21, pages 103 and 110 [K3/K8].)

K2 K3 Case study

Recognising the importance of effective communication and exchanging information

Kate, a speech therapist, is in school to meet the Special Educational Needs Co-ordinator (SENCo)(Additional Support for Learning (ASL) teacher) and advise on strategies to support pupils who have been referred to the Speech and Language Therapy Service. She comes once and sometimes twice each year as there are so many pupils in school with speech and language disorders. She has specifically asked to speak to Rob, a teaching assistant working with several of pupils with speech and language disorders.

Rob only received the memo about the meeting that morning. He has not met Kate before, but has not had time to prepare for the meeting. He arrives late, is clearly busy and is not thinking about the pupils or what Kate is asking him. As a result the meeting is very brief and Kate comes away feeling that the school does not particularly want her support.

From the point of view of the SENCo (ASL teacher), Rob and Kate, explain how this meeting could have been better organised and more useful to each of them.

School policy for confidentiality of information – who is entitled to pass on what information to whom

As a member of staff in school you have a responsibility to ensure that you observe **confidentiality** at all times. Under the Data Protection Act 1998, information kept about children needs to be kept in a secure place such as locked filing cabinets or password-protected computers. If you are asked to update information, you should do this while you are on school premises and not take any information off site. You should consider all information about pupils as confidential and ensure that you do not share it with others without parental permission. When discussing pupils with others, you should also take care to ensure that you only share necessary information and be mindful that it should only be given to those who need to receive it. Adults working with a particular pupil need to receive information, while those who are simply curious do not.

There may be cases where information on pupils needs to be accessible to all staff, for example where pupils have specific medical conditions such as asthma or epilepsy. In this case there should be an agreed system within the school for making sure that all staff are aware of these pupils. Some schools display photographs of these pupils in staffrooms or dining areas, removing them if the premises are used by others during the evening.

> **ⓘ Key Term**
>
> **Confidentiality** – only providing information to those who are authorised to have it

Keys to good practice

Providing information to others

✓ Ensure parental consent has been given for information to be shared.
✓ Provide any information requested promptly.
✓ Record or say facts rather than opinions.
✓ Remember confidentiality – only pass information on to those who need it.
✓ Ensure that details are complete and accurate.
✓ Follow the usual school routines.

School's protocols and procedures for recording and sharing information

If you are asked to share information on pupils' progress with other practitioners, this should take place formally where possible. However in reality, information may also be passed verbally where there is not time to arrange a formal meeting or other practitioners are not available.

Written information

It is possible that you will be asked to attend meetings at which you need to present a report or outline concerning a pupil or pupils you support. If you find that you are unable to produce a thorough report and do not feel that you have sufficient information, or if you are unsure about any aspect of what you have been asked to do, you should speak to the member of staff who has requested it. When writing down information about pupils you must always remember confidentiality issues (see above).

You also need to make sure that any contact you make with professionals outside the school goes through the usual channels. If the school usually writes to inform others about meetings, it will be good practice to continue to do this rather than make a phone call. It is also useful to maintain written records of contacts made.

Verbal information

You may be asked to give feedback or information to others verbally on a regular basis, but important issues should always be recorded so that what has been said is documented. You may also pass on information about pupils at whole school or support staff meetings.

K5 Portfolio activity

Identifying ways of sharing information

Think about the different ways you share information with other professionals with whom you have contact. Record the ways in which you do this (you can extend the table on page 369 if required).

▼ **Figure 62.1** Meetings are a perfect way to share expertise

Your role within the school and the limitations of your own competence and area of responsibility

Your role within the school should be outlined in your job description, and it is important to remember that as a teaching assistant you are a member of support staff. This means that your role and area of responsibility should be defined by teachers and senior managers within the school. Although you will be expected to work under your own initiative to a certain extent, you need to be aware of when you should refer to others within or outside the school. You may regularly be the first line of contact with parents, for example, but should be aware of when you need to inform teachers about information from them. When carrying out learning activities, you should always be directed and guided by teachers. You need to be able to show that whoever you work with feels that you are a reliable and competent practitioner. (For more about your role, see Unit 24, page 155.)

Case study K6

Recognising the limitations of your responsibilities

Alex is a teaching assistant attached mainly to the English department. He is very experienced, has achieved his NVQ 3 and is considering applying for HLTA (higher-level teaching assistant) status. He is often asked to take the Year 8 (S2) English class as he works with the deputy headteacher who is regularly called out of lessons.

During period 3, Alex is taking the class on his own as the deputy is in a meeting. He is taking the register when a pupil arrives late, hands him a note and tells Alex that she will be going home just before the lesson finishes. Alex reads the note as it is not sealed or addressed to the teacher. However the message is a confidential matter concerning the pupil's parents and needs to be acted on. Alex decides that he is able to deal with the matter rather than worrying the teacher.

- Should Alex do this?
- Why is it important that he does not keep the content of the note to himself?
- Would the situation be any different if he were an HLTA?

Your role within different group situations, including multi-agency working, and how you contribute to the overall group process

You will belong to different 'groups' in your work with pupils. If you have worked in classrooms for some time, you may have found that in recent years you have been more involved in discussing pupils with different groups or other agencies, including social services, professionals who advise on children with special educational (ASL) needs and health professionals. You should have notice and an agenda of any meetings you are expected to attend so that you have time to prepare for them.

- **Your role as a member of support staff** – As part of this role you should be invited to meetings to discuss special educational (ASL) needs matters or other 'general' school information.

- **Your role as part of the year group** – You may be invited to planning meetings with teachers and other assistants in your year group, in which you will also find out about what will be happening in your part of the school.
- **Your role as part of a subject group** – If you support one particular subject across the school such as Music, you may be asked to talk about your role and the level of support required.
- **Your role as part of the class** – You may be invited to annual review days to discuss the pupil(s) with whom you work or to attend information meetings for parents.
- **Your role when working with an individual** – Your opinion may be sought on a specific child with whom you work and this may involve meetings with a number of different agencies, for example during review meetings. You may also need to go off site to do this.

Roles and responsibilities of staff in the school and other professionals in contact with school

In a school environment there are many different professionals who work both inside and outside the school to support pupils. Depending on how much you are involved with a particular pupil, you may meet some of these people on a regular basis and get to know them well.

(See Unit 20, page 80 for a list of other professionals with whom you may come into contact in school and their roles.)

? Thinking point
Do you know the roles and responsibilities of all staff within the school with whom you come into contact?

You may also develop professional relationships with outside agencies or non-teaching organisations who visit school in order to work with or advise on pupils who need additional support (see also page 373) or to provide information or work in extended school provision. If you support pupils with special education (ASL) needs, you may be asked to join in with meetings and discuss the progress of those pupils. Professionals from outside school with whom you are likely to come into contact may include the following.

- **Speech and language therapists** offer therapy and advice for children with speech and communication difficulties. Parents will usually take children for blocks of therapy over a period of weeks and will then be advised on work they can do with children at home before starting the next block of therapy.
- **Educational psychologists** provide diagnostic assessments on pupil learning and will visit the school by arrangement with the SENCo (ASL teacher).
- **English as an additional language (EAL) support tutors** – These tutors take EAL pupils for assessment and small group work during school hours and also advise school staff on strategies and targets to use with these pupils.
- **Sensory support tutors** offer advice and support for pupils with sensory (e.g. visual or auditory) impairments.
- **Behaviour support staff** may come into school to observe individual pupils and offer guidance and support to staff who are working with them. They may also give individual or group sessions to pupils if needed.
- **Specialist teachers, for example for children with autism** – These teachers may come into school to advise you on strategies for managing pupils with specific needs.
- **Occupational therapists and physiotherapists** – They may offer advice, but will usually work with children outside school.

- **Teachers of additional subjects (subject-specialist teachers), for example sport, dance or languages** – These professionals may come in to school to take groups of pupils for additional sessions either during or after school hours.

As there are many different aspects to the role of teaching assistants in schools, the particular expectations of your role need to be written down clearly in your own job description so that you are aware of the different responsibilities you are expected to undertake. There have been many changes in the role of teaching assistant in recent years, which has moved away from the traditional role of supporting the teacher to a more professional role in supporting pupils' learning. National Occupational Standards for teaching assistants, first published in 2001 and revised in May 2007, outline the variety of roles that those employed to support teaching and learning may be expected to undertake (see www.tda.gov.uk/support/NOS/teaching_and_classroom_assistants.aspx/ for a list of these.) Qualifications for teaching assistants increasingly take into account the diversity of what you may be asked to do. You need to be clear about the duties that you are expected to perform and should also be aware of your own limitations within your role.

Portfolio activity K8

Roles and responsibilities of staff

Use and extend the following table to outline the roles and responsibilities of staff with whom you come into contact as part of your role. Make your own table based on the format below. (A photocopiable version is also available in the *Tutor Resource File*.) You can then use this in your portfolio.

Member of staff	Role and responsibility	How to contact

Your own and others' professional boundaries

All professionals who work in schools will have experience and knowledge about working with pupils and the kinds of issues that can sometimes arise. In your work with pupils you will encounter different situations and may need to call on others to support you. You need to make sure that you know the kinds of issues you can resolve yourself and when you should refer on, and to whom (see also K14 on page 373).

Case study

Recognising your professional boundaries

Look at the following scenarios.

1. A parent informs you that she is involved in a custody dispute with her child's father and that he should not be allowed on school premises or to collect his child.

2. A Year 7 (S1) pupil approaches you on the playground and tells you that she is being followed by a group of older pupils who are teasing her and trying to take her belongings. When you talk to her about it she says that she always has to keep away from them as they regularly pick on her.

3. Another member of staff tells you that a pupil in her class has been behaving out of character and that she is worried about him. You know that his grandfather has been very ill.

4. A speech therapist who works with a pupil in your tutor group comes into school wishing to speak to the tutor, who is unavailable. The therapist tells you that she is very concerned about the pupil and hands you some confidential reports and information to pass on.

5. Unfortunately, pupils at your school tend to congregate around the school gate at the end of the school day. You are aware of an ongoing dispute between one of your Year 9 (S3) tutees and a boy from a neighbouring school. The two pupils are shouting at each other as other pupils leave school. You seek the help of another member of staff before approaching the pupils.

- Should you have been involved in any/all of the above situations?
- Which cases should you refer to another member of staff and which would you deal with yourself?
- Should any other members of staff be involved or informed?

▼ **Figure 62.2** Be aware of when you should seek help from another member of staff

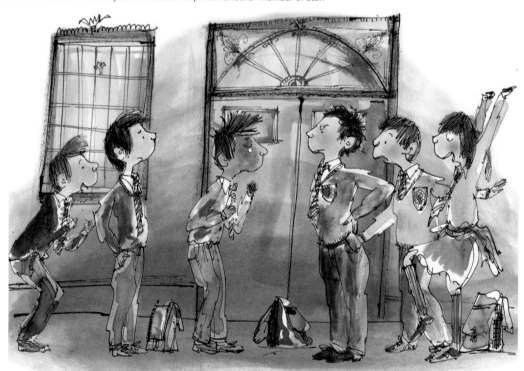

Due to the number of different individuals and professionals with whom you may come into contact, especially in a larger school, it may take a while for you to be clear on everyone's role. If you are not sure about the role of others when you meet them, you should not be afraid to ask. Schools are busy places and can be full of jargon; sometimes teaching and other staff may assume that you are aware of what they do. All professionals who work with children need to pass on information to others and it is important that you are clear on who should be informed about what and how much detail they should be given.

Importance of working within the school's values, beliefs and culture

Your school's prospectus will give you information about its ethos and the way in which staff are expected to work together to promote a particular set of values. This should also be reinforced regularly so that pupils, staff and parents are given a clear idea of what the school is promoting. For example, a religious school may have a value system that promotes the importance of regular worship, whereas a special needs school might focus on positive achievements and clear communication.

Importance of respecting the skills and expertise of other practitioners and the value of sharing how you approach your role with them

You should always remember the importance of respect for the professional judgement of others. Those with whom you come into contact in school will have a wide range of knowledge and expertise, and have been trained in different areas relating to their work with children.

In your work with different professionals and personalities, you could have a disagreement or difference of opinion at some time – most people will get on better with some individuals than others. However, remember that if you have a difference of opinion you should remain professional at all times. If you have cause to question the opinion of another professional, think first about their expertise and experience, and whether you really think that it is appropriate to challenge them. If after consideration you think that this is the case, you should speak in confidence to a teacher or senior member of staff who should be able to advise you on what to do next. If information is shared between professionals appropriately and colleagues are given opportunities to voice their concerns, it is more likely that pupils will be supported effectively.

As you have contact with pupils on a daily basis, you should have the opportunity to discuss your approach with other practitioners. This is because you will get to know pupils and be able to talk about their personalities and how different recommendations will work. Due to legislation that focuses on the rights and best interests of the child, all professionals who work with children, as well as the children themselves, are likely to be asked to contribute to discussions and meetings about their progress.

Case study

Respecting the skills and expertise of others and sharing your approach

1. Sandy works with Raymond, who has autism. She has known him and his family for some time and feels that she is very aware of his needs. The SENCo (ASL teacher) has asked a specialist teacher to carry out an assessment on Raymond as she is concerned about his progress.

   Following the assessment, the specialist produces a report listing a number of recommendations. Sandy is unhappy with what has been written and says that she does not agree with several of the points raised.

2. David has complex needs and is supported for 16 hours a week by Sara. He communicates through sign language and a computerised 'voice' system. He is in Year 8 (S2) and Sara has helped him to make great progress since he arrived at the school in Year 7 (S1). She has regular meetings with other professionals, who have supported her work with David and given her specific work to do with him. In this way, Sara has been able to relate the approaches that have worked and those that have been less successful.

- Which of these two approaches respects the skills and expertise of all those who work with the pupil?
- Why is it important for all those who support teaching and learning to have opportunities to contribute?

School policy and procedures for making and maintaining contact with professionals outside of the school setting

If you are required to make contact with professionals outside school, you need to ensure that you follow school policy. This means that you should remain professional in your approach at all times and be clear on what you have been asked to do.

Ensure that you address people in the correct manner, for example using appropriate titles such as 'Mrs' or 'Miss' as necessary, and that you are willing to communicate required information willingly. It is unlikely you will be asked to write letters, but if you are, it is always a good idea to ask someone else (preferably the person who asked you to write them) to read through them before they are sent out. It is important that you are consistent in your approach with others and can be relied upon to undertake the required work with and for them as necessary. If there is any reason why you are unable to do what has been requested, for example due to timescales or other duties, you should tell the person concerned straightaway.

How to judge when you should provide information and/or support yourself and when you should refer the situation to another practitioner

You may sometimes find that you are in a position to offer information or support to others. If this is simply a matter of offering them information to make their job easier or letting them know something of which you are aware, this is good practice. It may be a student teacher or a colleague in the school who needs help. You may find out what is needed through support staff meetings or through chatting to others. However, if you are at all unsure or if the information required is very specific, you should check with colleagues or other professionals to ensure that providing the information is the correct course of action. You need to be aware of confidentiality when offering support yourself and to be sure that it is appropriate to pass information on to others – if in doubt, always make sure (see also page 365).

Specialist support and advice that is available to you in the school and from other professionals in contact with the school

As you get to know the other professionals with whom you come into contact, you will be able to identify those from whom you are more likely to seek advice. However, if you are new to the school or do not know who to approach, it is likely that you would go through either the SENCo (ASL teacher) or other senior managers in the first instance. You could also ask your class teacher for advice or ideas on where you can seek further help.

It may be that there are others within the school that you can observe if they are working with pupils with similar needs and this may help you with ideas for the kinds of strategies you can use. If you are working in a school that has a special unit attached, for example for pupils with behavioural needs, there will be staff there who may be able to offer advice and support.

For your portfolio...

K2
K9
K14
K15

Linda is working with Raoul, who has global learning delay. His mother also has some special educational (ASL) needs. Linda has been working with Raoul for a term when she is approached by his mother. She asks Linda to help her as she wants to take him to swimming lessons, but does not know how to go about it. She tries to give Linda some money and asks her whether she can arrange the lessons for her son. She has sought Linda's help on other occasions and she often calls the school to speak to Linda. She has also asked Linda to do some shopping for her and asked her to come to her house.

- Should Linda agree to help Raoul's mother?
- Where else could Linda seek help or find out how to support her?

This unit focuses on your relationships with other practitioners and on how you support them. You may be able to cover a considerable amount of information if you can gather witness testimonies that verify how you do this. Written statements should be on headed paper from the practitioner's organisation or verbal testimonies could be given directly to your assessor.

Index

AAC (Alternative and Augmentative Communication) 91, 249, 253, 257, 263

abilities 34–5, 45, 85, 144, 161, 227

accidents 3–4, 4–6, 7, 13, 14–17, 17–18, 334, 335

action plans 324–5, 328

active learning 194, 270

active listening 47–8, 299, 310

Additional Support for Learning (ASL) *see* special educational (Additional Support for Learning(ASL)) needs

ADHD (attention deficit hyperactivity disorder) 68, 271

adult/pupil ratios 13, 21, 27

age 34, 35, 68, 85, 227, 281, 323

agencies, for supply 351–2, 358

allergic reactions 16, 18

Alternative and Augmentative Communication *see* AAC

animals, keeping 12

anti-discriminatory practice 84–6, 305–6

appraisals 119, 125, 129–34, 139, 173, 174–5, 328

ASD (autistic spectrum disorder) 11, 96, 253, 257, 258, 268, 268–9

    supporting pupils 73, 249, 256, 260, 268–9, 272, 273

ASL (Additional Support for Learning) *see* SENCos; special educational (Additional Support for Learning (ASL)) needs

assertiveness 309, 310, 311

assessment 145, 189, 190, 230

    of EAL pupils 235

    for learning 187, 190–8

    records of 153, 334, 339, 340

    see also peer assessment; self-assessment

assessment criteria 194, 197

assessments, for special needs pupils 245–6, 250, 368

assumptions 25, 26, 55, 69, 101, 281, 285–6

autistic spectrum disorder/autistic pupils *see* ASD

backgrounds 23–4, 34–5, 183–4, 202, 210, 263, 278, 284, 320

    EAL pupils 218–20, 223–5, 230, 238

behaviour 10, 56–60, 68–9, 93–5, 219, 224, 284, 296

    challenging 26, 64, 275, 280

    inappropriate 26, 62–3, 72–3, 86–7, 283

    management 25–6, 47–8, 51, 54–6, 62–3, 65–7, 123

    policy 24, 26, 53–5, 63–4, 70, 123, 255–6, 277, 283

    poor 44, 47–8, 60, 95

    promoting good 25, 44, 51, 53, 60–1, 94, 95, 147–9

    reviewing 67, 73–4

    targets 73–4, 278

    whole school approach 51, 55, 56, 94, 123, 149

    see also boundaries; rules; sanctions

behavioural difficulties 70, 71–2, 72–3, 265, 275

    supporting pupils with 277–87

Behaviourist Theory 60, 161

best practice 116–17, 135–6

bilingual pupils 90, 213, 215

    see also EAL pupils

bilingual teaching assistants 213, 218, 225, 228, 231, 233–9

Bloom, Benjamin 206–7

body language 48, 91, 105, 257, 260, 307, 310, 312

boundaries 25–6, 53–4, 87, 123, 132, 148, 148–9, 319, 323

    professional 369–71

business cases 312–14

challenging behaviour 26, 64, 275, 280

child abuse 21–5

child protection 1, 21–5, 27–8, 87, 153, 322, 337, 342

    policy 22–3, 24, 53, 70, 277

Children Act 1989 6, 244

Children Act 2004 27–8, 53, 82, 138, 342

Citizenship 67, 85, 87, 88, 301, 302–3, 304, 308

    see also communities

class teachers 31, 32, 33, 34, 56, 72, 106, 336

    feedback to 22, 229, 236, 297

    support from 66, 204, 256

classroom management 66–7, 138–9

co-learners, acting as 205–6

co-operation 25, 58, 88, 281

Co-ordinated Support Plans *see* Statements of Special Educational Needs

cognitive development theory 161

cognitive difficulties 41, 267–74

collaboration 46, 105–6, 176, 197, 206

communication 97–101, 112, 225, 250–1, 262–3, 306–8

    and behaviour 94–5, 255–6

    with colleagues 164, 205, 363

    with families 233, 238–9, 250

    with pupils 89, 192, 299

    see also AAC

communication difficulties 41, 91, 99–100, 249, 253, 257–9, 262, 282, 368

    supporting pupils with 253, 255–7, 259–62, 262–4

communication skills 257, 267, 273, 309, 319

    teaching assistants' 90, 105, 117, 126–7, 132, 319, 364

communities 303–9

    see also Citizenship

concentration 34, 36, 85, 271, 281

    lack of 36, 37, 45, 257, 272, 292, 295

confidence 58, 89, 198, 284, 292, 323

    building 47, 190, 224, 229, 297, 309, 310, 311, 319, 321

    lack of 35, 48, 101, 218, 310

teaching assistants' 121, 124
confidentiality 18, 69–70, 82–4, 101, 132, 153, 337, 366, 373
    appraisals 130
    dealing with parents 101, 110
    grievance procedure 113
    legal requirements 82, 342, 365
    mentoring 322
    record keeping 264, 331, 336, 339, 342, 344
    school policy 77
    see also Data Protection Act 1995; information
conflict 94, 96, 100–1, 111–12, 280, 283, 304, 309
consistency 25, 55, 56, 58, 94, 123
cover, organising/administering 345, 347, 348–59
cover supervision 345, 347, 351, 353
cultural background 34–5, 38, 68–9, 183–4
cultural diversity 86, 215, 238
culture 38, 85, 225–6, 239, 263
    EAL pupils 218, 223–4, 225
curriculum 33, 137–8, 171–3, 202–3
    see also Citizenship; National Curriculum
curriculum areas, supporting 169, 171–4, 175–84

Data Protection Act 1998 153, 342, 365
decision-making 47, 58, 87–8, 96, 308–9, 321, 322–3, 324
    skills 87–8, 270, 285, 310
development 56–60, 68, 219, 292
    social 58–60, 172, 277, 281, 287
    stages 34, 56–60, 248, 281
differentiation 161, 226, 249, 271
disabilities 248, 292
Disability Discrimination Act 1995 68, 82, 244, 305
disabled pupils 27, 68, 292
    supporting 241, 243, 246–51
discrimination 21–2, 37, 82, 84, 244, 248, 304, 305–6
diversity 86, 98, 215, 225, 246, 320
dyslexia 253, 268
dyspraxia 61, 253, 258, 268

EAL (English as an additional language) pupils 38, 90, 203, 215, 218–19, 258, 368
    backgrounds 223–4, 230, 233–5, 238
education, changes in 119, 128–9, 171, 172, 364
emergencies 4, 5, 14–17, 20–1, 334
emotional development 58–9, 277, 287
emotional needs 41, 182, 224, 227, 275, 278, 323
emotions 34, 35, 83, 93–4, 127–8, 261–2, 279–80, 296
enabling 42, 45, 270, 298
encouragement 24, 36, 42, 47, 161, 191, 192, 224, 262
    during mentoring 321, 323
    special needs pupils 283, 285, 292, 297
English as an additional language *see* EAL
equal opportunities 11, 37, 246–7, 281, 305–6
    school policy 37–9, 70, 151, 203–4, 215–16, 246–7, 248
equipment 8–9, 10, 12, 21, 43–4, 62, 179, 180
    safety equipment 6, 11–12, 18

specialist 7, 91, 250, 294–5
evaluating 121–2, 152–3, 155, 159, 325, 356
Every Child Matters framework 1, 37, 144, 181, 303, 342
    and mentoring 325, 326
    multi-agency approach 27–8, 53, 82, 138, 144, 245
expectations 35–6, 69, 72, 100, 147, 171, 202–3, 285
    of behaviour 25–6, 284
    high 32, 55, 190–1, 202, 246, 326
experiences 34, 281, 323, 324
    traumatic 224, 233, 278, 279
Extended Schools 138, 210, 238
extension 36, 45, 47, 162, 204, 298
extra-curricular activities 108, 173, 352
eye contact 48, 63, 85, 91, 263

families 68, 69, 86, 243, 263, 324, 327
    bilingual support 231, 233, 236, 238, 238–9
    see also backgrounds; parents
feedback 23, 166–8, 173, 195–6, 229, 310, 319, 366
    on cover 356–7
    on EAL pupils 236–7
    to pupils 187, 190, 192, 194, 195–6, 224, 262
    to teachers 123, 153, 157, 229, 297, 339
    to teaching assistants 125, 130, 173–4
fire procedures 4, 20
first aid 3–4, 13, 14–17, 18, 27, 137

G&T (Gifted and Talented) Co-ordinators 201, 204, 206
Gardner, Howard 39–40
gender 35–6, 68, 68–9, 85
gifted pupils 201, 203, 207
    see also gifted and talented pupils
Gifted and Talented (G&T) Co-ordinators 201, 204, 206
gifted and talented pupils 38, 41, 199, 201–2, 203–11
grievance policies 113–14
group work 39, 45, 58, 89, 179, 222, 225, 298
grouping pupils 32, 221, 222, 278

hazards 1, 4, 5–6, 9, 10, 12
headteachers 6, 31, 66, 80, 171, 305, 335–6, 337, 358
    and appraisals 129, 130
    child protection role 22
    and cover 351, 352
health and safety 4–6, 8, 13, 21, 24, 28, 137, 179, 180
    policy 4, 5–6, 20, 53, 64, 137
    representatives 5, 9, 18, 137
    see also emergencies; first aid; illnesses; safety
human rights 24, 37, 81, 304, 342
humour 132, 363

IEPs (Individual Education Plans) 146, 162, 171, 182, 229–30, 259, 269
    for behaviour 70, 278
    special needs 193, 245, 259, 269, 291, 298, 335
illnesses 13, 17, 19–20, 295, 296, 358

inclusion 37–8, 84, 181, 246, 248
    disabled pupils 68, 82, 292, 296
    policy 37–9, 41, 70, 151, 203–4, 215–16, 248, 255
independence 47, 58, 85, 89, 273, 285, 287
    disabled pupils 292, 295, 297, 298
independent learning 29, 46–7, 58, 285
Individual Education Plans see IEPs
individuality 89, 92, 96, 98
information 99–100, 101, 137, 238, 323, 339–40, 365–6
    for cover staff 353–4, 355
    passing on 77, 99, 101, 367
    personal 333, 336, 337, 339
    presenting 181, 182–3
    on pupils 69–70, 82, 246–7
    sharing 105, 115, 164, 233, 336–7, 341, 342–3, 364, 365,
      371, 373
    sources 181–2, 314, 323–4
    see also confidentiality; record keeping
intelligence 34, 39–40
interaction needs 41, 253, 255–64
interactive styles 108–9, 314

job descriptions 31, 108, 122, 160, 328, 367, 369
    and appraisals 130, 131, 174

language 25, 41, 213, 222–3, 255–6
    acquisition 216–18, 224, 227, 258–9, 267
    and learning 34, 35, 222, 258–9, 267, 269
    modelling 224, 229, 261, 263
    young people's 306–8
language skills 90, 215, 219, 253, 267, 269, 272
learning 36, 161–2, 210–11
    active 194, 270
    independent 29, 46–7, 58, 285
    language and 35, 222, 258–9, 269
    personalised 46–7, 144–5, 164
    reviewing 48–9, 189, 196, 274
learning activities 31
    see also teaching and learning activities
learning difficulties 13–14, 70, 228–9, 250, 253, 257, 265, 268–9
    supporting pupils with 268, 269–74
learning environments 9–12, 44, 55, 57, 147–8, 164, 272, 294
learning mentors 66, 317, 319, 326, 327–8
    see also mentoring
learning needs 40–1, 146, 181, 219, 227, 234, 253, 269–74
learning objectives 34, 143, 158, 189, 193–4, 209, 249, 298
    clarity 46–7, 72
learning styles 39–40, 114, 144, 182, 182–3, 219, 314
legislation 81–2, 138, 291, 304–6, 326, 347
    child protection 27–8
    data protection 82, 153, 342, 365
    disability 68, 82, 244, 305
    health and safety 4–6, 8
    human rights 24, 81, 304, 322
    special needs 82, 244–5

lesson plans 143, 162–3, 184, 189, 249
lifting 7–8, 294
line managers 80, 83, 127, 137, 160, 358
    and appraisals 129, 140, 174, 175, 328
listening skills 47–8, 90, 105, 132, 299, 310, 312
    EAL pupils 213, 218, 220, 226, 234–5
local authorities 6, 23, 206, 210, 228, 233, 244, 246
    and mentoring 323, 326
    restraint guidelines 87, 280
    training 259, 293, 319

materials 4, 9, 10, 16, 177–84, 292–3, 355
maturity 34, 35, 58, 85
medication 68, 271, 280, 334
meetings 80, 99, 101, 105, 108, 117, 164, 368
    outside professionals 364, 365–6, 367, 368
    for planning 155, 157, 368
    staff meetings 5, 53, 127, 137, 182, 366
    year groups 127, 137, 159, 164, 367
mentoring 66, 173, 317, 319–28
monitoring 42–3, 62, 66, 129, 189, 229–30, 236, 325
motivating pupils 42, 45, 149–50, 161, 191, 272–3, 310
    with feedback 195–6, 262
    by mentoring 321, 325
motivation 34, 35, 47, 72, 184, 190, 285–6
multi-agency approach 27–8, 53, 82, 138, 144, 245, 367–9
multiculturalism 215, 215–16
multilingual pupils 90, 213, 215
    see also EAL pupils

National Curriculum 33, 157, 171–2, 203, 234, 244
needs 38, 72–3, 85, 132, 144, 182, 314
    basic 22, 223
    learning needs 40–1, 162
    meeting 149–50, 182, 321
negotiation 88, 209, 280, 283, 311–12, 319
non-verbal communication 257, 259, 259–60, 261, 283, 297, 307
    body language 48, 91, 105, 257, 260, 310, 312

observations 125, 129–30, 143, 146, 175, 189
Ofsted 6, 27, 67, 136, 151, 174
organisational skills 89, 257, 267, 268, 272, 273, 285
outside agencies 23, 53, 66, 81, 134–5, 219, 326, 367, 368–9
    behaviour support 72, 283
    reports from 334–5
    special needs 245, 255, 268, 294–5
    see also multi-agency approach

parents 17, 20, 22, 38, 157, 335, 336, 367
    and confidentiality 83, 110
    EAL pupils 215, 218, 233, 238
    'expert parents' 247
    gifted and talented pupils 204, 210
    special needs/disabled pupils 243, 244, 247–8, 261

working with 122, 247, 278, 282
see also families
peer assessment 47, 72, 125, 145, 176, 192, 194, 197
personalised learning 46–7, 144–5, 164
personality 34, 105, 108–9
physical development 34, 35, 56–8, 68, 219
physical impairments 40, 253, 257, 258, 261, 265, 292, 297
see also disabled pupils
Piaget, Jean 162
planning 108, 123, 143–7, 155, 157–9, 162, 205, 249, 298
of activities 32, 141, 155, 160
cover 350, 352
curriculum 33, 203, 226
EAL pupils 222–3, 224, 228
future learning 196, 198, 209–10, 274
plans 143, 153, 158, 334, 335, 337, 339
curriculum 33, 203, 226
lesson plans 143, 162–3, 184, 189, 249
praise 41–2, 48, 60, 161, 224, 262, 270, 285, 310
for disabled pupils 292, 297, 299
for effort 42, 286, 292, 310
for good behaviour 44, 55, 94
for work 36
presentations 182–3, 309, 312–14
problem-solving 46, 267, 270, 285, 321
professional development 119, 121–2, 127, 128, 132–6, 328, 350
professionalism 86–7, 369–72
professionals (from outside school) 101, 106, 122, 229, 273, 282, 291, 368–9
special needs 250, 256–7, 262–3, 291, 293, 294–5, 334–5
working with 366, 367, 368–9, 372–3
PSHE (personal, social and health education) 59, 70, 93, 172, 225
psychiatric disorders 282–3
psychological disorders 282–3
pupil records 74–5, 146, 153, 263–4, 331, 333–9, 340–1
see also record-keeping

qualifications 135–6, 138, 369
questioning 42, 43, 45, 61, 90, 192, 198, 312, 322
gifted and talented pupils 207, 208

reading 213, 221–2, 234–5
record keeping 153, 184, 331, 337–44, 349, 358–9
pupil records 74–5, 146, 153, 263–4, 331, 333–9, 340–1
referring to others 45–6, 65, 112, 256, 295, 358, 369–70
SENCos 256, 293
teachers 44, 45, 157, 161, 192, 207, 228, 229, 293
reflection 187, 198, 209–10
reflective practice 119, 120–7, 128, 138, 141, 151
relationships 110, 283, 323
positive 77, 90, 92, 97–8
among pupils 36–7, 59, 60, 97, 279, 280
with pupils 29, 36, 47–8, 61, 85, 148–9
see also working relationships
religious issues 93, 219

resources 10, 146–7, 184, 355
curriculum areas 177–9, 180–4
EAL pupils 222, 228
gifted and talented pupils 206
problems with 43–4, 179
special needs 272, 292–3
respect 87, 89, 92, 98, 107, 147–8, 279, 309, 371–2
responsibilities 56, 149, 304–5, 310, 367–9
pupils' 58, 72, 85, 86, 194, 205, 206, 209
Restorative Justice 94, 280
restraint 64, 87, 280
reviewing 189, 314, 325, 343
behaviour 67, 73–4
learning 48–9, 189, 196, 274
rewards 32, 41–2, 60, 61, 63, 74, 94, 149
rights 24–5, 148, 244, 246–7, 304–5, 309, 310, 322
see also human rights
risks 1, 5, 14, 26–7, 64
rules 10, 25–6, 53–4, 67, 94, 149

safety 1, 4–6, 8–10, 12, 24, 26–7, 64, 304, 323
of equipment 10, 21, 62
safety equipment 6, 11–12, 18, 179
sanctions 26, 62, 63, 94, 95, 123, 149, 279
schemes of work 171, 184, 189, 334, 335, 337
school councils 67, 88
school policies 137, 328
anti-bullying 53, 70, 277
anti-racism 70, 215–16, 277
assessment, recording and reporting 153, 333, 343, 365–6
behaviour 24, 26, 53–5, 63–4, 70, 123, 255–6, 277, 283
child protection 22–3, 24, 53, 70, 277
cover 347, 352, 356
EAL pupils 215, 234
equal opportunities 37–9, 70, 151, 203–4, 215, 215–16, 248, 277
health and safety 4, 5–6, 20, 21, 53, 64, 137
inclusion 37–9, 41, 70, 151, 203–4, 215–16, 248, 255, 277
intervention 64, 87, 279, 280
language 255–6
praise, assistance and rewards 41–2, 63
PSHE 70, 277
special needs 38, 70, 255, 277
working relationships 111, 113–14
school structure 31, 105, 131
Scotland 14, 27, 33, 59, 66, 173, 275
legislation 6, 53, 245
security 4, 20, 153, 212, 333, 344
self-assessment 47, 72, 145, 187, 192, 193, 194, 197, 198
self-control 279–80, 310
self-esteem 58–9, 69, 90, 124, 225, 262, 285–7, 309, 323
developing 55, 184, 202, 228, 229, 246, 278, 283, 283–4, 297, 320–1
low 45, 69, 191, 218, 278, 284
self-image 24, 25, 284, 286–7, 321

SENCos (Special Educational Needs Co-ordinators/Additional Support for Learning (ASL) teachers) 72, 79–80, 83, 106, 129, 244, 291, 368, 373
  advice from 65–6, 70–1, 177, 182, 204, 283
  and EAL pupils 229, 234, 236
  and mentoring 323–4, 327
  records 263–4, 334–5, 335–6
  referring to 256, 293
  support from 135, 246, 295
sensory needs 40, 253, 265, 292–9
sharing information 105, 115, 164, 336–7, 341–3, 364, 365, 371, 373
  with parents 233, 367
Skinner, Burrhus Frank 60, 161
social development 58–60, 172, 277, 281, 287
social difficulties 278–80, 285–6
social relationships 36–7, 225, 253, 281
social skills 165, 273, 281–2
speaking skills 261, 310
  EAL pupils 213, 218, 220, 226, 227, 228, 234–5
special educational (Additional Support for Learning (ASL)) needs 38, 40–1, 70, 145, 238, 243, 255, 275
special educational (Additional Support for Learning (ASL)) needs pupils 7, 35, 38, 45, 157, 162, 171, 193
  assessments 245–6, 250, 368
  equipment 7, 91, 250, 294–5
  records 32, 263–4, 334–5
  supporting 56, 61, 81, 122, 203, 241, 248–51, 285
Special Educational Needs Co-ordinators see SENCos
specialist support 65–6, 246–7, 255, 256–7, 268, 273, 368–9
Statements of Special Educational Needs 39, 246, 275
stereotyping 25, 26, 69, 285–6, 319–20
subject knowledge 175–80, 368
success criteria 152, 159, 193
supply teachers 347, 348, 350, 351, 351–2, 354, 358

talented pupils 201, 210, 211
  see also gifted and talented pupils
targets 132–4, 140, 175, 273, 324–5
  behaviour 72, 74, 278
  on IEPs 70, 171, 193, 245, 259, 278, 298
  setting 88, 132–4, 140, 145, 175, 236, 324–5, 338
  SMART 72, 133–4, 140, 176, 324–5, 357
teachers 10, 80, 129, 156–7, 198, 367
  planning 141, 143, 155, 189
  see also class teachers

teaching assistants 131–2
  bilingual 213, 218, 225, 228, 231, 233–9
  as enablers 42, 45, 270, 298
  HTLAs 138, 173, 174, 179, 180
  qualifications 135–6, 138, 369
  responsibilities 32, 65, 367–8
  role 54–5, 121, 123, 143, 156–60, 204–6, 367–8, 369
  targets 132–4, 140, 175
teaching and learning activities 42–5, 146, 161
  evaluating 121–2, 152–3, 155, 159
  planning 32, 141, 155, 160
  supporting 29, 31, 39–49, 149–50, 177–9
thought 206–7, 267
time management 165–6
training 32, 117, 132, 134–6, 138, 176, 182
  for cover supervision 358
  first aid 18
  health and safety 180
  induction 5, 135
  INSET 117, 140, 173
  lifting 7, 294
  for mentoring 319
  providing 173
  on record keeping 333
  for special needs 135, 249, 259, 263, 292, 293
  subject-specific 122
trips 13, 21, 26–7, 278–9, 334, 335, 340, 349
trust 61, 83, 148, 311, 312

UN Convention on the Rights of the Child 1989 24, 81, 322
unions 87

valuing pupils 61, 86, 90–1, 92, 225, 299, 310, 319
virtual communication 307

Wales 67, 90
Welsh 90, 218, 219, 221–2
  see also bilingual pupils
work teams 103, 105–17
working relationships 79–81, 110–14, 122, 166–8, 361, 362–3, 371–2
writing 213, 221–2, 234–5

year groups 80, 106, 159, 164, 368
young people, interactions 306–8